REGENERATION

REGENERATION

*A Complete History of Healing
In the Christian Church*

VOLUME THREE:
BIBLIOGRAPHY

J.D. King

Regeneration: A Complete History of Healing in the Christian Church, Volume Three
Copyright © 2017 by J.D. King.

All rights reserved. No part of this publication may be reproduced, distributed, or transmitted in any form or by any means, including photocopying, recording, or other electronic or mechanical methods, without the prior written permission of the publisher.

Printed in the United States of America
First Printing, 2017

ISBN 978-0-9992826-2-5

Christos Publishing
Lee's Summit, Missouri

Cover Design by Randy Keeler, http://keelerdesign.com/
Layout by Penoaks Publishing

This book is not intended as a substitute for the advice of licensed medical professionals. The reader should regularly consult a physician in matters relating to his/her health and particularly with respect to any symptoms that may require diagnosis or medical attention.

Dedicated to Bobbie.
Your kindness and love has transformed me.

"There are many more things that Jesus did. If all of them were written down, I suppose not even the world itself would have space for the books that would be written."

—JOHN 21:25

Table of Contents

Foreword	i
Introduction to the Bibliography	1
1. Post-Apostolic	7
2. Medieval	23
3. Reformation	35
4. Post-Reformation	43
5. European Faith Cure	57
6. American Faith-Cure	65
7. Radical Holiness	85
8. Early Pentecostalism	97
9. Later Holiness	119
10. Salvation-Healing	137
11. Later Pentecostalism	161
12. Anglicanism	193
13. Fundamentalist-Evangelical	217
14. Mainline and Liturgical	259
15. Roman Catholic	303
16. Charismatic Renewal	319
17. Word of Faith	333
18. Third Wave	343
19. Case Studies	365
20. Physicians and Academics	375

"Religion as a form of experience can and does profoundly influence the literary imagination. It has done so powerfully in the past; the influence today is still operative."[1]

—CHARLES I. GLICKSBERG

---

1. Charles I. Glicksberg, *Literature and Religion: A Study in Conflict* (Dallas: Southern Methodist University Press 1960), 226.

Foreword

J.D. King's bibliography of academic and popular literature on healing was distributed to my doctoral students within hours of my reception of it—I felt it was that useful to their research. This thorough work covers a neglected area in Christian ministry practice to an extent that I have rarely seen.

Because of its valuable guidance to often obscure literature, this bibliography deserves the attention of archivists and indexers of academic literature.

While the practice of Christian divine healing appears consistently through the centuries on a widespread popular level in the Christian community, it has received a disproportionately limited attention from scholars.

Since the charismatic movement, with its emphasis on healing, is expanding toward one billion practitioners, both on its own and throughout established Christian groups, it is imperative that the popular and academic literature that reflects that movement be understood and engaged.

J.D. King's excellent bibliography on healing significantly contributes to that worthy effort.

— Jon Mark Ruthven, Ph.D., author,
On the Cessation of the Charismata:
The Protestant Polemic on Post-Biblical Miracles

Introduction to the Bibliography

"The Teacher searched to find appropriate expressions, and what is written here is right and truthful. Sayings from the wise are like cattle prods and well fastened nails; this masterful collection was given by one shepherd. So learn from them, my son. There is no end to the crafting of many books, and too much study wearies the body." (Ecclesiastes 12:10-12)

Myriads of books fill cardboard boxes and dusty bookshelves. They are stacked in the corners of offices and occupy valuable space on disheveled desks. Reflecting on the bewildering diversity of the many publications, David L. McKenna declared:

> Millions of Christian books have been written since the time of Christ, and thousands have been published in the last fifty years. Some are classics that have stood the test of time, some are bestsellers that have enjoyed a season of popularity, some are throwaways that should never have been printed, and many others are located somewhere in between.[1]

McKenna's insights could easily be applied to the literature on divine healing: Thousands of books, articles, and case studies intersect with the Christian understanding of physical deliverance. This genre is tremendously diverse: sermons, pamphlets, testimonies, hymnals, histories, essays, critiques, tracts, theologies, biographies, and how-tos.

---

1. David McKenna, *How to Read a Christian Book* (Grand Rapids: Baker Book House, 2001), 28–29.

When I began to make inquiries into healing literature, decades ago, I had a difficult time finding resources. Although many works were readily available, the scarcity and inequality of the offerings were disheartening.

When visiting a research institution, I would inquire about source material on healing only to receive puzzled looks.[2] I would then either be directed to the section on Pentecostalism or handed cursory studies that hardly broached the subject. Unable to obtain bibliographic sources or adequate information, my frustration was mounting.

At that time, I was attempting to obtain supplementary works on healing's history and underpinnings. I wanted a better grasp of its theology, methods, and effects.

Fortunately, I ultimately located several substantial works. I remember obtaining Morton Kelsey's *Healing and Christianity: In Ancient Thought and Modern Times* (1973), David Edwin Harrell Jr.'s *All Things Are Possible: The Healing and Charismatic Revivals in Modern America* (1975), Paul Gale Chappell's "The Divine Healing Movement in America"(1983), Michael L. Brown's *Israel's Divine Healer* (1995), as well as Ronald Kydd's *Healing through the Centuries: Models for Understanding* (1998). Each of these works became foundational for my studies.

I did not realize then that there was soon to be a groundswell of healing studies. While little was being discussed in 2001, what has been released since then is remarkable. Candy Gunther Brown suggested, "Scholars have until recently paid scant attention to Christian spiritual healing." However, over the past decade, there has been a "proliferation of dissertations and books."[3]

I recall coming across Jonathan Baer's "Perfectly Empowered Bodies: Divine Healing in Modernizing America" (2002). Then, I obtained Nancy Hardesty's *Faith Cure: Divine Healing in the Holiness and Pentecostal Movements* (2003). I was certainly overjoyed that works of this caliber were being released.

---

2. William McLoughlin declared, "Since revivalism is by its nature concerned with experience, not theory, and since revivalists are by temperament and tradition concerned with the spoken rather than the written word, the sources for a study of revivalism are often random and elusive." William G. McLoughlin, *Modern Revivalism: From Charles Finney to Billy Graham* (New York: Ronald Press Company, 1959), 531.

3. Candy Gunther Brown, "From Tent Meetings and Storefront Healing Rooms to Walmarts and the Internet: Healing Spaces in the United States, the Americas, and the World, 1906–2006," *Church History: Studies in Christianity and Culture* 75:3 (September 2006), 633.

In 2005, I obtained Heather D. Curtis' outstanding Harvard dissertation "The Lord for the Body: Sickness, Health and Divine Healing in Nineteenth-Century Protestantism." Her research was later revised and released as *Faith in the Great Physician: Suffering and Divine Healing in American Culture, 1860–1900.*

That same year, Amanda Porterfield published, through Oxford University Press, *Healing in the History of Christianity.* This is an outstanding work that thoughtfully examines healing claims in the Christian tradition. Porterfield's work deepened my understanding of historical developments.

I also examined James William Opp's *The Lord for the Body: Religion, Medicine, and Protestant Faith Healing in Canada, 1880–1930* (2005). This was another remarkable work exploring the trajectory of healing in the nineteenth and early twentieth centuries.

Kimberly Ervin Alexander's *Pentecostal Healing: Models in Theology and Practice* was published to great acclaim in 2006. This work broke new ground as it examined the foundations of physical deliverance within classical Pentecostalism.

In 2008, Joseph W. Williams wrote a dissertation on the changing understanding of healing in Pentecostalism, calling it 'The Transformation of Pentecostal Healing, 1906–2006." This was ultimately reworked and released by Oxford University Press as *Spirit Cure: A History of Pentecostal Healing* in 2012.

In 2010, I received an email from James Robinson, a gifted scholar from the United Kingdom, who was developing a series of books on divine healing. I was thrilled when he went on to release the following: *Divine Healing: The Formative Years: 1830–1880: Theological Roots in the Transatlantic World* (2011); *Divine Healing: The Holiness-Pentecostal Transition Years, 1890–1906: Theological Transpositions in the Transatlantic World* (2013); and *Divine Healing: The Years of Expansion, 1906–1930: Theological Variation in the Transatlantic World* (2014).

Two extraordinary books have been released more recently: *Miracles: The Credibility of the New Testament Accounts* (2011) by Craig Keener and *Jesus as Healer: A Gospel for the Body* (2016) by Jan-Olav Henriksen and Karl Olav Sandnes. Both works have broken new ground and will, no doubt, be catalysts for further theological discourse.

As I eagerly obtained publications, I occasionally purchased the same volume twice. If the cover had been changed or the title tweaked, I was not cognizant that I had purchased something that I already owned. I knew that I needed to start keeping better records.

So, the arduous task of compiling and arranging resources began. I obtained a simple notebook and began listing my books. I continued adding to it as I picked up new works. Those crude scribbles were the beginning of this bibliography.

At that point in time, I had no idea that I was actually beginning the process of developing a major healing resource. Yet, that is precisely what was transpiring.

In this attempt to answer my own questions, my hope is that I will be helping others to answer theirs.

A work such as this always has its deficiencies. Though uncovering hundreds of loosely circulated publications, the challenge of cataloging was indisputable. Due to the sheer number and diversity of holdings, it is nearly impossible to compile a complete listing of healing publications.

Though varying in length, scope, and depth, the following bibliographic entries reflect the most significant works on healing in the English tongue. Obviously, relatively insignificant works are included in this bibliography as well.

Be advised that the entries were organized on the basis of the authors' theological background and the era of composition. Thus, an article on an individual or movement may be found listed in an unexpected chapter. Exceptions were made with post-apostolic, medieval, Reformation, and post-Reformation periods. These entries are chiefly secondary sources[4] derived from later authors.

Within each respective era, the entries are listed alphabetically by the author's last name. Each listing also includes a brief annotation that provides a glimpse into the nature of the resource along with general source material.

---

4. Secondary sources "are useful to historians when they do not have access to all of the places where the relevant primary sources are located. Also, secondary sources provide useful interpretation about historical events and movements." Helen J. Poulton, *The Historian's Handbook* (Norman, Oklahoma: University of Oklahoma Press, 1972), 175–176.

Groundbreaking research is poised to be written as scholars gain better access to literature on physical deliverance. The more that healing is understood and written about, the more it will find its place within broader Christian discourse.

The time has come for a reassessment of Christian healing practices and literature. Although reputable studies have increased over the last two decades, informed analysis is more important than ever. Much has been written about the ministry of healing, but many things remain silent—longing to be heard.

1. POST-APOSTOLIC

Amundsen, Darrel W. *Medicine, Society, and Faith in the Ancient and Medieval Worlds*. Baltimore: Johns Hopkins University Press, 1996. Amundsen's work is an exploration of perspectives on health, healing, and medical treatment from antiquity to the medieval period.

Amundsen, Darrel W. "Medicine and Faith in Early Christianity." *Bulletin of the History of Medicine* 56 (1982): 326–350. This article, published in a medical journal, explores how early Christians engaged medicine and health in an earlier period of Christian history.

Amundsen, Darrel W., and Gary B. Ferngren. "Medicine and Religion: Pre-Christian Antiquity," in *Health, Medicine and the Faith Traditions: An Inquiry into Religion and Medicine,* ed. M.E. Marty and K.L. Vaux, 53–92. Philadelphia: Fortress, 1982. In this well-researched chapter, Amundsen and Ferngren explore views of health in the pre-Christian Greco-Roman world.

Athanasius. *Life of Antony*. tr. Caroline White. London: Penguin, 1998. The *Life of Antony* by Athanasius (251–356) was written around 365. It is a biographical work about the father of Christian asceticism. Saint Antony of Egypt was known for driving out demons and healing the sick. Athanasius recounts how Antony "healed and converted many."

Augustine. "The Retractions," in *Augustine: Earlier Writings*, tr. John H. S. Burleigh. Philadelphia: Westminster, 1953. In this pivotal work, Augustine of Hippo recounts changing insights late in life. One of the most significant is his new-found openness to healing.

Avalos, Hector. *Health Care and the Rise of Christianity*. Peabody, Massachusetts: Hendrickson Publishing, 1999. This work considers the scope of health care in early Christian and Roman societies.

Barrett-Lennard, R.J.S. *Christian Healing After the New Testament: Some Approaches to Illness in the Second, Third, and Fourth Centuries*. Lanham,

Maryland: University Press of America, 1994. This is a penetrating academic analysis of healing in the first centuries of the church.

Barrett-Lennard, R.J.S. "Request for Prayer for Healing," in *New Documents Illustrating Early Christianity: A Review of the Greek Inscriptions and Papyri*, ed. G. H. R. Horsley, 245–250. Sydney, Australia: Macquarie University, 1987. Barrett-Lennard provides further insights into the ministry of healing during the Ante-Nicene period.

Barrett-Lennard, R.J.S. "The Canons of Hippolytus and Christian Concern with Illness, Health, and Healing." *Journal of Early Christian Studies* 13:2 (2005): 137–164. In this article, Barrett-Lennard examines early liturgical documents considering what it has to say about healing practices in the church.

Baumgarten, A.I. "Miracles and Halakah in Rabbinic Judaism." *Jewish Quarterly Review* 73 (1983): 238–253. This article explores the Jewish understanding of miracles and their relationship to authority structures within subsequent rabbinics.

Bazzana, Giovanni Battista. "Early Christian Missionaries as Physicians: Healing and Its Cultural Value in the Greco-Roman Context." *Novum Testamentum* 51:3 (2009): 232–251. Bazzana argues that early followers of Jesus positioned themselves as Greco-Roman medical practitioners to gain prestige and freely travel around the empire. Their success was, in part, derived from the fact that they did not require payment for their services.

Blenkinsopp, Joseph. "Miracles: Elisha and Hanina ben Dosa," in *Miracles in Jewish and Christian Antiquity: Imagining Truth*, ed. by John C. Cavadini, 57–81. Notre Dame, Indiana: University of Notre Dame Press, 1999. This well-researched essay examines the Jewish understanding of miracles.

Bokser, Baruch M. "Wonder-Working and the Rabbinic Tradition: The Case of Hanina ben Dosa." *Journal for the Study of Judaism* 16 (1985): 42–92. This article draws upon the stories of Hanina ben Dosa, a first-century Jewish healer and miracle worker. It explores how miracles were understood throughout later rabbinical traditions.

Brothwell, Don, and A.T. Sandison, eds. D*iseases in Antiquity: A Survey of the Diseases, Injuries and Surveys of Early Populations.* Springfield, Illinois: Charles C. Thomas Publishing, 1967. This book is a compilation of essays on disease in antiquity. Of primary interest is chapter 16, "Diseases in the Bible and the Talmud" by Max Sussman.

Burgess, Stanley M. *The Holy Spirit: Ancient Christian Traditions.* Peabody, Massachusetts: Hendrickson Publishing, 1984. In this well-researched work, Burgess recounts the understanding and experiences of the early church fathers. There are a number of references to healing.

Butler, Dom Cuthbert. *The Lausiac History of Palladius: A Critical Discussion Together with Notes on Early Egyptian Monasticism.* London: Cambridge University Press, 1898. This is a seminal work archiving the experiences of early Christian monks who lived in the Egyptian desert. This work was written in 419–420 by Palladius of Galatia at the request of Lausus, chamberlain at the court of Byzantine Emperor Theodosius II.

Campenhausen, Hans von. *Ecclesiastical Authority and Spiritual Power in the Church of the First Three Centuries.* Stanford, California: Stanford University Press, 1969. Examining historical and sociological dynamics, Campenhausen explores the tensions of charismata and institutionalism.

Case, Shirley Jackson. "The Art of Healing in Early Christian Times." *The Journal of Religion* 3:3 (May 1923): 238–255. This is an older academic article that explores the practice of healing in early Christianity.

Coats, George W. "Healing and the Moses Traditions," in *Canon, Theology, and Old Testament Interpretation: Essays in Honor of Brevard S. Childs*, eds. Gene M. Tucker, David L. Petersen, and Robert R.

Wilson, 131–146. Philadelphia: Fortress, 1988. This is an excellent academic essay on healing in the ancient Jewish traditions.

Conybeare, Frederick Cornwallis, ed. *The Apology and Acts of Apollonius and Other Monuments of Early Christianity.* London: Swan Sonnenschein and Company, 1894. This is a collection of testimonies and accounts from the early church. Of particular interest are the healing stories of Saint Eugenia.

Cooper, Kate and Jeremy Gregory. *Signs, Wonders, Miracles: Representations of Divine Power in the Life of the Church.* Suffolk: United Kingdom: The Boydell Press, 2005. This is a unique collection of academic articles on signs and wonders within church history. These include: "The Place of Miracles in the Conversion of the Ancient World," W.H.C. Frend. "Signs, Wonders, Miracles: Supporting the Faith in Medieval Rome," Brenda Bolton. "Miracles in Post-Reformation England," Alexandra Walsham. "Late Seventeenth-Century Quakerism and The Miraculous: A New Look at George Fox's Book of Miracles," Rosemary Moore.

Cotter, Wendy J. *Miracles in Greco-Roman Antiquity: A Sourcebook for the Study of New Testament Miracles Stories.* New York: Routledge Publishing, 1999. This book provides an overview of miraculous accounts from the Greco-Roman world and some excellent commentary from Cotter.

Coyle, J. Kevin, and Steven C. Muir. *Healing in Religion and Society from Hippocrates to the Puritans, Selected Studies.* Lewiston, New York: The Edwin Mellen Press, 1999. This is a fascinating collection of essays exploring the understanding of healing in the ancient world. Two of the most valuable are: "Faith Healing and Deliverance in Mark's Gospel," and "Patristic Reception of a Lukan Healing Account: A Contribution to a Socio-Rhetorical Response to Will Brun's Feasting and Social Rhetoric in Luke 14."

Craffert, Pieter F. *Illness, Health, and Healing in The New Testament World: Perspectives on Health Care.* Pretoria: Biblia, 1999. This is a well-researched book that examines first century perspectives on sickness and healing.

Darling, Frank C. *Biblical Healing: Hebrew and Christian Roots.* Boulder, Colorado: Vista Publications, 1989. This is a general overview of Christian healing in history. It primarily focuses on the Jewish roots and expansion into Ante-Nicene Christianity.

Daube, David. *New Testament and Rabbinic Judaism.* London: Athlone Press, 1956. The chapter titled "The Laying on of Hands" (224–246) discusses laying on of hands in the Jewish tradition. It distinguishes two Old Testament words. One means to lay one's hands upon another lightly (as in a blessing). The other refers to pressing with weight. The second term was used sacrificially. It signified "the creating of a substitute and the transfer of sin by leaning into the sacrifice."

Daunton-Fear, Andrew. "The Healing Ministry in the Pre-Nicene Church," Ph.D. diss., London University, 2000. Daunton-Fear's outstanding monograph carefully explores healing practices in the early Christianity.

Daunton-Fear, Andrew. *Healing in the Early Church: The Church's Ministry of Healing and Exorcism from the First to The Fifth Century.* Eugene, Oregon: Wipf and Stock Publishers, 2009. Building upon the work of his dissertation, Daunton-Fear considers the scope of healing practices during the first five centuries of the church.

Dave, Victor Gladstone. "The Attitude of the Early Church toward Sickness and Healing," Ph.D. diss., Boston University, 1955. This work examines divine healing and the works of the Spirit in the Ante-Nicene church. The author's focus is on the dynamics of "spiritual healing."

Drake, H.A. *A Century of Miracles: Christians, Pagans, Jews, and the Supernatural, 312-410.* New York: Oxford University Press, 2017.

This book explores the changing understanding of miracles in the fourth and fifth centuries.

Ferngren, Gary B. "Early Christianity as a Religion of Healing." *Bulletin of the History of Medicine* 66 (1992): 1–15. This essay from a conservative evangelical scholar considers Christianity's influence on health care in the Ante-Nicene period.

Ferngren, Gary B. "Early Christian Views of the Demonic Etiology of Disease." in *From Athens to Jerusalem: Medicine in Hellenized Jewish Lore and in Early Christian Literature*, eds. S. Kottek, M. Horstmanshoff, G. Baader, and G. Ferngren, 195–215. Rotterdam: Erasmus, 2000. While it is often assumed that early Christians coupled disease with the onslaught of demons, this article suggests that there were deviations. Apparently, some did not share this outlook.

Ferngren, Gary B. *Medicine and Health Care in Early Christianity*. Baltimore, Maryland: The Johns Hopkins University Press, 2009. In this work, Ferngren presents a comprehensive account of medicine and medical philanthropy in the first five centuries. Ferngren examines the relationship of early Christian medicine to the natural and supernatural modes of healing found in the Bible. Despite biblical accounts of demonic possession and miraculous healing, Ferngren argues that early Christians generally accepted naturalistic assumptions about disease and cared for the sick with medical knowledge gleaned from the Greeks and Romans.

Ferngren, Gary B. *Medicine and Religion: A Historical Introduction*. Baltimore, Maryland: The Johns Hopkins University Press, 2014. Ferngren describes how medical practice was articulated by the polytheistic religions of ancient Mesopotamia, Egypt, Greece, and Rome and the monotheistic faiths of Judaism, Christianity, and Islam. In this work, he addresses the ancient, medieval, and modern periods.

Floris, Andrew T. "Chrysostom and the Charismata." *Paraclete Journal* 5:1 (Winter 1971): 17–22. This article explores what Chrysostom, a proficient early preacher, believed about the continuation of healing and the other gifts of the Holy Spirit. Chrysostom had leanings toward cessationism.

Floris, Andrew T. "Didymus, Epiphanius, and the Charismata." *Paraclete Journal* 6:1 (Winter 1972): 26–31. Floris aptly examines two lesser-known figures from the post-Apostolic church, considering their engagement with spiritual gifts.

Floris, Andrew T. "Spiritual Gifts and Macarius of Egypt." *Paraclete Journal* 3:2 (Summer 1969): 18–20. This is a captivating historical article that examines spiritual gifts in the ministry of a fourth century Egyptian monastic.

Floris, Andrew T. "Spiritual Gifts in the Post-Apostolic Period." *Paraclete Journal* 5:2 (Spring 1971): 26–31. In this short essay, Floris briefly examines the gifts of the Spirit in the post-Apostolic church.

Floris, Andrew T. "The Charismata in the Post-Apostolic Church." *Paraclete Journal* 3:4 (Fall 1969): 8–13. Floris briefly explores the continuation of spiritual gifts in the early church.

Floris, Andrew T. "Two Fourth Century Witnesses on the Charismata." *Paraclete Journal* 4:4 (Fall 1970): 17–22. Drawing upon insights from post-Nicene leaders, Floris suggests that the usage of spiritual gifts provides a window into ongoing Christian practice.

Flusher, David. "Healing Through the Laying on of Hands in a Dead Sea Scroll." *Israel Exploration Journal* 7:2 (1957): 107–108. A document called the Genesis Apocryphon (1Qap Genesis 20:19–20) was found at Qumran in Israel in 1949. It includes an account of Abram employing the method of laying on of hands as he prayed for Pharaoh. It is the only specific example of this practice in Jewish literature. The account reads "Then Hirqanos came to me, and begged me to come and pray over the king and lay my hands upon him that he might be cured" (20:21–22a); "So I prayed for that ... and I laid my hand upon his head; the plague was removed from him, and the evil [spirit] was rebuked, and he was cured" (20:29).

Frend, W. H. C. *The Rise of Christianity.* Philadelphia: Fortress Press, 1984. This is a thoroughly researched historical analysis of the first centuries of Christianity. Frend alleges that Christianity grew, in part, due to healing and miracles.

Fridrichsen, Anton. *The Problem of Miracle in Primitive Christianity.* Minneapolis, Minnesota: Augsburg Publishing, 1972. This book is a critical look at miracles in early Christianity and what it might mean for modern Christian practice.

Frost, Evelyn. *Christian Healing: A Consideration of the Place of Spiritual Healing in the Church of Today in Light of the Doctrine and Practice of the Ante-Nicene Church.* London: A.R. Mowbray and Company LTD., 1940, 1954. This well-researched twentieth century work explores the significance of healing in the early centuries of Christendom.

Geller, Markham J. "Jesus' Theurgic Powers: Parallels in the Talmud and Incantation Bowls." *Journal of Jewish Studies* 28 (1977): 141-155. This article explores the background and Jewish context of New Testament miracle stories.

Gregory of Nyssa. "On the Christian Mode of Life." *Ascetical Works*, ed. and tr. Virginia Woods Callahan. Washington, DC: Catholic University of America Press, 1967. Gregory of Nyssa, a noted monastic, shares his insights about prayer and spiritual engagement.

Gregory of Nyssa. *The Life of Saint Macrina*, tr. Kevin Corrigan. Portland, Oregon: Wipf & Stock, 2005. This is a biographical account of Macrina (330–370) composed by her brother, Gregory of Nyssa. Macrina was considered holy and insightful. She apparently operated in the gift of "wonderworking." In this work, there is a notable story of a girl with an eye affliction healed.

Gregory the Great. *The Life and Miracles of St. Benedict.* Collegeville, Minnesota: Liturgical Press, 1949. This is Gregory the Great's biographical account of Benedict, also known as the *Second Book of Dialogues*.

Hamilton, Mary. *Incubation or the Cure of Disease in Pagan Temples and Christian Churches*. London: Simpkin, Marshall, and Kent Publishers, 1906. This book explores the nuances of healing and medical practice in the ancient world.

Hogan, Larry P. *Healing in the Second Temple Period*. Göttingen: Vandenhoeck and Ruprecht, 1992. This thoroughly researched work, drawn from Hogan's dissertation, explores the Jewish understanding of healing in the inter-testamental period.

Hurtado, Larry W. "Miracles—Pagan and Christian." *Paraclete Journal* 4:2 (Spring 1970): 20–25. This article examines the differences between pagan and Christian miracles in history. It is an insightful article from a gifted Pentecostal writer.

Hurtado, Larry W. "Healing and Related Factors." *Paraclete Journal* 4:4 (Fall 1970): 13 –16. In this brief article, Hurtado examines healing paradigms. This includes faith, prayer, the name of Jesus, and the laying on of hands.

James, M. R. *The New Testament Apocrypha*. Berkley, California: Apocryphile Press, 2004. This is a comprehensive anthology of apocryphal literature. These documents claim to be articulating the hidden teachings of the apostles, transmitted to their followers. In these dubious works, several references to healing can be found.

Jefferson, Lee M. *Christ the Miracle Worker in Early Christian Art*. Minneapolis, Minnesota: Fortress Press, 2014. This book examines early Christian art and its miraculous imagery. The author seeks to examine "the deep connection between art and its underwriting and elucidation of pivotal theological claims and developments."

Jensen, Robin M. *Baptismal Imagery in Early Christianity: Ritual, Visual, and Theological Dimensions*. Grand Rapids: Baker Academic, 2012. Jensen, a liturgical scholar, considers how images, language, architecture, and gestures convey baptism's theology. In the opening chapter, Jensen specifically explores healing within the baptismal rite.

Jerome. "The Life of Saint Hilarion the Hermit." *Nicene and Post-Nicene Fathers of the Christian Church*, second series, volume 6, ed. William Henry Freemantle, George Lewis, and William Gibson Martley. New York: Christian Literature, 1893. This work, originally written in 390, recounts the story of Hilarion. Although he wanted solitude and obscurity in the monastery, he could not avoid praying for the sick.

Kee, Howard Clark. *Miracle in The Early Christian World: A Study in Sociohistorical Method.* New Haven, Connecticut: Yale University Press, 1983. This book explores the understanding of miracles in the first-century Greco-Roman world. It clarifies the context from which Christian healing practices emerged.

Kee, Howard Clark. *Medicine, Miracle and Magic in New Testament Times.* New York: Cambridge University Press, 1986. This is an insightful monograph that explores the views of healing and medicine among first-century Jews, Christians, and Romans.

Kydd, Ronald A.N. "Charismata to 320 AD: A Study of the Overt Pneumatic Experience of the Early Church," Ph.D. diss., Saint Andrews University, 1973. This is an exceptional paper that explores the experiences of healing and the charismata in the ante-Nicene church.

Kydd, Ronald A.N. *Charismatic Gifts in the Early Church: An Exploration into the Gifts of the Spirit During the First Three Centuries of the Church.* Peabody, Massachusetts: Hendrickson Publishers, 1984. Kydd provides an outstanding overview of supernatural phenomena in the early church, including several references to healing.

Kydd, Ronald A.N. "Healing in the Christian Church." *The New International Dictionary of Pentecostal and Charismatic Movements*, eds. Stanley M. Burgess and Eduard M. Van Der Maas, 698–711. Grand Rapids, Michigan: Zondervan Publishing House, 2002. This is an exceptional article exploring healing's depth and scope within the Christian church.

Luff, S. G. A. "The Sacrament of the Sick: A First-Century Text." *The Clergy Review* 52 (1967), 56–60. This short essay explores the meaning and practice of sacramental healing during the first centuries of Christianity.

MacMullen, Ramsey. *Christianizing the Roman Empire (A.D. 100–400)*. New Haven, Connecticut: Yale University Press, 1984. MacMullen's book is a fascinating analysis of the growth of Christianity from 100–400 AD. He argues demonic deliverance and healing were the principal reasons the early church grew so rapidly.

Michaelides, Demetrios, ed. *Medicine and Healing in the Ancient Mediterranean*. Oxford, United Kingdom: Oxbow Books, 2014. The forty-two papers presented in this volume cover several aspects of medicine and therapeutic practice in the early Mediterranean world.

Neuman, Terris. "Healing in the Patristic Period." *Paraclete Journal* 18:1 (Winter 1984): 12–15. This essay evaluates the healing practices and experiences of early Church Fathers. Neuman declares, "The major conclusion of this article is that the church had a valid, continual healing ministry through the first five centuries of its existence. Although some were healed by the gifts of healing through certain individuals, the majority occurred in the context of community worship through anointing with oil."

Preuss, Julius. *Biblical and Talmudic Medicine*, tr. Fred Rosner. Lanham, Maryland: Rowman and Littlefield Publishers, 1978, 1993, 2004. This is a collection of medical and hygienic references in the Talmud and other extant Jewish sources.

Puller, Frederick William. *The Anointing of the Sick in Scripture and Tradition, With Some Considerations on the Numbering of the Sacraments*. London: Society for Promoting Christian Knowledge (SPCK), 1904. This is one of the seminal Anglican works on the sacrament of healing in church history. Puller does a fantastic job examining the historical trajectory of the healing rite, advocating for its return to the Anglican Church.

Rayner, S.L. "The Early Church and the Healing of the Sick," Ph.D. diss., University of Durham University, 1973. This carefully researched dissertation explores healing practices in the early church.

Roberts, Alexander, A. Cleveland Coxe, Alexander Roberts, James Donaldson, Phillip Schaff, and Henry Wallace, eds. *Ante-Nicene Fathers: The Writings of the Fathers Down to A.D. 325* (10 volumes). Peabody, Massachusetts: Hendrickson Publishers, 1994. This ten-volume collection contains English translations of a majority of the extant Ante-Nicene church documents. There are a number of references to healing in these works.

Roberts, Alexander, James Donaldson, Phillip Schaff, and Henry Wallace, eds. *Nicene and Post-Nicene Fathers: First Series* (14 volumes). Peabody, Massachusetts: Hendrickson Publishers, 1996. Series 1 of the *Nicene and Post-Nicene Fathers* consists of eight volumes of the writings of Saint Augustine and six volumes of the sermons and writings of Saint Chrysostom. There are cursory references to healing in these writings.

Roberts, Alexander, James Donaldson, Phillip Schaff, and Henry Wallace, eds. *Nicene and Post Nicene Fathers: Second Series* (14 volumes). Peabody, Massachusetts: Hendrickson Publishers, 1996. *The Nicene and Post-Nicene Fathers: Second Series* contains—in fourteen volumes—the works of the Greek Fathers, Eusebius to John of Damascus. It also includes the Latin Fathers from Hilary to Gregory the Great. These works also include references to healing.

Russell, Norman, tr. *The Lives of the Desert Fathers: Historia Monachorum in Aegypto*. Collegeville, Minnesota: Cistercian Publications, 1981. This work, attributed to Rufinus of Aquileia (340–410), recounts the history of the monks of Egypt. The events of twenty-six men's lives are recorded. In their stories are fascinating accounts of healings and exorcisms. The *Historia Monachorum in Aegypto* contributed to the notoriety of the monks of Egypt throughout Christendom.

Sharp, Omer Jaye. "Did Charismata Cease with the Apostles' Death?" *Paraclete Journal* 10:2 (Spring 1976): 17–20. This essay examines the theological and historical formation of the early church, rebuffing the dubious claims of cessationism.

Sheils, William J., ed. *The Church and Healing: Papers Read at the Twentieth Summer Meeting and the Twenty-First Winter Meeting of the Ecclesiastical Historical Society.* Oxford, United Kingdom: Blackwell, 1982. This is an insightful collection of academic papers on sickness and health in the history of Christianity.

Socrates. *The Ecclesiastical History of Socrates, Surnamed Scholasticus, Or The Advocate: Comprising a History of the Church, in Seven Books, From the Ascension of Constantine, A.D. 305 to the 38th Year of Theodosius II, Including a Period of 140 Years.* London: Bohn, 1853. Socrates Scholasticus (380-439), was a 5th-century historian. He references a number of healing accounts in this historical work (See 1.17, 19, 20; 4.23, 24, 27; 7.4).

Sozomen. *The Ecclesiastical History of Sozomen: Comprising a History of the Church from A. D. 324 to A. D. 440*, tr. Edward Walford. London: Bohn, 1855. In addition to reflecting on the rise of monasticism, Sozomen focuses on the missionary activity among the Armenians, Saracens, and Goths. This work includes several healing accounts (See II.1, 6, 7; III.14; IV.3, 16; V.21; VI.16, 20, 28 and 29; VII.27).

Stephanou, Eusebius A. "The Charismata in the Early Church." *Greek Orthodox Theological Review* 21 (Summer 1976): 125–46. This is an astute Orthodox scholar examining spiritual gifts in the early church.

Womack, David A. "Divine Healing in the Post-Apostolic Church." *Paraclete Journal* 2:2 (Spring 1968): 3–8. This brief essay provides an analysis of healing in the early Christianity.

Zimany, Roland. "Divine Energies in Orthodox Theology." *Diakonia* 11:3 (1976) 281–85. This article, written from the perspective of the

Eastern Orthodox theological tradition, explores "divine energy" and its varied impact on humanity

2. MEDIEVAL

Adamnan. *Life of Saint Columba Founder of Hy*, ed. William Reeves. Edinburgh, Scotland: Edmonston and Douglas, 1874. Columba (521–597) was a leader among Irish missionary monks. Exiled from his homeland, he established a monastery at Iona, and from there he spread the gospel to Scotland and Northern England. This work, on his life and miracles, was written in the ninth century.

Aelfric. *Lives of Saints*, 2 volumes, ed. Walter Skeat. London: N. Trübner & Company, 1881. Aelfric (955–1025) was an Anglo-Saxon writer, considered the greatest of his time. His work on the saints was written to provide inspiration and guidance for other monks.

Allen, David. "Signs and Wonders in Bede's History." *Paraclete Journal* 24:4 (Fall 1990): 28–30. Bede's work on the history of the English church was published in the eighth century. This brief essay examines Bede's references to signs, wonders, and healings.

Amundsen, Darrel. *Medicine, Society, and Faith in the Ancient and Medieval Worlds*. Baltimore, Maryland: Johns Hopkins University Press, 2000. In this penetrating work, Amundsen explores the understanding and appropriation of healing in the ancient world.

Ataoguz, Jenny Kirsten. "Visual Preaching in the Early Middle Ages: The Healing Arts at the Carolingian Monastery of St. John in Müstair, Switzerland," paper presented at the Annual Meeting of the College Art Association, February 2008. In this paper, Ataoguz documents how, around 800 AD, the Church of the Monastery of John the Baptist in Müstair, Switzerland, received an elaborate painting. Meanwhile, a sacramentary and a preaching handbook were composed at the same time. Ataoguz demonstrates how these three items worked together to facilitate ministry. She points out that the strategically-placed cluster of scenes, which depicts Jesus healing, corresponds to healing prayers in the sacramentary and exhortations in the preaching handbook.

Athanasius. *The Life of Antony and The Letter to Marcellinus*, tr. Robert C. Gregg. Mahwah, New Jersey: Paulist Press, 1979. Athanasius was the noted bishop of Alexandria. Around 360, he was asked to write an account of Antony, a mystic, and originator of Christian monasticism. Among other things, Athanasius recounts some of the healings that took place under Antony's ministry.

Bagnoli, Martina, Holger A. Klein, C. Griffith Mann, and James Robinson, eds. *Treasures of Heaven: Saints, Relics, and Devotion in Medieval Europe.* New Haven: Yale University Press, 2010. This well-researched work explores medieval reliquaries and the individuals that engaged them.

Bartlett, Robert. *Why Can the Dead Do Such Great Things? Saints and Worshippers from the Martyrs to the Reformation.* Princeton, New Jersey: Princeton University Press, 2013. Bartlett, the Bishop Wardlaw Professor of Medieval History at the University of Saint Andrews in Scotland and a fellow of the British Academy, explores the significance of reliquary healing in the medieval church.

Bede. *Ecclesiastical History of the English People*, eds. J.A. Giles and G. Gray. Chicago: Tiger of the Stripe, 2007. The Venerable Bede (AD 672–735) was a historian who documented the expansion of the church in the British Isles. This work that includes several healing accounts, was originally published in 731.

Bonaventure, *The Life of Saint Francis Of Assisi: From the "Legenda Santi Francisci of Saint Bonaventure,"* ed. Henry Edward. London: R. Washbourne, 1868. Written shortly after his death, this is the official Franciscan account of Francis Assisi's life and exploits.

Bornstein, Daniel E. "Relics, Ascetics, Living Saints." *A People's History of Christianity: Medieval Christianity*, ed. Daniel E. Bornstein, 75–106. Minneapolis: Fortress Press, 2009. This is a well-researched examination of the meaning of relics in the middle ages.

Brewer, Ebenezer Cobham. *A Dictionary of Miracles, Imitative, Realistic, and Dogmatic.* London: Chatto and Windus, 1901. This book is a compilation of miraculous accounts of early and medieval saints.

Brown, Peter. "Relics and Social Status in the Age of Gregory of Tours." *Society and the Holy in Late Antiquity*, by Peter Brown, 222–250. Berkley, California: University of California Press, 1989. In this academic article, Brown examines healing, relics, and unusual phenomena in the early middle ages.

Brown, Peter. "Society and the Supernatural: A Medieval Change." *Society and the Holy in Late Antiquity*. Berkley, California: University of California Press, 1989. 302–332. In this essay, Brown provides insights into the understanding of the supernatural in the medieval period.

Brown, Peter. *The Cult of the Saints: Its Rise and Function in Latin Christianity*. Chicago: University of Chicago Press, 1981. In this work, Brown explores the role of tombs, shrines, relics, and pilgrimages in the medieval church.

Brown, Peter. "The Rise and Function of the Holy Man in Later Antiquity." *Journal of Roman Studies* 61 (1971): 80–101. This is an article that explores the understanding of the miraculous in the middle ages.

Burgess, Stanley M. *The Holy Spirit: Eastern Christian Traditions*. Peabody, Massachusetts: Hendrickson Publishing, 1989. In this well-researched book, Burgess recounts the understanding and experience of the Holy Spirit in Eastern Church traditions. It includes references to the ministry of healing.

Burgess, Stanley M. *The Holy Spirit: Medieval Roman Catholic and Reformation Traditions*. Peabody, Massachusetts: Hendrickson Publishing, 1997. In this concluding work, Burgess examines medieval and reformed pneumatology. Within these accounts, there are references to healing.

Bulter, Alban. *Butler's Lives of the Saints*, volume 2, eds. Herbert J. Thurston and Donald Attwater. Notre Dame, Indiana: Christian Classics, 1956. Butler (1711-1773), was an English Catholic who, between 1756 and 1759, compiled hundreds of popular accounts of the saints. This work includes several healing accounts.

Bynum, Caroline Walker. *Christian Materiality: An Essay on Religion in Late Medieval Europe*. New York: Zone Books, 2011. This work from Bynum clarifies the understanding of healing via relics within the Roman Catholic tradition.

Colgrave, Bertram, ed. and tr. *The Earliest Life of Gregory the Great*. New York: Cambridge University Press, 1968, 1985. Around 700AD, an unknown Anglo-Saxon at Whitby wrote this notable book. It recounts aspects of the life and miracles of Gregory the Great.

Colgrave, Bertram, ed. and tr. *The Life of Bishop Wilfrid by Eddius Stephanus*. New York: Cambridge University Press, 1927, 1985. Stephanus' work, aside from *Bede's Historia Ecclesiastica*, is the only source on Wilfrid. It was written shortly after monk's death in 709. Stephanus recounts a number of Wilfrid's healings and extraordinary events. However, unlike most medieval hagiographies, which consisted of random miracles attributed to saints, this work provides a chronological narrative with specific names and events.

Colgrave, Bertram, ed. and tr. *Two Lives of Saint Cuthbert*. New York: Cambridge University Press, 1940. This is an annotated compilation of two closely associated accounts of Saint Cuthbert of Durham, England (633–687). Both works recount the astounding life and miracles of Cuthbert.

De Voragine, Jacobus. *The Golden Legend: Readings on the Saints*, tr. William Granger Ryan. Princeton, New Jersey: Princeton University Press, 2012. This hagiography was compiled around 1260 by Jacobus de Voragine, a scholarly friar, and archbishop of Genoa. Compiling true and exaggerated accounts of the saints, De Voragine wanted to edify the common people.

Darling, Frank C. *Christian Healing: In The Middle Ages and Beyond.* Boulder, Colorado: Vista Publications, 1990. This historical work briefly explores the history of healing from the middle ages to the present.

Eales, Samuel J. *Saint Bernard, Abbot of Clairvaux, A.D. 1091–1153.* London: Society for Promoting Christian Knowledge, 1890. Bernard (1090–1153) was abbot of the monastery at Clairvaux, and the primary instrument who brought reformation to the Cistercian Order. A number of healings took place through his ministry.

Finucane, Robert C. "Authorizing the Supernatural: An Examination of English Miracles Around 1318," in *Aspects of Power and Authority in the Middle Ages*, eds. Brenda Bolton and Christine Meek, 289–303. Turnhout: Brepols Publishers, 2007. This is a gripping examination of miracles in late medieval English society.

Finucane, Robert C. "Faith Healing in Medieval England: Miracles at Saints' Shrines," *Psychiatry* 36 (1973): 341–346. This engaging article explores the understanding of reliquary healing in medieval England.

Finucane, Robert C. *Miracles and Pilgrims: Popular Belief in Medieval England.* London: Palgrave Macmillan, 1977. In this work, Ronald C. Finucane analyzes more than 3,000 posthumous accounts of miracles. He pieces together the world of pilgrims, miracles, and faith-healing, demonstrating its hold over the medieval imagination.

Finucane, Robert C. "The Use and Abuse of Medieval Miracles." *History* 60 (1975) 1–10. In this article, Finucane provides some compelling research into the viability of healing during the medieval period.

Floris, Andrew T. "Primacy of the Spiritual." *Paraclete Journal* 6:3 (Summer 1972): 27–32. In this article, Floris deliberates on Symeon, the New Theologian (949–1022), a leader purportedly gifted with great power to operate in healing.

Gardner, Rex. "Miracles of Healing in Anglo-Celtic Northumbria as Recorded by the Venerable Bede and His Contemporaries: A Reappraisal in the Light of Twentieth-Century Experience," *British Medical Journal* 287 (1983): 1927–1933. This is a perceptive article that examines healing accounts in the Venerable Bede's eighth century work.

Goodich, Michael E. *Miracles and Wonders: The Development of the Concept of Miracle, 1150–1350.* Hampshire, United Kingdom: Ashgate Publishing, 2007. Goodich explores the understanding of miracles in later medieval society.

Greer, Rowan A. *The Fear of Freedom: A Study of Miracles in the Roman Imperial Church.* University Park, Pennsylvania: Penn State University Press, 1989. In this work, Greer explores how miracles shaped catechesis, scriptural exegesis, and piety in the fourth and fifth centuries.

Hildegard of Bingen, *Causae et Curae (Holistic Healing),* tr. Manfred Pawlik and Patrick Madigan, eds. Mary Palmquist and John Kulas. Collegeville, Minnesota: Liturgical Press, Inc., 1994. Hildegard of Bingen (1098–1179) was a German Benedictine abbess, writer, composer, philosopher, and mystic. *Causae et Curae* is an exploration of the human body, its connections to the natural world, and the causes and cures of various diseases. Hildegard's works are primarily medical, but she often integrates the spiritual. She typically combined physical treatments with holistic methods centered on "spiritual healing."

Hildegard of Bingen. *Physica,* tr. Priscilla Throop. Rochester, Vermont: Healing Arts Press, 1998. *Physica* contains nine books that describe the scientific and medicinal properties of various plants, stones, fish, reptiles, and animals. Although medical by design, Hildegard refracted these practices through her mysticism.

Heffernan, Thomas J. *Sacred Biography: Saints and Their Biographers in the Middle Ages.* New York: Oxford University Press, 1992. Though medieval collections on the Roman Catholic saints are among the oldest literary texts of Western Christianity, scholars often denigrate them. Heffernan offers a reassessment of the nature and importance of the accounts of the saints, arguing that modern scholarship, bound by its historical-critical methodology, has not understood the underlying principles of these works.

Koopmans, Rachel. *Wonderful to Relate: Miracle Stories and Miracle Collecting in High Medieval England.* Philadelphia: University of Pennsylvania Press, 2011. In this work, Rachel Koopmans explores medieval religious culture by examining the miracle stories collected in England from roughly 1080 to 1220.

Kleinberg, Aviad. *Flesh Made Word: Saints' Stories and The Western Imagination.* Boston: Balknap Press, 2008. Aviad Kleinberg argues that the saints' stories of medieval Europe were more than edifying entertainment: They inspired and created a subversive theology that continues to impact the understanding and practice of Christianity.

Kreiser, B. Robert. *Miracles, Convulsions, and Ecclesiastical Politics in Early Eighteenth-Century Paris.* Princeton: Princeton University Press, 1978. Against the backdrop of fierce social and religious conflicts in France, worshipers at the tomb of a Jansenist deacon in Paris' Cemetery of Saint-Médard witnessed a variety of miraculous occurrences.

Kydd, Ronald, A.N. "Jesus, Saints, and Relics: Approaching The Early Church Through Healing." *Journal of Pentecostal Theology* 2 (April 1993): 91–104. This insightful article examines the attitudes and practices of early Christians in matters of healing.

Larchet, Jean-Claude. *Mental Disorders and Spiritual Healing: Teachings from the Early Christian East,* tr. Rama P. Coomaraswamy and G. John Campoux. New York: Sophia Perennis, 1992, 2005. This intriguing volume explores the early Eastern church's understanding of mental illness and demonic affliction. The first chapter, on the Christian valuation of the body, alone is worth the price of the book.

Larchet, Jean-Claude. *The Theology of Illness*. Crestwood: Saint Vladimir's Seminary Press, 2002. This book explores biblical and patristic perspectives on sickness and what some call "redemptive suffering." Larchet, a scholar from the Eastern Orthodox tradition, explores the origin of sin, its impact on physical health, and the healing of human nature by the incarnate Son of God.

Maconachie, C. Leslie. "Anointing and Healing: Truth, Opinion and Misconception: A Study of the Propagation of the Faith in Twelfth Century Britain," Ph.D. diss., Greenwich University, 1990. This work is an exploration of ritual and healing practices in England during the late Middle Ages.

Macdougall, Simone. "The Surgeon and the Saints: Henri de Mondeville on Divine Healing." *Journal of Medieval History* 26:3 (2000): 253–267. A common theme of medieval miracle collections was to highlight the inadequacies of secular medicine while promoting the divine healing power of the saints. The fourteenth-century Parisian surgeon Henri de Mondeville provides an opposing view. Mondeville refutes healing miracles and the competition that they pose to his profession. He believes that people should place their confidence in the operations of the surgeon rather than the intercession of a saint.

McCready, William D. *Miracles and the Venerable Bede*. Toronto: Pontifical Institute of Mediaeval Studies, 1994. This scholarly work carefully examines the healing and miracle accounts in the *Ecclesiastical History of Bede*.

Moog, Ferdinand Peter, and Axel Karenberg. "St. Francis came at dawn—the miraculous recovery of a hemiplegic monk in the Middle Ages." *Journal of Neurological Sciences* 213 (2003): 15–17. The authors of this article present a case study of a thirteenth-century miracle ascribed to St. Francis. They draw their report from a detailed summary of the recovery of a hemiplegic monk whom St. Francis healed through the use of touch.

O'Malley, J. Steven. "Probing the Demise and Recovery of Healing in Christianity." *Pneuma Journal* 5:1 (1983): 46–59. This well-researched article examines the waning of healing after the Nicene Council and attests to its later resurgence.

Patrick. *The Confession of Saint Patrick and Letter to Coroticus*, tr. John Skinner. Colorado Springs, Colorado: Image, 1998. This work is a brief account of St. Patrick's life. It provides a stirring reflection on the miraculous works and healings in Ireland.

Porter, Harry Boone. "The Origins of the Medieval Rite for Anointing the Sick or Dying." *Journal of Theological Studies* 7:2 (October 1956): 211–225. In this article, Porter explores the history of the last rite as it progressively changes from a sacrament for the sick to a sacrament for the dying.

Preuss, Julius. *Medicine in the Bible and Talmud*, tr. Fred Rosner. New York: Ktav Publishing House, 1977. This book explores references to medicine and disease in the Old Testament and early Jewish literature.

Scott, Robert A. *Miracle Cures: Saints, Pilgrimage and The Healing Powers of Belief*. Oakland, California: University of California Press, 2010. Using research in biomedical and behavioral science, Scott examines several accounts of miracle cures at medieval, early modern, and contemporary shrines.

Stouck, Mary Ann. "Relics," in *Medieval Saints: Reader*, ed. Mary Ann Stouck, 355–409. Toronto: University of Toronto Press, 1998. This well-researched entry explores the understanding and scope of relics in the medieval Roman Catholic Church.

Talbot, Charles Hugh, ed. and tr. *The Anglo-Saxon Missionaries in Germany. Being the Lives of SS. Willibrord, Boniface, Sturm, Leoba and Lebuin, Together with the Hodoeporicon of St. Willibald and a Selection from the Correspondence of St. Boniface*. New York: Sheed and Talbot, 1954. This work examines the lives of European missionaries from the early medieval period. It includes a number of healing accounts.

Theodoret of Cyrrhus, *A History of the Monks of Syria*, tr. R.M. Price. Trappist, Kentucky: Cistercian Publications, 1985. This is an important early hagiographic work, documenting Syrian monasticism in the fourth and fifth centuries.

Ward, Benedicta. *Miracles and the Medieval Mind: Theory, Record and Event 1000–1215*. Hampshire, England: Wildwood House, 1982, 1987. Ward's study of miracles in the medieval Roman Catholic Church is noteworthy.

Ward, Benedicta. *Signs and Wonders: Saints, Miracles and Prayers from the 4th Century to the 14th*. Surrey, England: Ashgate Variorum, 1992. This is, arguably, the seminal work on signs and wonders in the Roman Catholic tradition.

York, William H. *Health and Wellness in Antiquity through the Middle Ages*. Santa Barbara, California: Greenwood, 2012. This academic work explores the diverse health care approaches through different cultures in the ancient world. It also includes reflections on healing practices in the medieval church.

Ziegler, Joseph. "Practitioners and Saints: Medical Men in Canonization Processes in the Thirteenth to Fifteenth Centuries." *Social History of Medicine* 12 (1999): 191–225. In the later middle ages, the church appealed to medical judgment to authenticate miracles. Records of the canonization processes from 1200 – 1500 demonstrate that doctors actively appeared as witnesses in ecclesiastical proceedings.

3. REFORMATION

Baxter, Richard. "Directions for The Sick." *The Practical Works of Richard Baxter with A Preface Giving Some Account of the Author and of The Edition of His Practical Works; An Essay On His Genius, Works, And Times; And A Portrait*, volume 1. London: George Virtue, 1838, 522–534. In this work, the noted Puritan, Richard Baxter, provides some of his pastoral insights for dealing with sickness and disease.

Baxter, Richard. "Directions to Friends of the Sick, That Are About Them." *The Practical Works of Richard Baxter with A Preface Giving Some Account of the Author and of The Edition of His Practical Works; An Essay On His Genius, Works, And Times; And A Portrait*, volume 1. London: George Virtue, 1838, 534–547. This short work is a practical guide from Baxter on dealing with illnesses in the church community.

Calvin, John. "An Admonition Showing the Advantages Which Christendom Might Derive from an Inventory of Relics." Liverpool, United Kingdom: E. Howell Publisher, 1844. Originally published in the sixteenth century, this tract showcases Calvin's biting satire in his criticism of Roman Catholicism. He says that if an inventory of relics were actually taken, we would discover that every apostle had more than four bodies, and every saint two or three.

Calvin, John. *Calvin's Commentaries*. Grand Rapids, Michigan: Baker Books, 1974. This twenty-two volume collection is a compilation of Calvin's expositions on the Bible. In a handful of the entries, Calvin makes references to healing and the gifts of the Spirit.

Calvin, John. *Institutes of Christian Religion*, tr. Ford Lewis Battles, ed. John T. McNeil. Philadelphia: Westminster John Knox Press, 1559, 1960. Calvin's magnum opus does not delve into the ministry of healing in any major way. There were, however, some passing references to it in his general theological discourse.

Cheng, Yang-en. "Calvin on the Work of the Holy Spirit and Spiritual Gifts," in *Calvin in Asian Churches*, volume 3, ed. Sou-Young Lee, 113–40. Seoul, Korea: Presbyterian College and Theological

Seminary Press, 2008. This work explores Calvin's pneumatology and understanding of the charismata.

Elbert, Paul. "Calvin and Spiritual Gifts." *Journal of The Evangelical Theological Society* 23: 2. (September 1979): 235–256. This article, written by an Evangelical scholar, briefly examines Calvin's understanding of healing and the gifts of the Holy Spirit.

Foller, Oskar. "Martin Luther on Miracles, Healing, Prophecy and Tongues." *Studia Historia Ecclesicticas* 31:2 (October 2005) 333–351. This article explores Luther's understanding of healing and the supernatural works of God. Foller declares, "Luther mentions the idea of a restriction of the gifts to early Christianity, but he did not make a principle of it. Rather, he maintains an openness to the present-day occurrence as well."

Gilbert, Daniel. "The Pneumatic Charismata in the Theology of John Calvin: A Study of Calvin's Pneumatology, Focusing on his Concepts and Interpretation of the Pneumatic Charismata in his Life and Works," Ph.D. diss., Aberdeen University, 2005. This well-researched dissertation explores Calvin's conception of the Holy Spirit and the possibility of continuing spiritual gifts.

Harley, David. "John Hart of Northampton and the Calvinist Critique of Priest-Physicians: An unpublished Polemic of the early 1620s." *Medical History* 42 (1998): 362–386. This article examines the understanding of medicine and religion in the post-Reformation world.

Hejzlar, Pavel. "John Calvin and the Cessation of Miraculous Healing." *Communio Viatorum* 49:1 (2007): 31–77. This is an article that examines Calvin's understanding of divine healing. Hejzlar believes Calvin's doctrine of cessation of miraculous is principally based on two propositions. 1). Healing fulfilled its function of certifying the gospel as it emerged in the first century. 2). What is really important is the healing of the soul from sin.

Hoffman, Bengt Runo. *Luther and the Mystics: A Re-examination of Luther's spiritual experience and his relationship to the mystics.* Minneapolis, Minnesota: Augsburg Publishing House 1976. This book explores the mystical element in Luther's thought. Among other things, Hoffman recounts Luther's battles with illnesses and how prayer brought healing.

Hoffman, Bengt Runo. "Luther and the Mystical." *The Lutheran Quarterly* 36:3 (August 1974): 316–329. In this well-researched article, Hoffman explores some of the "mystical" elements of Luther's theology and practice. Hoffman characterizes Luther differently than many imagine him.

Jensen, Peter F. "Calvin, Charismatics, and Miracles." *The Evangelical Quarterly* 51:3 (1979): 131–144. This well-researched article wrestles with Calvin's understanding of miraculous works against the context of the 70s era Charismatic Renewal. Jensen argues that Calvin believed, "The gospel, the preached word, is power, the real power. The seat of power is word, not deed. Things which men had feared or used as supernatural were illusory and satanic effects, to be eschewed, never harnessed, even with ecclesiastical sanction." Thus, he says that Calvin would have rejected healing and other works of the Spirit.

Langstaff, Beth Yvonne. "*Temporary Gifts: John Calvin's Doctrine of the Cessation of Miracles*," Ph.D. diss., Princeton University, 1999. This well-researched work explores the idea of the cessation of the charismata in the theology of John Calvin. Langstaff records that "John Calvin posits that miraculous gifts such as healing, exorcism, and prophecy ceased at the close of the apostolic era."

Lindberg, Carter. "The Lutheran Tradition." *Curing and Caring: Health and Western Medicine in the Western Religious Traditions*, eds. Ronald L Numbers and Darrel W. Amundsen, 173–203. New York: Macmillan Publishing Company, 1986. In this well-researched essay, Lindberg explores the understanding of sickness and disease in the Lutheran tradition.

Lopez, Augustus Nocodemus and José Manoel Da Conceicao. "Calvin, Theologian of the Holy Spirit: The Holy Spirit and the Word of God." *Scottish Bulletin of Evangelical Theology* 15 (1997): 38–49. This article draws upon John Calvin's pneumatological formation to provide a fierce critique of the Pentecostal-Charismatic movement.

Luther, Martin. *Letters of Spiritual Counsel*, tr. Theodore Gerhardt Tappert. Vancouver, British Columbia, Canada: Regent College Publishing, 2003. While this work does not specifically refer to healing, Luther's thoughts about pastoral care and intercession are in evidence. In one letter, Luther shares some guidance for praying for a sick man.

Mashau, Derrick. "John Calvin's theology of the charismata: its influence on the Reformed Confessions and its implications for the church's mission." *Missionalia: Southern African Journal of Mission Studies* 36.1 (2008): 86–97. This study explores the ways that Calvin addressed the gifts of the Spirit in his writings. It also investigates the influence of Calvin's thought on missions and Protestant confessions.

Mather, Cotton. *The Angel of Bethesda: An Essay on the Common Maladies of Mankind*, ed. Gordon Jones. Worcester, Massachusetts: American Antiquarian Society, 1724, 1972. In this book, Matther attempts to explain various illnesses in their spiritual context. He attributes some illnesses to demonic sources and others to God. Mather advocates for repentance and traditional folk medicine for a treatment for mental illness. Afflicted individuals are understood to be responsible for their own sickness. Mather writes, "O thou afflicted, and under distemper, go to physicians in obedience to God, who has commanded the use of means. But place thy dependence on God alone to direct and prosper them. And know that they are all physicians of no value if He does not do so. Consult with physicians; but in full persuasion, that if God leaves them to their own counsels, thou only suffer many things from them; they will do thee more hurt than good. Be sensible, tis from God, and not from the physician, that cure is to be looked for."

Mentzer, Raymond A. "The Persistence of 'Superstition and Idolatry' among Rural French Calvinists." *Church History* 65:2 (1996): 220–233. The Reformers suggested that the medieval church was filled with "superstition and idolatry." Mentzer writes that "John Calvin and Theodore Beza, erudite theologians and celebrated preachers, local pastors and village elders alike stood ever ready to apply the designations to a variety of religious convictions and habits that they considered the incorrect belief and inappropriate behavior of the 'uninformed' and 'vulgar.'"

Michelet, Jules. *The Life of Luther Written by Himself*, 2nd edition, tr. William Hazlett. London: Bell and Daldy, 1872. This historical work, drawn primarily from Luther's own writings, provides insight into his experiences with divine healing.

Minnema, Theodore. "Calvin's Interpretation of Human Suffering," in *Exploring the Heritage of John Calvin*, ed. David E. Holwerda, 140–162. Grand Rapids, Michigan: Baker Book House, 1976. This work briefly delves into John Calvin's Augustinian understanding of suffering and pain.

Morris, John Gottlieb. *Quaint Sayings and Doings Concerning Luther.* Philadelphia: Lindsay and Blakiston, 1859. This collection of Luther's sayings includes some of his less cited notions on healing.

Peter, J.F. "The Ministry in the Early Church as Seen by John Calvin." *The Evangelical Quarterly* 35 (1963): 68–78. This academic article explores what the John Calvin understood about the government and theology of the early church.

Rieder, Philip. "Miracles and Heretics: Protestants and Catholic Healing Practices in and around Geneva 1530–1750." *Social History of Medicine* 23:2 (2010): 227–243. From the time of the Reformation, Calvin's Geneva had numerous conflicts about the appropriation of healing. Protestant control of medical practice in the city naturally led to the prohibition of Catholic healing rituals. However, various sources suggest that demand for the forbidden healing rites continued in Geneva into the eighteenth century.

Schiefelbein, Kyle K. "'Receive this oil as a sign of forgiveness and healing': A Brief History of the Anointing of the Sick and Its Use in Lutheran Worship." *Word & World* 30:1 (Winter 2010): 51–62. This article is a thoroughly researched examination of the practice of anointing with oil within Lutheranism.

Smylie, James H. "The Reformed Tradition, Health and Healing." *Curing and Caring: Health and Western Medicine in the Western Religious Traditions*, ed. Ronald L. Numbers and Darrel W. Amundsen, 204–239. New York: Macmillan Publishing Company, 1986. This is an excellent work that explores the history of healing in the Reformed tradition.

Soergel, Philip M. *Miracles and the Protestant Imagination: The Evangelical Wonder Book in Reformation Germany*. New York: Oxford University Press, 2012. In this carefully researched work, Soergel examines a few of the miraculous accounts in Post-Reformation Germany.

4. POST-REFORMATION

Anonymous. "To the Patriarchs, Archbishops, Bishops, and others in places of chief rule over the church of Christ throughout the earth and to the Emperors, Kings, Sovereign Princes and Chief Governors over the nations of the baptized." *The History and Doctrine of Irvingism*, 1, ed. Edward Miller, 347–436. London: Kegan Paul and Company, 1878. This work, originally published in 1838, explores the theological outlook of Edward Irving and the Catholic Apostolic Church. It includes insights into their conceptions of healing.

Barager, C.A. "John Wesley and Medicine." *Annals of Medical History* 10 (1928): 59–65. This is an early twentieth century article that explores John Wesley's conception of medicine and physical healing.

Barlow, Frank. "The King's Evil." *The English Historical Review* 95:374 (January 1980): 3–27. Barlow explores the healing practices of French and English monarchs in the late Middle Ages and early modern period.

Baxter, Robert. *Irvingism: in its Rise, Progress and Present State*. London: Nisbet, 1836. Baxter explores some of the ideas and practices of Edward Irving and his followers who believed in the continuation of the gifts of the Spirit in the early 1800s.

Baxter, Robert. *Narrative of Facts Characterizing the Supernatural Manifestations in Members of Mr. Irving's Congregation*. London: Nisbet, 1836. This is a work that examines what transpired in Edward Irving's congregation in the 1830s. In addition to glossolalia and prophetic declarations, there were also expressions of healing.

Beckett, William. *A Free and Impartial Enquiry into the Antiquity and Efficacy of Touching for the Cure of the King's Evil: Written Some Time Since, in Two Letters: the One to Dr. Steigertahl, the Other to Sir Hans Sloane, To which is Added, a Collection of Records*. London: J. Peele, 1722. This short, eighteenth century work explores the validity of European monarchs praying for the sick.

Bloch, Marc Léopold Benjamin. *The Royal Touch: Sacred Monarchy and Scrofula in England and France*, tr. by J.E. Anderson. Montreal, Quebec, Canada: McGill-Queen's University Press, 1973. Bloch, a noted historian and scholar, takes a skeptical approach to analyzing the later medieval healing exploits of French and English kings. Bloch associates this practice with superstition and mass hysteria.

Boys, Thomas. *The Christian Dispensation Miraculous: Republished from The Jewish Expositor, With A Dedication to the Lord Bishop of London*, Second Edition. London: L.B. Seely publisher, 1832. Boys, a colleague of Edward Irving, presents arguments for the continuation of miracles, centering his argument on "the case of Miss Fancourt," a woman who received a marvelous healing.

Boys, Thomas. *The Suppressed Evidence: Or, Proofs of the Miraculous Faith and Experience of the Church of Christ in All Ages, from Authentic Records of the Fathers, Waldenses, Hussites, Reformers, United Brethren, Etc.: A Historical Sketch Suggested by The Honorable and Reverend B.W. Noel's Remarks On the Revival of Miraculous Powers in The Church*. London: Adams, Hamilton Publishers, 1832. Boys' work argues for the continuance of miracles, tracing their occurrences from the early church to 1832. He cites Augustine, Chrysostom, Isidore, Huss, Fox, Luther, Zwingli, Calvin, Bucer, Beza, Knox, and Zinzendorf as he argues against cessationalist claims.

Brogan, Stephen. "The Royal Touch: A Monarch's Divine Ability to Cure Scrofula was an Established Ritual When James I Came to the English Throne in 1603. Initially Skeptical of the Catholic Characteristics of the Ceremony, the King Found Ways to 'Protestantize' It and to Reflect His Own Hands-On Approach to Kingship." *History Today* 61:2 (February 2011). Brogan, one of the leading authorities on the Royal Touch, provides fascinating insights into the practice.

Brogan, Stephen. *The Royal Touch in Early Modern England: Politics, Medicine, and Sin*. London: Royal Historical Society, 2015. Drawing on a wide range of sources—images, coins, medals, playing cards, manuscripts and printed texts— this book provides a valuable window into the practice of the Royal Touch. This is arguably the standard work on the healing practices of French and English kings.

Bulteel, Henry Bellenden. *The Doctrine of the Miraculous Interference of Jesus on Behalf of Believers.* Oxford: Baxter, 1832. Bulteel was a controversial minister ousted from the Church of England. After being directly impacted by the ministry of Edward Irving in the early 1830s, he recounts successfully ministering healing to three women.

Crawfurd, Raymund. *The King's Evil.* London: Oxford University Press, 1911. In this work, Crawfurd explores the controversial history and meaning of the Royal Touch. Crawfurd remains skeptical in his analysis, associating the practice with superstition and ignorance.

Cule, John "The Contribution of John Wesley (1703–1791) to Medical Literature." *History of Science and Medicine* 17:1 (1982): 328–331. This article briefly explores how John Wesley's understanding of health and disease influenced later medical therapies and literature.

Currelly, C. T. "The King's Evil and the Royal Touch." *Canadian Medical Association Journal* 16.5 (1926): 581–583. This is a fascinating overview of the history of French and English kings who provided healing in the name of Jesus through the use of touch.

Duffy, Earmon. "Valentine Greatrakes: The Irish Stroker," in *Miracle, Science, and Orthodoxy in Restoration England: Religion and Humanism*, ed. K. Robbins, 251–273. London: Oxford, 1981. This article critically examines the claims of Valentine Greatrakes, a seventeenth century Irish healer.

Editor. "A Medical Tract by John Wesley." *The British Medical Journal* 29 (1902): 780–799. This academic article, from an early twentieth century medical researcher, explores John Wesley's understanding of medicine and healing.

Editor. "John Wesley and the Art of Healing." *The British Medical Journal* 28 (1906): 987–988. This is an article from a medical journal that explores John Wesley's understanding of health and healing.

Editor. "Miraculous Cures." *The Morning Watch: Quarterly Journal on Prophecy and Theological Review* 4 (1832): 474-481. This article is a collection of healing testimonies from individuals associated with Edward Irving's congregation in London.

Editor. "Particulars of a few Recent Cases of Healing," *The Morning Watch: Quarterly Journal on Prophecy and Theological Review* 4 (1832): 215-227. This article recounts healing stories from individuals who intersected with Edward Irving's church.

Elmer, Peter, ed. *The Healing Arts: Health, Disease, and Society in Europe, 1500–1800*. United Kingdom: Manchester University Press, 2004. This book explores how social, religious, political, and cultural dynamics affected health from the Renaissance to the Enlightenment.

Elmer, Peter. *The Miraculous Conformist: Valentine Greatrakes, the Body Politic, and the Politics of Healing in Restoration Britain*. London: Oxford University Press, 2013. This work explores the fascinating story of Valentine Greatrakes. In the 1660s, he cured multitudes suffering from a large range of diseases. Elmer's book on Greatrakes is based on extensive research from the Irish and English archives.

Flegg, Columba Graham. *Gathered under Apostles: A Study of the Catholic Apostolic Church*. London: Oxford University Press, 1992. This extensively researched book is one of the seminal works on Edward Irving and the Catholic Apostolic Church.

Fox, George. *George Fox's Book of Miracles*, ed and comp. Henry J. Cadbury. London, England: Cambridge University Press, 1948. George Fox (1624–1691), founder of the Quakers, was renown in the 17th century for his prayers for healing. He wrote extensively on how he accessed God's power to institute over one hundred and fifty cures of physical and mental problems. This work was critical to expanding the influence of early Quakerism. Most of Fox's papers were lost after his death, but from original notes and fragments, Cadbury (1883–1974) was able to construct this book.

Fox, George. *The Journal of George Fox,* ed. Rufus M. Jones. Friends United Press, 2006. George Fox (1624–1691) was the founder of the Religious Society of Friends, commonly known as the Quakers. Fox's journal, first published in 1694, includes a number of occurrences that took place throughout his ministry. It includes accounts of healing.

Goerke, Edmund. "The Gift of Healing in the Life of George Fox." Gloucester, United Kingdom: Fellowship Press, 1972. This booklet examines some of the healing testimonies that transpired through the ministry of George Fox, founder of Quakerism.

Goddard, Paul R. "The King's Evil." *West of England Medical Journal* 112:2 (June 2013): 1–2. This is a short synopsis of the practice of the French and English kings praying for the sick in the late medieval period.

Greatrakes, Valentine. *A Brief Account.* London: Valentine Greatrakes, 1666. This book was written by Irish healing practitioner to defend himself against attacks by the English political and religious authorities. Greatrakes was controversial, carrying on a tradition that was originally associated with European kings who would lay hands on the afflicted and heal them. Although a commoner, Greatrakes carried on what was thought to be a royal tradition. George Rush, a nobleman of the period, noted, the following: "I . . . saw him lay his hands upon a thousand persons, and really there is something more than ordinary… I have seen pains strangely fly before his hand, till he has chased them out of the body, dimness cleared and deafness cured by his touch."

Grub, Edward. "Spiritual Healing Among Early Quakers," in *Quaker Thought and History: A Volume of Essays.*, ed. Edward Grubb. New

York: The MacMillan Company, 1925. Edward Grubb was an influential twentieth-century Quaker. In this article, he provides analysis on the ministry of healing in the life of George Fox.

Haas, Angela. "Miracles on Trial: Wonders and Their Witnesses in Eighteenth-Century France." *Proceedings of the Western Society for French History* 38 (2010): 111–128. This article explores some of the controversial miraculous accounts in early modern Europe.

Hiatt, R. Jeffrey. "John Wesley and Healing: Developing Wesleyan Missiology." *The Asbury Theological Journal* 59:1–2. (Spring, Fall 2004): 89–109. This article is an insightful exploration of the early Wesleyan views on healing.

Hiatt, R. Jeffrey. "Salvation as Healing: John Wesley's Missional Theology," D.Miss., thesis, Asbury Theological Seminary, 2008. In this thesis, Hiatt argues that John Wesley's emphasis on the therapeutic nature of the gospel provides a missional basis for treating the spiritual and physical spheres of life comprehensively.

Hodges, David. *George Fox and the Healing Ministry*. United Kingdom: Claridge House, 1995. This book briefly explores George Fox's role as a "healer" in the burgeoning Quaker movement in England.

Hunter, Richard A. and Ida Macalpine. *Valentine Greatrakes and Divers of the Strange Cures by Him Lately Performed On Patients from St. Bartholomew's Hospital in 1666: Three Hundred Years Psychiatry*. London: Oxford University Press, 1963. This is an account of Valentine Greatrakes, the unusual "Irish Stroker" who brought healing by the laying on of hands into seventeenth-century England.

Huizenga, Lee S. "The Royal Touch." *International Journal of Leprosy* 5:2 (1937): 175–179. In this article, Huizenga explores the practice of Royal Touch in France and England. He takes a relatively open view.

Irving, Edward. *Edward Irving: Works, collected and edited by his nephew, the Rev. G. Carlyle*. London: Alexander Strahan Publisher, 1865. This is a collection of Irving's voluminous writings. Very little of it directly deals with healing, but there are entries that clarify his understanding of spiritual gifts.

Irving, Edward. "Miracles, Signs, Powers." *The Morning Watch: Quarterly Journal on Prophecy and Theological Review 3* (1831): 138-160. This is a theological examination of the meaning of miracles in the Bible.

Irving, Edward. "On the Gifts of the Holy Spirit." *The Morning Watch: Quarterly Journal on Prophecy and Theological Review* 2 (1831): 850-869. In this article, Irving shares his insights on the gifts of the Holy Spirit.

Irving, Edward. "The Outpouring of the Holy Spirit." *The Morning Watch: Quarterly Journal on Prophecy and Theological Review* 2 (1831): 608-622. This article is an examination of the revival that began in London.

Irving, Edward. Personal Letter to Mrs. Wooner. London, Judd Place, July 27, 1831. This letter provides insight into Irving's understanding of healing. He writes, "Make known to your friend that it is as much her duty to believe in the name of the Lord Jesus for the healing of her body as of her soul; I refer to her the whole history of his life, to his instructions to his apostles and disciples, and to the passage in James, also to Exodus 15, Psalm 103:3, 107:19–20, Isaiah 53:1 as quoted in Matthew, Job 33:19–26. All our Lord's dealings which were intended to draw us to him—1 Corinthians 11:20, 12:9 and all the passages which speak of unqualified prayer. Tell her from me that the reason she is not healed is that she supposes Christ to be somehow or other the cause of her affliction, but He is the Redeemer from it and not the cause of it, direct her attention to the concluding verses of Mark's Gospel, and Oh tell her to believe that the Lord she worships on the throne of Heaven is the same who walked about curing all manner of diseases and healing them that were oppressed of the Devil; Tell her that she is standing in the way of His Glory by not believing in His willingness and desire to heal her, Disease is sin manifested in the body; This was the word which cured Miss Hughes. Oh be not afraid to communicate all these things to her, and call upon the Lord for her sake, I also will wait upon the Lord for her, and Oh tell her to believe, and it will be well with her according to her faith."

Jennings, Daniel R. *The Supernatural Occurrences of John Wesley.* Oklahoma City: Sean Multimedia, 2005, 2012. This book examines some of John Welsey's inexplicable experiences. The entire third chapter deals with the subject of healing, recounting a number of documented stories.

Kaplan, Barbara Beigun. "Greatrakes The Stroker: The Interpretations of His Contemporaries." *Isis* (1982): 178–185. Valentine Greatrakes drew considerable attention from the scientific and intellectual communities of mid-seventeenth-century England. In this article, Kaplan explores some of the viewpoints of those who encountered him.

Kidd, Thomas S. "The Healing of Mercy Wheeler: Illness and Miracles among Early American Evangelicals." *The William and Mary Quarterly* 63:1 (January 1, 2006): 149–170. This is a fascinating article that explores healing practices during the Great Awakening period in America.

Knolly, Hanserd. "Michael Haykin, (c. 1599–1691) on the Gifts of the Spirit." *Westminster Theological Journal* 54:1 (Spring 1992): 99–113. This article is a theological analysis of Hanserd Knollys (1599–1691), a seventeenth-century Calvinistic Baptist. It briefly considers his ideas on the gifts of the Holy Spirit.

Laver, A. Brian. "Miracles No Wonders: The Mesmeric Phenomena and Organic Cures of Valentine Greatrakes." *Journal of the History of Medicine* 33 (1978): 35–46. This critical article examines the ministry of Valentine Greatrakes, a seventeenth-century minister who healed by the laying on of hands.

Littlewood, Roland. "The King's Evil Revisited." *Anthropology & Medicine* 3:2 (1996): 1–4. Littlewood explores the meaning and scope of the Royal Touch transacted by French and English kings. Their touch apparently brought healing to a form of tuberculosis.

Lusk, R. B. *The Testimony of Facts Concerning the Continuation of Miracles in the Church.* London: Greenock, 1832. This short book, written in the context of Edward Irving's ministry in London, explores testimonies of supernatural activity in Church history. It is an excellent book that seeks to affirm the reality of God's stupendous works.

MacDonald, Michael. *Mystical Bedlam: Madness, Anxiety and Healing in Seventeenth-Century England.* London: Cambridge University Press, 1983. This well-researched book explores the understanding of miracles during the Restoration period in England.

Madden, Deborah, ed. *Inward and Outward Health: John Wesley's Holistic Concept of Medical Science, the Environment and Holy Living.* Eugene, Oregon: Wipf and Stock Publishers, 2012. This work is a collection of academic articles, examining John Wesley's conception of health and human embodiment.

Madden, Deborah. "Wesley as Advisor on Health and Healing," in *Cambridge Companion to John Wesley*, eds. Randy L. Maddox and Jason E. Vickers, 176–189. Cambridge: Cambridge University Press, 2010. This is a fascinating article on John Wesley and his understanding of health.

Maddocks, Morris. "Health and Healing in the Ministry of John Wesley," in *John Wesley: Contemporary Perspectives*, ed. John Stacey, 138–149. London: Epworth, 1988. This well-researched essay effectively frames up John Wesley's understanding of healing.

Maddox, Randy L. "John Wesley on Holistic Health and Healing." *Methodist History* 46 (2007): 4–33. This thoroughly developed article delves into John Wesley's comprehensive understanding of health and what it might mean for believers today.

Middleton, Conyers. *A Free Inquiry into the Miraculous Powers*. London: R. Manby and H. S. Cox, 1749. In this highly influential eighteenth century work, Conyers Middleton draws into question the reality of the miraculous. Wesley, Irving, and a number of others felt inclined to respond to Middleton's work.

Oliphant, Margaret. *The Life of Edward Irving, Minister of the National Scotch Church, London: Illustrated by his Journals and Correspondence*. London: Hurst and Blackett Publishers, 1862. In this massive biographical work on Edward Irving, Oliphant references some of the healing experiences.

Ott, Philip W. "John Wesley on Health as Wholeness." *Journal of Religion and Health* 30 (1991): 43–57. In this article, Ott explores Wesley's holistic conception of health.

Ott, Philip W. "John Wesley on Health: A Word for Sensible Regimen." *Methodist History* 18 (1980): 193–204. In this essay, Ott considers the Methodist founder's practical approach to medicine and health.

Owen, Henry John. *The Prayer of Faith Viewed in Connection with the Healing of the Sick*. London: Nisbet, 1831. Writing from the general context of Edward Irving's ministry in London, this work seeks to explore the ministry of healing.

Pitt, Leonard. *A Small Moment of Great Illumination: Searching for Valentine Greatrakes the Master Healer*. Emeryville, California: Shoemaker and Hoard, 2006. Greatrakes was a healer from Ireland during the 1600s. He was known for laying hands upon people who had cancer, leprosy, and leukemia. He was viewed as a threat by both church and state. This work describes Pitt's personal account of studying Greatrakes's life and ultimately acquiring an edition of his 1666 biographical account.

Pym, William Wollaston. *An Inquiry Concerning Spiritual Gifts*. London: James Nisbet, 1832. Pym, Vicar of Willian, Hert, examines the biblical meaning of spiritual gifts in light of what was transpiring through Edward Irving's church in London.

Rack, Henry D. "Doctors, Demons, and Early Methodist Healing," in *The Church and Healing*, ed. W. J. Sheils, 137–152. Oxford: Basil Blackwell, 1982. This article explores the diverse terrain of Wesley's experiences with spiritual and physical maladies.

Shaw, Jane. *Miracles in Enlightenment England*. New Haven Connecticut: Yale University Press, 2006. In this intriguing book, Shaw presents miraculous accounts in early modern England (1650–1750). She considers the reactions of intellectuals, scientists, and physicians.

Stewart, David. "John Wesley, the Physician." *Wesleyan Theological Journal* 4 (Spring 1969): 27–38. This is an article from a Wesleyan physician exploring John Wesley's relationship with healing and medicine.

Stotts, George R. "Manifestations of the Spirit in Late 17th-Century France." *Paraclete Journal* 9:1. (Winter 1975): 8–12. This essay explores manifestations of the Spirit among the Camisards and Jansenists in seventeenth and eighteenth-century France. While the bulk of this article deals with prophecy, it does include some references to healing.

Stanger, Frank B. "Healing in the Life and Ministry of John Wesley." *Herald* (June 27): 15–16. 1973. This short essay explores the multifaceted understanding of healing in the life and ministry of John Wesley.

Steneck, Nicholas H. "Greatrakes the Stroker: The Interpretations of Historians." *Isis* (1982): 161–177. In this insightful article, Steneck provides insight into the views of the contemporaries of Valentine Greatrakes, the controversial Irish stroker.

Sturdy, David J. "The Royal Touch in England," in *European Monarchy: Its Evolution and Practice from Roman Antiquity to Modern Times*, ed. Heinz Duchhardt, Richard A. Jackson, and David J. Sturdy, 171–184. Stuttgart, Germany: Franz Steiner Verlag, 1992. Sturdy provides a well-researched exploration of the Royal Touch.

Tainmont, Jacques. "A Historical Vignette (18). The King's Evil: scrofula, physicians and the Royal Touch." *B-ENT* 6.2 (2009): 153–159. In this article, Tainmont explores what the physicians believed about the king's ability to provide healing of tuberculosis of the neck through touch. Tainmont suggests that there was some collusion between the physicians and the king, each not wanting to undermine the other.

Theilmann, John M. "The Miracles of King Henry VI of England." *Historian* 42:3 (1980): 456–471. In this well-researched article, Theilmann studies Henry VI's usage of the King's Touch to heal a form of tuberculosis.

Thom, David. *The Miracles of the Irving School Shewn to be Unworthy of Serious Examination*. London: Longman and Company, 1832. In this treatise, Thom examines the miraculous claims of Edward Irving and his associates and comes to the conclusion that they are in error. Discounting the healings, Thom ends by saying, "The Bible, the Bible only is the religion of Protestants."

Thomas, Burton G. "John Wesley on the Art of Healing." *The British Medical Journal* (April 28, 1906): 987–881. This article from a medical practitioner draws insights from John Wesley's understanding and application of healing.

Turrell, James F. "The Ritual of Royal Healing in Early Modern England: Scrofula, Liturgy, and Politics." *Anglican and Episcopal History* (1999): 3–36. This essay delves into the background and social implications of the King's Touch.

Walton, William. *The Miraculous Powers of the Church of Christ Asserted Through Each Successive Century From the Apostles Down to the Present Time.* London: Anonymous, 1756. In this work, William Walton (1716-1780), a theology professor at Douay College, challenges the cessationist assertions of Middleton and Douglas.

Webster, Robert Joseph Jr. "Balsamic Virtue: Supernatural Healing in John Wesley," in *Methodism and The Miraculous: John Wesley's Contribution to the Historia Miraculorurn*, 241–285, Ph.D., diss., Oxford University, 2006. This is an academic investigation of Wesley's healing practices.

Wesley, John. *Primitive Physick; or, an Easy and Natural Method of Curing Most Diseases.* 12th ed. Philadelphia: Andrew Steuart, 1764. While this work does not deal with divine healing, it is concerned with practical matters of health and medicine. It provides a window into the understanding of sickness and health during the Methodist revival.

Wesley, John. *The Works of John Wesley*, 3rd Edition. Grand Rapids, Michigan: Baker Publishing Company, 1996. This collection of the major works of Wesley includes his sermons and personal journal. Throughout this work, Wesley makes a number of general references to his belief in the ongoing work of the Holy Spirit. However, of particular interest to the study of healing are the vast numbers of references to healing in his journal. One can find examples of healing in the following entries: November 16, 1740; May 8, 1741; November 20, 1741; March 17, 1746; November 12, 1746; May 24, 1749; April 8, 1750; May 19, 1752; April 6, 1756; October 3, 1756; May 5, 1757; March 23, 1758; December 26, 1761; March 19, 1766; October 16, 1778; April 24, 1782; September 3, 1782; May 23, 1783; April 12, 1784; May 31, 1785; October 25, 1787; October 7, 1790.

5. EUROPEAN FAITH CURE

Ambrose, R.G. *Prayer Healing: Thoughts on Saint James 5:14–16*. London: Nisbet, 1891. This short work is a sympathetic look at the ministry of healing, exploring its foundations from James 5:14–16.

Anonymous. "The Ministry of the Holy Ghost in Healing Soul and Body Together." London: J. Snow and Company, 1885. This pamphlet, written by "One who knows," explores the reality of healing against the backdrop of the European faith-cure movement.

Baxter, Mrs. M. [Elizabeth]. *Divine Healing*. Christian Herald Company, 1930. This is a collection of teachings on the ministry of healing from Elizabeth Baxter, one of the directors of the Bethshan Healing Home in London, England, and editor of the magazine *Thy Healer*.

Baxter, Mrs. M. [Elizabeth]. "Questions Concerning Healing." *The Word, Work and World* 5:11 (November 1885): 297–298. Baxter addresses some common questions about the ministry of healing at a Fall 1885 Christian and Missionary Alliance Convention.

Belcher, Thomas Waugh. *Miracles of Healing Considered in Relation to Some Modern Objections and to Medical Science*. London: James Parker and Company Publishing, 1872. This reasoned work is an apologetic for healing from a gifted English writer.

Bennett, Risdon. *Diseases of the Bible*. London: Religious Tract Society, 1887. This book is a late nineteenth-century work that seeks to examine major expressions of disease and illnesses of the Bible.

Blumhardt, Johann Christoph and Christoph Friedrich Blumhardt. *Thy Kingdom Come: A Blumhardt Reader*. Grand Rapids, Michigan: Eerdmans Publishing, 1980. This book is a collection excerpts from the writings of Johann Christoph Blumhardt, a noted German healing proponent. It also includes insights from his son who carried on Blumhardt's work after his demise.

Blumhardt, Johann Christoph. *Blumhardt's Battle: A Conflict with Satan*. tr. Frank S. Boshold. New York: Thomas E. Lowe LTD, 1970. This is a first-hand account of the beginnings of Johann Christoph Blumhardt's noted healing ministry in Germany.

Blumhardt, Johann Christoph and Christoph Friedrich Blumhardt. *Now is Eternity: Comfort and Wisdom for Difficult Hours from Christoph Friedrich Blumhardt and Johann Christoph Blumhardt*. Farmington, Pennsylvania: Plough Publishing, 1999. This is a collection of excerpts from the writings of the Blumhardts, compiled with the intent to bring comfort to the afflicted.

Blumhardt, Johann Christoph and Christoph Friedrich Blumhardt. *Thy Will Be Done: Sickness, Faith, And The God Who Heals*. Farmington, Pennsylvania: Plough Publishing, 2011. This is a collection of short teachings on healing from Johann Christoph Blumhardt and his son.

Boardman, Mary Morse. *Mrs. Boardman's Words of Counsel and Comfort*, ed. Miss Barclay. London: Bethshan Bookroom, 1904. This is a collection of insights from one of the directors of the Bethshan Healing Home in London. Bethshan was one of the prominent centers of healing in Europe during the late nineteenth and early twentieth centuries.

Boardman, Mary Morse. *The Life and Labors of the Reverend William E. Boardman*. New York: D. Appleton and Company Publishers, 1887. This biographical account of W. E. Boardman, a noted healing proponent and founder of the Bethshan healing home, was composed by his wife.

Boardman, William E. *Faith Work under Dr. Charles Cullis in Boston*. Boston: Willard Tract Repository, 1874. This is W. E. Boardman's first-hand account of Dr. Charles Cullis's healing ministry in Boston, Massachusetts.

Boardman, William E., ed. *Record of the International Conference of Divine Healing and True Holiness Held at The Agricultural Hall, London, June 1–5, 1885*. London: J. Show and Company, 1885. This publication is a compilation of the teachings and accounts of the first international healing conference that took place in London, England, in 1885.

Boardman, William E. *The Lord That Healeth Thee (Jehovah Rophi)*. London: Morgan and Scott, 1881. Boardman's work on the biblical foundations of healing was extremely influential within the faith-cure movement in the United States and Europe.

Bodamer, William G. "The Life and Work of Johann Christoph Blumhardt: A Study in the Relationship Between Theology and Experience," Ph.D. diss., Princeton Theological Seminary, 1966. This respected dissertation covers the life and ministry of Johann Christoph Blumhardt.

Butlin, H. T. "Remarks On Spiritual Healing." *British Medical Journal* 1:2581 (June 18, 1910): 1466–1470. In this essay, an inquisitive medical doctor examines the efficacy of divine healing.

Cox, James C. *Johann Christoph Blumhardt and the Work of the Holy Spirit*. The Netherlands: Van Corcum Assen, 1959. In this work, Cox provides an excellent biographical account of Johann Christoph Blumhardt.

Draper, Gideon. "The Faith Homes of Europe: Christian Work at Home and Abroad." *The Word, Work and World* 5:4 (April 1883): 110–12. New York. This article, published by the Christian and Missionary Alliance, documents the prominent European healing homes.

Du Plessis, Johannes. *The Life of Andrew Murray of South Africa*. London: Marshall Brothers Limited, 1920. Du Plesis has penned an insightful Andrew Murray biography. He touches on Murray's healing ministry.

Editor. "Homes of Divine Healing." *The Word, Work, and World* 5:10 (October 1885) 253–254. This news article documents prominent faith-healing homes in the United States and Europe.

Fishbourne, E. Gardiner. "Divine Healing of Body and Soul Essential to the Complete Christ Life." Pamphlet. London: Harrison, 1885. Fishbourne was friends with W. E. Boardman and Otto Stockmayer. He became convinced of the validity of healing. In this pamphlet, Fishbourne's final work, he made a plea to church leaders to recover the spiritual vitality that was demonstrated in the early church.

Gliddon, Aurelius L. G. *Faith Cures: Their History and Mystery*. London: Christian Commonwealth Publishing Company, 1890. This author tries to take an objective look at faith healing, assessing both the theological and scientific dimensions.

Guest, William. *Pastor Blumhardt and His Work*. London: Morgan and Scott Publishers, 1881. This is one of the noted English biographies of Johann Christoph Blumhardt. Guest brought together eyewitness accounts of what happened in Blumhardt's life. He interviewed a professor of medicine from Tübingen who reviewed letters sent to Blumhardt in which people testified to healings. Apparently, the professor found it increasingly difficult to doubt the reality of the cures.

Murray, Andrew. *Divine Healing: A Series of Addresses*. Nyack, New York: Christian Alliance Publishing Company, 1900. This work, by a noted Holiness leader from South Africa, was one of the most influential works on healing. It has remained in print for over a century.

Murray, Andrew. "Is Sickness a Chastisement?" *Christian and Missionary Alliance* 24:19 (May 12, 1900): 310. This is a practical healing article published in one of the Christian and Missionary Alliance publications. It examines the reality of sickness.

Murray, Andrew. "The Sick Child." *Christian and Missionary Alliance* 21:2 (Wednesday, July 13, 1898): 34. In this teaching article, Murray talks about a healing passage from John 4:46–47. In this teaching, he discusses practical applications, drawing insights from the ministry to children.

Stockmayer, Otto. *Church of God, Awake!* London: Bethshan Bookroom and Christian Herald Office, 1904. Stockmayer was a significant figure in the European faith-cure movement. This small book brings together some of his sermons and a testimony of healing from the Bethsham Healing Home in London.

Stockmayer, Otto. "Divine Healing." *The Christian Alliance* 12:12 (March 23, 1894): 314. This is one of Stockmayer's healing teachings that was published in one of the *Christian and Missionary Alliance* periodicals.

Stockmayer, Otto. *Sickness and the Gospel.* New York: A.C. Gaebelein Publisher, 1887. This book, written during the height of the European faith-cure movement, associated healing with Jesus' atonement. This is one of the first books in the modern era to attempt this. Stockmayer was a prominent Swiss healing proponent who was associated with the Keswick movement. This book's tremendous influence led A. J. Gordon to affirm that Stockmayer was the "theologian of the doctrine of healing by faith."

Special Correspondent Abroad. "Pastor Stockmayer." *The Word, Work and World* 3:3 (March 1883): 36–37. This Christian and Missionary Alliance article recounts what was transpiring in Stockmayer's healing home in Switzerland.

Spittler, Marcus. *Pastor Blumhardt and his Work.* London: Morgan and Scott, 1880. This was a influential biographical work on Johann Christoph Blumhardt, the noted German healing proponent.

Stapfer, Eliza. "A Visit to Mannedorf, Near Zurich." *The Christian: A Weekly Record of Christian Life, Christian Testimony, And Christian Work* (December 1871): 5–6. This article examines Dorothea Trudel's healing home in Mannedorf, Switzerland, the Elim Institute. After her passing, leadership was transferred to Samuel Zeller.

Trench, Richard Chenevix. *Notes on the Miracles of our Lord*. London: Paternoster House, 1895. In this work, Trench has developed an exegetical study of the healings and miracles of Jesus in the gospels.

Trudel, Dorothea. *The Prayer of Faith: Showing the Remarkable Manner in which Large Numbers of Sick Persons were Healed in answer to prayer, with an introduction by Charles Cullis,* third edition. Boston: Willard Tract Society, 1872. This is the autobiographical account of Dorothea Trudel, a noted Swiss healing proponent. This work was edited by Charles Cullis, a noted American healing advocate in Boston.

Wiseman, Nathaniel. *Elizabeth Baxter*. London: The Christian Herald Company, 1928. This is an inspiring biographical account of the life of Elizabeth Baxter, wife of a prominent European Holiness figure, Michael Baxter. She became the matron of William Boardman's healing home in London—Bethshan.

Zuendel, Friedrich. *Pastor Johann Christopher Blumhardt: An Account of His Life*. Hugo Brinkmann, tr. Eugene, Oregon: Cascade Books, 1883, 2010. This is an English translation of Zundel's noted biographical work on Johann Christoph Blumhardt.

Zuendel, Friedrich. *The Awakening: One Man's Battle with Darkness*. Farmington, Pennsylvania: The Plough Publishing House, 1999. This is an abridged version of Zuendel's Blumhardt narrative.

6. AMERICAN FAITH-CURE

Allen, Ethan O. *Faith Healing; Or, What I have Witnessed of the Fulfillment of James 5:14, 15, 16*. Philadelphia, Pennsylvania: G.W. McCalla, 1881. This is a captivating polemic on healing by one of the noted figures of the early American faith-cure movement. This short work has a number of great insights.

Bainbridge, Harriette S. *Life for Soul and Body*. Brooklyn, New York: Christian Alliance Publishing Company, 1906. This work envisions healing within the context of holiness. Bainbridge argues that one should entrust all of one's life to the indwelling Christ whose atonement makes healing possible.

Barton, William E. *Faith as Related to Health*. Boston: L.C. Page and Company, 1901. William E. Barton (1861–1930) was a Congregational pastor from Oak Park, Illinois. In this book, Barton compiled some of his messages on faith healing.

Bell, James B. "Divine Healing from a Medical Standpoint." New York: Christian Alliance Publishing Company, undated. This sympathetic work explores the meaning of divine healing from a physician's perspective.

Boole, W.H. "The Consumptives Home." *The Earnest Christian and Golden Rule* 21:4 (April 1871): 138. This is an inspiring article on Charles Cullis's healing home in Boston, Massachusetts.

Brown, Sarah A. *A New Lesson from an Old Book*. New York: Word, Work and World Publishing Company, undated. This work, published around 1883, recounts the story of a former missionary to China who was suffering from complications stemming from malaria. She received instruction in healing prayer from a hospital matron and was healed in response to her own prayers.

Burbank, Frank. "She is not Dead, But Asleep." *Victory Through Faith* 2 (May 1884): 38. Burbank wrote a eulogy of the noted African American healing proponent Sarah Ann Freeman Mix. It was published in her official publication.

Carter, R. Kelso. "Difficulties Concerning Healing." *The Word, Work and World 5:11.* (November 1885): *299–300.* In this work, originally shared at the Christian and Missionary Alliance Convention in 1885, Carter addresses some of the challenges associated with the ministry of healing.

Carter, R. Kelso. *Divine Healing or Atonement for Sin and Sickness.* New York: John B. Alden Publishing, 1888. This is the revised edition of Carter's work on the theological foundations of healing.

Carter, R. Kelso. "Divine Healing, or Faith-Cure." *The Christian Century* 33. (March 1887): 777–780. In this article published in *The Christian Century* magazine, Carter defends divine healing and the faith-cure movement. This essay was extremely influential.

Carter, R. Kelso. *Faith Healing Reviewed, After Twenty Years.* Boston: Christian Witness Company, 1897. In this later work, Carter modified his positions on healing. It provides a window into the changing dynamics of the faith-cure movement.

Carter, R. Kelso. *Miracles of Healing: The Cure in Answer to the Prayer of Faith.* Boston: Willard Tract Depository, 1880. Carter, a prominent faith-cure leader, shares inspiring stories of healing in this brief work.

Carter, R. Kelso. *Pastor Blumhardt: A Record of the Wonderful Spiritual and Physical Manifestations of God's Power in Healing Souls and Bodies, through the prayers of His servant, Christoph Blumhardt.* Boston: Willard Tract Depository, 1883. This book is an outstanding and highly readable biography of Johann Christoph Blumhardt, the noted German healer.

Carter, R. Kelso. *The Atonement for Sin and Sickness; or a Full Salvation for Soul and Body.* Boston: Willard Tract Depository, 1883. This is the first edition of Carter's influential work on healing.

Cobbe, Frances Power. "Faith Healing and Fear Killing." *Littell's Living Age* 174: 5: 59 (July 16, 1887): 131–142. This article provides a contentious analysis of the faith-cure movement of the late 1880s.

Cullis, Charles. *Annual Reports of the Consumptives' Home, and Other Institutions Connected with a Work of Faith*. Boston: Willard Tract Repository, 1864–1895. Every year, Dr. Charles Cullis provided reports about what was transpiring through his ministry. This continued until a few years after his death in 1892.

Cullis, Charles. *Faith Cures, or Answers to Prayer in the Healing of the Sick*. Boston: Willard Tract Society, 1879. This book is the original collection of healing testimonies compiled by Dr. Charles Cullis.

Cullis, Charles. *Annual Reports of the Consumptives' Home, and Other Institutions Connected with a Work of Faith*. Boston: Willard Tract Repository, 1864–1895. These are the different collections and reports of the ministry homes of Dr. Charles Cullis. Each was published independently.

Cullis, Charles, ed. *Faith Training Lectures*. Boston: Willard Tract Repository. Boston, 1878. This is a collection of notes and training materials given to students at Dr. Charles Cullis's Bible school in Boston, Massachusetts. It includes insights on healing.

Cullis, Charles. *Fifteen Helps*. Boston: Willard Tract Repository, 1885. This small book is a compilation of short tracts written by Dr. Charles Cullis. It includes expositions on healing.

Cullis, Charles. *More Faith Cures, or Answers to Prayer in the Healing of the Sick*. Boston, Massachusetts: Willard Tract Society, 1881. This book is Cullis' second collection of healing testimonies.

Cullis, Charles. *Other Faith Cures, or Answers to Prayer in the Healing of the Sick*. Boston, Massachusetts: Willard Tract Society, 1885. This is the third and final compilation of healing accounts gathered by Cullis.

Cullis, Charles. *Faith Healing.* Boston, Massachusetts: Willard Tract Society, undated. This is a short work by Cullis on the finer points of healing. It represents some of the best teaching material from the early American faith-cure proponents.

Cullis, Charles. *Tuesday Afternoon Talks.* Boston, Massachusetts: Willard Tract Society, 1892. This is a wonderful collection of healing and faith-building teachings from Cullis's Tuesday afternoon meetings, which were held on his campus in Boston, Massachusetts.

Cullis, Charles, ed. *Work for Jesus: The Experiences and Teachings of Mr. and Mrs. Boardman.* Boston, Massachusetts: Willard Tract Society, 1875. This is Cullis's biographical account of W. E. Boardman and his wife. The Boardmans were prominent in Holiness circles and went on to establish a prominent healing home in London, England.

Cuyler, Theodore L. "Faith Cures." *New York Evangelist* 54:1 (May 3, 1883). This critical article examines the faith healing claims presented by the adherents of the faith-cure movement.

Daniels, William. *Dr. Cullis and His Work.* Boston: Willard Tract Repository, 1885. This early account of the Cullis' work in Boston includes details about his healing home and other expressions of his ministry.

Editor. "Berachah Home." *Word, Work and World* 7:4 (October 1886): 232–234. This is an excellent article on the healing home established by the Christian and Missionary Alliance in New York.

Editor. "Divine Healing and Its Counterfeits." *Christian and Missionary Alliance* 23:1 (June 3, 1899): 8–9. This editorial explores differences between biblical healing and the erroneous approaches emerging during this period.

Editor. "Faith Convention at Old Orchard." *The Congregationalist* 67 (August 9, 1882). This is a news article that examines the events at a faith convention that was at a Holiness campground in Old Orchard, Maine.

Editor. "Faith Convention at Old Orchard." *New York Witness* (August 11, 1883). Dr. Charles Cullis' faith conventions brought in crowds from all over the Northeast. This article discussed: meetings for consecration, healing by faith, and marvelous cures answer to prayer.

Editor. "Faith-Cures." *Christian Advocate* 58. (May 31, 1883): 343. This is a dismissive essay on the subject of faith healing from the prominent periodical, *The Christian Advocate*.

Editor. "Faith Healing." *The Christian* 18 (June 1885): 5. This article, from a conservative mainline author, denounces A. B. Simpson's stance on faith healing.

Editor. "Miracles." *The Congregationalist* 67:2 (August 16, 1882). This article from *The Congregationalist* periodical examines faith healing and the viability of miracles.

Editor. "Miss Lindenberger." *Word, Work and World* 7:3 (September 1886): 178–179. This is an essay on Sarah Lindenberger, the matron of Berachah, a healing work associated with the Christian and Missionary Alliance.

Editor. "New Faith Cure Society." *New York Times* (August 18, 1899). This is a dismissive article on the controversial ministry of Frank W. Sandford of Shiloh, Maine.

Editor. "Old Orchard-Holiness and Faith Cures." *New York Witness* 1 (August 18, 1881): 1. This article examines the holiness roots of the nineteenth-century healing movement.

Editor. "Report from Old Orchard." *Christian Advocate* 57 (August 24, 1882): 530. This article explores one of the faith-cure conferences that transpired at the Old Orchard campgrounds in 1882.

Editor. "Sarah Ann Freeman Mix – Mrs. Edward Mix." *Torrington Register* (April 19, 1884). This article reflects on the life of Sarah Ann Freeman Mix, a female African American healing proponent.

Editor. "The Balance of Truth." *Christian and Missionary Alliance* 23:12 (August 19, 1899): 184. This editorial points out the differences between biblical healing and false approaches emerging during this period.

Editor. "The Discipline of Suffering as Related to 'Faith Cure.'" *Christian Advocate* 60. (May 28, 1885): 341–342. This article provides a critique of the faith-cure practice of healing prayer. This article suggests that physical suffering is a Christian virtue.

Editor. "Two Phases of Divine Healing." *Christian and Missionary Alliance* 23:12 (August 19, 1899): 184–185. This is an editorial reflection on the meaning of healing.

Editor. "What to Do with the Faith Healers." *Independent* 51 (June 8, 1899): 1576–1577. This hastily written article seeks to dismiss those who practice faith healing and other activities.

Erskine, Thomas. *The Supernatural Gifts of the Spirit with Remarkable Cases of Modern Miracles*, ed. R. Kelso Carter, ed. Philadelphia: Office of Words of Faith, 1883. Erskine, a lay Scottish theologian, shares some of his insights into healing.

Ferguson, John. "Faith Healing, Mind Curing, Christian Science." *Canadian Magazine of Politics, Science, Art and Literature* 6 (December 1895): 183–187. This article is a critical analysis of faith healing, associating it with unorthodox means.

Fishbourne, Edmund Gardiner. "Divine Healing of Body and Soul Essential to the Complete Christ Life." London: Harrison and Sons Publisher, 1885. This is a pamphlet on the subject of divine healing written by a naval admiral.

Fletcher, Rebecca I. "Bethany Home, Toronto." *Triumphs of Faith* (May 1890): 105–8. This is a brief account of the beginnings of a Christian and Missionary Alliance healing home in Toronto, Canada.

Fletcher, Rebecca I. "Himself Hath Done It, or How the Lord Taught Me Divine Healing." *Triumphs of Faith* (January 1890): 15–19. Fletcher shares her insights into healing and how Christian and Missionary Alliance leaders John Salmon and A. B. Simpson were influential in her development.

Ford, Willis E. "Exit: The Faith Cure." *Journal of the American Medical Association* 10 (June 16, 1888): 749. Here is a critique from a late nineteenth-century physician who dismisses the value of the faith-cure movement.

Ford, Willis E. *Miraculous Cures: An Address Delivered to The Y.M.C.A. Courses*. Utica, New York, November 7, 1887. Utica, New York, undated. Ford's booklet is a critical work on the faith-cure movement.

Funk, A .E. "Divine Healing in Divine Supply." The Christian and Missionary Alliance 25:26 (December 22, 1890): 347. This article reinforces the belief in healing espoused by the Christian and Missionary Alliance.

Gill, William I. "Isms: The Faith Cure." *New England Magazine and Bay State Monthly* 5 (March 1887): 438–449. This article was written to undermine the faith-cure movement. There were dozens of articles during the 1880s that ridiculed healing practices.

Goddard, Henry H. "The Effects of Mind on Body as Evidenced by Faith Cures." *American Journal of Psychology* 10:3. (1898–1899): 431–502. Goddard's article dismisses the ministry of healing. His insights were derived from a nineteenth-century psychology journal.

Gordon, A. J. "Gordon on Healing." *The Revivalist* 24 (August 1899): 10. This practical article was written by Adoniram Judson Gordon, a prominent Baptist pastor and theologian. It is one of the several articles that he wrote for *The Revivalist* magazine.

Gordon, A. J. "Healed by Prayer." *The Revivalist* 24 (August 1899): 10. This article is a brief examination of how prayer influences the ministry of healing.

Gordon, A. J. "Hints on Healing" *The Revivalist* 24 (August 1899): 10. This is a practical reflection on healing from Gordon. Here he shares some "healing hints" and practical methods that he has learned.

Gordon, A. J. "Jesus Is Victor." *The Revivalist* 27 (April 1899): 10. Gordon provides a brief biographical reflection on Johann Christoph Blumhardt and his healing ministry in Germany.

Gordon, A. J. "Luther and Melanchthon." *The Revivalist* 7 (September 1899): 10. This article examines how Martin Luther ministered healing to his close friend and colleague, Philip Melanchthon.

Gordon, A. J. *The Ministry of Healing; Or Miracles of Cure in All Ages*, third edition, Revised. Chicago: Fleming Revell Company, 1882. This book is, perhaps, the most significant work on healing in the late nineteenth and early twentieth centuries. Gordon makes an effective case for its efficacy.

Gordon, Ernest B. *Adoniram Judson Gordon: A Biography with Letters and Illustrative Extracts Drawn from Unpublished or Uncollected Sermons and Addresses*. New York: Fleming Revell Company, 1896. This thoroughly documented biography of A. J. Gordon was written by his brother shortly after his passing. It includes some detailed healing stories.

Hamilton, J. W. "The Faith Cure." *Chautauqua* 11 (May 1890): 204–208. This news story disparaged divine healing practices. Hamilton was convinced that healing was something to be derided.

Hammon, William. "The Scientific Relations of Modern Miracles." *International Review* 10 (March 1881): 225–242. In this scientifically imbued article, Hammon sets out to undermine faith-cure claims.

Hepworth, George H. "The Faith Cure." *Independent* 35 (October 19, 1882): 1. This is a cautious article that critically examines the faith cure healing practices.

Hertzog, Isaac. *Wonderful Experiences: In The Work of Faith in God, Showing How the Sick Are Healed "With the Gifts of Healing."* Nazareth, Pennsylvania: Isaac Hertzog, 1905. Hertzog was a gifted photographer and healing advocate from Pennsylvania.

Hussey, A. H. *Divine Healing in Mission Work.* Nyack, New York: Christian Alliance Publishing Company, 1902. This book, written by a Christian and Missionary Alliance leader, describes some healing encounters that took place through mission work.

Johnson, Anna Jane Sample. *The Healing Voice on the Power of Prayer, Faith Literature and the Science of Healing: Proving to the World that a Living Faith Gives us a Practical Christianity.* New York: Press of James N. Johnston, 1884. This book is a compilation of poetry and literary reflections on the topic of healing.

LeLacheur, D. W. "Divine Healing." *Christian and Missionary Alliance* 25:13 (September 29, 1900): 179. This short, sermonic article affirms the significance of divine healing in the church.

Lindenberger, Sarah A. *A Cloud of Witnesses.* New York: Christian Alliance Publishing Company, 1900. In this work, Lindenberger recounts testimonies and stories of breakthrough in the Christian and Missionary Alliance.

Lindenberger, Sarah A. "Miss S. Lindenberger, Deaconess Berachah Home." *Word, Work and World* 9:1 (July 1887): 18–19. This article recounts the story of Sarah Lindenberger, the matron and overseer of the Berachah Home.

Lindenberger, Sarah A. "Divine Healing: Address at Old Orchard Convention." *The Christian and Missionary Alliance* 25:9 (September 1, 1890): 123. This valuable article, written by one of the leaders of A. B. Simpson's healing home, explores the meaning of healing.

Lindenberger, Sarah A. "Divine Healing: How I learned the Secret." *The Christian Alliance* 12 (January–July 1894): 12–14. In this article, Lindenberger recounts divine healing precepts that she learned while working at the Berachah home in New York.

Lindenberger, Sarah A. "Some Truths of Divine Healing." *Triumphs of Faith* 33 (January 1913). This is a healing article from Lindenberger that was published in Carrie Judd Montgomery's paper in 1913.

Lindenberger, Sarah A. "The Work of Berachah Home." *The Christian Alliance and Missionary Weekly* 4. (March 21–28, 1890): 207–208. This article is a riveting account of what transpired at the Berachah home.

Lindenberger, Sarah A. *Streams from the Valley of Berachah.* New York: The Christian Alliance Publishing Company, 1893. In this book, Lindenberger recounts her personal testimony as well as what she learned as the matron of the Berachah Home in New York.

Lloyd, James Hendrie. "Faith Cures." *Medical Record: A Weekly Journal of Medicine and Surgery* 29 (March 27, 1886): 349–352. In this article, a medical doctor questions the efficacy of divine healing practices.

Lombard, Victor. *Victor Lombard of Geneva: A Story of Healing and Spiritual Transformation.* New York: Alliance Press Company, 1906. Lombard, a Swiss advocate of divine healing, recounts his testimony.

MacArthur, William T. *Ethan O. Allen.* Philadelphia, Pennsylvania: *The Parlor Evangelist*, undated. This is a biographical account of Ethan Allen, an early American healing proponent who contributed to the advancement of the faith-cure movement.

Mackenzie, Kenneth. *Divine Life for the Body.* Brooklyn, New York: Christian Alliance Publishing, 1900. Mackenzie, a prominent early

Christian and Missionary Alliance leader, wrote on the validity of healing.

Mackenzie, Kenneth. "The Spiritual Ground for Divine Healing." *The Word, Work, and World* 5:11 (November 1885): 294–297. Mackenzie shares some insights into the ministry of healing at a Christian and Missionary Alliance convention. This article is a summary of his talk.

Mallory, E.F., ed. *Touching the Hem: A Record of Faith Healing*. Montreal, Canada: F. E. Grafton, 1884. This book provides an inspiring collection of healing testimonies. It was written to stir faith and encourage people to accept the claims of the faith-cure proponents.

Marsh, R.L. *Faith Healing: A Defense, or, The Lord Thy Healer*. New York: Revell Publishing, 1889. This defense of the theology and practice of healing was based on a Yale Divinity School thesis. It was an important apologetic, written at the height of the faith-cure movement in America.

McArthur, W. T. "Hindrances to Divine Healing." *Christian and Missionary Alliance* 19:16 (Wednesday, October 13, 1897): 375. This article examines what stands in the way of healing's reception. It was published in one of the Christian and Missionary Alliance periodicals.

McDonald, William. "Dr. Charles Cullis." *The Christian Witness and Advocate of Bible Holiness* 23:28 (July 14, 1892). William McDonald, a prominent holiness adherent, reflects on the life of Charles Cullis. This eulogy was written shortly after his demise in 1892.

McDonald, William. *Modern Faith Healing: Scripturally Considered*. Boston: McDonald and Gill Publishers, 1892. William McDonald was the president of the National Holiness Association. Although open to the ministry of healing, he wanted it to be practiced reasonably.

Mitter, George. *The True Method of Healing: Or The Christian's Substitute for the Various Methods of Healing, Practiced by the Healers of the So-called "Faith Cure" and "Sympathy Cure," and of "Christian Science," by Hypnotic and Magnetic Healers and even for the Method Practiced by the Doctors of Medicine through the Application of Chemically-Combined Medicaments.* Elmore, Ohio: Western Methodist Book Concern, 1902. This book, from a sympathetic Methodist author, presents a scriptural approach to healing. He contrasts his method against some of the controversial approaches that were being embraced around the turn of the century.

Mix, Mrs. Edward [Sarah Ann Freeman]. *Faith Cures, and Answers to Prayers.* Springfield, Massachusetts: Press of Springfield Publishing Company, 1882. This is a work on the theology and practice of divine healing, written by a gifted African American healer. Evangelist Ethan O. Allen raised up Mix, an African American woman. He had her operating in healing alongside her husband, Edward. Sarah prayed for many (including Carrie Judd Montgomery. She is an important faith-cure figure.

Mix, Mrs. Edward [Sarah Ann Freeman]. *Faith Cures and Answers to Prayer: The Life and Work of the First African American Healing Evangelist; With a Critical Introduction by Rosemary D. Gooden.* New York: Syracuse University Press, 1882, 2002. This is a special collection of Sarah Ann Freeman Mix's works brought together with a scholarly reflection on her life by Rosemary D. Gooden.

Mix, Mrs. Edward [Sarah Ann Freeman]. *The Life of Mrs. Edward Mix Written by Herself in 1880.* Stonington, Connecticut: Press of Register Printing Company, 1884. This small work is an autobiographical account of the life and ministry of Sarah Ann Freeman Mix.

Mix, Mrs. Edward [Sarah Ann Freeman]. "Holding Fast." *Triumphs of Faith* 1:1 (January 1881): 4–5. This is an article about learning to walk in faith by Mix. This article was originally published in Carrie Judd's widely-circulated periodical.

Mix, Mrs. Edward [Sarah Ann Freeman]. "Faith in God." *Triumphs of Faith* (June 1881): 83–84. This is a short article by noted African American healing proponent Sarah Mix on the importance of having faith for healing.

Montgomery, Carrie Judd. "Divine Healing in Relation to the Use of Our Lips." Oakland, California: *Triumphs of Faith*, undated. In this pamphlet, Montgomery looks at the role of speech in a Christian's life, particularly in regards to healing.

Montgomery, Carrie Judd. "Faith Without Works." Oakland, California: *Triumphs of Faith*, undated. In this work, Montgomery explores the operation of faith in the Christian's life.

Montgomery, Carrie Judd. "God's Messengers to The Sick." Oakland, California: *Triumphs of Faith*, undated. This is a practical work by Montgomery that is directed to providing guidance to the sick.

Montgomery, Carrie Judd. "Jesus Christ, Our Covenant of Healing." Oakland, California: *Triumphs of Faith*, undated. This is a doctrinal article from Carrie Judd Montgomery. She roots the recuperative work of Jesus within an Old Testament covenantal matrix.

Montgomery, Carrie Judd. *The Prayer of Faith*. Alameda County, California: *Triumphs of Faith*, 1880. This work, which happened to be Montgomery's first, was extremely influential in the faith-cure movement. Montgomery not only shares faith-building aspects of her personal story, but also reveals insights into the ministry of healing.

Montgomery, Carrie Judd. *Under His Wings: The Story of My Life*. Oakland, California: *Triumphs of Faith*, 1936. This book is an autobiographical account of the life of Carrie Judd Montgomery. It includes several inspiring accounts of healing.

Moxon, Walter. "Faith Healing." *Contemporary Review* 48 (November 1885) 707–722. This is a critical article published during the height of the faith-cure movement in 1885. Moxon dismisses both the arguments and practices of healing proponents.

Needham, Mrs. George C. [Elizabeth Annabelle]. *Mrs. Whilling's Faith Cure*. Boston: Bradley and Woodruff, 1891. This is a fictional work that was written to ridicule and parody the faith-cure movement. Elizabeth and her husband were at one time supporters of the healing practices, but they came to reject it.

Nichols, C.F. "Divine Healing." *Science* 19 (January 1892): 43–44. This article was written during the height of the faith-cure movement. It subtly critiques divine healing practices.

Oerter, John Henry. *Divine Healing in the Light of Scripture*. New York: Christian Alliance Publishing Company, 1900. Oerter argues that all disease is a consequence of the wrath of God against human sin. Therefore, one of the consequences of Christ's atonement is the removal of the manifestation of God's wrath in the bodies of believers, for God did not intend to give life (in the present age) only to the incorporeal part of humanity. Divine healing is the physical earnest of the coming resurrection.

Orr, James W. "Faith Healing and the Mind Cure in America." *London Quarterly Review* 101 (January 1904): 100–127. This article examines faith healing claims, associating them with the "mind-cure" and unorthodox approaches to healing.

Osborn, Lucy Drake. *Heavenly Pearls Set in a Life: A Record of Experiences and Labors in America, India, and Australia*. New York: Fleming H. Revell, 1893. This book recounts the experiences of Lucy Drake Osborn, one of the first people to be healed under Charles Cullis' ministry in Boston, Massachusetts.

Peak, Giles H. *Christ's Healing Wings: A Series of Talks*. New York: Christian Alliance Publishing Company, 1900. This book is made up of thirteen talks presented while Peak was pastor of Gospel Tabernacle Church in Los Angeles.

Platt, Smith H. *My 25th Year Jubilee; or Cure by Faith after Twenty Five Years of Lameness*. Brooklyn, New York: S. Harrison Publisher, 1875. In this work, Platt, a holiness adherent, shares an incredible testimony of healing that he experienced.

Platt, Smith H. *The Secrets of Health; Or How Not to Get Sick and How to Get Well from Sickness*. New York: Orange Judd Company, 1895. Smith H. Platt had experienced healing more than two decades earlier. In this work, he talks about the roots of disease and how one can experience healing.

Porter, Nelson L. "Experience of Healing by Faith." Boston: Nelson L. Porter Publisher, 1885. This is a pamphlet on divine healing composed during the height of the faith-cure movement in the 1880s.

Prosser, Anna Weed. *From Death to Life: An Autobiography*. Buffalo, New York: Anna Prosser Publisher, 1901. Prosser was an official in the Christian and Missionary Alliance and ran a faith home. This work is her autobiography. It recounts stories of healing that took place in her faith home as well as other experiences.

Riley, William Bell. *Divine Healing, or Does God Answer Prayer for the Sick?* South Nyack, New York: Christian Alliance Publishing Company, 1899. Riley, a prominent Baptist pastor from Minneapolis, expresses his confidence in the validity of divine healing.

Russell, R. Gertrude. "Personal Testimonies: His Healing Power." *The Christian Alliance and Mission Weekly* 8:2 (Friday, January 8, 1892): 26–27. This is a testimony of healing from a woman attending one of Cullis' healing meetings.

Schofield, Alfred Taylor. *A Study of Faith Healing*. New York: Revell Publishing, 1899. This book, published just before the turn of the century, is a conservative examination of the doctrine and practice of faith healing.

Sellew, Edgar A. "Ethan Allen." *Christian and Missionary Alliance* 30:21 (May 23, 1903). This insightful article on Ethan Otis Allen was published in a major Christian and Missionary Alliance publication. Allen was an early healing proponent who influenced the faith-cure movement in America.

Short, John N. *Divine Healing; With a Testimonial and Introduction by Reverend N. Hammond Follin.* Chicago: Christian Witness Company, undated. This is a general overview on healing written between 1895 and 1897. Short shares insights about what he believes the Bible teaches about divine healing.

Simpson, A. B., ed. *A Cloud of Witnesses for Divine Healing, Second Edition.* New York: Word, Work and World Publishing Company, 1887. This book is a collection of healing testimonies from various members of the Christian and Missionary Alliance.

Simpson, A. B. *Discovery of Divine Healing.* Brooklyn, New York: Christian Alliance Publishing Company, 1903. This booklet was one of several divine healing works that A. B. Simpson composed.

Simpson, A. B. *Friday Meeting Talks, or Divine Prescriptions for the Sick and Suffering, Series Number One.* New York: The Christian Alliance Publishing Company, 1894. This work is a collection of Simpson's messages on divine healing.

Simpson, A. B. *Friday Meeting Talks, or Divine Prescriptions for the Sick and Suffering, Series Number Two.* New York: The Christian Alliance Publishing Company, 1899. This is a second collection of healing messages from A.B. Simpson.

Simpson, A. B. *Friday Meeting Talks, or Divine Prescriptions for the Sick and Suffering, Series Number Three.* New York: The Christian Alliance Publishing Company, 1900. This book is the third collection of Simpson's messages on divine healing.

Simpson, A. B. "How to Receive Divine Healing." *The Word, Work and World* 5 (July–August 1885): 204–205. This was one of A. B. Simpson's most popular articles on divine healing. In it, he provides practical strategies for receiving healing.

Simpson, A. B. *The Four-Fold Gospel.* Harrisburg, Pennsylvania: Christian Publications, 1890. In this work, A. B. Simpson shares his four-fold understanding of the gospel. One of the expressions of the gospel that Simpson emphasizes is the ministry of healing.

Simpson, A. B. *The Lord for The Body: Discovering God's Plan for Divine Health and Healing.* Camp Hill, Pennsylvania: Christian Publications Incorporated, 1996. This is an anthology of A. B. Simpson healing articles.

Simpson, A. B. *Tracts for the Times: Divine Healing Series.* New York: The Christian Alliance Publishing Company, undated. This is a collection of Simpson tracts on the subject of healing. The titles include: Divine Healing and Natural Law, Is It God's Will?, The Lord for the Body, By His Stripes, Temples of the Holy Ghost, How to Take It, How to Keep It, Should We Care for our Bodies?, Faith and Fanaticism, Questions and Objections, How to Help Others.

Simpson, A. B. "True and False Teachings Concerning Divine Healing." *The Word, Work and World* 5:11 (November 1885): 293. This article from Simpson includes insights into the uncertainties of divine healing. It is a printed summary of one of his messages at a Christian and Missionary Alliance convention in 1885.

Smith, Jennie. *From Baca to Beulah: From a Couch of Suffering to My Feet, to Exalt His Holy Name.* Philadelphia: Garrigues, 1884. Smith was a semi-invalid evangelist. She received healing prayer a number of times but finally encountered total healing. She got up, and pain left her body for the first time in 21 years. This book is the account of her testimony.

Spear, Samuel T. "The Faith Cure." *Independent* 34 (September 14, 1882): 7–8. This is a newspaper article examining healing by means of the faith cure.

Spiher, H. H. *The World's Physician, Christ The Lord: or Five Hundred Testimonials of Divine Healing in Answer to Prayer Through the Ages.* Saint Louis: H.H. Spiher Publisher, 1895. Spiher, a Church of God minister, pastored churches started by evangelist Maria Woodworth-Etter. This work was written, in part, as an apologetics work to support the contemporary healing ministry.

Stanton, Robert Livingston. "Did Christ Ever Use Means in Healing?" *Triumphs of Faith* 3 (August 1883): 177-179. This is an article from a prominent Presbyterian that became a part of the faith-cure movement. It asks whether Jesus utilized medicine or doctors.

Stanton, Robert Livingston. *Gospel Parallelisms: Illustrated in The Healing of Body and Soul.* Buffalo, New York: Triumphs of Faith, 1883. Stanton was the former president of Miami University in Ohio and a moderator of the general assembly of the Presbyterian Church. In this work, he set out to clarify that Christ's atoning work laid the foundation for the deliverance of both sin and disease.

Stanton, Robert Livingston. "Healing through Faith." *The Presbyterian Review* 5 (June 1884): 49-79. This is Stanton's response to Marvin Vincent's oppositional article on healing. This article represents a significant interchange during the height of the Faith Cure Movement.

Stanton, Robert Livingston. *"Healing Through Faith," Again: A Paper Prepared for the Presbyterian Review but its Publication Declined, Together with Supplement Notes.* Buffalo, New York: Baker, Jones and Company, 1884. This was Stanton's written rebuttal of Marvin R. Vincent's "Dr. Stanton on 'Healing Through Faith.'" This would have been the fourth interchange in the Presbyterian Review. Since the editors decided not to publish it, Stanton published it himself.

Tuckley, C. Lloyd. "Faith Healing as a Medical Treatment." *Nineteenth Century* 24 (December 1888): 839–850. This is a critical article on divine healing that was published in response to the growing influence of the faith-cure movement in the late 1880s.

Whittle, Daniel Webster. *The Wonders of Prayer: A Record of Well-Authenticated and Wonderful Answers to Prayer.* Chicago, Illinois: Fleming H. Revell, 1886. This work includes a number of vignettes and stories on prayer. It references a few accounts of healing from Charles Cullis and others.

Wood, S. A. "The Disciples 'Gift of Healing." *Christian and Missionary Alliance* 19:13 (Wednesday, September 22, 1897): 299. This is a sermonic reflection on 1 Corinthians 12 by a Christian and Missionary Alliance leader.

7. RADICAL HOLINESS

Anderson, Allan. *Zion and Pentecost: The Spirituality and Experience of Pentecostal and Zionist Apostolic Churches in South Africa.* Pretoria, South Africa: University of South Africa Press, 2000. This book explores the history of a group of churches established in Africa by John G. Lake.

Blezek, W. C. "Prophet or Profit: The Rhetoric of John Alexander Dowie and the Christian Catholic Church," M. Div., thesis, Northern Illinois University, 1999. This well-researched thesis is a critical analysis of John Alexander Dowie, a prominent healing proponent in the late nineteenth and early twentieth centuries.

Buckley, James Monroe. "Dowie, Analyzed, and Classified." *The Century Magazine* 64 (October 1902): 928–932. Buckley, the editor of the *The Century*, a prominent Methodist periodical, was extremely critical of the Holiness movement, Pentecostalism, and their openness to healing. In this article, he attacks John Alexander Dowie.

Conley, John W. *Divine Healing and Doctors: What Says the Bible? An Examination of the Attitude of the Biblical Writers toward the Use of Medicines and the Employment of Physicians.* Chicago: Fleming H. Revell Company, 1898. This book examines what the scriptures have to say about doctors and medical practice.

Cook, Phillip. *Zion City, Illinois: A Twentieth Century Utopia.* Syracuse New York: Syracuse University Press, 1996. This is a riveting academic treatment of the ministry of John Alexander Dowie.

Darms, Anton. *Life and Work of John Alexander Dowie.* Zion, Illinois: Zion Publishing, 1938. Darms was a Pentecostal who was loosely connected to Dowie before his fall. In this text, Darms reflects on Dowie's life and ministry.

Day, Holman F. "The Saints of Shiloh." *Leslie's Magazine* 101 (April 1905): 682–692. This in-depth magazine article reflects on the ministry of Frank Sandford and his followers in Shiloh, Maine.

Dowie, John Alexander. *American First Fruits: Being a Brief Record of Eight Months' Divine Healing Mission in the State of California Conducted by the Reverend John Alexander Dowie and Mrs. Dowie from Melbourne Australia.* Chicago: Zion Publishing House, 1893. This is an account of some of the first healings Dowie conducted as he began his healing ministry in the United States.

Dowie, John Alexander. "Christ's Methods of Healing: Reply to the Exposition of the Sunday School Lesson by the Reverend Dr. John Lindsay Withrow, Pastor of the Third Presbyterian Church, Chicago, in the Record of January 8, 1898, Delivered in Zion Tabernacle, 1621–1633 Michigan Avenue, Chicago, Jan. 9, 1898, by the Reverend John Alexander Dowie." Chicago: Zion Publishing House, 1898. This is the transcription of the message that John Alexander Dowie shared in response to one of his critics.

Dowie, John Alexander. "Divine Healing Vindicated." Chicago: Divine Healing Association, 1893. This book is a short defense of the ministry of healing written by proto-Pentecostal, John Alexander Dowie.

Dowie, John Alexander. "Jesus the Healer or The Exercise of Apostolic Powers the Gifts of the Holy Spirit a Sermon by Reverend John Alexander Dowie First Apostle of the Christian Catholic Apostolic Church in Zion, Illinois." Chicago: Zion Publishing House, 1895. This is a healing teaching composed by Dowie.

Dowie, John Alexander. "'What Should a Christian Do When Sick?' A Sermon by The Reverend John Alexander Dowie, General Overseer of the Christian Catholic Church in Zion. Delivered in Central Zion Tabernacle, 1621–1633 Michigan Avenue, Chicago, Illinois, Lord's Day, July 2, 1897." Chicago: Zion Publishing House, 1898. This is a pithy transcription of a Dowie healing sermon.

Dowie, John Alexander. "Zion's Holy War Against the Hosts of Hell in Chicago: A Series of Addresses by The Reverend John Alexander Dowie, General Overseer of the Christian Catholic Church in

Zion." Zion, Illinois: Zion Publishing House, 1900. This is a bombastic book in which John Alexander Dowie shares his outright hatred of doctors and medicine. He found medical practices to be opposed to faith.

Dyer, T. F. Thiselton. "Faith Healing." *Gentleman's Magazine* 259 (July–September 1885): 61–74. This feature article, printed in a popular publication, was written to critique the faith-cure movement.

Editor. "100, Healed By Faith to Tell About Miracles: Lake Arranging Testimony Meeting as Part of Worship Services Here." *The Spokane Press* (Sunday, July 5, 1924). This newspaper article recounts some of what was transpiring in John G. Lake's meetings.

Editor. "Aided 8,130 Ill Persons: The Reverend John G. Lake Claims Greater Record Than Hospitals." *The Spokesman-Review* (January 3, 1916). This Spokane newspaper published a news story about John G. Lake's healing claims in that city.

Editor. "He Died in the City He Founded: Neither Wife, Nor Son, Whom He Had Repulsed Was at His Bedside." *New York Times* (March 9, 1907). This is a news article on the passing of John Alexander Dowie.

Editor. "Modem Miracles: Spokane Minister Announces He Will Cure by Faith and Invites Physicians to Check Up on His Promised Performances." *The Spokane Press* (Thursday, July 3, 1924). This brief newspaper article was undoubtedly initiated by John G. Lake in Spokane, Washington.

Editor. "Said to Be Religion: Strange Scenes at 'Revival Meetings' Held in Indiana." *The New York Times*. (January 24, 1885) 1. This is a critical journalistic article describing some of the wild scenes of a Mariah Woodworth-Etter revival meeting.

Editor. "Sister Etter with the Lord." *Pentecostal Evangel* 27 (September 1924): 9. This is a eulogy for Mariah Woodworth-Etter published in the official organ of the Assemblies of God.

Editor. "Tell Cures, All Night Meeting: Apostolic Society Greets 200 in Healing Room New Year's Eve." *The Spokesman-Review* (Tuesday morning, January 2, 1917). This news article recounts a New Year's Eve healing service conducted by John G. Lake in Spokane, Washington.

Gates, Harrison. *More Than a Prophet: Twelve Years with Frank W. Sandford*. Francistown, New Hampshire: Marshall Jones Company, 1990. This is a biographical account of controversial, proto-Pentecostal healing evangelist Frank W. Sandford.

Gilchrist, H. H. *Dr. Dowie Before the Court of Public Opinion*. Topeka, Kansas: Crane and Company Publishers, 1899. This book is a fierce exposé of the controversial John Alexander Dowie of Chicago.

Gleason, Ralph E. "Wilt Thou Be Made Whole." Durham, Maine: Shiloh Bible School, undated. This is a divine healing Bible study that students used in Frank Weston Sandford's Bible school in Maine.

Harlan, Rolvix. *John Alexander Dowie and the Christian Catholic Apostolic Church in Zion*. Evansville, Wisconsin: R. M. Antes Publisher, 1906. This is a biographical account of famous healing evangelist John Alexander Dowie.

Heath, Alden R. "Apostle in Zion." *Journal of the Illinois State Historical Society* 70 (1977): 98–113. This is a thoroughly researched article on the life and ministry of controversial healing evangelist John Alexander Dowie.

Hiss, William. "Shiloh: Frank W. Sandford and His Kingdom: 1893–1948," Ph.D. diss., Tufts University, 1978. This is an important dissertation that explores the life and ministry of proto-Pentecostal healer, Frank W. Sandford, and his religious community in Shiloh, Maine.

Lake, John Graham. *Adventures in God.* Tulsa, Oklahoma: Harrison House Publishers, 1981, 1991. This book is a biographical account of noted healing evangelist John G. Lake. It includes several marvelous healing accounts.

Lake, John Graham. "A Lecture on Divine Healing: Saint Patrick and His Power." *The Spokesman-Review* (Sunday morning, March 17, 1918). This article, penned by Lake, examines the life of Saint Patrick and his utilization of supernatural power.

Lake, John Graham. "Do You Know God's Way of Healing?" *The Spokesman-Review* (Sunday, March 31, 1918). In this article, published in the Spokane newspaper, Lake provides a brief biblical reflection on healing.

Lake, John Graham. "How I Came to Devote My Life to the Ministry of Healing." *The Spokesman-Review* (Sunday morning, March 3, 1918). This brief testimonial article was submitted by Lake to *The Spokesman-Review* newspaper in Spokane, Washington.

Lake, John Graham. *John G. Lake—Apostle to Africa*, ed. Gordon Lindsay. Dallas, Texas: Christ for the Nations, 1981. This biographical account focuses on Lake's ministry in Africa.

Lake, John Graham. *John G. Lake: His Life, His Sermons, His Boldness of Faith.* Fort Worth, Texas: Kenneth Copeland Publications, 1995. This collection of John G. Lake's teachings contains several healing accounts.

Lake, John G. *John G. Lake on Healing*, ed. Roberts Liardon. New Kensington, Pennsylvania: Whitaker House, 2009. This book is a collection of sermons, articles, letters, and teachings from John G. Lake.

Lake, John Graham. *The Astounding Diary of John G. Lake*, ed. Gordon Lindsay. Dallas, Texas: Christ for the Nations, 1994. This work includes excerpts from John G. Lake's diary. It recounts some of the great healings and miracles that occurred in his ministry.

Lake, John Graham. *The Complete Collection of His Life Teachings*. Tulsa, Oklahoma: Albury Publishing, 1999. Roberts Liardon collected sermons, articles, and journal entries from the writings of John G. Lake. Throughout this work is a number of references to healing.

Lake, John Graham. "The Healing Stream." *Spokane Daily Chronicle* (Sunday, April 26, 1919). This is a teaching that Lake paid to have published in a Spokane, Washington newspaper.

Lake, John Graham. *The John G. Lake Sermons on Dominion over Demons, Disease, and Death*, ed. Gordon Lindsay. Dallas, Texas: Christ for the Nations, 1949, 1976. This is a collection of sermons on healing and deliverance by John G. Lake.

Lake, John Graham. *The New John G. Lake Sermons*, ed. Gordon Lindsay. Dallas, Texas: Christ for the Nations. Dallas, Texas, 2000. Gordon Lindsay compiled several of Lake's sermons to produce this work in the 1950s. Several of the messages deal with healing.

Lake, John Graham. "The Power of God." *The Spokesman-Review* (Sunday Morning, October 8, 1918). This brief article, from Lake, considers the transformative effects of God's power.

Lee, Carl Q. *John Alexander Dowie*. Chicago: Published by Carl Q. Lee, 1944. This brief biographical account of John Alexander Dowie includes some useful insights into his ministry.

Lindsay, Gordon, comp. and ed. *Champion of the Faith: The Sermons of John Alexander Dowie*. Dallas, Texas: Christ for the Nations, 1987. Drawing from *Leaves of Healing* and other publications, Lindsay edited and compiled this collection of John Alexander Dowie sermons.

Lindsay, Gordon. *John Alexander Dowie: A Life Story of Trials, Tragedies and Triumphs*. Dallas, Texas: Christ for the Nations, 1986. This work is the biography of John Alexander Dowie. Lindsay brought together aspects of his story that were not included elsewhere.

Murray, Frank S. *The Sublimity of Faith: The Life and Work of Frank W. Sandford*. Amherst, New Hampshire: Kingdom Press, 1981. This in-depth, sympathetic work examines the controversial ministry of Frank Sandford.

Nelson, Shirley and Rudy. "Frank Sandford: Tongues of Fire in Shiloh, Maine." *Portraits of a Generation: Early Pentecostal Leaders*, eds. James R. Goff Jr. and Grant Wacker, 51–69. Fayetteville, Arkansas: University of Arkansas Press, 2002. This well-researched essay, from the Nelsons, explores the life and ministry of Frank Weston Sandford.

Nelson, Shirley. "Trust and Trouble: The Story of Shiloh a Fascinating Chapter in American Faith." *Glimpses* 171 (2004). This article explores the notorious life of Frank W. Sandford and his ministry in Shiloh, Maine. Shirley Nelson's family was part of Sanford's ministry during the height of its impact.

Newcomb, Arthur. *Dowie: Anointed of the Lord*. New York: Century Company, 1930. This work by Newcomb is a major early biographical account of John Alexander Dowie.

Reidt, Wilford. *John G. Lake: A Man without Compromise*. Tulsa, Oklahoma: Harrison House, 1989. This book, composed by John G. Lake's son-in-law, is a short account of his remarkable ministry.

Reidt, Wilford H. *Jesus: God's Way of Healing & Power to Promote Health: Featuring the Miracle Ministry of Dr. John G. Lake*. New York: Vantage Press, 1977. This book recounts some of John G. Lake's doctrinal and practical methodologies.

Sandford, Frank W. *Seven Years with God.* Mount Vernon, New Hampshire: Kingdom Press, 1900, 1957. This is an autobiography of the controversial Frank Weston Sandford. It documents his spiritual journey up to the year 1900.

Sheldrake, Edna, ed. *The Personal Letters of John Alexander Dowie.* Zion City, Illinois: Wilbur Glenn Voliva Publisher, 1912. This work is an edited collection of the correspondence of John Alexander Dowie.

Votaw, Clyde W. "Christian Science and Faith Healing." *New Englander and Yale Review* 54 (March 1891): 249–259. This dismissive article falsely conflates the faith cure with Christian Science.

Weiss, C. S. *Sanfordism Exposed: A Warning and Protest.* Lisbon Falls, Maine: C. S. Weiss publisher, 1899. This is a fierce critique of Frank W. Sandford and his ministry.

White, Arnold. *The Almighty and Us: The Inside Story of Shiloh, Maine.* Fort Lauderdale, Florida: White, 2009. In this book, White examines some of what transpired through Frank Sandford's ministry in Shiloh, Maine.

Woodward, E. P. *Sanfordism: An Exposure of the Claims, Purposes, Methods, Predictions and Threats of Frank W. Sandford, the "Apostle" to Shiloh, Maine.* Portland Maine: Safeguard Publishing Company, 1902. Woodward dismissively examines the theology and practices of Frank Sandford.

Woodworth-Etter, Maria. *Acts of the Holy Ghost, or The Life and Experience of Mrs. M. B. Woodworth-Etter.* John F. Worley Publishing. Dallas, Texas, 1912. This is one of several autobiographical accounts of the life and ministry of Maria Woodworth-Etter. This work includes Maria's experiences with the emerging Pentecostal movement

Woodworth-Etter. Maria. *A Diary of Signs and Wonders.* Tulsa, Oklahoma: Harrison House, 1916, 1981. This book is a different autobiographical work. In addition to remarkable stories, the work includes unusual healing testimonies.

Woodworth, Maria. *Life and Experience of Maria B. Woodworth.* Dayton, Ohio: United Brethren Publishing House, 1885. This is Woodworth's first account of her life and ministry. The work covers the time period of 1883–1885. Woodworth's books published before 1902 are under the name Mrs. M. B. Woodworth or Mariah Beulah Woodworth. Books published after 1902 show the author's name as Maria Woodworth-Etter. This reflects her marriage to Samuel Etter. It is difficult to document all of Maria's books because she often updated them and changed their titles.

Woodworth-Etter, Maria. *Life and Testimony of Mrs. M. B. Woodworth-Etter, Evangelist: Finished Biography of Nearly Fifty Years Ministry.* Indianapolis, Indiana: August Feick, 1925. This publication is a much later account of Etter's life and ministry.

Woodworth, Maria. *Life, Work and Experience of Maria B. Woodworth.* Saint Louis, Missouri: Commercial Printing Company, 1894. This is an early account of Maria's life and ministry. Like the others, it recounts many of the unusual healing experiences that took place in her meetings.

Woodworth-Etter, Maria. *Marvels and Miracles God Wrought in the Ministry for 45 years.* Indianapolis, Indiana: Maria Woodworth-Etter, 1922. This book is another extended account of Maria's ministry.

Woodworth-Etter, Maria. *Questions and Answers On Divine Healing, Revised and Enlarged.* Indianapolis, Indiana: Maria Woodworth-Etter, 1922. This book is a collection of responses to questions about healing. Some of the language of this work shares affinities with the work of F. F. Bosworth.

Woodworth-Etter, Maria. *Signs and Wonders God Wrought in the Ministry for Forty Years by Mrs. M. B. Woodworth-Etter, Evangelist, Compiled and Written by Herself, Complete Including Sermons.* Indianapolis, Indiana:

Maria Woodworth-Etter, 1916. This is another viable account of Maria's ministry exploits.

Woodworth-Etter, Maria. *The Complete Collection of Her Life Teachings*, comp. and ed. Roberts Liardon. Tulsa, Oklahoma: Albury Publishing, 2000. Roberts Liardon compiled sermons, letters, and articles from Maria Woodworth-Etter.

Woodworth, Maria. *Trials and Triumphs of Maria Beulah Woodworth*. Dayton, Ohio: United Brethren Publishing House, 1886. In this early work, Mara recounts some interesting incidents from her life.

Wyatt, Brett A. *Fire of God: John G. Lake in Spokane*. Spokane, Washington: Riley Media, 2002. This well-researched compilation of newspaper reports, tracts, and other publications provides valuable information on the healing ministry of John G. Lake in Spokane, Washington.

8. EARLY PENTECOSTALISM

Adams, Agnes. *Stephen Jeffreys: Present Day Miracles*. Springfield, Missouri: Gospel Publishing House, 1928. This book is a popular treatment of the ministry of twentieth-century British evangelist Stephen Jeffreys. There were a number of healing accounts included.

Adams, John Welsh. *Miracles of Today*. Lichfield, England: Wall Vicarage, 1930. J. W. Adams was part of the outreach team of Stephen Jeffreys, a British evangelist who witnessed hundreds of healings. This book is an account of the remarkable things that Adams witnessed.

Argue, Zelma. "The Ministry of Healing." *The Pentecostal Evangel* 1732 (August 2, 1947): 2. This is an article, published in the official publication of the Assemblies of God, detailing one of Smith Wigglesworth's ministry engagements.

Baur, Benjamin A. *The Great Physician*. Rochester, New York: Glad Tidings Publishing Society, 1938. This book provides a brief biblical analysis of Jesus' role as the "Great Physician."

Baxter, Betty. *The Betty Baxter story: A 1941 Miracle of Healing as Told by Herself*. Elmore, Minnesota: D. Heidt, 1951. This book recounts an amazing healing that a girl with severe spinal problems experienced.

Boddy, Alexander A. "Dr. Yoakum 'An Overseer.'" *Confidence* 4:11 (November 1911): 254–255. In this article, Anglican rector, A. A. Boddy provides reflections on Finis Yoakum's healing ministry in Los Angeles, California.

Boddy, Alexander A. "Dr. Yoakum's Work at Los Angeles: An Appreciation and Candid Criticism." *Confidence* 5:11 (November 1912): 248–251. This is another insightful article on Finis E. Yoakum's healing ministry in California.

Boddy, Alexander A. "Transatlantic Experiences: A Visit to Zion City Illinois." *Confidence* 6:2 (February 2, 1913): 33, 36–39. In this article,

A. A. Boddy, a Spirit-filled Anglican rector, shares some of his personal reflections on the ministry of John Alexander Dowie.

Bogard, Ben M., and Aimee Semple McPherson. *Bogard-McPherson Debate: McPhersonism, Holy Rollerism, Miracles, Pentecostalism, Divine Healing: A Debate with both Sides Presented Fully: Elder Ben M. Bogard Affirming that Miracles and Divine Healing as Taught and Manifested in the Word of God, Ceased.* Nashville: Gospel Advocate, 1934, 1938. This book is the edited transcript of a public debate between Aimee Semple McPherson and Ben Bogard. Each presented different sides in their debate on healing and the gifts of the Spirit. This publication not only provides insight into the differing outlooks of cessationists and continualists, it also shows some of the rhetorical strategies being employed.

Bosworth, F. F. *Christ the Healer.* Miami Beach, Florida: F. F. Bosworth Publisher, 1924, 1951. This is an anthology of healing messages from F.F. Bosworth, a prominent Christian and Missionary Alliance evangelist. This book has been extremely influential, shaping the approaches of many healing proponents.

Bosworth, F. F. "Discerning the Lord's Body: Living Faith Makes Disease Impossible." *Latter Rain Evangel* 6:9 (June 1914): 2–7. This article is derived from a Bosworth's keynote message on healing delivered at a Pentecostal convention in Dallas, Texas on May 22, 1914.

Bosworth, F. F. "For This Cause Was the Son of God Manifest That He Might Destroy the Works of the Devil." *Latter Rain Evangel* 13:10 (July 1921): 6–9. This is a healing sermon that Bosworth preached at a tent meeting in Chicago, Illinois on June 20, 1921.

Bosworth, F. F. "Hints Regarding Healing." *Pentecostal Evangel* 1776 (May 22, 1948): 4. This is an article from F. F. Bosworth that clarifies some of the practical ways that healing can be appropriated.

Bosworth, F. F. "Pentecostal Outpouring in Dallas, Texas." *Latter Rain Evangel* 10 (July 1912): 10. This is a news story covering the revival meetings and stupendous miracles transpiring at F.F. Bosworth's church in Dallas, Texas.

Bosworth, F. F. "The Faith That Takes." *Pentecostal Evangel* 1707 (January 25, 1947): 6–7. This Bosworth healing article, published in the Assemblies of God's official publication, discusses the relationship between faith and healing.

Bosworth, F. F. "The Wonders of God in Dallas." *Word and Witness* 20 (August 1912): 3. This is a first-hand account of the healings and other notable occurrences at an extended F. F. Bosworth revival meeting in Dallas, Texas.

Bosworth, F. F. "'They Rehearsed All That God Had Done with Them': The Re-Creative Power of God – Miracles of Healing." *Latter Rain Evangel* 13 (March 1921): 5–10. This article on healing and miracles was drawn from some first-hand testimonies.

Boulton, E. C. W. *George Jeffreys: A Ministry of the Miraculous.* Tonbridge Kent, United Kingdom: Sovereign World LTD., 1928. This is a biography of George Jeffreys, an early healing proponent emerging from British Pentecostalism.

Bowling, Hugh. "My Position on Divine Healing." *Pentecostal Holiness Advocate* 3:53 (1920): 4–5. Bowling, a prominent minister in the Pentecostal Holiness denomination, reflects on his understanding of healing.

Brewster, Percy S. "The Approach to Divine Healing: or, Can We Expect Miracles Today?" London: Elim, undated. This work by an Elim minister advocates for the ongoing practice of the ministry of healing. It was published around 1939.

Bridges, Cecil. "Divine Healing." *Church of God Evangel* 44:4 (1953): 11. Bridges, a popular leader in the Church of God (Cleveland,

Tennessee), shares insights into healing's meaning and application. This work was written during the height of the salvation-healing revival.

Brooks, Noel. *Fight for Faith and Freedom*. London: Pattern Book Room, 1948. This work is a detailed first-hand account of the Jeffreys brothers' healing ministries.

Brooks, Noel. "Sickness, Health, and God." Franklin Springs, Georgia: *Advocate*, 1965. In this article, Noel Brooks, a British-born Pentecostal minister, shares his notable insights about the ministry of healing.

Brooks, Noel. *The Place of Faith in Sickness and Health*. Bristol, England: Noel Brooks, undated. In this work, Brooks describes how faith is intended to work in the lives of infirmed Christians.

Brown, Charles Reynolds. *Faith and Health*. New York: Thomas Y. Crowell Company, 1910. This book is an analysis of orthodox and unorthodox healing practices in the early twentieth century. Brown provides a fierce critique of healing proponents.

Close, Carra H. *God's Word on Divine Healing: Containing the Instances and Promises Recorded Therein*. Beulah Heights, California: Triumphs of Faith, undated. This is an insightful reflection on healing from one of Carrie Judd Montgomery's closest associates.

Conn, Charles W. "Divine Healing and the Church of God," *Church of God Evangel* (February 25, 1956): 4. This is an article from a prominent Church of God (Cleveland, Tennessee) historian, exploring healing practices in his denomination.

Cove, Gordon. *God's Covenant of Divine Healing or An Amazing Contract*. United Kingdom, undated. This is a practical work composed by a British Pentecostal healing evangelist who encourages people to place their faith in Jesus as their heavenly physician.

Cove, Gordon. *How to Build a Strong Faith for Divine Healing*. United Kingdom: Gordon Cove, undated. This practical work from a gifted evangelist provides insight for faith development.

Cove, Gordon. *How to Make Your Healing Permanent*. Sandbach: Wrights, 1956. This practical work from Cove provides insight on how to "seal" a healing work. This was written in response to the fact that some "lost" their healings after the meetings.

Cove, Gordon. *Why Some Are Healed by Christ and Some Are Not*. Nelson, United Kingdom: Coulton and Company, undated. Cove, a prominent healing evangelist, tries to explain why some are healed in the healing meetings, and some are not.

Dallimore, Arthur Henry. *Healing by Faith: Including Many Testimonies of Healing Received by People in New Zealand*. Auckland, New Zealand: Arthur Henry Dallimore Publisher, 1932. Evangelists John G. Lake and Charles Price directly impacted Dallimore while he still resided in North America. When he moved to New Zealand, the church that he founded quickly grew as the ministry of healing was highlighted. This book was largely reflective of that ministry. Dallimore later became more eccentric and embraced unorthodox doctrines as time progressed. Because of this, he was discredited.

Darragh, R. E. *In Defense of His Word: Being a Number of Carefully Selected Testimonies of Dire Suffering Healed by the Power of Christ Under the Ministry of Principle George Jeffreys*. United Kingdom: Elim Publishing, 1932. This is a inspiring collection of healing testimonies from the ministry of George Jeffreys of England.

DeVore, J.E. "We Believe in Divine Healing," *Church of God Evangel* (December 4, 1954): 3. This article briefly articulates the position of the ministry of healing held by the Church of God (Cleveland Tennessee).

Dixon, Rebecca. "Healed of Diphtheria," *Church of God Evangel* (August 6, 1927): 4. This is a healing testimonial that was documented in the official publication of the Church of God.

Dooley, John Alexander and Hannah Dooley. *Jesus Christ the Great Physician*. Minneapolis, Minnesota: John A. and Hannah M. Dooley, 1928. This explores the healing ministry of Jesus, drawing conclusions about its implications for believers today.

Dudley, Dora G. *Beulah: or Some of the Fruits of a Consecrated Life, Revised and Enlarged Edition*. Grand Rapids, Michigan: Published by Dora G. Dudley, 1896. This book is a collection of practical teachings and biblical reflections from a gifted Christian and Missionary Alliance leader. Dudley, whose teaching was widely recognized, managed a faith-healing home in Michigan. She later became Pentecostal.

Dudley, Dora G. "Christian Science, Counterfeit of Divine Healing." Grand Rapids, Michigan: Published by Dora G. Dudley, undated. In this tract, Dudley distinguishes between sound healing practices and those of Christian Science.

Dudley, Dora G. "Divine Healing." Tract. Grand Rapids, Michigan: Published by Dora G. Dudley, undated. In this booklet, Dora Dudley shares her insights into the biblical foundations of divine healing.

Eason, Glenn. "Why Preach and Practice Divine Healing Today?," *Church of God Evangel* (July 3, 1943): 10. This is a practical article on the ministry of healing from a Classical Pentecostal minister.

Editor. "Cheerful Givers: No Miracles Without Cash; Services Halt While Money Is Collected; 'Healing' Services at Pisgah Home Bring Out Some Queer Testimony. Dr. Yoakum Asserts That Everyone Should Give Their All to God's Servants, Never Mind Debts." *Los Angeles Times*. March 1, 1909. This is a derisive article from a prominent California newspaper on Dr. Finis E. Yoakum.

Editor. "Evangelist Price Tries Healing Sick." *Oregonian*. (December 4, 1925). This dismissive article from a major newspaper in Portland, Oregon ridicules the healing ministry of Charles Price.

Editor. "Founder of Pisgah Dies." *Los Angeles Daily Times* 2. (August 19, 1920). This is an obituary of Pentecostal evangelist Finis E. Yoakum published in a prominent Los Angeles newspaper.

Editor. "Healer Draws in Pomona: Afflicted Ones Gather at Five O'clock in the Morning in Search of Relief." *Los Angeles Times*, March 28, 1909. This article reflects on the healing ministry of Finis E. Yoakum.

Editor. "Healing and Health." *Church of God Evangel* 9:2 (1918): 1. In this brief article, published in the official organ of the Church of God (Cleveland, Tennessee), biblical foundations of healing are presented.

Editor. "Pouring Oil on the Sick: Service Instituted Yesterday at Temperance Temple; Crippled Girl Claims That She Was Made Whole Again; Leader of the Band Says Faith Isn't Necessary—Stories Don't Jibe." *Los Angeles Times*. (August 8, 1903). This is a news article critiquing the ministry of Finis E. Yoakum in Los Angeles, California.

Editor. "Revival in Galena Heals the Sick—Cripples Enabled to Walk." *Joplin Globe* (Friday morning, October 28, 1903). This Missouri newspaper article recounted the exploits of Pentecostal progenitor, Charles F. Parham.

Editor. "Sickness and Health." *Church of God Evangel* 5:28 (1914): 1–3. This essay reflects on the healings that have transpired in the Church of God (Cleveland, Tennessee).

Editor. "The Great Physician." *Pentecostal Evangel* 1776. (May 22, 1948). This article, from the official Assemblies of God publication, is a strong exhortation about the significance of healing. The sentiment is much stronger than what would be expected at this time from this classical Pentecostal denomination.

Edsor, Albert W. *George Jeffreys: Man of God*. London: Ludgate Press Limited, 1964. This is a popular biographical account of Pentecostal healing evangelist George Jeffreys.

Erickson, Clarence H. *Jesus, the Healer Divine*. Indianapolis, Indiana: Published by Clarence H. Erickson, 1927. This down-to-earth book provides an overview of Jesus as a healer. The goal was to encourage people to seek after him for healing.

Fitch, Theodore. *Our Afflictions Their Cause and Remedy*. Council Bluffs, Iowa: Theodore Fitch, undated. This practical booklet from the early 1950s provides a basic overview of the biblical foundations of healing from a lesser known oneness Pentecostal.

Frodsham, Arthur W. "The Sixteenth Chapter of Mark: How God Vindicates His Word in the Last Days." *Pentecostal Evangel* (April 28, 1923): 1–16. This is a popular article on healing that was published in the official organ of the Assemblies of God.

Frodsham, Stanley. *Smith Wigglesworth: Apostle of Faith*. Springfield, Missouri: Gospel Publishing House, 1948. This is a biographical work on Smith Wigglesworth written by a prominent Pentecostal leader. It is one of the seminal works on his ministry.

Gainforth, Mary E. *Experience of Divine Healing and Salvation*. Salem, Oregon: F. P. Kyle, 1911. This was a widely received collection of healing testimonies. It contains some of the encounters that took place in the outworking of Gainforth's ministry.

Gainsforth, Mary E. "Divine Healing Secrets." Oakland, California: *Triumphs of Faith*, undated. In this publication, Gainsforth shares some healing insights that she picked up while on the evangelistic field.

Gardiner, Gordon P. "The Apostle of Divine Healing: The Story of John Alexander Dowie." Brooklyn, New York: *Bread of Life*, 1957. Gardiner (1915–1986) lived in John Alexander Dowie's Zion City as a boy. In this article, he shares some of what he experienced.

Gardiner, Gordon P. "Unquestionably The Apostle of Divine Healing in His Day." *Bread of Life* 6 (March 1957): 3–15. This fascinating article about John Alexander Dowie was written by a man whose family lived in Zion, Illinois.

Gee, Donald. *Trophimus I Left Sick: Our Problems of Divine Healing*. London: Elim Publishing Company, 1952. This noted Pentecostal explores passages of the Bible that suggest that healing did not take place. It was written to provide understanding about why some Christians are not healed.

Greene, Merle H. "Divine Healing," *Church of God Evangel* (October 12, 1946): 15. This is a short, pragmatic article on the ministry of healing.

Gurden, B. F. *Healing for the Body*. Hollywood, California: B. F. Gurden Publisher, 1934. Gurden, a prominent minister in the Foursquare denomination, lays out a practical case for the healing of the body.

Gurden, B. F. *Studies in Divine Healing*, volume 1. Hollywood, California: B. F. Gurden Publisher, 1933. This little book is a short collection of teachings on faith and healing. It was written to stir up faith in those who were sick.

Holcomb, Sam. "Divine Healing." *Church of God Evangel* (May 6, 1944): 14. Holcomb's article is a down-to-earth reflection on the ministry of healing.

Hoover, J. N. "Divine Healing." *Pentecostal Evangel* 8. (January 1931): 5. This is a practical article on the subject of healing published in the Assemblies of God's official publication, *Pentecostal Evangel*.

Hoover, J. N. "Divine Healing—Is It Practical or Fanatical?" *Latter Rain Evangel* (November 1934): 9–11. This article, published in a leading Pentecostal periodical, is a spirited defense of healing.

Hoover, J. N. "Is Scriptural Healing Fanaticism?" *Latter Rain Evangel* (January 1931) 7–10. Although Hoover was a Baptist minister, he was sympathetic to the Pentecostal message. Here he seeks to defend the doctrine of healing.

J. M. B. "Miracles of Healing." *The Bridal Call* 4:8 (January 1921): 14–15. This article on remarkable acts of healing was published in one of Aimee Semple McPherson's widely circulated periodicals.

Jeffreys, George. *A Modern Miracle of Healing at Grimsby*. Clapham Elim Publishing Company, 1927. This short book is a testimony of a healing that took place in one of George Jeffreys' healing meetings.

Jeffreys, George. *Healing Rays*. London: Elim Publishing Company, 1932. This is an important work on healing from a prominent European Pentecostal. The Jeffreys brothers were saved during the Welsh revival and impacted all of the United Kingdom with their healing ministries.

Jeffreys, George. *Helpless Cripple Perfectly Healed at Leeds*. Clapham, United Kingdom: Elim, 1927. This is an account of a healing that took place in one the healing meetings of the Jeffreys brothers.

Jeffreys, George. *Miraculous Healing after Twenty Years' Suffering*, London: Elim, 1927. This book is a collection of testimonies that took place through the evangelistic campaigns of George Jeffreys.

Jeffreys, George. *The Miraculous Foursquare Gospel—Doctrinal*, volume one. London: Elim Publishing Company, 1933. This work by Jeffreys is an anthology of doctrinal teachings. It includes insights about the ministry of divine healing.

Jeffreys, Edward. *Stephen Jeffreys the Beloved Evangelist*. London: Elim Publishing, 1946. This is an inspiring biographical account of one of the most prominent healing evangelists in early British Pentecostalism.

Jeffreys, Edward. *Present Day Miracles of Divine Healing.* Birmingham: Bethel Press, 1933. This is an account of several healings that took place in the early Pentecostal meetings in England.

Johnson, Phil. *How to Obtain and Retain Your Healing.* Tulsa, Oklahoma: Pentecostal Publications, 1949. This is a practical work on the ministry of healing from a lesser-known Pentecostal minister.

Johnson, W.E. "What I Believe About Divine Healing," *Church of God Evangel* (July 10, 1954): 3. This is a brief reflection on the biblical foundations of healing by a minister associated with the Church of God (Cleveland, Tennessee).

Kerr, Daniel Warren. *Waters in the Desert.* Springfield, Missouri: Gospel Publishing House, 1927. This is a doctrinal treatise by an early Assemblies of God leader that includes several insights into healing.

Lee, Flavius J. *Divine Healing.* Cleveland, Tennessee: Church of God Publishing House, 1925. This is an overview of the biblical foundations and practice of healing from a popular early Church of God minister.

Luce, Alice E. "The Great Physician and His Medicines." *Pentecostal Evangel* 2138 (May 1, 1955): 3, 7. This article, published in the official Assemblies of God periodcials, is a reprint from the 1930s. It makes a pronounced case for divine healing.

Martin, Mrs. George. "Healed When Doctor Was Dismissed." *Church of God Evangel* 13:32 (1922): 3. This is an inspirational testimony of a lay member of the Church of God (Cleveland, Tennessee).

McPherson, Aimee Semple. *Aimee: Life Story of Aimee Semple McPherson.* Los Angeles, California: Foursquare Publications, 1979. This account is one of several autobiographical works that Aimee Semple McPherson wrote during her lifetime.

McPherson, Aimee Semple. *Divine Healing Sermons.* Los Angeles, California: Biola Press, 1921. This is a collection of Aimee Semple McPherson's sermons on divine healing. The titles of these messages include: "Is Jesus Christ the Great I Am? or Is He the Great I Was?," "A Double Cure for a Double Curse," "The Scriptural Relationship of Salvation and Divine Healing," "The Three Parties Concerned in Your Receiving Healing," "How to Receive Your Healing," "How to Keep It," "Questions Frequently Asked Regarding Divine Healing," and "Some Wonderful Testimonies of Those Healed Through Prayer."

McPherson, Aimee Semple. *In the Service of the King.* New York: Boni and Liveright, 1927. This book is the first autobiography of Aimee Semple McPherson. In it, she recounts some stories of healing breakthrough.

McPherson, Aimee Semple. *Lost and Restored: Sermons and Personal Testimony of Aimee Semple McPherson, Centennial Edition.* Los Angeles, California: Four Square Publications, 1990. This is a collection of sermons and personal observations from Aimee Semple McPherson. It naturally includes some of her insights into the ministry of healing.

Mitchell, S. R. "Divine Healing." *Church of God Evangel* 12:28 (1921): 2. This is a brief overview of healing from a Church of God (Cleveland, Tennessee) minister.

Nelson, P. C. *Does Christ Heal Today? Messages of Faith, Hope, and Cheer for the Afflicted.* Waxahachie, Texas: Southwestern Press, 1941. P. C. Nelson was a prominent Assemblies of God teacher. This work is a compilation of his messages on divine healing.

Parham, Charles F. and Sarah E. Parham. *Selected Sermons of the Late Charles E. Parham and Sarah E. Parham*; Baxter Springs, Kansas. Apostolic Faith Bible College, 1941, 2000. This book is a Charles F. Parham sermon collection. One of the messages focuses on healing.

Parham, Sarah E. *The Life of Charles F. Parham Founder of the Apostolic Faith Movement.* Baxter Springs, Kansas: Apostolic Faith Bible College, 1930, 2000. This biography of Charles F. Parham, the founder of Pentecostalism, includes accounts of his Bethel Healing Home in Topeka, Kansas.

Parr, J. Nelson. *Divine Healing: An Exhaustive Series of Bible Studies on This Important Subject.* Springfield, Missouri: Gospel Publishing House, 1955. This is a biblical examination of healing from an Assemblies of God teacher.

Parker, Percy G. *Divine Healing: Is It for Today? What Is It? How Can It Be Obtained?* London: United Kingdom: Victory Press, 1931. This is a practical guide to healing from a British Pentecostal.

Perkins, Eunice M. *Joybringer Bosworth: His Life Story.* Dayton, Ohio: John J. Scruby Distributors, 1921. This book is a well-researched biographical account of early twentieth-century healing evangelist F. F. Bosworth.

Perry, Mattie Elmina. *Christ and Answered Prayer.* Cincinnati, Ohio: M. E. Perry Publisher, 1939. Perry was an educator and a healing proponent with ties to the Christian and Missionary Alliance. She was very bold in faith, founding a Bible a school and an orphanage. She was radically healed after being in a wheel chair for 14 years. Later in life, she became affiliated with the Assemblies of God. This book recounts her amazing story.

Price, Charles Sydney. *The Meaning of Faith and The Sick Are Healed: Resolving the Mysteries of Faith.* Shippensburg, Pennsylvania: Mercy Place, 2002. This book combines two of Charles Price's previously published works on faith and healing.

Price, Charles Sydney. *Spiritual and Physical Health.* Pasadena, California: Charles S. Price Publishing Company, 1946. This is the final book Charles Price composed on healing. He died not long after this work came out.

Price, Charles Sydney. *And Signs Followed: The Life Story of Charles S. Price.* Plainfield, New Jersey: Logos International, 1972. This edited edition of Charles Price's autobiography was promoted in the Charismatic market.

Price, Charles Sydney. *The Story of My Life 1887–1947.* Elkhart, Indiana: Strategic Press, a division of Strategic Global Assistance, 1944. This is a later autobiography of Charles S. Price, one of the most celebrated healing evangelists of the early twentieth century.

Price, Charles Sydney. *The Real Faith for Healing.* Plainfield, New Jersey: Logos International, 1972. This book is Charles Price's most recognized work. In it, he explores the foundations of operating in faith.

Price, Charles Sydney. *The Great Physician.* Winnipeg, Canada: De Montfort Press, 1924. In this work, Price carefully examines the biblical foundations of healing.

Price, Charles Sydney. *The Sick Are Healed.* Pasadena, California: Charles S. Price Publishing Company, 1939. Price continues to provide biblical teaching on the reality of divine healing.

Redding, W. A. "Doctors and Medicine." *The Latter Rain Evangel* 11:8 (1919): 20–22. This article, written from an early classical Pentecostal perspective, reflects on the issues of divine healing and the employment of doctors.

Richey, Eloise May. *What God Hath Wrought in the Life of Raymond T. Richey.* Houston, Texas: The Full Gospel Advocate, 1925. Richey was a Pentecostal evangelist and participant in the salvation-healing revival of the 1940s–1950s. Though he practiced healing, he felt the greatest pull toward evangelism. He had been reported as saying, "Divine healing is the dinner bell. Keep ringing that bell and people will come." This biographical account of his life was written by his wife.

Roberts, H. V. *New Zealand's Greatest Revival under Smith Wigglesworth.* Enola, Pennsylvania: Rex and Lois Burgher Ministries, 1951, 2003. This book is a captivating account of Smith Wigglesworth's ministry in New Zealand. Part of this account includes testimonies of healing.

Rouse, L. G. *Marvels and Miracles of Healing.* Knoxville, Tennessee Published by L. G. Rouse, undated. Rouse was a gifted Pentecostal minister who was prominent in the Church of God (Cleveland, Tennessee). This book recounts some of the healings and miracles that he witnessed.

Sisson, Elizabeth. "Healing of a Man Born Blind: Power of The Word in Dallas, Texas." *Latter Rain Evangel* (April 1914): 2–6. Sisson shares eyewitness accounts of the healings that were taking place in F. F. Bosworth's church in Dallas, Texas.

Sisson, Elizabeth. "Our Health, His Wealth." *Confidence* 9:10 (October 1916): 164–166. This is a practical article on healing written by a gifted female evangelist who was originally associated with the Christian and Missionary Alliance. She later joined the Assemblies of God after being impacted by the Pentecostal Outpouring.

Sisson, Elizabeth. "The Lord's Healing: Raised to Health in The Valley of Death." *Latter Rain Evangel* 1:7 (April 1909): 2–4. Elizabeth Sisson, a gifted Pentecostal, recounts how a blind man regained his sight during one of the meetings at a large Pentecostal conference.

Sisson, Elizabeth. "Wonderful Miracles Wrought in Jesus' Name: An Open Letter to The Evangel Leaders by an Eye Witness. Worldwide Campmeeting, Long Hill, Connecticut, June 19, 1913." *Latter Rain Evangel* (July 1913): 2–4. In this article, Sisson shares a number of healing accounts that took place during a prominent Connecticut camp meeting.

Shuler, Robert P. *McPhersonism: A Study of Healing Cults and Modern Day Tongues Movements,* second edition. Los Angeles, California: Bob

Shuler Publisher, 1924. Shuler was a prominent pastor of a Methodist Church in Los Angeles, California, in the 1920s. In this work, he attempts to write an exposé of Aimee Semple McPherson.

Sumrall, Lester. *Adventuring With Christ*. South Bend, Indiana: Lester Sumrall Evangelistic Association, 1988. This was Sumrall's first book, which was originally published in England in 1938. It recounts some of the amazing things that he encountered as he traveled with Howard Carter.

Sumrall, Lester. "Killed By Compassion." *The Pentecostal Evangel* (August 2, 1947): 14. Lester Sumrall wrote a eulogy of Smith Wigglesworth's life that was published in the Assemblies of God official periodical.

Sumrall, Lester. *Lester Sumrall's Short Stories*. South Bend, Indiana: Lester Sumrall Evangelistic Association, 1988. This book, originally published in 1946, recounts some of the notable experiences Sumrall had as he traveled around the world as a missionary evangelist.

Sumrall, Lester. *Pioneers of Faith*. Tulsa, Oklahoma: Harrison House, 1995. This book contains 24 biographical sketches of leaders such as Smith Wigglesworth, F. F. Bosworth, Howard Carter, Lillian Thrasher, Lillian Barbara Yeomans, James Salter and others. Sumrall (1913–1996) knew these people and wanted to reflect on the impact of their lives.

Turner, William Henry. *Christ the Great Physician*. Franklin Springs, Georgia: Advocate Press, 1941. Turner was originally a missionary to China and later an evangelist. Yet, he became most known, in the Pentecostal Holiness Church, for his writing. In this work, Turner reflects on Jesus as a healer.

Turner, William Henry. *Five Thousand Years of Healing*. Franklin Springs, Georgia: Advocate Press, 1947. In this forty-three-page booklet, Turner briefly reflects on the history of healing in the church, recounting a number of different stories.

Turner, William Henry. *I Am the Lord That Healeth Thee*. Franklin Springs, Georgia: Advocate Press, 1947. In this booklet, Turner reflects on Exodus 15:26 and the fact that healing is resident in the nature of God.

Turner, William Henry. *Is it the Will of God to Heal All Who Are Sick?* Franklin Springs, Georgia: Advocate Press, 1947. In this short work, Turner asks whether God wants to heal everyone. This was a question that he often heard as he traveled in Pentecostal circles.

Turner, William Henry. *Shall God's People Take Medicine?* Franklin Springs, Georgia: Advocate Press, 1947. In this abbreviated work, Turner considers whether Christians could take medicine or just trust in God for healing.

Turner, William Henry. *What Must I Do to Be Healed?* Franklin Springs, Georgia: Advocate Press, 1947. This booklet presents some functional strategies for healing.

Turner, William Henry. *Why Are Not All Healed?* Franklin Springs, Georgia: Advocate Press, 1947. In this forty-two-page booklet, Turner attempts to answer why everyone is not healed.

Valdez Jr., A. C. *Divine Health in the Light of God's Word*. Chattanooga, Tennessee: A. C. Valdez Jr. Publisher, 1953. This is a collection of pragmatic articles on divine healing authored by a gifted Pentecostal minister.

Wigglesworth, Smith. *Ever-Increasing Faith: A Legacy of Love and Faith from One of the Great Spiritual Leaders of Modern Times*. Springfield, Missouri: Gospel Publishing House, 1924, 1971. This is a collection of edited sermons that were originally published during Wigglesworth's lifetime.

Wigglesworth, Smith. *Faith That Prevails: The Effectual Fervent Prayer of a Righteous Man Availeth Much*. Springfield, Missouri: Gospel Publishing House, 1938, 1966, 1995. This is a collection of teachings on faith that was compiled, edited, and published during Wigglesworth's lifetime.

Wigglesworth, Smith. *Greater Works: Experiencing God's Power.* New Kensington Pennsylvania: Whitaker House Publishers, 1999. This is a broad collection of Wigglesworth teachings drawn from a variety of Pentecostal periodicals.

Wigglesworth, Smith. *Smith Wigglesworth on Healing*, comp. and ed. Roberts Liardon. New Kensington, Pennsylvania: Whitaker House, 1999. This is an anthology of Wigglesworth teachings that pertain to the subject of healing.

Wigglesworth, Smith. *Smith Wigglesworth Speaks to Students of the Bible: One of a Kind Question and Answer Sessions with Smith Wigglesworth*, ed. Roberts Liardon. Tulsa, Oklahoma: Albury Publishing, 1998. This work provides a glimpse into Wigglesworth's doctrine and methods. In it, he talks to students at Aimee Semple McPherson's Bible school in California.

Wigglesworth, Smith. *The Complete Collection of His Life Teachings*, ed. Roberts Liardon. Tulsa, Oklahoma: Albury Publishing, 2000. This impressive anthology culls a number of Wigglesworth documents from a variety of sources.

Wigglesworth, Smith. "The Gifts of Healing and the Working of Miracles." *Pentecostal Evangel* (August 4, 1923): 2–5. This article, published in the official organ of the Assemblies of God, is a Wigglesworth message on healing and miracles.

Wigglesworth, Smith. "Wonderfully Healed: Smith Wigglesworth's Testimony." *Pentecostal Evangel* (January 13, 1934): 7. This is a heartfelt testimony of someone who was healed under the ministry of Smith Wigglesworth.

Wigglesworth, Smith. "I Am the Lord That Health Thee." *Pentecostal Evangel* (April 3, 1943): 2–3. This article is an empassioned

Wigglesworth sermon edited for the constituents of the Assemblies of God.

Wigglesworth, Smith. "Himself Took Our Infirmities and Bare Our Sickness." *Pentecostal Evangel* (May 12, 1923): 2. This is a short doctrinal teaching culled and edited from a Wigglesworth sermon.

Wigglesworth, Smith. "Wilt Thou Be Made Whole?" *Pentecostal Evangel*. (March 17, 1923): 6. This teaching, drawing upon the healing of the crippled man at the pool of Bethesda (John 5), encourages people to have faith for healing.

Wigglesworth, Smith. "The Grace of Longsuffering, the Counterpart of 'Gifts of Healing,' Salvation of God is All-inclusive." *The Latter Rain Evangel* (April 1923): 6. Wigglesworth's messages, particularly those that dealt with healing, were extremely popular in the Pentecostal publications.

Wigglesworth, Smith. "Wise Words from Wigglesworth." *Redemption Tidings* (November 18, 1938): 6. This is a practical article on healing from the Wigglesworth. It was derived from one of his sermons.

Willitts, Ethel Ruby. *Healing in Jesus' Name: Fifteen Sermons and Addresses on Salvation and Healing*, second edition. Crawfordsville, Indiana: Ethel R. Willitts Publisher, 1931. This is an anthology of Evangelist Ethel Willitts' messages on divine healing.

Willitts, Ethel Ruby. *When Prayer Fails and Scriptural Reasons Why*. Chicago, Illinois: Published by Ethel R. Willitts, 1938. This practical booklet was written by Willitts to explain why healing prayer sometimes does not seem to bring results.

Willitts, Ethel Ruby. *To All Who Seek to Know the Truth On the Subject of Divine Healing*. Detroit, Michigan: Ethel R. Willitts Publisher, 1932. Willitts wrote this short apologetic to defend the efficacy of healing.

Willitts, Ethel Ruby. *Does Faith Healing Cure? Sermon Taken Down Stenographically, While Being Delivered by Ethel R. Willitts, Evangelist,*

Before Thousands Gathered Under the Mammoth Tent in Muskegon, Michigan, Tuesday, August 10, 1935. Chicago, Illinois: Ethel R. Willitts, 1935. This pamphlet on divine healing was taken directly from one of Willitts' sermons.

Willitts, Ethel Ruby. *Is Healing Emotional Psychology or Does It Actually Come from God?* Detroit, Michigan: Ethel Ruby Willitts Publisher, 1939. In this booklet, Willitts attempted to defend divine healing from accusations of being "emotional psychology."

Wyatt, Thomas. *Wings of Healing, 2nd Edition*. Portland, Oregon: Ryder Printing Company, 1944. Though lesser known, Wyatt actively prayed for the sick in 1930s and 40s. He had his greatest influence in the Pacific Northwest. This book is an anthology of Wyatt's teachings on healing.

Yeomans, Lilian B. *Balm of Gilead*. Springfield, Missouri: Gospel Publishing House, 1936. Yeomans was a former physician and drug addict who became saved and supernaturally healed. She wrote a number of books on healing and the deeper work of Jesus.

Yeomans, Lilian B. "Bible Studies in Divine Healing: Dietetics." *Pentecostal Evangel* 497 (1923): 6–7. In this popular article, Lillian Yeomans provides some empirical and scriptural insight on how diet affects one's health.

Yeomans, Lilian B. "Divine Healing." *Pentecostal Evangel* 484–485 (1923): 5. Yeoman's shares her valuable insights on the biblical foundations of divine healing.

Yeomans, Lilian B. "Divine Healing in the Sunburst Psalm." *Pentecostal Evangel* 1222 (October 9, 1937): 3. In this popular article, Yeomans shares insights into healing from the Psalms.

Yeomans, Lilian B. *Divine Healing Diamonds*. Springfield, Missouri: Gospel Publishing House, 1933. This is another one of Lillian Yeoman's assessable works on divine healing.

Yeomans, Lilian B. *Healing from Heaven.* Springfield, Missouri: Gospel Publishing House, 1926. This is the first book on the subject of healing that Dr. Lilian Yeomans published through the Assemblies of God.

Yeomans, Lilian B. *Healing Treasury—Four Classic Books on Healing Complete in One Volume: Healing from Heaven, The Great Physician, Balm of Gilead, Health and Healing.* Tulsa, Oklahoma: Harrison House Publishers, 2004. This volume is an anthology of four of Yeomans' books.

Yeomans, Lilian B. *The Royal Road to Health-Ville: Some Simple Talks About Divine Healing.* Springfield, Missouri: Gospel Publishing House, 1938. This is the last book that Yeomans produced on the subject of divine healing.

Yoakum, Finis E. *Dr. F. E. Yoakum's Healing by The Lord: His Testimony at The Annual Convention of the Southern California Branch of the Christian Alliance, Together with C. A. Jeffers' Healing and Other Cases, Fifth Edition.* Los Angeles: Pisgah Home, 1907. This small work is a published testimony of Finis E. Yoakum's dramatic healing encounter.

Yoakum, Finis E. "Dr. Finis E. Yoakum's Healing by The Lord; Together with Other Cases of the Lord's Healing, 3rd Edition." Los Angeles, California: Published by Finis E. Yoakum, undated. This is a booklet that Yoakum hastily compiled. It contains his testimony along with other stories to encourage faith for healing.

9. LATER HOLINESS

Ahrendt, Edward Henry. *Healing for All.* Anderson, Indiana: Warner Press, 1931. Ahrendt was a prominent minister in the Church of God (Anderson, Indiana) and actively taught on the viability of healing.

Adams, Stephen and K Neill Foster, eds. *Healing Voices: A Celebration of Deliverance Among God's Hurting People.* Camp Hill, Pennsylvania: Christian Publications, 2000. This is a collection of testimonies from past and present leaders of the Christian and Missionary Alliance.

Anderson, Jacob Grant. *Divine Healing.* Anderson, Indiana: Gospel Trumpet Company, 1926. In this fascinating book, Anderson shares a Scriptural basis for healing and also shares some healing testimonies.

Andrus, M. L. *Twenty Years' Experience in Divine Healing.* M.L. Andrus Publisher, 1916. In this early Twentieth Century booklet, a holiness evangelist shares some of his personal accounts of ministering healing.

Bailey, Keith M. *Divine Healing: The Children's Bread - God's Provision for Human Health and Healing.* Camp Hill, Pennsylvania, 1977. This is an exceptional overview of the ministry of healing from a Christian and Missionary Alliance scholar. Bailey is an excellent researcher.

Bailey, Keith M. "A New Significance for the Doctrine of Healing in the Atonement." *His Dominion* 13 (summer 1987): 2-12. Bailey argues that the church must continue to insist that divine healing involves "the direct intervention of the living Christ on the basis of his [atoning] death and resurrection."

Baker, Elizabeth V. *Chronicles of a Faith Life.* New York and London: Garland Publishing, 1916, 1984. This book is an autobiographical account of Elizabeth Baker, an overseer of one of the influential healing homes in the early twentieth century. It includes many healing stories.

Bedford, William Boyd. "'A Larger Christian Life': A. B. Simpson and the Early Years of The Christian and Missionary Alliance," Ph.D. diss., University of Virginia, 1992. This dissertation explores the ministry of healing and other expressions in the Christian and Missionary Alliance.

Bevington, G. C. *Remarkable Incidents and Modern Miracles Through Prayer and Faith.* Cincinnati, Ohio: God's Bible School and Revivalist, undated. This is the story of G. C. Bevington's amazing life. He recounts remarkable incidents and miracles.

Blaney, John C. "Dowie-ism vs. the Bible," *Gospel Trumpet* 21:32 (August 15, 1901): 1-3. This essay, from a Church of God (Anderson, Indiana) leader, is a critique of John Alexander Dowie.

Bostrom, John H. *The Causes of Sickness and How to Get Well.* San Gabriel, California: Bostrum Publications, 1940. In this practical book, Bostrom focuses on the roots of various diseases and how to counteract them in a scriptural way.

Byers, A. L., ed. *200 Genuine Instances of Divine Healing: The Doctrine Explained.* Anderson, Indiana: Gospel Trumpet, 1911. Jacob Byers, a holiness minister closely associated with the Church of God (Anderson Indiana), was an adamant proponent of healing. This is a book of healing testimonies that he compiled.

Byers, Jacob Whistler. *The Grace of Healing; Or Christ Our Physician.* Moundsville, West Virginia: Gospel Trumpet Company, 1899. Byers, a prominent holiness minister in the Church of God (Anderson, Indiana), actively espoused healing. This book shares some of his biblical insights.

Byers, Jacob Whistler "Questions on Divine Healing Answered," *Gospel Trumpet* 20:12. (March 20, 1902): 8. In this article, Byers provides answers to questions about healing. This was published in the official publication of the denomination.

Byers, Jacob Whistler. *Questions and Answers On the Subject of Divine Healing.* Anderson, Indiana: Gospel Trumpet Company, undated. This practical book is a compilation of articles from the *Gospel Trumpet*. In it, Byers provides answers to questions about healing directed to him from the denomination's constituents.

Byers, Jacob Whistler. "We Must Preach Divine Healing." *Gospel Trumpet* 15:51 (December 26, 1895): 4. In this article, Byers attempts to persuade ministers in the Church of God (Anderson, Indiana) to preach messages on the subject of divine healing.

Byrum, Enoch Edwin. "Believe for Healing" *Gospel Trumpet* 15:49 (December 12, 1895): 4. Byrum, the editor of the Gospel Trumpet, shares a practical teaching, encouraging Church of God adherents to believe for healing.

Byrum, Enoch Edwin. "Christ The Healer." *Gospel Trumpet* 15:47 (November 28, 1895): 4. This is a brief healing article from Byrum. In it, his practical insights on Jesus are observed.

Byrum, Enoch Edwin. *Divine Healing of Soul and Body: Also How God Heals the Sick, And The Conditions by Which They Are Restored; Giving Wonderful Testimony of His Miraculous Power in These Last Days.* Moundsville, West Virginia: Gospel Trumpet Company, 1892. This book is a general work on healing from a popular, widely traveled holiness preacher.

Byrum, Enoch Edwin. "Divine Healing: The Commission." *Gospel Trumpet* 15:44. (November 7, 1895): 4. In this short article, Byrum discusses how Jesus commissioned His disciples to minister healing. He wants his readers to consider what those implications might be for all believers.

Byrum, Enoch Edwin. "Divine Healing: The Will of God to Heal." *Gospel Trumpet* 15:45 (November 14, 1895): 4. Byrum was a prolific writer and composed a number of different articles on divine healing in the pages of the *Gospel Trumpet*. This particular article discusses God's will to bring healing.

Byrum, Enoch Edwin. "Means Used in Divine Healing." *Gospel Trumpet* 16:1. (January 2, 1896): 4. In this article, Byrum discusses some of the practical strategies for ministering and executing healing.

Byrum, Enoch Edwin. *Miracles and Healing: Scriptural Incidents and Evidences of the Miraculous Manifestation of the Power of God, And The Healing of a Sicknesses and a Disease*. Anderson, Indiana: Gospel Trumpet Company, 1919. In this work on healing, Byrum draws on Scripture and personal testimonies.

Byrum, Enoch Edwin. "Questions Answered: Sending Anointed Handkerchiefs." *Gospel Trumpet* 20:49 (December 13, 1900): 4. In this article, Byrum discusses the practice of sending handkerchiefs that have been prayed over and anointed.

Byrum, Enoch Edwin. "Questions Answered," *Gospel Trumpet* 26:8 (Feb. 22, 1906): 4. Byrum provides answers to questions about healing in the official Church of God publication.

Byrum, Enoch Edwin. *Startling Incidents and Experiences in The Christian Life; Narratives of Wonderful Dealings of the Lord with Those Who Put Their Trust in Him and of Their Deliverance in Time of Adversity, Trial, And Temptation*. Anderson, Indiana: Gospel Trumpet Company, 1915. In this work, Byrum recounts fascinating experiences and healing stories.

Byrum, Enoch Edwin. *The Great Physician and His Power to Heal*. Anderson, Indiana: Gospel Trumpet Company, 1899. In this book, Byrum explores Jesus' healing ministry and what it means for believers today.

Byrum, Enoch Edwin. *The Doctrine of Healing*. Anderson, Indiana: Gospel Trumpet Publishing, undated. In this substantive work, Byrum expands on the doctrine of divine healing from the Scriptures.

Byrum, Enoch Edwin. *The Power of Healing.* Anderson, Indiana: Gospel Trumpet Publishing, undated. In this work, Byrum provides an examination of the transforming influences of healing in the church.

Byrum, Enoch Edwin. *Why Some Are Not Healed: 35 Reasons or Excuses with Answers Given.* Anderson, Indiana and Kansas City, Missouri: Gospel Trumpet Publishing, undated. This booklet attempts to answer the question of why some are not healed.

Case, M.B. *Health and Healing: The Key to Holiness, Happiness, Health and Long Life.* Greeley, Colorado: Published by M. B. Case, 1909. This is a practical healing book compiled by a prominent holiness minister. The appendix of the book includes articles on divine healing from: E. T. Slaybaugh, S. S. Quinn, Dora Doudley, William D. Gentry, W. B. Godbey, R. Kelso Carter, and John Wesley.

Chesnut, Lawrence J. *Divine Physical Healing for You.* Oklahoma City: Lawrence J. Chesnut Publisher, 1945, 1975. This is an overview of the doctrine of divine healing. The author talks about: The origin and cause of sickness and disease. Divine healing did not cease with the Apostles. How to be healed. Works that accompany faith for healing. Hindrances to healing.

Clear, Valorous B. *Where Saints Have Trod: A Social History of the Church of God Reformation Movement.* Chesterfield, Indiana: Midwest Publications, 1977. This account, based on Clear's 1953 dissertation, "The Church of God: A Study in Social Adaption," explores the early history and background of the Church of God (Anderson, Indiana). It includes valuable insights into early healing practices.

Cole, Mary. *Trials and Triumphs of Faith.* Anderson, Indiana: Gospel Trumpet Company, 1914. This is the account of the life of Mary Cole, an early evangelist and practitioner of divine healing in the Church of God (Anderson, Indiana).

Comer, A. Vance. *The Manifestation of God to John R. Harrell.* Louisville, Kentucky: Herald Press, 1959. This little booklet is the testimony of

John R. Harrell, a prominent Holiness businessman who was healed of cancer.

Davis, Henry Turner. *Modern Miracles*. Cincinnati, Ohio: M. W. Knapp Publisher, 1901. This book was written to defend the idea of divine healing in the Bible and to encourage faith. Davis believed that there was growing skepticism in the early Twentieth Century and he sought to counteract that.

Dayton, Donald W. *Discovering an Evangelical Heritage*. Peabody, Massachusetts: Hendrickson Publishing, 1976, 1992. Dayton's work explores components of nineteenth century Evangelical origins. This book includes references to divine healing.

Dayton, Donald W. "The Rise of the Evangelical Healing Movement in Nineteenth Century America." *Pneuma 4* (Spring 1982): 1–18. This article examines the significance of the faith-cure movement. Dayton's essay became a catalyst for further study.

Dayton, Donald W. *The Theological Roots of Pentecostalism*. Peabody, Massachusetts: Hendrickson Publishing, 1987. This is an important work that explores the foundations of Pentecostalism. Within this text is a discussion about the influence of the faith-cure on Pentecostalism

Dieter, Melvin E. *The Holiness Revival of the Nineteenth Century, Second Edition*. Lanham, Maryland: Scarecrow Press, 1996. This is an important work includes references to the faith cure movement and its associations with the Holiness Movement.

Dupont, Anthony. "Divine Healing in the Experience, Thought, and Ministry of Albert Benjamin Simpson," M.A., thesis, Asbury Theological Seminary, 1993. This is an analysis of A.B. Simpson, the founder of the Christian and Missionary Alliance.

Evearitt, Daniel J. *Body and Soul: Evangelism and The Social Concern of A.B. Simpson*. Camp Hill, Pennsylvania: Christian Publications, 1994. This book considers the worldview and ministry practices of A.B. Simpson.

Fant, David J., ed. *Modern Miracles of Healing: Personal Testimonies of Well-Known Christian Men and Women to The Power of God to Heal Their Bodies.* Harrisburg, Pennsylvania: Christian Publications, 1943. This is a collection of healing testimonies from prominent Evangelicals and Christian and Missionary Alliance figures.

Forrest, Aubrey Leland. "A Study in the Development of the Basic Doctrines and Institutional Patterns in the Church of God (Anderson, Indiana)," Ph.D. diss., University of Southern California, 1948. Forrest explores the early theology, history, and ministry practice of the Church of God (Anderson, Indiana). He briefly explores the reality of healing.

Forrest, J.E. "Healings of Christ and His Followers," *Gospel Trumpet* 35:9 (July 1, 1915). Forrest, a Church of God (Anderson, Indiana) evangelist briefly reflects on stories of healing from the Gospels.

Foster, K. Neill Foster. *Sorting Out The Supernatural: If It Happens In Church, Is It Always God?* Camp Hill, Pennsylvania: Christian Publications, 2001. This work by a Christian and Missionary Alliance evangelist explores healing and other phenomena in the contemporary church context.

Godbey, William Baxter. *Divine Healing.* Greensboro, North Carolina: Apostolic Messenger Office, 1909. Godbey was an eccentric holiness evangelist and adamant opponent of Pentecostalism. However, he had a favorable view of the ministry of healing. This is evidenced in this small book that he published in 1909.

Goshulak, Ted D. "A Bibliography on Healing." *His Dominion* 14 (Summer 1987): 35-43. This is a bibliographical essay, focusing on works of healing within the Christian and Missionary Alliance tradition.

Gracey, Samuel L. and Daniel Steele. *Healing by Faith: Two Essays*. Boston: Willard Tract Repository, 1882. This booklet brings together healing messages from two prominent Holiness leaders, Samuel L. Gracey and Daniel Steele. Dr. Charles Cullis, the noted healing minister from Boston, Massachusetts, published this work.

Green, Cleve. "Guaranteed Healing On a Conditional Warranty." *The Gospel Trumpeter* 1:1 (March 7, 1971): 10-11. This is an article from a Church of God (Anderson, Indiana) leader who believes that healing is possible but conditional.

Hahn, Fred L. *Hints On Healing*. Grand Junction, Michigan: *Gospel Trumpet Company*, 1894. Hahn, a Church of God (Anderson, Indiana) minister, shares some of his insights on the ministry of healing.

Hawkins, Henry C. "Earthly Physicians and Divine Physician Contrasted," *Gospel Trumpet* 27:32 (August 15, 1907): 16. This practical article contrasts early twentieth biomedicine with the approaches of faith healing.

Helm, Kathryn E. *The Lure of Divine Love: Or Experiences and Their Lessons, Selected from A Half Century of Practical Christian Living, Including Many Miracles of Divine Healing*. Cincinnati, Ohio: God's Bible School and Missionary Training Home, 1929. This is a collection of testimonies and stories. There are several stories of healing and physical breakthrough.

Henley, Micajah. *Divine Healing: A Biblical Exegesis of the Subject, Showing the Relations It Has Sustained to God's People in the Past Ages, and Its Proper Place Amongst Them Today*. Cincinnati: Mrs. M. W. Knapp, 1902. This work, from a gifted holiness preacher, explores the meaning of healing and what it meant for early twentieth century believers.

Jones Charles E. "Perfectionist Persuasion: The Holiness Movement and American Methodism, 1867 – 1936," Ph.D. diss., University of Wisconsin, 1974. This is the seminal work on the American

Holiness Movement. Among other things, Jones explores the Holiness movement's intersection with the faith cure tradition.

King, Paul L. *God's Healing Arsenal: A 40-Day Divine Battle Plan For Overcoming Disease and Distress.* Alachua, Florida: Bridge-Logos Publishing, 2011. King, a trained academic from Oral Roberts University shares practical strategies for the ministry of healing.

King, Paul L. *Only Believe: Examining the Origin and Development of Classic and Contemporary Word of Faith Theologies.* Tulsa, Oklahoma: Spirit and Word Press, 2008. In this well-researched work, King shows the continuities between holiness and deeper life modalities and the Word of Faith Movement.

King, Paul L. "Pentecostal Roots in the Early CMA." *Assemblies of God Heritage* 24:3 (Fall 2004) 12–17. This well-researched article explores some of the early developments of the Christian and Missionary Alliance, touching on their understanding of healing.

Kostlevy, William, and Gari-Anne Patzwold, eds. *Historical Dictionary of the Holiness Movement.* Lanham, Maryland: Scarecrow Press, 2001. This reference work on the Holiness Movement includes entries on figures associated with the Faith Cure Movement.

Leever, Richard. "Healing: Mass Meeting or Local Church Elders?" *His Dominion* 14 (Summer 1987): 27-34. This is an article exploring some of the practical ways that healing ministry could operate in a contemporary Christian and Missionary Alliance Church.

Linn, C.H. Jack. *Does God Heal The Body Today?* Oregon, Wisconsin: Hallelujah Print Shop, 1928. Linn, a holiness author, explores whether healing is available in the atonement. He comes to a negative conclusion.

Mackenzie, Kenneth. "My Memories of Dr. Simpson." The Alliance Weekly 72:23 (July 31, 1937): 485-487. This is a heartfelt article reflecting on the life, ministry, and practice of A. B. Simpson, a significant healing proponent in the late 19th and early 20th Centuries.

Mackenzie, Kenneth. *Our Physical Heritage in Christ*. New York: Fleming H. Revell, 1923. This is an apologetic for "healing in the Atonement" by an Episcopalian associate of A. B. Simpson. In addition to sharing his own healing testimony, Mackenzie argues that Simpson differed from Dowie, believing that God can use sickness to chasten people.

Mahan, Asa. "Faith-Healing." *Earnest Christian* 47 (September 1884): 80. Mahan, an influential holiness figure and a gifted instructor from Oberlin College, wrote an article on "Faith Healing" in the "Earnest Christian" for the September 1884 issue. Mahan used Matthew 8:16-17 to contend that healing was still a valid gift. He says "If the fact that Jesus bore our sins in his own body on the tree is a valid reason why we should trust Him now to pardon our sins, the fact that He 'bares our sicknesses' is an equally valid reason why we should now trust Him to heal our diseases. We have the same revealed basis for the trust in the one case as in the other." Mahan merged his understanding that the gifts were for today with revelation that healing was explicitly an expected gift.

Mauro, Philip. *Sickness Among Saints: To Whom Shall We Go?* Boston: Hamilton Brothers, 1909. In this small book, Mauro seeks to clarify the difference between the meaning of sickness in the wicked and sickness in the saints.

Miller, Basil. *The Miracle of Divine Healing*. Kansas City, Missouri: Beacon Hill, 1951. Desiring to avoid polemics, Miller simply pursues a message of sincere faith and prayer for healing.

Miller, Emma. "God's Wonderful Dealings with Sister Emma Miller." Gospel Trumpet 6:20 (December 15, 1884): 2. In June of 1883, Emma Miller was healed of blindness at the Church of God (Anderson, Indiana) camp meeting in Bangor, Michigan. Her breakthrough was a catalyst for additional healings throughout the movement.

Neinkirchen, Charles W. *A. B. Simpson and Pentecostal Movement: A Study in Continuity, Crisis, and Change.* Peabody, Massachusetts: Hendrickson Publishers 1979. This is a valuable work that explores the relationship between A.B. Simpson and the emerging Pentecostal Movement.

Nienkirchen, Charles W. "Albert Benjamin Simpson." *Dictionary of Pentecostal Charismatic Movements.* Grand Rapids, Michigan: Zondervan, 1988. 786-787. Nienkirchen provides a brief character sketch of the founder of the Christian and Missionary Alliance.

Niklaus, Robert L. Niklaus, John S. Sawin, and Samuel J. Stoesz. *All for Jesus: God at work in the Christian and Missionary Alliance Over One Hundred Years.* Harrisburg, Pennsylvania: Christian Publications, 1996. This book explores the history of the Christian and Missionary Alliance. It brings insights into the organization's early emphasis on healing.

Norton, Mary c. and Irene E. Lewis. *Life Sketch of Mary C. Norton and Remarkable Healings On the Mission Fields.* Los Angeles, Pilgrim's Mission, 1954. In this work, missionaries involved with the Christian and Missionary Alliance share powerful accounts of healing.

Olson, Heddie T. *My Personal Experience of Divine Healing.* New York: Hollis, 1939. This short book, originally published by the Nazarene Publishing House in 1936, is an interesting healing apologetic from a holiness preacher.

Parker, J. Fred "Heal, Healing," in *The Beacon Dictionary of Theology*, ed. Richard S. Taylor, 248-249. Kansas City, Missouri: Beacon Hill Press of Kansas City, 1983. This is an article written by a Holiness scholar, framing up the meaning and context of healing.

Pett, David M. "Divine Healing: The Development of Simpson's Thought." *His Dominion* 16 (March 1990): 23-33. This is a well-researched analysis of A.B. Simpson's theology and understanding of healing.

Pierson, Arthur Tappan "Divine Healing: Does The Bible Encourage Us to Expect the Healing of the Body in Answer to Prayer?" *National Baptist* 32 (July 15, 1886): 435-436. A. T. Pierson, a prominent Holiness minister, reflects on the biblical foundations of healing. He continued his teaching in the following issue (July 22, 1886): 451-452.

Purkiser, Westlake Taylor. *Spiritual Gifts: Healing and Tongues; An Analysis of the Charismatic Revival*. Kansas City, Missouri: Nazarene Publishing House, 1964. This is an account of healing and spiritual gifts composed by a Nazarene author.

Roark, Warren C., complier. *Divine Healing*. Gospel Trumpet Company. Anderson, Indiana: The Warner Press, 1945. This book is a compilation of divine healing articles written by various figures in the Church of God (Anderson Indiana).

Robinson, Bud. *Does The Bible Teach Divine Healing?* Kansas City, Missouri: Nazarene Publishing House, 1934. This book, from a prominent figure in the Nazarene denomination, explores what scripture has to say about the ministry of healing

Ronzheimer, Philip P. *"Trust Me! Trust Me!" Healing and the Sovereignty of God*. Camp Hill, Pennsylvania: Christian Publications, 1992. This booklet, by a Christian and Missionary Alliance author, wrestles with the tension of pursuing healing and resting in God's sovereign initiatives.

Schell, William G. "Dr. Dowie Against the Bible," *Gospel Trumpet* 18:15 (April 14, 1898): 1-2. This article from the official organ of the Church of God (Anderson, Indiana) renounces the controversial views of John Alexander Dowie.

Scruby, John J. *Gems of Truth On Divine Healing.* Dayton, Ohio: The Standard Bearer, 1904. This is a compilation of articles and practical reflections on healing from a Holiness publisher. Scruby went on to produce two other similar volumes.

Sears, Lawrence Wayne. *The Reality of Divine Healing.* Kansas City, Missouri: Beacon Hill Press, 1955. This book is an apologetic for the ministry of healing from a sympathetic Nazarene author.

Smith, David John. *How Can I Ask God for Physical Healing?* Grand Rapids, Michigan: Chosen Books, 2005. This practical healing work was penned by a gifted Christian and Missionary Alliance pastor. David J. Smith, was the Senior Pastor, Rose Hill Alliance Church in Roseville, Minnesota and an adjunct professor at Crown College in St. Bonifacius, Minnesota.

Smith, John W.V. *Heralds of a Brighter Day: Biographical Sketches of Early Leaders in the Church of God Reformation Movement.* Anderson, Indiana: Warner Press, 1979. This work recounts the stories of many of the early Church of God leaders. Most of them were active healing participants.

Smith, Oswald J. *The Great Physician.* New York: Christian and Missionary Alliance Publishing Company, 1927. This is an overview of biblical foundations of healing from a prominent Christian and Missionary Alliance pastor.

Snider, William E. "Introduction of Faith Healing into American Evangelicalism: A Study of the Life and Influence of Dr. Charles Cullis," M.A., thesis, Cincinnati Christian University, 2008. This dissertation explores the contribution that Charles Cullis, had upon American Evangelism in the late 19th Century. Snider writes from a Wesleyan-Holiness background.

Strege, Merle. *I Saw the Church: The Life of the Church of God Told Theologically.* Anderson: Warner Press, 2002. In this volume, Strege explores the history and theology of the Church of God (Anderson,

Indiana). He provides a fascinating analysis of the early acceptance of healing and its later waning.

Stephens, Michael S. "In Prison For Christ's Sake: Divine Healing Trials And the Church of God (Anderson)." *Wesleyan Theological Journal* 39:1 (Spring 2004): 194-208. This article examines early twentieth century court cases where Holiness parents refused medical help and relied on divine healing alone.

Stephens, Michael S. *Who Healeth All Thy Diseases: Health, Healing, And Holiness in The Church of God Reformation Movement*. Lanham, Maryland: Scarecrow Press, 2008. Stephens' research into healing in the Holiness traditions is extraordinary. This is unquestionably the seminal work on healing in the Church of God (Anderson, Indiana) tradition.

Sterner, R. Eugene. *Healing And Wholeness*. Anderson, Indiana: Warner Press, 1978. In this bold work, Sterner, advocates for a return to an emphasis on healing in the Church of God (Anderson, Indiana).

Stewart, Alexander Hamilton. *Bodily Healing Since Pentecost and "All Things" (Romans 8:28)*. New York: Loizeaus Brothers, undated. This work, published around 1900, provides a conservative overview of healing practices.

Straton, John Roach. *Divine Healing in Scripture and Life*. New York: Christian Alliance Publishing Company, 1927. This is an outstanding general work on healing from a prominent leader in the Christian and Missionary Alliance Movement.

Susag, S. O. *Personal Experiences of S.O. Susag*. Guntrie, Oklahoma: Standard Printing Company, 1948. Susag was a prominent healing evangelist in the Church of God (Anderson, Indiana). He apparently wrote this book as the thoughts came to his mind. There is no order to the healing incidents.

Teasley, D.O. "Our Physician—Chapter 1," *Gospel Trumpet* 21:20 (May 16, 1901): 3. In this article, a prominent holiness leader examines the reality of Jesus as the healer of humanity.

Thompson, A.E. *A.B. Simpson: His Life and Work.* Harrisburg, Pennsylvania: Christian Publications, 1960. Upon publication, Thompson's book became the seminal biography of A. B. Simpson.

Tozer, A.W. *Wingspread, Albert B. Simpson: A Study in Spiritual Attitude.* Harrisburg, Pennsylvania: Christian Publications, 1943. This is a truncated biographical account of Simpson. Unfortunately, Tozer leaves out many details about Simpson's ministry of healing.

Travis, Drake. *Christ Our Healer Today: The Ministry of Healing in the Christian and Missionary Alliance.* Camp Hill, Pennsylvania: Christian Publications, 1984. This is a well-conceived reflection on healing from a Christian and Missionary Alliance leader.

Travis, Drake. *Healing Power: Voice Activated: Discover Today How Your Words Bless, Heal, and Restore.* Lake Mary, Florida: Creation House, 2009. This well-formed book examines thirteen Hebrew words for healing as well as the multi-faceted nature of Jesus' healing miracles. It also includes over 100 pages of modern-day healing testimonies.

Warner, D. S. "Anointing for Healing," *Gospel Trumpet* 10:6 (June 1, 1888): 1. In this practical article, Warner, the progenitor of the Church of God (Anderson, Indiana), talks about anointing the sick. Warner writes that the gifts of the Spirit "were meant to stay in the church ... They return when people come out of sects [established denominations]."

Warner, D. S. "Faith Healing an Important Factor in Soul Saving," *Gospel Trumpet* 6:3 (November 1, 1883): 2-3. In this practical article, Warner shares how healing can enable the growth of the church.

Warner, D. S. "Healing in Christ," Gospel Trumpet 6:1 (October 1, 1883): 2. In this short article, Warner explores how healing is available to believers today through the work of Jesus.

Warner, D. S. "The Power of God Sent By Mail." *Gospel Trumpet* 8:18 (December 1, 1886): 1. Warner shares his thoughts about sending prayerfully anointed handkerchiefs. The practice was based on Acts 19:11-12. The Apostle Paul sent handkerchiefs and aprons to the sick.

Wilcox, Vernon L. *God's Healing Touch: A Study of the Doctrine of Divine Healing*. Kansas City, Missouri: Beacon Hill Press of Kansas City, 1968. This book sets out to answer a number of questions that people have about healing. This is a favorable work from a Holiness publishing house.

Wilson, Ernest Gerald. The Christian and Missionary Alliance: Developments and Modifications of its Original Objectives, Ph.D. diss., New York University, 1984. This is a significant analysis of the history and trajectory of the Christian and Missionary Alliance. Wilson draws heavily on periodicals and reports in his findings.

Yerty, Oscar L. *Christ The Master of All Diseases*. Anderson, Indiana: Gospel Trumpet Company, undated. This book is a collection of healing messages from a prominent Holiness evangelist.

10. SALVATION-HEALING

Allen, A. A. *Born to Lose, Bound to Win.* New York: Doubleday Publishing, 1970. This is an autobiography of A. A. Allen that was published shortly after he died in 1970. It has a unique literary style and rhetorical embellishments. It provides an interesting window into this controversial figure.

Allen, A. A. *Can God?* Miracle Valley, Arizona: A. A. Allen Revivals Incorporated, undated. In this book, Allen argues for God's healing and provisional activities in the lives of people. It was published around 1965.

Allen, A. A. *Does God Heal Through Medicine?* Miracle Valley, Arizona: A. A. Allen Revivals Incorporated, undated. In this booklet, Allen explores whether God uses medicine to heal people.

Allen, A. A. *God's Guarantee to Heal You.* Tyler, Texas: Schambach Revivals Incorporated, 1954. This was one of A. A. Allen's most popular healing works. It provides an interesting practical glimpse into the biblical foundations of this ministry.

Allen, A. A. *God Will Heal You.* Miracle Valley, California: A. A. Allen Revivals Incorporated, 1953. This inspirational book uses scripture and testimony to assure people about the possibility of healing.

Allen, A. A. *Is Your Sickness a Thorn in The Flesh?* Miracle Valley, Arizona: A. A. Allen Revivals Incorporated, undated. In this pamphlet, Allen addresses the issue of the Apostle Paul's "thorn in the flesh" from 2 Corinthians 12:7. Many interpret it as a sickness. Allen interprets it differently. He wrote this to counteract the assumption that God made Paul sick.

Allen, A. A. *My Cross: The Life Story of A.A. Allen as Told by Himself.* Miracle Valley, Arizona: A.A. Allen Revivals Incorporated, 1958. This book is an interesting early autobiography of one of the leading figures of the salvation healing revival (1946-1958).

Allen, A. A. *Power With God Through Fasting And Prayer*. Miracle Valley, Arizona: A. A. Allen Revivals Incorporated, 1953. In this book, Allen wanted to talk about how one could begin to operate in supernatural power to pray for the sick. In this, he argues that fasting and prayer are what takes one into a place of power.

Allen, A. A. *The Price of God's Miracle Working Power*. Miracle Valley, Arizona: A. A. Allen Revivals Incorporated, 1950. In this practical, sermon-based book Allen shares his insights into experiencing increased power for healing. Operating in supernatural strength will always cost you in one way or another.

Allen, A. A. *Who Can Heal the Sick?* Miracle Valley, Arizona: Allen Revivals Incorporated, 1953. In this practical book, Allen delves into the question of who can legitimately pray for the sick.

Allen, A. A. *Why Did Job Have Boils*. Miracle Valley, Arizona: A. A. Allen Revivals Incorporated, date unstated. A. A. Allen wrote an insightful pamphlet that examined the reality of Job's sickness and its implications for believers. Allen had a knack for speaking plainly. This booklet certainly reflects his typical, down-home rhetoric.

Allen, Lexie. *God's Man of Faith and Power: The Life Story of A. A. Allen written by his wife, Lexie E. Allen*. Hereford, Arizona: A. A. Allen Revivals, 1954. This book is a fascinating biographical account of healing evangelist, A. A. Allen, written by his wife.

Allen, Paul Asa. *In the Shadow of Greatness: Growing Up "Allen."* Tucson, Arizona: Paul Allen Publisher, 2008. This book is a biographical account of A. A. Allen written by his son. It provides a unique window into the Salvation-Healing revival of the 1940s-1950s.

Baker, Ronald L. "Miracle Magazine in the Sixties: Mass Media Narratives of Healings and Blessings." *Journal of American Folklore* 118: 468 (Spring 2005): 204-218. This journal article explores rhetoric in A.A. Allen's *Miracle Magazine*. Baker looks at it as a unique dimension of American folklore. While this article is critical, it does provide interesting analysis from an academic point of view.

Bozarth, Randy. *The Voice of Healing: A Voice Still Speaks.* Duncanville, Texas: World Missions Advance, 2004. This book is a popular account of Gordon Lindsey and the Voice of Healing ministry that was very prominent in the late 1940s and early 1950s.

Branham, William Marion. "Do You Fear Cancer?" Jefferson, Indiana: William Braham Evangelistic Association, undated. In this practical booklet, Branham seeks to counteract disease and the fear that immobilizes people.

Branham, William Marion. *Twentieth Century Prophet.* Jeffersonville, Indiana: Voice of God Recordings, 1985. This is the autobiography of William Branham, the most prominent healing evangelist in the salvation-healing revival.

Cain, Paul W. *The Life, Call, And Ministry of Paul Cain.* Paul Cain Publisher, 1950. The book explores Paul Cain's early life and his calling as a minister. In 1947, at the age of 18, Cain began to hold healing campaigns. He was one of the youngest of the Voice of Healing evangelists. He was renowned as a minister because of his usage of the word of knowledge to supplement his healing ministry.

Caldwell, William. *Meet the Healer.* Tulsa: Miracle Moments Evangelistic Association, 1965. This practical booklet provides an overview of divine healing from a lesser known evangelist.

Cater, Richard. "That Old-Time Religion Comes Back." *Coronet* (February 1958): 125-130. This is a critical analysis of the evangelists and participants in the Salvation-Healing Revivals.

Carter, Richard. "Beware The Commercialized Faith Healers." *Readers Digest* (June 1971): 179-180. This is the second dismissive article that Carter wrote about Pentecostal and Charismatic healing evangelists.

Coe, Jack. *A Sure Cure: And Other Sermons on Divine Healing*. Dallas, Texas: Herald of Divine Healing, 1953. This booklet is a collection of healing sermons that were drawn from Jack Coe's tent meetings in the early 1950s.

Coe, Jack. *Curing the Incurable*. Dallas, Texas: Herald of Healing, undated. This is one of Coe's most impactful healing sermons. After being widely shared in his crusades, it was later developed into a book.

Coe, Jack. *Divine Healing On Trial*. Dallas, Texas: Herald of Healing, undated. This booklet, from late 1957, deals with the controversial arrest of Jack Coe in Florida over "practicing medicine without a license." Coe, ever the campaigner, sought to use this experience to elicit attention. Sadly, he passed away shortly after this.

Coe, Jack with Gordon Lindsey. *The Story of Jack Coe, from Pup Tent to the World's Largest Gospel Tent*. Shreveport, Louisiana: Jack Coe Ministries, 1951. This work is an autobiography of Coe developed with the assistance of Gordon Lindsay.

Coe, Jack. *Tried...But Freed! The True Story of the Arrest and the Case Against Jack Coe*. Dallas, Texas: Herald of Healing, undated. This book, published around 1957, recounts the controversial arrest of Jack Coe in Miami, Florida for "practicing medicine without a license."

Coe, Juanita. *The Jack Coe I Know*. Dallas, Texas: Herald of Healing Publishing, 1956. This is a biographical account of Jack Coe written by Juanita Coe, his devoted wife.

Coyne, R. R. *When God Smiled On Ronald Coyne*. Sapulpa, Oklahoma, Ronald Coyne, 1957. This is an account of a boy who experienced a stupendous healing in the 1950s. Although losing his eye in a farming accident, after prayer, he was able to see things through his empty eye socket.

Culpepper, Richard Weston. *100,000 Miles of Miracles*. Dallas, Texas: R.W. Culpepper, undated. R.W. Culpepper briefly functioned as a

Voice of Healing evangelist. In 1958, he teamed up with David Nunn, W.V. Grant, and Morris Cerullo to form the World Convention of Deliverance Evangelists. From there, he became more involved with world missions. This book recounts some of the more remarkable stories from his ministry.

Culpepper, Richard Weston. *How You Too Can Receive Your Healing.* Bellflower, California: R. W. Culpepper, 1955. In this booklet, Culpepper provides practical strategies that the sick could use to receive their healing.

Daoud, Mounir Aziz. *Bringing Back the King: God's Plan for World Evangelization.* Dallas, Texas: Voices of Miracles and Missions, 1955. This is an account of lesser known evangelists. It includes incredible reports about missionary crusades in India, Pakistan, and France in 1953 and 1954.

Daoud, Mouniz Aziz and Jane Daoud. *Difference Between Miracles and Healings: Time Required for Each, Why Many Are Not Healed, When Should We Die?* Dallas, Texas: The Voice of Miracles and Missions, 1955. In this pamphlet, Daoud and his wife discuss the difference between praying for healing and praying for a miracle.

Daoud, Mouniz Aziz and Jane Daoud. *Divine Healing for All: The Blind See, Paralytics Walk and All Kinds of Sickness Can Be Healed by Faith in Jesus Christ.* Dallas, Texas: The Voice of Miracles and Missions, 1955. This book contains a number of Daoud's messages on healing.

Daoud, Mouniz Aziz and Jane Daoud. *Faith: How to Receive It ... How to Exercise It.* Dallas, Texas: The Voice of Miracles and Missions, 1955. In this booklet, Daoud and wife discuss how to operate in faith.

Daoud, Mouniz Aziz and Jane Daoud. *Sickness: Is It From God or The Devil?* Dallas, Texas, Voice of Miracles and Missions Inc., 1955. In this work, Daoud and wife explore whether sickness comes from God or the devil.

Daoud, Mouniz Aziz and Jane Daoud. *Undeniable Proofs: God's Will Is to Heal All Today*. Dallas, Texas: The Voice of Miracles and Missions, 1955. Daoud, and his wife, evaluate the biblical meaning of Paul's thorn in the flesh.

Darms, Anton. *Divine Healing in the Scriptures*. Zion, Illinois: Anton Darms, 1950. Darms, who had been associated with Dowie's work in Zion, wrote a well-received overview of healing in the Bible. This work was later promoted in the *Voice of Healing* magazine.

Editor. "A Failure of Faith in a Faith Healer." *Life* (March 5, 1956): 63-64. This article from *Life Magazine* explored the controversy surrounding Jack Coe's failed healing attempt in Miami, Florida.

Editor. "Coe's Cure" *Newsweek* (February 27, 1956): 56. In this article, the healing ministry of Jack Coe is examined.

Editor. "Frenzy of Faith in Man's Touch." *Life* (August 3, 1962): 12-21. This *Life Magazine* article explored the methodology and influence of evangelist Oral Roberts.

Editor. "Oklahoma Faith Healer Draws a Following." *Christian Century* 72 (June 29, 1955): 749-750. The *Christian Century*, a mainline Protestant publication, explores the impact of the ministry of Oral Roberts.

Editor. "Oral Roberts: Deadline From God." *Time* 66:2 (July 11, 1955): 41. This is a Time Magazine article that focuses on the ministry of Granville Oral Roberts. Roberts explained that he felt like he needed to win one million souls by July 1, 1956.

Editor. "Thrill of My Life." *Newsweek* (October 24, 1955): 104. This is an uplifting Newsweek article that delves into the ministry of healing evangelist Oral Roberts.

Editor. "Travail of The Healer." *Newsweek* (March 19, 1956): 82. In this penetrating news article, a journalist from *Newsweek* reflects on Roberts' pervading influence.

Erickson, Clifton O. *Supernatural Deliverance*. Denver Colorado: Clifton O. Erickson, 1950. This book, from a lesser known evangelist, is not only an autobiography but also a theological discourse on healing.

Fox, Lorne F. "Is Physical Healing in The Atonement," *The Pentecostal Evangel* (October 8, 1950): 3. This article, published by the Assemblies of God, discusses the viability of divine healing. Fox was one of the lesser-known evangelists of 1950s.

Fox, Lorne F. "Sickness and Demon Possession." *The Pentecostal Evangel* (April 15, 1950): 3. In this article, Lorne Fox talks about illness and the reality of dark forces.

Fox, Lorne F. *This Is My Story: Life Story and Healing Testimony of Lorne F. Fox*. Naselle, Washington: Published by Lorne F. Fox, 1970. This is an autobiographical account of Fox, a noteworthy Assemblies of God evangelist. It includes some of his personal accounts of healing.

Freeman, William. *How to Receive and Keep Your Healing*. Branson, Missouri: William W. Freeman, date unstated. This is a practical booklet on the ministry of healing published around 1953.

Freeman, William. *Living Waters and Other Sermons*. Springfield, Missouri: William W. Freeman, undated. This book is a collection of popular sermons on healing and deeper-life topics. It was published around 1952.

Freeman, William. *The Miracle Book: 101 Miraculous Testimonies and Messages On How You Too May Receive a Miracle*. Carthage, Missouri: William Freeman Evangelistic Association, undated. William Freeman was one of the lesser known Voice of Healing evangelists. This booklet, published around 1951, includes many inspirational testimonies.

Gardner, Velmer. *Healing for You: Scriptural Proof That You Can Be Healed*. Springfield, Missouri: Velmer Gardner Ministries, 1952. This is a practical book on the ministry of healing from an evangelist associated with the *Voice of Healing* magazine in the 1950s.

Gardner, Velmer. *My Life Story*. Springfield, Missouri: Velmer Gardner Evangelistic Association, 1954. This is an autobiographical account of Gardner. He shares his call to ministry and some of his notable experiences ministering healing.

Gardner, Velmer. *The God of Miracles Lives Today – A 20th Century Challenge to A Modernist: Healing and How to Receive It*. Wenatchee, Washington: Velmer Gardner Evangelistic Association, 1950. This book brings together Gardner's healing sermons and some of the testimonies of healing from his crusades.

Grant, W. V. *7 Reasons Why You Can't Receive Your Healing*. Dallas, Texas: Faith Clinic, 1970. W. V. Grant, an evangelist associated with the Voice Healing, wrote a number of booklets. In this work, Grant shared 7 reasons why people struggle with receiving their healing. The seven hindrances were: 1. I Can't Keep My Mind on the Lord. 2. Someone Hindered Me. 3. Must Call for Elders and Use Oil. 4. If "So and So" Will Pray for Me. 5. Hezekiah Used a Poultice. 6. Trophimus Was Left Sick. 7. Healing Is Just for Some People.

Grant, W. V. *Are You Sick and Tired of Feeling Sick and Tired?* Dallas, Texas: Grant's Faith Clinic, 1955. This booklet is a practical guide for Christians who are feeling sick and wanted to experience breakthrough.

Grant, W. V. *Chronic Cases Cured*. Dallas, Texas: Faith Clinic, undated. In this practical booklet, evangelist W.V. Grant provides some reasoned defenses for the efficacy of divine healing.

Grant, W. V. *Creative Miracles*. Dallas, Texas: Faith Clinic, undated. This book recounts the insights and experiences of Neal Frisby, an evangelist who imagined himself William Branham's successor. David Edwin Harrell described Frisby as "The most bizarre prophet of the 1970s."

Grant, W. V. *Divine Healing Answers*, volume one. Waxahachie, Texas, Southwestern Bible Institute Press, undated. In this paperback, Grant provides practical answers to questions that various Spirit-filled people had presented to him.

Grant, W. V. *Divine Healing Answers*, volume two. Waxahachie, Texas, Southwestern Bible Institute Press, 1952. This book is a continuation of the first volume. Grant continues to provide answers about the theology and practice of healing.

Grant, W. V. *Divine Healing in The Grant Campaigns*. Shreveport, Louisiana: The Voice of Healing, 1950. This book is an overview of the healing accounts that took place in some of Grant's healing crusades.

Grant, W. V. *Faith Cometh or How to Get Faith: A Textbook On Divine Healing*. Dallas, Texas: W.V. Grant, undated. This practical book presents 117 specific issues that hinder the ministry of healing.

Grant, W. V. *Faith For Healing*. Dallas, Texas: Faith Clinic, undated. Grant wrote this booklet like he was providing simple instructions to an individual who wanted healing. He wanted to take the needy man or woman through the whole process.

Grant, W. V. *From Plow Boy to Preacher Boy*. Dallas, Texas: Grant's Faith Clinic, undated. This is Grant's autobiography that was first published in the early 1960s.

Grant, W. V. *Gifts of Healing*. Dallas, Texas: Grant's Faith Clinic, 1955. In this work, Grant considers what the scriptures have to say about the diverse gifts and expressions of healing.

Grant, W. V. *Have You Tried and Tried to Believe? Read These Seven Chapters by W.V. Grant*. Dallas, Texas: Faith Clinic, undated. In this booklet, Grant clarifies impediments to healing. He covers things like: healing in the atonement, is sickness punishment, leadings, discomfort with public meetings, distrust and other areas.

Grant, W. V. *Health and Healing: Faith Tonic*. Malvern, Arkansas: W. V. Grant, undated. This practical booklet, published in the early 1950s, discusses how the sick can experience healing.

Grant, W. V. *How to Be Healed in 3 Minutes: The Faith That Never Fails*. Dallas, Texas: Grant's Faith Clinic, undated. This booklet, published in the 1950s, provides practical strategies for the reception of healing.

Grant, W. V. *Just Before the Healing Service Read These Seven Sermons*. Dallas, Texas: Grant's Faith Clinic, undated. This sermon compilation, published in the 1950s, was used to get the sick positioned to receive prayer. People were encouraged to read these messages before they came to the healing line.

Grant, W. V. *Luke Was a Physician: And Six Other Deliverance Sermons*. Dallas, Texas: Grant's Faith Clinic, undated. This collection of healing messages was published after the height of the salvation healing revival in the late 1950s or early 1960s.

Grant, W. V. *Maybe You Have a Thorn in The Flesh*. Dallas, Texas: Grant's Faith Clinic, undated. Grant's booklet was published to clarify that Paul's thorn in the flesh was not a sickness that came from God.

Grant, W. V. and James Dunn. *Power to Discern Disease*. Dallas, Texas: Grant's Faith Clinic, undated. This booklet that Grant co-authored with another evangelist, highlighted strategies for understanding and fighting against disease.

Grant, W. V. *Seven Reasons Why You Can't Receive Your Healing*. Dallas, Texas: Grant's Faith Clinic, undated. In this practical guide, Grant provides insight into some of the hindrances to healing: 1. I Can't Keep My Mind on the Lord. 2. Someone hindered me. 3. I must call for the elders and use oil. 4. If "so and so" will pray for me. 5. Hezekiah used a poultice. 6. Trophimus was left sick. 7. Healing is just for some people.

Grant, W. V. *The Grace of God in My Life*. Dallas, Texas: W. V. Grant, 1952. Grant's autobiography was written to clarify his calling to ministry and to recount the amazing healings that took place.

Grant, W. V. *The Hand of the Healer*. Dallas, Texas: Faith Clinic, undated. This is a practical booklet that deals with appropriation of healing through touch. Grant talks about a point of contact, how to turn loose your faith, and the touch of Jesus' hand.

Grant, W. V. *The Last Step of Healing*. Dallas, Texas: Grant's Faith Clinic, 1957. In this booklet, Grant provides another practical guide for receiving healing.

Grant, W. V. *The Life and Ministry of Walter Vinson Grant* enlarged edition. Dallas, Texas: W. V. Grant publisher, 1952. This book is an autobiographical work, explaining significant details from Grant's life and ministry.

Grant, W. V. *The Truth About Faith Healers: What Happens to the People They Claim to Cure?* Dallas, Texas: Grant's Faith Clinic, undated. In this pamphlet, W. V. Gant defends himself and other faith healing proponents. Part of the point of this work was to respond to the claim that some do not remain healed.

Grant, W. V. and James Dunn. *The Sign-Gift Ministry in The 20th Century*. Dallas, Texas: Faith Clinic, undated. This book is an interview with evangelist James Dunn exploring the application and meaning of the supernatural.

Grant, W. V. *When Prayer Fails: Read These Nine Sermons*. Dallas, Texas: Faith Clinic, undated. This booklet was written to assist individuals who have struggled to receive healing.

Hall, Franklin. *Bodyfelt Salvation: Healed from the Adamic Sickness*. Phoenix, Arizona: Hall Deliverance Foundation, 1968. In this work, Hall talks about: 1. Freedom from adamic sickness and harm 2. Freedom from adamic sin. 3. Freedom from adamic poverty 4. Freedom from adamic sorrow.

Hall, Franklin. *Our Divine Healing Obligation*. Phoenix, Arizona Franklin Hall, 1964. Hall shares how he believes that a person can be healed through "the healing power of Holy Ghost fire."

Hayes, Alton with Gordon Lindsay. *The Life Story of Alton Hayes*. Dallas, Texas: Voice of Healing, 1953. This is a short account of Hayes' life and calling to ministry that was produced in cooperation with Gordon Lindsay. Also included is Gordon Lindsay's "How To Receive Your Healing."

Hedgepeth, William. "Brother Allen On the Gospel trail." *Look* (October 7, 1969): 23-31. This article is a photo-journalistic piece on evangelist A.A. Allen.

Hicks, Tommy M. *Capturing The Nations in The Name of the Lord*. Los Angles, California: Deliverance and World Wide Evangelism, 1956. This book is the autobiography of missionary-evangelist Tommy Hicks.

Jacobs, Hayes B. "Oral Roberts: High Priest of Faith Healing." *Harpers Magazine* (February 1962): 37-43. This is pictorial essay on evangelist Oral Roberts published by a general interest magazine.

Jackson, Gayle. *Divine Deliverance for the Human Race as Provided by the Death and Atonement of the Lord Jesus Christ and Manifested in the Divine Healing Ministry of Evangelist Gayle Jackson in the 20th Century*. Sikeston, Missouri: Gayle Jackson, 1951. This is an autobiography of evangelist Gayle Jackson. Much of what was written was produced from his sermons.

Jaggers, Orval Lee. *Everlasting Spiritual and Physical Health*. Dexter, Missouri: Published by O.L. Jaggers, 1949. Jaggers was a friend of William Branham and associated with the Voice of Healing. Over time, he became increasingly controversial, embracing eccentric teachings.

Jaggers, Orval Lee. *How God Gave This Ministry to Me*. O.L. Jaggers, undated. This is the autobiography of O.L. Jaggers. Some have suggested that he was one of the greatest orators of the salvation-healing revival. Nevertheless, his vivid imagination contributed to extravagant claims. Over time, his doctrinal views became extreme. Jaggers separated from his Voice of Healing colleagues, ultimately abandoning the ministry of healing altogether.

Jenkins, Leroy. *Somebody Up There Loves Me*. Tampa, Florida: Leroy Jenkins Evangelistic Association, 1965. Jenkins experienced a spectacular healing when his arm was about to be amputated. This book not only shares his story, but also includes biblical teachings, practical strategies, and testimonies.

Johnson, Cyrus C. *How to Receive Your Healing in the Paul Cain Meetings*. Garland, Texas: Paul Cain Evangelist Association, 1954. This practical guide was made available in Paul Cain's meetings to assist people in receiving healing.

Jorgenson, Owen. *Supernatural - The Life of William Branham*, volume 1. Saint Silsbee, Texas: Supernatural Christian Books, 2011. In this series, Jorgenson recounts aspects of Branham's life and ministry. The first book relates childhood stories and the beginning of Branham's ministry.

Jorgenson, Owen. *Supernatural - The Life of William Branham*, volume 2. Saint Silsbee, Texas: Supernatural Christian Books, 2011. The second book in this series recounts the rise of the salvation healing revivals and some of Branham's largest meetings.

Jorgenson, Owen. *Supernatural - The Life of William Branham*, volume 3. Saint Silsbee, Texas: Supernatural Christian Books, 2011. The third and final book in this series recounts the final years of Branham's ministry.

Karol, Stanley W. *Scars and Stripes of Calvary*. Philadelphia: Karol Evangelistic Association, 1953. Karol was a lesser known Voice of Healing evangelist. Unlike many of his peers, he remained associated with the Assemblies of God. This book contains Karol's life story and several of his sermons.

Karol, Stanley W. *Whys and Wherefores*. Philadelphia: Karol Evangelistic Association, 1953. This book attempts to answer questions about why some suffer and never get healed.

Kobler, John. "The Truth About Faith Healers." *McCalls* (February 1957): 29-42. This exposé attempts to discredit the evangelists associated with the salvation-healing revival.

Lindsay, Gordon. *Answers to the Difficult Questions Concerning Divine Healing*. Dallas, Texas: The Voice of Healing Publishing Company, 1960. Gordon Lindsay, founder of the *Voice of Healing* magazine, evaluates some of the controversies associated with healing.

Lindsay, Gordon. *Bible Days Are Here Again: Divine Healing for Today and God's Plan for Ending Sickness*. Dallas, Texas: Voice of Healing Publishing Company, 1949. In this work, Lindsay argues that a new season of God's Spirit is underway through the salvation-healing revival.

Lindsay, Gordon. *Christ the Great Physician*. Dallas, Texas: Voice of Healing Publishing, 1960. Through a concentrated biblical study, Lindsay clarifies Jesus' role as a healer. Drawing upon this truth, he makes modern day applications.

Lindsay, Gordon. *Divine Healing in the Grant Campaigns*. Shreveport, Louisiana: W.V. Grant Publisher, 1949. This excerpt from Lindsay's "How to Receive Your Healing" was released to supplement the healing crusades of W.V. Grant.

Lindsay, Gordon. *God's Answer to the Puzzling Cases*. Dallas, Texas: Voice of Healing Publications, 1956. Lindsay tries to explain some of the difficult issues that come into focus through the ministry of healing.

Lindsay, Gordon. *How to Receive Your Healing*. Dallas, Texas: Voice of Healing Publishing, undated. Lindsay's work is a practical guide to helping people be positioned to receive healing.

Lindsay, Gordon. *How You Can Have Divine Health: Seven Steps by Which You can Enjoy Divine Health – How to End the Sickness Problem*. Dallas, Texas: Voice of Healing Publishing, undated. Lindsay wrote a seven-point, practical guide to assist individuals with receiving their breakthrough.

Lindsay, Gordon. *Is the Healing Revival from Heaven or of Men?* Dallas, Texas: Voice of Healing Publishing, undated. In this booklet, Lindsay provides a defense for the efficacy of the salvation-healing revival.

Lindsay, Gordon. *How You Can Be Healed*. Dallas, Texas: Christ for the Nations, 1977. Lindsay was proficient at developing teaching and practical guides for the multitudes who attended the tent meetings in the 1950s. In this work, he provides healing tips.

Lindsay, Gordon, ed. and comp. *Men Who Heard From Heaven: Sketches from The Life Stories of Evangelists Whose Ministries are Reaching Millions As Told By Themselves*. Dallas, Texas, Voice of Healing, undated. In this book, Lindsay compiled sketches of healing evangelists who "heard from heaven." Lindsay shares accounts of T. L. Osborn, W. V. Grant, Velmer Gardner, Raymond Richey, A. C. Valdez, Richard Vineyard, Gayle Jackson, David Nunn and others.

Lindsay, Gordon. *The Bible Secret of Divine Health*. Dallas, Texas: Christ For the Nations, 1995. In this exegetical work, Lindsay provides a practical overview of what the Bible teaches on divine healing.

Lindsay, James Gordon. *The Gifts of Healing*. Dallas, Texas: Voice of Healing Publishing, 1963. Lindsay articulates some of what the Bible has to say about the various "gifts of healings."

Lindsay, Gordon. *The Gordon Lindsey Story*. Dallas, Texas: The Voice Of Healing Publishing Company, 1953. This work is the autobiography of Gordon Lindsay. It includes a number of insights into the salvation healing revival.

Lindsay, James Gordon. *The Real Reason Why Christians Are Sick and How They May Get Well*. Dallas, Texas: Voice of Healing Publishing, undated. In this booklet, Lindsay considers the reasons Christians get sick and what needs to be done about it.

Lindsay, Gordon. *They Saw It Happen: The Dramatic Story of Men of God Who Were Greatly Used in the Pentecostal Outpouring of the Twentieth Century*. Dallas, Texas: Christ for the Nations, 1986. This book includes accounts of early twentieth-century healings and outpourings of the Spirit.

Lindsay, James Gordon. *Thirty Reasons Why Christ Heals Today*. Dallas, Texas: Christ for the Nations Publishing, 1968. In this booklet, Lindsay articulates a number of different reasons why he believes that Jesus continues to heal the infirmed today.

Lindsay, Gordon. *Why Some Are Not Healed And The Bible Answer*. Dallas: Christ for the Nations, 1971. In this practical guide, Lindsay considers twenty-five reasons why healing does not transpire.

Lindsay, Gordon. *World Evangelization Now by Healing and Miracles*. Dallas, Texas: Christ For the Nations, 1951. Lindsay provides a defense for the healing revivals and articulates a broader strategy.

Mann, W. E. "What About Oral Roberts?" *Christian Century* 73 (September 5, 1956): 1018-1021. This is an essay published in a mainline periodical that critiques the methodology of Oral Roberts.

McKay, William B. *Christ's Deliverance For Soul and Body.* Orlando, Florida: William B. McKay Publisher, 1952. This is a practical healing guide from a minor Voice of Healing evangelist. The book includes a number of healing testimonies.

McKay, William B. and Edith Evelyn McKay. *Christ the Divine Healer.* Orlando, Florida: W. B. McKay, 1949. This book includes sermons and testimonies of individuals who were healed under the McKay's ministry

Morrison, Chester "Faith Healer At Work." *Look Magazine* (June 29, 1954): 88-94. Look magazine published a feature article on Oral Roberts during the height of the salvation healing revival.

Nunn, David O. *God's Dynamic Trio: Faith, Healing, Miracles.* Dallas, Texas: Bible Revival Evangelistic Association, undated. This booklet from the late 1950s was written to stir faith and facilitate a greater breakthrough.

Nunn, David O. "God's Law of Health and Wealth." Dallas, Texas: David O. Nunn, undated. This booklet, which was published in the 1970s, takes Nunn's teachings in the direction of Kenneth Hagin and the Word of Faith Movement.

Nunn, David O. "Jesus The Healer Divine." Dallas, Texas: David Nunn Revivals, 1980. In this booklet, Nunn provides a practical strategy for the sick to receive healing.

Nunn, David O. *The Life And Ministry Of David Nunn.* Dallas, Texas: David Nunn, undated. This work is an autobiographical account of David Nunn. It talks about his beginnings and some of the greatest miracles he witnessed.

Osborn, T.L. *Faith's Testimony: The Important Secret of Confession Unveiled and How to Keep Your Healing.* Tulsa, Oklahoma: T. L. Osborn Evangelistic Association, 1956. This booklet, penned by Osborn, relates practical strategies for maintaining healing.

Osborn, T.L. *Healing En Masse.* Tulsa, Oklahoma: T.L. Osborn, 1958. In this book, Osborn recounts his approach to simultaneously ministering to a larger group of people. He calls it "healing en masse." Osborn would apply this approach successfully as he conducted foreign missions.

Osborn, T.L. *Healing the Sick.* Tulsa, Oklahoma: Harrison House, 1951, 1977, 1981, 1986. In this work, Osborn shares many of the lessons that he learned through biblical study and by praying for thousands.

Osborn, T.L. *One Hundred Divine Healing Facts.* Tulsa, Oklahoma: Harrison House Publishers, 1983. In this practical booklet, Osborn takes a page from F.F. Bosworth's *Christ The Healer* and recounts one hundred things that he has learned about divine healing.

Osborn, T.L. *Seven Steps To Receive Healing From Christ.* Tulsa, Oklahoma: T.L. Osborn Ministries, 1955. In this booklet, Osborn shares seven practical strategies for receiving healing.

Rhodes, Jackie. *Life And Healing of Jackie Rhodes; Including Scriptures, Testimonies, Pictures and Lay Talks.* Delight, Arkansas: Jackie Rhodes, 1955. This book is the first-hand account of a woman who was healed of schleraderma at a Jack Coe crusade.

Roberts, Evelyn. *Evelyn Roberts' Miracle Life Stories.* Tulsa, Oklahoma: Oral Roberts Ministries, 1998. In this book, Oral Roberts' wife shares healing accounts and stories of the miracles that she witnessed.

Roberts, Granville Oral. *A Daily Guide To Miracles.* Grand Rapids, Michigan: Fleming H. Revell Company, 1978. This practical book, by Roberts, explains how one can receive physical and spiritual breakthrough.

Roberts, Granville Oral. *Deliverance From Fear and From Sickness.* Tulsa, Oklahoma: Oral Roberts Evangelistic Association, 1954. In this book, Roberts shares biblical and practical advice for experiencing a breakthrough.

Roberts, Granville Oral. *Exactly How You May Receive Your Healing-Through Faith*. Tulsa, Oklahoma: Oral Roberts Evangelistic Association, 1958. This booklet is a how-to guide that Roberts made available to individuals who came to his healing crusades.

Roberts, Granville Oral. *God Still Heals Today: And Here is How He Heals You*. Tulsa, Oklahoma: Oral Roberts Evangelistic Association, 1984. This book is a practical work on healing from noted evangelist, Oral Roberts. In this book, Roberts reveals principles for healing.

Roberts, Granville Oral. *Healing For the Whole Man*. Tulsa, Oklahoma: Oral Roberts Evangelistic Association, 1965. In this practical booklet, Roberts talks about experiencing total healing. He affirms that the body, soul, and spirit can be rejuvenated and brought into alignment.

Roberts, Granville Oral. *If You Need Healing Do These Things: How You Can Use the Power of Faith in God for Spiritual, Mental and Physical Healing, and to Achieve Happiness and Peace*. Tulsa, Oklahoma: Oral Roberts Evangelistic Association, Inc., 1947, 1950, 1957. This is a collection of practical teachings from Oral Roberts.

Roberts, Granville Oral. *Miracles of Healing For You Today*. Tulsa, Oklahoma: Oral Roberts University, 1982. This is a collection of practical healing insights drawn from Oral Roberts.

Roberts, Granville Oral. *My Story*. Tulsa, Oklahoma: Oral Roberts Evangelistic Association, 1961. This is an autobiographical account of healing evangelist Oral Roberts.

Roberts, Granville Oral. *Oral Robert's Life Story*. Tulsa, Oklahoma: Oral Roberts Evangelistic Association, 1952. This is an early autobiography of Oral Roberts, one of the most celebrated evangelists in the Salvation-Healing revivals of the 1940s and 50s.

Roberts, Granville Oral. *Personal Commentary on the Four Gospels and the Acts of the Apostles*. Tulsa, Oklahoma: Oral Roberts Evangelistic

Association, 1967. This is a collection of notes from the Gospels and Acts that Roberts included alongside the biblical text. In the notes, there are many references to healing.

Roberts, Granville Oral. *Seven Divine Aids For Your Healing and Health*. Tulsa, Oklahoma: Oral Roberts University, 1960, 1965. This is a practical booklet on divine healing from Roberts. In this work, he shares some effective approaches to healing.

Roberts, Granville Oral. *Ten Greatest Miracles of Oral Roberts' Ministry*. Tulsa, Oklahoma: Oral Roberts Evangelistic Association, 1961. This is a fascinating account of several miracles that took place through Oral Roberts' ministry.

Roberts, Granville Oral. *The Healing Stream*, ed. G.H. Montgomery. Tulsa, Oklahoma: Oral Roberts Evangelistic Association, 1959. This small, popularly-written book is a collection of various healing articles from Oral Roberts. Each of these were originally published in his periodical.

Roberts, Granville Oral. *The Fourth Man and Other Famous Sermons Exactly as Oral Roberts Preached Them From the Revival Platform*. Tulsa, Oklahoma: Healing Waters, 1951, 1953. This is a collection of sermons from Oral Roberts that he preached during the height of the salvation-healing revivals.

Roberts, Granville Oral. *The Miracle Book*. Tulsa, Oklahoma: Pinook Publications, 1972. This book is a practical guidebook. Roberts provides tips and down-to-earth counsel for individuals who would like to see a miracle in their lives.

Roberts, Granville Oral. *Your Healing Problems And How To Solve Them*. Tulsa, Oklahoma: Oral Roberts Evangelistic Association, 1966. Roberts crafted a practical work to help people who are struggling for a breakthrough. He wanted to help people be better positioned for healing.

Robinson, Wayne A. *Oral: The Warm, Intimate Unauthorized Portrait of a Man of God.* Los Angeles, California: Action House Publishers, 1976. Robinson, who was a close associate of Oral Roberts, had a falling out with the ministry. In this work, he shares some of his reflections on Roberts.

Shambach, R. W. *Miracles: An Eyewitness To The Miraculous.* Tyler, Texas: Power Publications, 1969. This book is a compilation of healing stories from the early years of Shambach's ministry. Most of the testimonies reflect what he witnessed while working under A. A. Allen.

Shambach, R. W. *Miracles 2: Greater Miracles.* Tyler, Texas: Published by R.W. Shambach, 1993. Shambach wrote a follow-up to his popular collection of healing and miracle stories. While the accounts are not as dynamic as those included in his first book, they do represent the breakthroughs that occurred through Shambach's later itinerancy.

Stadsklev, Julius. *William Branham: A Prophet Visits South Africa.* Minneapolis, Minnesota: Julius Stadsklev Publisher, 1952. This compilation of Branham material—letters, healing testimonies, and other source material unique to this publication—provide insights into his ministry. This account focuses on Branham's ministry exploits in South Africa during the early part of the 1950s.

Stewart Don. *Only Believe: Eyewitness Accounts of the Great Healing Revivals.* Shippensburg, Pennsylvania: Revival Press, 1999, 2001. Don Stewart, the successor of A.A. Allen, reveals his insights about twentieth century healing figures. Stewart was prominent in the early 1970s, but lost his stature over time.

Stewart, Don. *How To Receive Your Healing.* Don Stewart Evangelistic Association, 1977. This practical guide from evangelist Don Stewart discusses strategies for experiencing breakthrough.

Sumrall, Lester. "Emotions and Divine Healing." *World Harvest* 3:6 (1964): 4-5. In this essay, Sumrall explores how emotions affect the health of believers and what we need to do to bring things into proper order.

Sumrall, Lester. *Human Illness And Divine Healing*, revised edition. South Bend, Indiana: Lesea Publication, 1984. In this work, Sumrall produced a syllabus and notes for detailed instruction on healing. He covers some of the following: The origin of sickness and disease, Is sickness a blessing or a curse?, The healing covenant, healing in the atonement, and other topics.

Weaver, C. Douglas. *The Healer-Prophet: William Marion Branham- A Study of the Prophetic in American Pentecostalism*. Macon, Georgia: Mercer University Press, 1987. Douglas' biographical account of William Marion Branham is well-researched and penetrating.

Wyatt, Thomas. *A Study in Healing and Deliverance*. Los Angeles, California, Wings of Healing, undated. Wyatt was a healing evangelist and radio ministry pioneer that predated the emergence of William Branham in 1947. This is the work that he wrote on the biblical foundations of healing and deliverance.

Wyatt, Thomas. *Commanding Power*. Los Angeles, California, Wings of Healing, 1956. This is a practical work on the importance praying with intensity and strength.

Wyatt, Thomas. *Wings of Healing*. Los Angeles, California, Wings of Healing, 1955. This is a work on healing from Wyatt, a forgotten figure in the Salvation-Healing revival of the 1950s.

Wyatt, Thomas. *Words That Work Wonders*. Portland, Oregon, Wings of Healing, 1951. In this work, Wyatt talks about the power of words and how they impact the lives of people.

11. LATER PENTECOSTALISM

Aker, Benny C. and Gary B. McGee. *Signs and Wonders In Ministry Today*. Springfield, Missouri: Gospel Publishing House, 1996. This book, written by two Pentecostal researchers, discusses contemporary miracles. It includes several modern healing accounts.

Albrecht, Daniel. "The Life and Ministry of Carrie Judd Montgomery," M.A., thesis, Western Evangelical Seminary, 1984. In this well-researched thesis, Albrecht explores Carrie Judd Montgomery and her notable ministry of healing.

Albrecht, Daniel E. "Carrie Judd Montgomery: Pioneering Contributor to Three Religious Movements." *Pneuma: The Journal for the Society of Pentecostal Studies* 8:2 (Fall 1985): 101-119. This insightful article on Montgomery explores her involvement with the Faith Cure Movement, Christian and Missionary Alliance, and the Assemblies of God.

Alexander, Kimberly Ervin. "A Critical Review of Healing Through the Centuries: Models for Understanding by Ronald A. N. Kydd," *Journal of Pentecostal Theology* 16 (2000): 117-127. Alexander reviews Ronald Kydd's *Healing Through The Centuries*, summarizing some of his findings.

Alexander, Kimberly Ervin "How Wide Thy Healing Streams Are Spread: Constructing a Wesleyan Pentecostal Model of Healing for the Twenty-first Century." *The Asbury Theological Journal* 59:1 -2 (2004): 63-76. This article is an examination of the theology and practice of healing of Pentecostals rooted in the Wesleyan tradition.

Alexander, Kimberly Ervin. "Models of Pentecostal Healing in Light of Early Twentieth Century Pentecostalism," Ph.D. diss., Open University, 2002. This well-researched dissertation explores the foundations and practice of healing within early Pentecostalism. This work is the basis for her subsequent work, *Pentecostal Healing: Models in Theology and Practice*.

Alexander, Kimberly Ervin. *Pentecostal Healing: Models In Theology and Practice*. Dorset, United Kingdom: Deo Publishing, 2006. This book is a well-researched analysis of healing praxis in the Classical Pentecostal tradition.

Anderson, Allan. "Pentecostal Approaches to Faith and Healing," *International Review of Mission* 91:363 (2002): 523-534. This article, from a British Pentecostal researcher, discusses Pentecostal healing modalities.

Anderson, Robert Mapes. *Vision of the Disinherited: The Making of American Pentecostalism*. Peabody, Massachusetts: Hendrickson Publishers, 1979. Many consider this work one of the definitive studies on early Pentecostalism. Among other things, Anderson clarifies Pentecostalism's connection to the faith cure movement.

Atter, Gordon. *The Student's Handbook on Divine Healing: Outlined Studies on the Subject of Divine Healing, Especially Prepared for Classroom Use, With Blank Pages For Additional Notes*. Peterborough, Ontario, Canada: Eastern Pentecostal Bible College, 1960. This biblical reflection on healing was written by a Canadian Pentecostal. It was developed for the usage of Bible school students.

Baer, Jonathan R. "Redeemed Bodies: The Functions of Divine Healing in Incipient Pentecostalism." *Church History* 70:4 (December 2001): 735-771. This is a well-researched article that explores the Faith Cure Movement and its intersection with Pentecostalism.

Banks, Melvin. *Divine Health Is For You*, United Kingdom: Melvin Banks, undated. Banks, a Pentecostal evangelist from England, provides a practical guide for individuals who are desirous for a healing breakthrough.

Banks, Melvin. *Healing Secrets*. Basingstoke, United Kingdom: Marshall Pickering, 1986. In this down-to-earth work, Banks reveals insights into the ministry of healing.

Barclift, Mark A. "Why Some Christians Are Not Healed." *Paraclete Journal* (Summer 1986): 13-17. In this article, Barclift explores some of the perceived theological and practical reasons that people are not healed.

Barnes III, Roscoe. *F. F. Bosworth: The Man Behind Christ the Healer*. Newcastle Upon Tyne, United Kingdom: Cambridge Scholars Publishing, 2009. This is a well-researched biographical account of twentieth century healing evangelist, F.F. Bosworth.

Barnes III, Roscoe and Graham Duncan. "F. F. Bosworth: A Historical Analysis of his Ministry Development using Social Cognitive Career Theory." *Verbum et Ecclesia* 32.1 (2011): 1-8. Drawing from the field of sociology, Roscoe and Duncan examine the life and ministry of F. F. Bosworth.

Belcher, John R., and Steven Michael Hall. "Healing And Psychotherapy: The Pentecostal Tradition." *Pastoral Psychology* 50:2 (2001): 63-75. This article explores the usage of psychotherapy within Pentecostalism and its implications for the ministry of healing.

Bendroth, Margaret Lamberts and Virginia Lieson Brereton, eds. *Women and Twentieth Century Protestantism*. Urbana, Illinois: University of Illinois Press, 2002. This well-researched work Includes the following articles: R. Marie Griffith, "Female Suffering and Religious Devotion in American Pentecostalism;" James W. Opp,,"Healing Hands, Healthy Bodies: Protestant Women and Faith Healing in Canada and the United States, 1880-1930." Both articles explore healing practice within the Classical Pentecostal tradition.

Bixler, Francis. "Lorne Franklin Fox." *Dictionary of Pentecostal Charismatic Movements*, eds. Gary McGee, Stanley Burgess, and Patrick Alexander, 315. Grand Rapids, Michigan: Zondervan, 1988. This is a biographical sketch of Fox, an Assemblies of God evangelist involved with the salvation-healing revival of the 1950s.

Blumhofer, Edith L. "Aimee Semple McPherson and the Decisive Wichita Meeting." *Assemblies of God Heritage Magazine 13:1* (Spring 1993): 18-21, 25-27. Blumhofer's article on McPherson's 1922 meetings in Wichita, Kansas provides some fascinating reflections on healing and the ethos of Pentecostalism.

Blumhofer, Edith L. "Charles F. Parham's 1906 Invasion: A Pentecostal Branch Grows in Dowie's Zion." *Assemblies of God Heritage Magazine* 6:3 (Fall 1986): 3-5. In this well-researched article, Blumhofer examines Charles Parham's early ministry in Zion, Illinois.

Blumhofer, Edith L. "Jesus Is Victor: A Study in the Life Johan Christoph Blumhardt." *Paraclete Journal* 19:2. (Spring 1985): 1-5. Blumhofer explores the life and ministry Johann Christoph Blumhardt, a German healing proponent from the mid-Nineteenth Century.

Blumhofer, Edith L. "John Alexander Dowie." *Dictionary of Pentecostal-Charismatic Movements*, eds. Gary McGee, Stanley Burgess, and Patrick Alexander, 248-249. Grand Rapids, Michigan: Zondervan Publishing, 1988. This is a well-researched article on the life and impact John Alexander Dowie.

Blumhofer, Edith L. "Life on Faith Lines: Faith Homes and Early Pentecostal Values." *Assemblies of God Heritage Magazine* 10:2 (Summer 1990): 10-12, 22. This article is the first part of a two-part series on how early faith homes shaped the identity and experience of Pentecostalism.

Blumhofer, Edith L. "Life on Faith Lines: Faith Homes and Early Pentecostal Values: Part Two." *Assemblies of God Heritage Magazine* 10:3 (Fall 1990): 5-7, 21-22. This is the second part of Blumhofer's series on the influence of faith homes.

Blumhofer, Edith L. "That Old-Time Religion: 'Aimee Semple McPherson and Perceptions of Pentecostalism, 1928-1926." *Journal of Beliefs and Values* 25:2 (August 2004): 217-227. Blumhofer composed an excellent article on Aimee Semple McPherson and the establishment of Pentecostal identity.

Brooks, Noel. *Sickness, Health, and God.* Franklin Springs, Georgia: Advocate Press, 1965. This work, from an English Pentecostal, explores the biblical foundations of healing.

Brown, Michael L. "'I am the Lord your Healer:' A philological study of the root 'rapa' in the Hebrew Bible and the ancient Near East," Ph.D., diss., New York University, 1985. Brown's well-researched dissertation explores the biblical foundations of the word "rapha" — "healer" in the Hebrew language. This work became the foundation of Brown's subsequent work, *Israel's Divine Healer.*

Brown, Michael L. *Israel's Divine Healer.* Grand Rapids, Michigan: Zondervan Publishing, 1995. Brown's well-researched exegetical analysis is possibly the definitive work on the theology of healing. The strength of this book is its examination of healing in the Old Testament. This tome is based on his earlier dissertation and research on the word "rapha" in the Old Testament.

Brown, Michael L. "rapa." *Theological Dictionary of the Old Testament,* eds. G. Johannes Botterweck, Helmer Ringgren, Heinz-Josef Fabry, 593-602. Grand Rapids, Michigan: Eerdmans Publishing, 2004. This exegetical article from Brown analyzes the linguistics of "healing" in the Old Testament.

Brown, Michael L. "repā'îm." *The New International Dictionary of Old Testament Theology and Exegesis,* ed. Willem A. VanGemeren, 1173-1180. Grand Rapids, Michigan: Zondervan, (1997): 1173-1180. In this article, Brown examines another derivative of "healing" in the Hebrew language.

Brown, Michael L., A. Kam-Yau Chan and Thomas B. Song. "r-p." *New International Dictionary of Old Testament Theology and Exegesis,* ed. Willem A. VanGemeren, 1162-1172. Grand Rapids, Michigan:

Zondervan, 1997. This is a theological and exegetical examination of the Hebrew word "rapa" (healing).

Brown, Michael L. "The Whole Man Wholly Healed: Israel's Divine Healer in the Prophetic Books," paper presented at the annual meeting of the Evangelical Theological Society, Capital Bible Seminary, Lanham, Maryland, April 3, 1992. In this well-researched paper, Brown examines depictions of healing in the Old Testament prophetic works.

Buller, Cornelius A. "Healing Hope: Physical Healing and Resurrection Hope in a Postmodern Context." *Journal of Pentecostal Theology* 10 *(April* 2002): 21-28. In this article, Buller provides a robust theological reflection on healing.

Bundrik, D.R. "The New Testament Fulfillment of Anointing." *Paraclete* 3:2 (1985): 15-18. This article explores the biblical meaning of anointing with oil. Bundrik clarifies how this practice finds ultimate expression in the New Testament through healing and other impartational outworkings.

Burgess, Stanley M. and McGee, Gary B., eds. *Dictionary of Pentecostal and Charismatic Movements*. Grand Rapids, Michigan: Zondervan Publishing House, 1988. This reference work includes well-researched entries on Pentecostal and Charismatic healing evangelists as well as the healing movements that span this diverse movement.

Burgess, Stanley M., ed. *The New International Dictionary of Pentecostal Charismatic Movements*. Grand Rapids, Michigan: Zondervan Publishing House, 2002. This ground-breaking resource is an update and expansion of the 1988 Pentecostal-Charismatic Dictionary.

Burgess, Stanley M. "Gifts of Healing." *Encyclopedia of Pentecostal and Charismatic Christianity*. New York: Routledge, 2006. This thoroughly researched article explores the foundations of healing in Pentecostal practice.

Butcher, J. Kevin. "The Holiness and Pentecostal Labors of David Wesley Myland 1890-1918," Ph.D. diss., Dallas Theological Seminary, 1983. This is a study on David Wesley Myland, an overlooked Christian and Missionary Alliance pastor. Myland ultimately accepted the Pentecostal message and focused much of his ministry on healing.

Callahan, Leslie D. "A Sanctified Body: Reassessing Sanctification in the Thought of Charles Parham," paper presented at the 33rd annual meeting of the Society of Pentecostal Studies, Milwaukee, Wisconsin, March 11-13, 2004. This paper explores the relationship between holiness and healing in the theology of Charles Parham.

Carlson, G. Raymond. "Anointing With Oil." *Paraclete* Journal 3:2 (Spring 1969): 15-17. This article examines how anointing with oil was used throughout the Bible. Carlson discusses its role in healing as well as other ministry practices.

Cartledge, Mark J. "'Catch The Fire:' Revivalist Spirituality From Toronto to Beyond," *PentecoStudies* 13:2 (2014): 217-238. This paper revisits scholarship on the Toronto Blessing and related renewal movements from the mid to late 1990s.

Cartledge, Mark J. "Pentecostal Healing as an Expression of Godly Love: An Empirical Study." *Mental Health, Religion & Culture* 16:5 (2013): 501-522. In this essay, Cartledge provides a scholarly analysis of Pentecostal healing

Cartwright, Desmond W. *The Real Smith Wigglesworth: The Man, The Myth, The Message.* United Kingdom: Sovereign World International Book, 2000. This is a biographical account of Smith Wigglesworth that attempts to move beyond myths.

Cartwright, Desmond W. *The Great Evangelists: The Lives of George and Stephen Jeffreys*. Baskingstoke Hants, United Kingdom: Marshall Pickering, 1986. Cartwright culled a biographical account of the Jeffreys brothers, prominent healing evangelists in the United Kingdom.

Chadwick, Harold J. *How to be Filled With Spiritual Power: Based on the Miracle Ministry of John G. Lake*. Gainesville, Florida: Bridge-Logos Publishing, 2006. This is a fascinating book that explores the contemporary scope of healing and supernatural power. It draws upon the theology and praxis of John G. Lake.

Chant, Ken. *The Healing Covenant From Genesis To Revelation*. Sydney, Australia: Ken Chant, 1989. Chant's overview of healing in the Old and New Testaments includes several graphics and charts.

Chant, Ken. *Healing In The Whole Bible: The Old Testament*. Ramona, California: Vision Publishing, 2012. This revised version of Chant's 1989 work delves into healing in the Old Testament.

Chant, Ken. *Healing In The Whole Bible: The New Testament*. Ramona, California: Vision Publishing, 2012. This revised edition examines the ministry of healing in the New Testament.

Chappell, Paul G. "Healing Movements." *Dictionary of Pentecostal and Charismatic Movements*, eds. Gary McGee, Stanley Burgess, and Patrick Alexander, 353-374. Grand Rapids, Michigan: Zondervan Publishing, 1988. Chappell's essay provides an excellent synopsis on the history of healing in Christianity.

Clark, E.C., ed. *Marvelous Healings God Wrought Among Us*. Cleveland, Tennessee: Church Of God Publishing House, undated. This is a compilation of healing testimonies from individuals in the Church of God (Cleveland Tennessee).

Clements, William M. "Faith Healing, Narrative from Northeast Arkansas." *Indiana Folklore* 8 (1957): 21. This is an anthropological analysis of faith healing, envisioning it as folklore.

Clements, William M. "Ritual Expectation in Pentecostal Healing Experience." *Western Folklore* 40:2 (April 1981): 139-148. This article is an anthropological analysis of Pentecostal healing practices.

Clifton, Shane. "The Dark Side Of Prayer For Healing: Toward A Theology Of Well-Being." *Pneuma* 36 (2014): 204-225. This article, penned by a handicapped Pentecostal, appraises healing modalities and experiences. He argues that in many cases, a different approach should be embraced.

Cross, James A., ed. *Healing in the Church*. Cleveland, Tennessee: Pathway Press, 1962. This overview of healing contains healing sermons from several Church of God (Cleveland, Tennessee) ministers, 1910-1960.

Dickin, Janice. "Take up the Bed and Walk: Aimee Semple McPherson and Faith Healing." *Canadian Bulletin of Medical Health* 17 (2000): 137-153. This is an insightful article on the healing ministry of Aimee Semple Mcpherson.

Dignard, Martin L. "God's Faithful Freedom: Healing As An Outflow Of God's Presence." *Journal of Pentecostal Theology* 23 (2014): 68-84. This article explores tensions resident in the ministry of healing. Dignard ultimately draws upon Agnes Sandford's approach to resolve this tension.

Dignan, Ken. *Til' Healing Comes*. Altamonte Springs, Florida: Advantage Inspirational Books, 2010. This work, by a handicapped Pentecostal, evaluates the meaning of pain. Dignan acknowledges that there are mysteries in the realm of suffering. He ultimately considers the actions that one should take when illness is present.

Doak, Brian R., and William P. Griffin. "Anointing With Oil," in *Encyclopedia of Pentecostal And Charismatic Christianity*, ed. Stanley M. Burgess, 339-342. New York: Routledge, 2006. This article, written by Pentecostal researchers, examines the biblical foundations of anointing with oil.

Dorries, David W. "The Making of Smith Wigglesworth, Part One—The Making of the Man." *Assemblies of God Heritage Magazine* 12:3 (Fall 1992): 4-9. This is the first of a two-part essay on the life and ministry of Smith Wigglesworth.

Dorries, David W. "The Making of Smith Wigglesworth—part two: The Making of His Message." *Assemblies of God Heritage Magazine* 12:4 (Winter 1992-1993) 20-23. This is the second part of Dorries' essay on Wigglesworth.

Dusing, Michael. "Trophimus Have I Left at Miletus Sickly—The Case for Those Who Are Not Healed," paper presented at the 31st Annual Meeting of the Society for Pentecostal Studies. Lakeland, Florida: South Eastern University, 2002. Dusing argues that Pentecostals need to develop a theology of suffering. He is concerned about the implicit link between sickness and sin in popular Pentecostal piety.

Edsor, Albert W. *George Jeffreys, Man of God.* London: Ludgate Press Limited, 1964. This book is a compelling biographical account of George Jeffreys, a gifted English healing evangelist.

Epstein, Daniel Mark. *Sister Aimee: The Life of Aimee Semple McPherson.* New York: Harcourt Brace Jovanovich Publishers, 1993. This is a penetrating biography of Aimee Semple McPherson.

Espinosa, Gaston. "Tongues And Healing At The Azusa Street Revival," in *Religions Of The United States In Practice, Volume 2*, Colleen McDannell editor. (Princeton New Jersey: Princeton University Press, 2001): 217-223. Espinosa's article examines some healings and other the phenomenal activity at the Azusa Street Revival in Los Angeles, California.

Eutsler, Steve D. "*Why Are Not All Christians Healed?*" *Paraclete* 27:2 (Spring 1993): 15-23. In this article, Eutsler explores why some of the individuals who actively receive ministry are not healed.

Exline, J.W. "Dr. Finis E. Yoakum's Healing By the Lord." *Herald of Hope* 28:3 (January-February 1968). This article reflects on the life of early Twentieth Century healing evangelist, Finis E. Yoakum.

Fischer, Christoph. "By His Stripes We Are Healed: An Investigation Into the Connection Between Healing and the Atonement in Classical Pentecostal Theology," M.A., thesis, Heverlee-Leuven, 2004. This study explores whether the ministry of healing is available in the atonement.

Foot, David Robert Paterson. *Divine Healing in the Scriptures.* Eastbourne, United Kingdom: Henry E. Walter Limited Publishers, 1967. This is an overview of healing in the Bible. Foot writes, "I felt the pressing need to assemble some of the principal Scriptures on divine healing, in a simple way that would appeal to all who love the Bible and receive it as the inspired Word of God."

Gardiner, Gordon P. *Concerning Spiritual Gifts.* Brooklyn, New York: Bread of Life, 1979. Gardiner, a Pentecostal formerly associated with John Alexander Dowie, shares his reflections on the gifts of the Spirit.

Gardiner, Gordon P. *Out of Zion into All the World.* Shippensburg, Pennsylvania: Companion Press, 1990. This work examines early twentieth century leaders who emerged from Dowie's Zion. Many of these leaders were strong proponents of healing.

Gardiner, Gordon P. *Radiant Glory: The Life of Martha Wing Robinson.* Brooklyn, New York: Bread of Life, 1962. This is a biography of Martha Wing Robinson, a noted healing proponent associated with

John Alexander Dowie. She later became a part of the Pentecostal Movement.

General Presbytery of The Assemblies of God. "Our Position On Divine Healing: A Statement Adopted By the Assemblies of God General Presbytery, August 20, 1974." *Paraclete* 9:2 (Spring 1975): 7-13. This paper, published in a Pentecostal journal, affirms the Assemblies of God's official position on the ministry of healing.

Gen, Raymond M. "The Phenomena of Miracles and Divine Infliction in Luke-Acts: Their Theological Significance." *Pneuma* 11 (Spring 1989): 3-20. Using Luke-Acts as a textual foundation, Gen explores what he considers the mutuality of miracles and divine infliction.

Goff Jr., James R. "Charles F. Parham and His Role in the Development of the Pentecostal Movement: A Reevaluation." *Kansas History: A Journal of the Central Plains* 7:3 (Autumn 1984): 226 – 237. This article on Charles F. Parham includes references to his healing ministry.

Goff Jr., James R. *Fields White Unto Harvest: Charles F. Parham and the Missionary Origins of Pentecostalism.* Fayetteville, Arkansas: University of Arkansas Press, 1988. This book is the definitive biography of Charles F. Parham, the progenitor of Pentecostalism.

Gohr, Glenn. "Frederick K.C. Price." *Dictionary of Pentecostal Charismatic Movements*, eds. Gary McGee, Stanley Burgess, and Patrick Alexander, 727. Grand Rapids, Michigan: Zondervan Publishing, 1988. Gohr, an Assemblies of God archivist, provides a brief sketch of Frederick K.C. Price, pastor of Crenshaw Christian Center and Word of Faith evangelist.

Gray, David E. "Lean Not Thou on the Arm of Flesh: Invoking Celestial Power in the Treatment of Disease. A Century of the Healing Arts 1850-1950." *Shawnee County Historical Society* 57 (November 1980). The article on Charles Parham includes reflections on his healing home in Topeka, Kansas.

Hacking, William. *Smith Wigglesworth Remembered.* Tulsa, Oklahoma: Harrison House, 1981. This is a biographical account of Wigglesworth from a minister who knew him well. It includes several inspiring stories of healing and supernatural breakthrough.

Hewlett, James Allen. "Voice of Healing." *Dictionary of Pentecostal Charismatic Movements.* Grand Rapids, Michigan: Zondervan, 1988. 872-874. This is an essay on the *Voice of Healing*, a magazine and association that propelled the salvation-healing revival (1946-1958).

Hewlett, James Allen. "William W. Freeman." *Dictionary of Pentecostal Charismatic Movements.* Grand Rapids, Michigan: Zondervan, 1988. 317. This is a biographical sketch of Voice of Healing evangelist William Freeman.

Hibbert, Albert. *Smith Wigglesworth: The Secret of His Power.* Tulsa, Oklahoma: Harrison House, 1982, 1993. This is a biography of Smith Wigglesworth includes a number of stories about healing.

Holdcroft, L. Thomas. *Divine Healing: A Comparative Study.* Springfield, Missouri: Gospel Publishing House, 1967. This is a study on healing that was written by a popular Assemblies of God teacher.

Hollenweger, Walter J. *Pentecostalism: Origins and Developments Worldwide.* Peabody, Massachusetts: Hendrickson Publishers, 1996. This is a pivotal work on early Pentecostalism. It includes references to healing's significance to Spirit-filled believers.

Hollenweger, Walter J. "Healing Through Prayer: Superstition or Forgotten Christian Tradition?" *Theology* 92 (May 1989): 166-174. This is an article on the plausibility of healing prayer by an academically-minded Pentecostal scholar.

Holm, Randall. "Healing in Search of Atonement: With A Little Help from James K.A. Smith." *Journal of Pentecostal Theology* 23 (2014): 50-67. This academic article, from a classical Pentecostal, critiques the belief of healing in the atonement.

Horton, Wade H. "We Believe Divine Healing," *Church of God Evangel* (June 25, 1962): 6. Horton, the General Overseer of the Church of God (Cleveland, Tennessee), persuades members of his denomination to continue to contend for healing.

Hoy, Albert L." Gifts of Healings." *Paraclete Journal* 12:1 (Winter 1978): 6-11. This is a brief article on the meaning of "Gifts of Healings" in 1 Corinthians 12. It was written from a classical Pentecostal perspective.

Hudson, Neil. "Early British Pentecostals and Their Relationship to Health, Healing and Medicine." *Asian Journal of Pentecostal Studies* 6:2 (2003): 283-301. This article explores the understanding of healing practices in early British Pentecostalism.

Hugh, Peter. *By His Stripes: A Biblical Study on Divine Healing*. Springfield, Missouri: Gospel Publishing House, 1977. This is a widely circulated Biblical study on healing from an Assemblies of God minister.

Hunt, Stephen. "The Anglican Wimberites." *Pneuma*. 17:1 (Spring 1995) 105-118. Hunt is a British Pentecostal who penned a fascinating article on John Wimber's influence on the Anglican movement.

Hyatt, Eddie. *2000 Years of Charismatic Christianity: A 21st Century Look At Church History from A Pentecostal-Charismatic Perspective*. Dallas, Texas: Hyatt International Ministries, 1996, 1998. Hyatt's work examines healing and supernatural activity within the history of Christianity.

Hywel-Davies, Jack. *The Life of Smith Wigglesworth: A Pioneer of the Pentecostal Movement*. Ann Arbor, Michigan: Vine Books, 1987. This is a biography of Smith Wigglesworth that references several healing stories.

Jenkins, Skip. "Why Are Some Not Healed?: Atonement Paradigms, Divine Healing And An Insight From Edward Irving," paper presented at the 32nd annual meeting of the Society for Pentecostal Studies in special session with the Wesleyan Theological Society,

Asbury Theological Seminary, Wilmore, Kentucky March 20-22, 2003. Drawing upon the thought of Edward Irving, this article explores the intersection of healing and atonement theory.

Jeter, Hugh. *By His Stripes: A Biblical Study On Divine Healing*. Springfield, Missouri: Gospel Publishing House, 1977. Jeter, a member of the faculty at Southwestern Bible College, Waxahachie, Texas, presents a moderating case for healing today.

Jeter, Hugh P. "Power ... Present To Heal." *Paraclete Journal* 8:1 (Winter 1974): 3-6. This is an essay on healing from an Assemblies of God Bible College instructor.

Johns, Cheryl Bridges, Vergil Elizondo, and Elisabeth Moltmann-Wendel. "Healing and Deliverance," in *Pentecostal Movements as an Ecumenical Challenge*, eds. Jürgen Moltmann, and Karl-Josef Kuschel, 45-62. London: SCM and Orbis, 1996. This is a well-researched essay on healing and deliverance within the Pentecostal movement.

Jones, Charles Edwin. "James Gardner Velmer." *Dictionary of Pentecostal Charismatic Movements*, eds. Gary McGee, Stanley Burgess, and Patrick Alexander, 328. Grand Rapids, Michigan: Zondervan Publishing, 1988. Jones provides a biographical sketch of Gardner, an evangelist in the salvation-healing revival.

Jones, W. Cornish "Is Healing in the Atonement?" *Elim Evangel* (October 13, 1962): 646. This article, published in a British Pentecostal magazine, explores whether physical deliverance is actually included in the atonement.

Kane, Gregory. "Anointed Prayer Handkerchiefs—Are We Missing a Paradigm for Healing?" *Journal of the European Pentecostal Theological Association* 32:1 (2012): 75-86. This article explores the viability of handkerchiefs and prayer cloths for transmitting healing.

Katter, John. "Divine Healing Principles and Practical Suggestions." *Paraclete* 27:2 (Spring 1993): 24-29. Katter provides a scholarly essay on healing in a Pentecostal journal.

Kay, William. "Approaches to Healing in British Pentecostalism." *Journal of Pentecostal Theology* 14 (April 1999): 113-125. This is a helpful article on the approaches to healing within British Pentecostalism.

Keefauver, Larry. *When God Doesn't Heal Now: How To Walk By Faith Facing Pain, Suffering, And Death*. Nashville, Tennessee: Thomas Nelson Publishers, 2000. Keefauver wrote this book to encourage those who struggle with healing.

Kellet, Timothy M. "The American Evangelical Faith Healing Movement And The Emergence of Pentecostalism," D.Min., thesis, Wheaton College, December 2001. This is a historical analysis of the faith cure movement's influence upon Pentecostalism.

Kingston. C.E. "Laying On of Hands." *Elim Evangel.* (July 23, 1966): 473. Kingston, an English Pentecostal, examines the meaning of "laying on of hands."

Knight III, Henry H. "God's Faithfulness and God's Freedom: A Comparison of Contemporary Theologies of Healing." *Journal of Pentecostal Theology* 2 (April 1993): 65-89. This is an insightful article on the complexities and tensions of various healing methodologies.

Kydd, Ronald A. N. *Charismatic Gifts in the Early Church. An Exploration into the Gifts of the Spirit during the First Three Centuries of the Christian Church*. Peabody, Massachusetts: Hendrickson Publishers, 1984. Kydd carefully examines the outworking of the gifts of the Spirit in the Ante-Nicene Church.

Kydd, Ronald A. N. "Healing in the Christian Church," *The New International Dictionary of Pentecostal and Charismatic Movements*, eds. Stanley M. Burgess and Eduard M. Van Der Maas, 698-711. Grand

Rapids: Zondervan, 2002. This is an outstanding essay on the history of healing in Christianity.

Kydd, Ronald A. N. *Healing Through the Centuries*. Peabody, Massachusetts: Hendrickson Publishers, 1989. Kydd's research and analysis of healing practices in this work is outstanding.

Littlewood, David. *Maria Beulah Woodworth-Etter: The Life And Work of Evangelist Maria Woodworth-Etter*. Leicestershire, United Kingdom, 2009. This biographical account of Maria Woodworth-Etter was written by a Pentecostal from the United Kingdom.

Macchia, Frank D. "Waiting and Hurrying for The Healing of Creation: Implications in The Message of the Blumhardts for A Pentecostal Theology of Divine Healing," paper submitted at the annual meeting of the Society of Pentecostal Studies. Mattersley, Donacaster, England, July 10-14, 1995. This paper suggests that Johann Christoph Blumhardt and his son might shed light on modern Pentecostal-Charismatic praxis.

Madden, Peter J. *The Wigglesworth Standard: The Standard for God's End-time Army*. Springdale, Pennsylvania: Whitaker House, 1993. Madden's work explores Smith Wigglesworth's doctrine and practices. He seeks to apply it to modern-day believers.

Martin, Francis. "Gift of Healing." *The New International Dictionary of Pentecostal and Charismatic Movements*, eds. Stanley M. Burgess and Eduard M. Van Der Maas, 352. Grand Rapids: Zondervan, 2002. Martin provides a well-reasoned article on the gift of healing.

McGee, Gary B. "Elizabeth V. Baker." *Dictionary of Pentecostal Charismatic Movements*, eds. Gary McGee, Stanley Burgess, and Patrick Alexander, 37. Grand Rapids, Michigan: Zondervan Publishing, 1988. McGee composes an insightful character sketch of Elizabeth Baker. She was a Pentecostal healing proponent and matron of a faith healing home.

McGee, Gary B. *Miracles, Missions And American Pentecostalism*. Maryknoll, New York: Orbis, 2010. This work explores the history of missions in early Pentecostalism. McGee shows how healing and supernatural exploits propelled these works.

Menzies, Robert P. "A Pentecostal Perspective on 'Signs and Wonders'" *Pneuma* 17:2 (1995): 265-278. This article explores the distinctions between Third Wave adherents and Classical Pentecostals.

Menzies, Robert P. "Healing In The Atonement," in *Spirit and Power*, by Robert and William Menzies, 159-170, Grand Rapids: Zondervan, 2000. This excerpt, from a major Pentecostal work, wrestles with the foundations of healing in the atonement.

Menzies, William. *Anointed to Serve: The Story of the Assemblies of God.* Springfield, Missouri: Gospel Publishing House, 1971. Menzies' well-researched history of the Assemblies of God briefly examines the influence of healing on the movement.

Miskov, Jennifer Ann. "Carrie Judd Montgomery: A Passion for Healing and the Fullness of the Spirit." *Assemblies of God Heritage* 32 (2012): 5-13, 59. Miskov provides a well-researched article on the life and ministry of Carrie Judd Montgomery.

Miskov, Jennifer Ann. "Life on Wings: The Forgotten Life and Theology of Carrie Judd Montgomery (1858-1946)," Ph.D. diss., University of Birmingham, 2011. This insightful dissertation examines Carrie Judd Montgomery's life and thought.

Miskov, Jennifer Ann. *Life on Wings: The Forgotten Life and Theology of Carrie Judd Montgomery*. Cleveland, Tennessee: CPT Press, 2012. This work is an abbreviated form of Miskov's dissertation.

Nichols, David. *The Healing Presence of Jesus*. Minneapolis, Minnesota: Heart of the Father Ministries, 2001. This practical work, by an Assemblies of God educator and evangelist, reflects on the contemporary ministry of healing.

Onyinah, Opoku. "God's Grace, Healing And Suffering." *International Review of Mission* 95 (January 01, 2006): 117-127. This article on healing was written from an African missiological perspective.

Onyinah, Opoku. "Matthew Speaks To Ghanaian Healing Situations." *Journal of Pentecostal Theology* 10:1 (2001): 120-143. This article addresses synchronistic healing practices among Ghanaian Pentecostals.

Osman, Jack. "The Ministry of Healing in the Life of the Church," in *Pentecostal Doctrine*, ed. P.S. Brewster, 179-194. Gloucestershire, United Kingdom: Elim Pentecostal Church, 1976. Jack Osman, an official in the Elim Church, explores the biblical accounts of Jesus' healing ministry.

Petts, David M. "Healing and the Atonement" *EPTA Bulletin: The Journal of the European Pentecostal Theological Association* 12 (1993): 23-37. This theological essay considers whether healing is in the atonement.

Powell, Timothy. "Anointing With Oil." *Dictionary of Pentecostal Charismatic Movements*, ed. Gary McGee, Stanley Burgess, and Patrick Alexander, 11. Grand Rapids, Michigan: Zondervan Publishing, 1988. This article examines the history and theological scope of anointing with oil.

Pratt, Thomas D., "The Need to Dialogue: A Review of the Debate on the Controversy of Signs, Wonders, Miracles and Spiritual Warfare Raised in the Literature of the Third Wave Movement." *Pneuma* 13:1 (Spring 1991): 7–32. This article discusses controversies rooted in the emergence of the Third Wave movement. Pratt is not only apprehensive about modern healing methodologies, but also prayer walks and spiritual mapping.

Prosser, Peter E. *Dispensationalist Eschatology and Its Influence on American and British Religious Movements*. Lewiston, New York: The Edwin Mellen Press, 1999. This is an important work that identifies Dispensational influences within Pentecostalism. Prosser argues that this has muted the movement's focus on healing and other works of the Spirit.

Pugh, Ben. *Bold Faith: A Closer Look at the Five Key Ideas of Charismatic Christianity.* Eugene, Oregon: Wipf & Stock, 2017. Pugh, a Pentecostal scholar, examines inner healing, the Shepherding Movement, Word of Faith, spiritual warfare, expressions associated with Bethel Church and other contemporary Spirit-filled expressions.

Purdy, Vernon. "Divine Healing," in *Systematic Theology: A Pentecostal Perspective*, ed. Stanley Horton, 489–523. Springfield, Missouri: Logion Press, 1994. Purdy provides a theological overview of the doctrine of divine healing.

Purdy, Vernon. "Biblical Anthropology And The Pentecostal Doctrine of Divine Healing," paper submitted to the Society for Pentecostal Studies 18th annual meeting, November 10-12, 1988. This is a well-researched overview of the doctrine of divine healing from a capable scholar.

Reider, Robert A. "The Laying on of Hands in Acts." *Paraclete* 11:3 (Summer 1977): 22-26. Reider's essay examines the biblical scope of laying on of hands, focusing on the various accounts in the Book of Acts.

Reinhardt, Douglas. "With His Stripes We Are Healed: White Pentecostals And Faith Healing," in *Diversities of Gifts: Field Studies In Southern Religion*, eds. Ruel W. Tyson Jr., James Peacock, and Daniel Patterson, 126-142. Urbana, Illinois: University of Illinois Press, 1988. Reinhardt provides an academic analysis of faith healing practices within a subset of Pentecostalism.

Rice Jr., Frank B. "The Holy Spirit In Healing." *Paraclete* Journal 5:4. (Fall 1971): 18-21. This essay attempts to root divine healing within the trajectory of Classical Pentecostal pneumatology.

Robeck Jr., Cecil M., ed. *Charismatic Experiences in History.* Peabody, Massachusetts: Hendrickson Publishers, 1985. This short anthology from a group of Pentecostal scholars explores supernatural experiences within renewal groups throughout Church history.

Robeck Jr., Cecil M. "Finis Ewing Yoakum." *Dictionary of Pentecostal Charismatic Movements*, eds. Gary McGee, Stanley Burgess, and Patrick Alexander, 907-908. Grand Rapids, Michigan: Zondervan Publishing, 1988. In this article, Robeck reflects on the life and ministry of Finis Yoakum, a Pentecostal healer from California.

Robeck Jr, Cecil M. "Frank Weston Sandford." *Dictionary of Pentecostal Charismatic Movements*, eds. Gary McGee, Stanley Burgess, and Patrick Alexander, 766-767. Grand Rapids, Michigan: Zondervan Publishing, 1988. Robeck provides a brief biographical sketch of Frank Weston Sandford, a prominent radical holiness figure.

Robinson, James. *Divine Healing: The Formative Years, 1830-1890: Theological Roots in the Transatlantic World.* Eugene, Oregon: Pickwick Publications, 2011. This is an exceptional work on the beginnings of the transatlantic faith cure movement. It includes phenomenal research and analysis.

Robinson, James. *Divine Healing: The Holiness Pentecostal Transition Years, 1890-1906.* Eugene, Oregon: Pickwick Publications, 2013. Robinson continues his exceptional research, examining healing practices as they advance through the radical Holiness movement and early Pentecostalism.

Robinson, James. *Divine Healing: The Years of Expansion, 1906-1930 - Theological Variation in The Transatlantic World.* Eugene, Oregon: Pickwick Publications, 2014. This is the third and final book of Robinson's examination of divine healing practices in the nineteenth and twentieth centuries.

Shelton, James B. "A Reply to Keith Warrington's Response to 'Jesus and Healing: Yesterday and Today.'" *Journal of Pentecostal Theology*

16:2 (2008): 113-117. In this article, Shelton interacts with Keith Warrington, disagreeing that Jesus and the Apostles should be excluded from contemporary ministry models. This was one of many theological interchanges.

Shelton, James B. "'Not Like It Used To Be?' Jesus, Miracles and Today." *Journal of Pentecostal Theology* 14:2 (2006): 219-227. This article compares the experiences of modern Pentecostals and Charismatics with those from the gospels.

Shemeth, Scott. "Clifton O. Ericsson." *Dictionary of Pentecostal Charismatic Movements*. eds. Gary McGee, Stanley Burgess, and Patrick Alexander, 263. Grand Rapids, Michigan: Zondervan Publishing, 1988. This is a biographical sketch of Clifton Ericsson, an evangelist associated with the Voice of Healing in the 1950s.

Shemeth, Scott. "Franklin Hall." *Dictionary of Pentecostal Charismatic Movements*. eds. Gary McGee, Stanley Burgess, and Patrick Alexander, 345-346. Grand Rapids, Michigan: Zondervan Publishing, 1988. This is a biographical sketch of Franklin Hall, a controversial evangelist associated with the Voice of Healing in the 1950s.

Shemeth, Scott. "Walter Vinson Grant." *Dictionary of Pentecostal Charismatic Movements*, eds. Gary McGee, Stanley Burgess, and Patrick Alexander, 343. Grand Rapids, Michigan: Zondervan Publishing, 1988. This essay explores the life of W.V. Grant Sr., a Voice of Healing evangelist prominent in the 1950s.

Shuttleworth, Abigail D. "'On Earth as it is in Heaven:' A Critical Discussion of the Theology of Bill Johnson." *Journal of the European Pentecostal Theological Association* 35:2 (2015): 101-114. A Classical Pentecostal from Europe provides a critique of the theology and practice of Bill Johnson.

Simmons, Daniel J. "They Shall Recover: Towards a Pneumatological and Eschatological Understanding of the Atonement in Pentecostal

Healing." *Selected Honors Theses*, paper 20, Southeastern University, 2015. This study examines the "atonement model" of healing, assessing its strength in capturing the contemporary Pentecostal thought.

Smeeton, Donald Dean. "John Alexander Dowie: An Evaluation." *Paraclete Journal* 15:2. (Spring 1981): 27-31. Smeeton examines the life and ministry of John Alexander Dowie in this well-researched essay.

Smythe, Peter. *Christ Our Healer: An Exposition of Healing Within Redemption*, Peter Smythe, 2012. This reflection on healing theology was penned by a capable Pentecostal teacher. Smythe writes, "I noticed that the best Pentecostal books on healing were written more than fifty years ago, and were more or less a compilation of sermons. After reading them again, I thought I could flesh the doctrine out a bit and include scriptures that weren't necessarily used in the older books."

Stock, Jennifer. "George Montgomery: Businessman for the Gospel, part one." *Assemblies of God Heritage* 9:1 (Spring 1989): 4-5, 17-18. This is the first of a two-part essay on George Montgomery, a healing proponent and the husband of Carrie Judd Montgomery.

Stock, Jennifer. "George Montgomery: Businessman for the Gospel, Part Two." *Assemblies of God Heritage* 9:2 (Summer 1989): 12-14, 20. This is the second part of Stock's reflection on Montgomery.

Stormont, George: *Wigglesworth: A Man Who Walked With God: A Friend's Eyewitness Account. Tulsa, Oklahoma:* Harrison House, 1989. This biography of the notable Smith Wigglesworth was written by one of his personal friends.

Storms, Jeannette. "A Theology of Healing Based on the Writings of Carrie Judd Montgomery," M.A., thesis, Fuller Theological Seminary, 1996. In this thesis, Storms considers the implications of Montgomery's healing theology and praxis.

Susanto, Johanes Lilik. "A Practical Theological Evaluation of the Divine Healing Ministries of Smith Wigglesworth and John G. Lake: A Continuationist Reformed Perspective," Ph.D. diss., University of South Africa, 2007. This paper explores the extraordinary healing ministries of Smith Wigglesworth and John G. Lake.

Synan, Vinson. "Baptists Ride the Third Wave." *Charisma* (December 1986): 52. In this news article from the mid-1980s, Synan documents how John Wimber was impacting Southern Baptists through his biblical teaching and ministry practices.

Synan, Vinson. "A Healing in the House? A Historical Perspective on Healing in the Pentecostal-Charismatic Tradition." *Asian Journal of Pentecostal Studies* 3:2 (2000): 189-201. Synan provides an excellent reflection on healing in the Pentecostal tradition.

Synan, Vinson. *Aspects of Pentecostal-Charismatic Origins: Eleven Leading Scholars Examine the Roots and Early Growth of the Greatest Religious Movement of the Twentieth Century.* Plainfield, New Jersey: Bridge/Logos Publishers, 1975. This anthology of articles from diverse Spirit-filled leaders examines the origins of the Pentecostal-Charismatic movement.

Synan, Vinson. *The Century of the Holy Spirit: 100 Years of Pentecostal and Charismatic Renewal.* Nashville, Tennessee: Thomas Nelson, 2000. This expansive reference provides an overview of the history of Pentecostalism. Within its pages, one witnesses the significance of healing to the movement's history and formation.

Synan, Vinson. *The Holiness-Pentecostal Movement in the United States.* Grand Rapids, Michigan: Eerdmans Publishing Company, 1971. This is a well-researched study of the Holiness movement's influence upon Pentecostalism.

Synan, Vinson. "Pentecostal Healing: Models in Theology and Practice." *Pneuma* 29:2 (2007): 347-348. In this article, Synan considers some of the different models that are being espoused by contemporary Pentecostals.

Taylor, Malcolm. "A Historical Perspective on the Doctrine of Divine Healing." *Journal of European Pentecostal Theological Association* 14 (1995): 54-84. Taylor, A British Pentecostal, explores the history of divine healing within the scope of renewalist Christianity.

Tee, Alexander B. The Doctrine of Divine Healing. In *Pentecostal Doctrine*, ed. P.S. Brewster, 197-209. Gloucestershire, United Kingdom: Elim Pentecostal Church, 1976. Tee, a Scottish evangelist in the Elim movement, provides an overview of the doctrine of healing in this essay.

Tee, Alexander B. "Why are so many Christians not healed?" *Elim Evangel* (March 30,1963): 200. In this article, Tee explores why some are not healed after receiving prayer.

Theron, Jacques P.J. "Towards A Practical Theological Theory for the Healing Ministry in Pentecostal Churches." *Journal of Pentecostal Theology* 14 (April 1999): 49-64. This article explores healing practices in the local Pentecostal church.

Thomas, John Christopher. "Healing in the Atonement: A Johannine Perspective." *Journal of Pentecostal Theology* 14:1 (2005): 23-39. In this exegetical analysis of the gospel of John, Thomas contemplates what the Apostle John believed about healing in the atonement.

Thomas, John Christopher. "Health and Healing: A Pentecostal Contribution." *Ex Auditu* 21 (2005): 88-107. In this article, Thomas provides a serious analysis of modern healing practices in Christianity. He is not afraid to take on the difficulties.

Thomas, John Christopher. "Spiritual Conflict in Illness and Affliction," in *Deliver Us From Evil: An Uneasy Frontier in Christian Mission*, ed. A. Scott Moreau, Tokunboh Adeyemo, David G. Burnett, Bryant L. Myers, and Hwa Yung, 37-60. Monrovia, California: World Vision

Publications, 2002. In this essay, Thomas explores the physical implications demonic affliction and how spiritual concerns affect the well-being of people.

Thomas, John Christopher. *The Devil, Disease, and Deliverance: James 5:14-16*. Journal of Pentecostal Theology 2 (April 1993): 25-50. Thomas provides a well-researched examination of healing and deliverance in the New Testament.

Thomas, John Christopher. *The Devil, Disease, and Deliverance: Origins of Illness in New Testament Thought*. Sheffield, United Kingdom: Sheffield Academic Press, 1998. In this theological work, Thomas delves into the implications of healing and deliverance.

Thomas, John Christopher. "The Spirit, Healing, and Mission: A Survey of the Biblical Canon." *International Review of Mission* 93 (2004): 421-442. In this article, the ministry of healing is considered in the context of Christian mission.

Tomberlin, Daniel. *Pentecostal Sacraments: Encountering God at the Altar*. Cleveland, Tennessee: Pentecostal Theological Seminary, 2010. This book reformulates several Pentecostal practices as "sacraments." It considers healing as a heightened liturgical form.

Van De Walle, Bernie A. "Cautious Co-belligerence?: The Late Nineteenth-Century American Divine Healing Movement and the Promise of Medical Science," paper submitted to the 37th annual meeting of the Society for Pentecostal Studies, 2008. This work explores the radical roots of Pentecostalism, demonstrating the significance of divine healing.

Wacker, Grant. *Heaven Below: Early Pentecostals and American Culture*. Cambridge, Massachusetts: Harvard University Press, 2001. Wacker's outstanding research and analysis has been widely praised. This an exceptional work on early Pentecostalism.

Wacker, Grant, Chris R. Armstrong, and Jay S.F. Blossom. "John Alexander Dowie: Harbinger of Pentecostal Power," in *Portraits of a Generation: Early Pentecostal Leaders*, ed. James R. Goff and Grant Wacker, 3-20. Fayetteville, Arkansas: University of Arkansas Press, 2002. This is a well-researched essay reflecting on the controversial life and ministry of John Alexander Dowie.

Wacker, Grant. "Marching to Zion: Religion in A Modern Utopian Community." *Church History Magazine* 54 (Spring 1985): 495-511. In this excellent work, Wacker draws out many different components on John Alexander Dowie and his contentious ministry.

Wacker, Grant. "The Holy Spirit and the Spirit of the Age in American Protestantism, 1880-1910." *The Journal of American History* 72:1 (1985): 45-62. Wacker, with his keen eye, clarifies the motivations of radical holiness adherents and early Pentecostals.

Wacker, Grant. "Travail of A Broken Family: Evangelical Responses to Pentecostalism in America, 1906-1916." Journal of Ecclesiastical History 47 (July 1996): 505-528. In this article, Wacker considers holiness and Fundamentalist responses to Pentecostalism.

Wacker, Grant. "Wimber and Wonders: What about Miracles Today?" *Reformed Journal* 37 (April 1987): 16-22. Wacker, a notable researcher, explores the controversial "signs and wonders" ministry of John Wimber.

Waldvogel, Edith Lydia. *"The 'Overcoming Life:' A study of Reformed Evangelical Origins of Pentecostalism,"* Ph.D. diss., Harvard University, 1977. In this outstanding thesis, Waldvogel explores the Reformed foundations of Pentecostalism.

Ward, C.M. "Healing By The Holy Spirit." *Paraclete Journal* 2:2 (Spring 1968): 13-15. Ward, a popular Pentecostal radio personality, shares some of his reflections on the ministry of divine healing.

Warner, Wayne E. "Cyclone Evangelism: Maria Woodworth-Etter and The Early Pentecostal Revival," paper submitted to the Society for Pentecostal Studies, November 14, 1986. Warner, a former archivist for the Assemblies of God, has written an excellent narrative on Maria Woodworth-Etter.

Warner, Wayne E. "Faith Healing." *Encyclopedia of Evangelicalism,* ed. Randall Balmer, 424-426. Louisville: Westminster, John Knox Press, 2002. Warner, drawing upon a number of sources, provides an excellent overview of divine healing within broader Evangelicalism.

Warner, Wayne. "Mariah Beulah Woodworth-Etter." *Dictionary of Pentecostal Charismatic Movements,* ed. Gary McGee, Stanley Burgess, and Patrick Alexander, 900-901. Grand Rapids, Michigan: Zondervan Publishing, 1988. Warner provides an biographical sketch of healing evangelist Mariah Woodworth-Etter.

Warner, Wayne. *The Woman Evangelist: The Life and Times of Charismatic Evangelist Maria B. Woodworth-Etter.* Lanham, Maryland Scarecrow Press, 1986. This work is, arguably, the definitive biography of Mariah Woodworth Etter.

Warrington, Keith. "Acts and The Healing Narratives: Why?" *Journal of Pentecostal Theology* 14:2 (2006): 189-217. Warrington asks, why does Luke record healings performed by Peter and Paul? Also, why does he record the healings performed by Stephen, Philip and Ananias? Warrington believes that the answer is simple. The healings indicate that Jesus is present among the believers.

Warrington, Keith. "Anointing with Oil and Healing." *EPTA Bulletin: The Journal of the European Pentecostal Theological Association* 12 (1993): 5-22. In this article, Warrington considers the biblical implications of anointing with oil.

Warrington, Keith. "Gifts of Healing," in *Encyclopedia of Pentecostal and Charismatic Christianity,* ed. Stanley M. Burgess, 232-236. New York:

Routledge, 2006. This essay explores the biblical meaning of the gifts of healing.

Warrington, Keith. "Healing and Kenneth Hagin." *Asian Journal of Pentecostal Studies* 3:1 (2000): 119-138. In this article, Warrington provides a critique of the theology and praxis of Kenneth Hagin.

Warrington, Keith. *Healing and Suffering: Biblical and Pastoral Reflections.* United Kingdom: Paternoster Press, 2005. In this work, Warrington examines some of the difficult pastoral issues that intersect with the ministry of healing.

Warrington, Keith. *Jesus The Healer: Paradigm or Unique Phenomenon.* United Kingdom: Paternoster Press, 2000. In this treatise, Warrington asks whether Jesus' healings were a pattern for believers or simply unique occurrences. While arguing for the continuance of healing, Warrington is hesitant about Jesus being a model for contemporary believers.

Warrington, Keith. "Major Aspects of Healing Within British Pentecostalism." *Journal of the European Pentecostal Theological Association* 19 (1999): 34-55. In this article, Warrington explores the history of healing among Pentecostals in the United Kingdom.

Warrington, Keith. "Some Observations on James 5:13-18." *Journal of the European Pentecostal Theological Association* 8:4 (1989): 160-176. This article considers the exegetical implications of James 5:13-18.

Warrington, Keith. "The Role of Jesus as Presented in the Healing Praxis and Teaching of British Pentecostalism: A Re-Examination." *Pneuma: The Journal for The Society for Pentecostal Studies* 25:1 (2003): 66-92. Warrington provides further reflection on healing within the constructs of British Pentecostalism.

Warrington, Keith. "The Use of the Name of Jesus in Healing and Exorcism with Partial Reference to the Teachings of Kenneth Hagin." *EPTA Bulletin: The Journal of the European Pentecostal*

Theological Association 17 (1997): 16-36. Warrington evaluates the methodology of praying in Jesus' name, evaluating, in part, the modality of Kenneth Hagin.

Wilhelm, Jared. "Familiar Ground: Origins of Pentecostal Thought and Belief as seen in the Writings, Life and Ministry of Alexander Dowie," paper given at the 28th Annual Meeting of the Society for Pentecostal Studies, *Toward Healing Our Divisions: Reflecting on Pentecostal Diversity and Common Witness*, Springfield, Missouri, March 1999. Wilhelm's argues that John Alexander Dowie's theology and practice was highly influential in the formation of Pentecostalism.

Williams, Joseph W. *Spirit Cure: A History of Pentecostal Healing*. New York: Oxford University Press, 2013. Williams has written a serious analysis of changing healing methodologies within classical Pentecostalism. He discusses the fact that Pentecostalism is more comfortable with biomedical procedures than it was decades ago.

Williams, Joseph W. "The Transformation of Pentecostal Healing, 1906-2006." Florida State University, 2008. Williams' thesis, evaluating the changing nature of healing within Pentecostalism, is the basis of his subsequent work, *Spirit Cure*.

Wilson, Julian. *Wigglesworth the Complete Story: A New Biography of the Apostle of Faith, Smith Wigglesworth*. United Kingdom: Authentic Publishing, 2002. Wilson wrote an excellent biography on the life of Smith Wigglesworth.

Womack, David, ed. *Pentecostal Experience: The Writings of Donald Gee: Setting the Question of Doctrine Versus Experience*. Springfield, Missouri: Gospel Publishing House, 1994. This is a compilation of some of the writings of Donald Gee. His wisdom was valued throughout transatlantic Pentecostalism.

Wright, Gordon. "In Quest of Healing." *Journal of the European Pentecostal Theological Association* 4:1 (1985). Wright's article provides an insightful examination of the biblical foundations of healing.

Wright, Gordon. *In Quest of Healing*. Springfield, Missouri: Gospel Publishing House, 1984. Wright's work on divine healing was widely received in Assemblies of God circles.

Wright, James. "Profiles of Divine Healing: Third Wave Theology Compared with Classical Pentecostal Theology," *Asian Journal of Pentecostal Studies* 5:2 (2002): 271-287. Wright's article is a fascinating comparison of healing practices in the Third Wave and Classical Pentecostal churches.

Zinter, Paul. *A Time to Heal: The Biblical Ministry of Divine Healing*. Maitland, Florida: Xulon Publishing, 2013. This pragmatic healing work was written by a graduate of the Assemblies of God Theological Seminary in Springfield, Missouri.

12. ANGLICANISM

Allister, Donald S. *Sickness and Healing in the Church*. Oxford, England: Latimer House, 1981. Allister, an Anglican bishop, discusses the meaning of sickness and healing.

Aldridge, David. *One Body: A Healing Ministry in Your Church*. Society For Promoting Christian Knowledge, 1987. Aldridge wrote this work to assist in the development of healing ministries in local Anglican churches.

Archbishop's Council. A *Time to Heal: The Development of Good Practice in The Healing Ministry – A Handbook*. London: House of Bishops of the General Synod of the Church of England, 2000. When it was published, *A Time To Heal* was the first healing report from the Anglican Church in forty years. It was designed to be a resource for leaders and congregants throughout the Anglican communion.

Ash, Edwin Lancelot. *Faith and Suggestion: Including an Account of the Remarkable Experiences of Dorothy Kerin*. London: Herbert and Daniel, 1912. This book recounts some of the healing testimonies brought to bear through the prayers of Dorothy Kerin, an Anglican laywoman.

Atkinson, David. "The Christian Church and the Ministry of Healing." *Anvil* 10:1 (1993): 25-42. This article not only provides a historical sketch of the Church's interest in healing, but it also explores various contemporary approaches.

Banks, Ethel Tullock. "Come Unto Me." San Diego, California: Fellowship of St. Luke's, 1924. This pamphlet describes Ethel's healing from a serious illness. While in a worship service, she had a vision of the Lord beckoning her to receive communion. Afterward, she was immediately healed. After that, she had a dream where she was told how to use communion as a vehicle for healing. Banks guides the reader through an Episcopal communion service, showing how to use every part of it as a healing prayer.

Banks, Ethel Tullock. "The Great Physician Calling." San Diego, California: St. Luke's Press, Undated. This pamphlet was written to provide guidance for healing practices. Ethel and her husband John, were prominent healing proponents in the Episcopal Church.

Banks, John Gayner. *Healing Everywhere*. San Diego: St Luke's Press, 1953. In this book, Banks presents a series of messages that were given during the Order of Saint Luke's "Mission of Christian Healing."

Banks, John Gayner. *Healing Everywhere: A Book of Healing Mission Talks*. San Diego, California: St. Luke's, 1961. Banks, an Anglican rector, was active in the English Society of the Nazarene. He came to the United States after World War I to do an advanced study on the relationship between religion, psychology, and healing. While in the States, he started the Order of Saint Luke in San Diego, California, a healing organization in the Episcopal church.

Banks, John Gayner. *Manual of Christian Healing*, 14th edition. San Diego, California: St. Luke's, 1965. This publication was a practical, healing guidebook used by members of the Order of Saint Luke.

Banks, John Gayner. *The Gospel of Power*. San Diego, California: St. Luke's, 1946. In this notable work, Banks talks about the overwhelming power of the gospel to transform lives.

Banks, John Gayner. *The Redemption of the Body*. Mountain Lakes: Christian Healing Foundation, 1931. Banks affirms that the body of man was intended to be a sacrament. It is a vehicle of God's goodness and grace. Banks renounced the asceticism of the Desert Fathers and their lacerations on the body.

Banks, John Gayner. *Thy Saving Health: Daily Readings for a Year*. Mountain Lakes, New Jersey: The Christian Healing Foundation, undated. This book is a collection of readings for those who are seeking healing and personal growth.

Bates, J. Barrington. "Extremely Beautiful, but Eminently Unsatisfactory: Percy Dearmer and the Healing Rites of the Church, 1909–1928." *Anglican and Episcopal History* 73:2 (June 2004) 196–207. In this article, Bates examines Percy Dearmer's efforts to reclaim healing in the Anglican Church.

Bennett, George. *Commissioned to Heal and Other Helpful Essays.* Evesham, United Kingdom: Arthur James Ltd., 1979. This work includes some of Bennett's essays on listening, laying on of hands, prayer, and exorcism.

Bennett, George. *In His Healing Steps.* Evesham, United Kingdom: Arthur James Ltd., 1976. Bennett shares testimonies of people around the world who have experienced healing—relating their experiences to the gospels.

Botting, Michael. *Christian Healing in the Parish Grove Ministry And Worship.* Bramcote, United Kingdom: Grove Books, 1976. This pamphlet discusses the ministry of healing in local Anglican churches.

Brooke, Avery. *Healing in the Landscape of Prayer.* Boston: Crowley Publications, 1996. This is an account of Brooke's personal experience in parish healing ministry. It also includes practical advice and guidance.

Butlin, J. T. *A Handbook of Divine Healing.* London: Marshall Brothers LTD., 1924. In this work, Anglican rector J.T. Butlin shares some of his insights into the ministry of healing.

Carlozzi, Carl G. *The Biblical Message of Healing.* Church Publishing, 1992. Using a contemporary translation of the Bible, Carlozzi cites Biblical texts on healing, arranging them according to different pastoral concerns.

Clerical and Medical Committee. *Spiritual Healing, A Report of a Clerical and Medical Committee of Inquiry into Spiritual, Faith and Mental Healing.* London: Macmillan, 1914. This is an Anglican report on the viability of "spiritual" healing. This document was, in part, a response to Pentecostalism and the reemergence of liturgical healing.

Cowie, Ian. *Jesus' Healing Works and Ours.* Glascow, United Kingdom: Wild Goose Publications, 2000. Cowie re-translates the Gospels, shedding new light on the healing miracles of Jesus.

Cowie, Ian. *Prayers and Ideas for Healing Services.* Glasgow, United Kingdom: Wild Goose Publications, 1995. This book is a collection of healing prayers, liturgies, and ideas for healing expressions in the church.

C. G. S. "The Centenary of Faith Healing." *Churchman* 54:2 (January-March 1940): 146-152. This article, published in an Anglican journal, celebrated the one hundredth anniversary of Johann Christoph Blumhardt's ministry (1840-1940). The author asks what Blumhardt might mean for a modern audience.

Cunningham, Raymond J. "James Moore Hickson and Spiritual Healing in the American Episcopal Church." *Historical Magazine of the Protestant Episcopal Church* 39:1(1970): 2–16. This is an insightful article on the contributions of James Moore Hickson, an Anglican lay evangelist.

DeArteaga, William L. *Agnes Sandford and Her Companions: The Assault on Cessationism and the Coming of the Charismatic Renewal.* Eugene, Oregon: Wipf and Stock Publishers, 2015. This is the seminal biography of Agnes Sandford. Sandford not only introduced the ministry of inner healing, but also trained Francis MacNutt, a notable Catholic Charismatic.

DeArteaga, William L. "Making Healing Respectable: The Order of Saint Luke." *Sharing* (January 1992): 9–13. This essay explores the influence of the Order of Saint Luke.

DeArteaga, William L. "Pearcy Dearmer: A Priest for All Seasons." *Sharing* (June–July 1992): 22–26. This is an article on Pearcy Dearmer, a noted twentieth century Anglican healing figure.

Dearmer, Percy. *Body and Soul: An Inquiry into the Effect of Religion Upon Health, With A Description of Christian Works of Healing from The New Testament to the Present Day*. New York: E.P. Dutton, 1909. This is an overview of the healing ministry by an Anglican scholar. The best part of the book is the appendix with references to healing accounts in history.

Dearmer, Nan. *The Life of Percy Dearmer*. London: Book Club, 1941. This book is a biographical account of Percy Dearmer, an Anglican proponent of healing. His second wife wrote it.

Duncan, Denis. *Health and Healing: A Ministry to Wholeness*. Edinburgh, Scotland: St. Andrew Press, 1988. This is a book written by an Anglican minister who was deeply concerned for individuals with disabilities. It focuses on loving and providing general pastoral care for those with illness.

East, Reginald. *Heal The Sick*. London: Hodder & Stoughton, 1977. This practical work, composed by an Anglican rector, was written to encourage Christians to function in the ministry of healing.

Eavis, Sid. *A Healing Ministry - My Recollections of Canon Jim Glennon*. Ourimbah, SNW: Bookbound Publishing, 2007. This is a biography of Jim Glennon, emphasizing his teaching and healing ministry. Hundreds of healings were documented through his ministry. One was a dancer with the Royal Ballet who had dystonia, a neuromuscular disease that caused her to be curled up in a fetal position. Glennon prayed for her and doctors described her healing as "inexplicable!" Another account involved a man who was suffering amyotrophic lateral sclerosis. After Glennon's prayers and some physical therapy, the once crippled man went snow skiing. A doctor at the Cleveland Clinic declared, "It's as if he never had it."

Editor, "Hath Made Thee Whole." *Time 3:24* (June 16, 1924). This article from Time Magazine documents the healing ministry of Episcopalian Robert B. H. Bell. He regularly conducted a healing meeting at old St. Paul's Chapel on lower Broadway, Manhattan. Several attending the meeting claimed that they were cured. By their own testimony, the blind saw, the deaf heard, the dumb spoke, the maimed walked. A cross-eyed little girl threw away her glasses.

Endicott, Mike. *Christian Healing: Everyday Questions And Straightforward Answers*. United Kingdom: Terra Nova Publications, 2004, 2011. This work is an anthology of questions and answers on healing. An Anglican healing proponent and founder of the Well Center in South Wales wrote it.

Endicott, Mike. *Heaven's Dynamite: God's Amazing Power to Heal the Sick*. United Kingdom: Terra Nova Publications, 2003. In this practical work, Endicott shares the "dynamic biblical keys to healing."

Endicott, Mike. *Let Healing Flow, Lord*. United Kingdom: Terra Nova Publications, 2001. Endicott's autobiography recounts how he began to open his life to the ministry of healing.

Endicott, Mike. *Pilgrimage: Reflections On Healing From Bardsey Island*. United Kingdom: Terra Nova Publications, 2009. In this work, Endicott explores historical and practical foundations of the ministry of healing.

Endicott, Mike. *Rediscovering Kingdom Healing*. United Kingdom: Terra Nova Publications, 2006. Endicott, a gifted Anglican proponent, talks about healing as an aspect of the Kingdom of God.

Endicott, Mike. *The Passion To Heal*. United Kingdom: Terra Nova Publications, 2003. In this work, Endicott discusses the ethos of healing ministry.

Endicott, Mike. *The Principles of Kingdom Healing.* United Kingdom: Terra Nova Publications, undated. This booklet highlights Endicott's teaching on healing's relationship to the Kingdom of God.

Endicott, Mike. *Your Kingdom Come: A Pocketbook Of Guidelines For Biblical Kingdom Ministry.* United Kingdom: Terra Nova Publications, 2007, 2011. This booklet provides practical strategies for the ministry of healing.

England, Anne, ed. *We Believe in Healing.* Crowborough, East Sussex, United Kingdom: Highland Books, 1986. In this book, thirteen Anglican contributors recount their experiences of receiving and ministering healing.

Fitch, May Wayburn. *The Healing Delusion: Dealing With The Doctrine, The Methods Prevailing And The Claims Made In the Present-Day Healing Campaigns.* New York: Loizeaux Brothers, undated. This is a critical assessment of healing practice in the early twentieth century.

Frost, Evelyn. *What is Divine Healing? Talks on Christian Healing.* London: The Guild of Saint Raphael, 1947. This book explores the meaning and outworking of healing in the Anglican Communion.

Garlick, Phyllis L. *Health and Healing: A Christian Interpretation.* London: The Cargate Press, 1948. This work examines the Christian understanding of healing. Garlick examines historical and medical foundations as she establishes her thesis.

Garlick, Phyllis L. *Man's Search for Health: Study for Health: A Study in The Inter-relation of Religion and Medicine.* London: The Highway Press, 1952. This is an overview of medicine and its connections to religious practice.

Garlick, Phyllis L. *The Wholeness of Man: A Study in the History of Healing.* London: The Highway Press, 1943. This book is a remarkable examination of the history of medical and religious healing from an English researcher.

Garton, Nancy. *Christian Healing for Beginners*. London: James Clarke and Company, LTD, 1964. Garton, in this practical work, wants to encourage Anglican lay people to pray for the sick.

Gillies, Robert A. *A Way for Healing: Some Christian Foundations*. United Kingdom: The Hansel Press, 1995. Gillies, who came from a medical background, became an official in the Anglican Church. In this work, he writes at length about healing ministry in the local church.

Gillies, Robert A. *Healing Broader and Deeper*. United Kingdom: Handsel Press, 1998. This book combines pastoral experience and exegesis in an effective way. Gillies engagingly shares his discoveries, insights, and reflections.

Glennon, Jim. *How Can I Find Healing?* Plainfield, New Jersey: Bridge-Logos Publishers, 1987. In this practical book, Glennon's message is simple and direct. In order to get well, one must claim God's promises as revealed in the Bible, repent, believe, obey and, above all, forgive and forget. Glennon gives specific suggestions for those seeking healing and added a chapter to assist those working in the healing ministry.

Glennon, Jim. *Your Healing Is Within You*. Plainfield, New Jersey: Logos International, 1980. This book is a practical healing work from a Charismatic Anglican rector.

Gross, Don H. *The Case For Spiritual Healing*. New York: Thomas Nelson and Sons, 1958. Gross, an Episcopal minister, graduated from the Carnegie Institute of Technology and served as a physicist in the navy. Gross had encounters with unexplainable healings. After entering the ministry, he wanted to find out more. Citing history, theology, and medical case studies, Gross advances an argument for our churches to practice Christian healing. He writes, "the church needs repentance and will find anew the power to heal when it returns once more to Christ's command to heal the sick."

Gunstone, John. *A Touching Place: The Ministry of Healing in the Local Church*. Norwich, United Kingdom: Canterbury Press, 2005. This is a practical handbook for churches developing a healing ministry. It explores the biblical foundations of healing, breakthrough through the sacraments, creating prayer ministry teams, developing healing services, and a number of other topics.

Gunstone, John. *Healed, Restored, Forgiven: Liturgies, Prayers and Readings for the Ministry of Healing*, Norwich, United Kingdom: Canterbury Press, 2004. This book is a liturgical resource that can be used devotionally. It includes prayers, readings and liturgies for healing services.

Gunstone, John. *Healing Power: What It Is And What To Do With It*. Ann Arbor, Michigan: Vine Books, 1987. This work on the ministry of healing, not only builds on solid theological analysis, but also on pastoral sensitivity. Gunstone was impacted by the ministry of John Wimber and became an influential proponent of healing in England.

Gunstone, John. *Meeting John Wimber*. United Kingdom: Monarch Publications, 1996. This anthology of English Evangelicals recounts their encounters with John Wimber. Wimber was the leader of the Vineyard, an organization that focused on healing and signs and wonders.

Gunsone, John. *Prayers for Healing*. Guildford, United Kingdom: Highland Books, 1987. In this work, Gunstone, compiles a collection of prayers and liturgical elements for the purpose of healing and physical renewal.

Gunstone, John. *Signs and Wonders: The Wimber Phenomenon*. London: Darton, Longman and Todd, 1989. This book is an examination of the ministry of John Wimber, focusing on healing and signs and wonders.

Gunstone, John. *Take Heart: Healing Prayer for the Whole of Life*. Norwich, United Kingdom: Canterbury Press, 2011. This work is a compilation of healing prayers and reflections on holistic ministry.

Gusmer, Charles W. "Liturgical Traditions of Christian Illness: Rites of the Sick." *Worship* 46:9 (November 1972): 534. This is a well-researched article exploring the liturgical roots of healing.

Gusmer, Charles W. *The Ministry of Healing in the Church of England: An Ecumenical-Liturgical Study*. London: Society For Promoting Christian Knowledge, 1974. Gusmer's work on liturgical healing is noteworthy. This work is a guide for participants in the Anglican Church.

Harris, Charles Wilson. "Visitation of the Sick: Unction, Imposition Of the Hands And Exorcism," in *Liturgy And Worship*, eds. W. Lowther Clarke and C.H. Harris, 472-540. London: Society For Promoting Christian Knowledge, 1932. This article discusses the methodology of ministering to the sick in the Anglican tradition.

Henson, H. Hensley. *Notes On Spiritual Healing*. London: Williams and Norgate Publishing, 1925. Henson, the Bishop of Durham, talks about a number of different topics including: Lourdes, faith-Healing, James Moore Hickson, and John Maillard.

Hickson, James Moore. *Behold the Bridegroom Cometh: addresses given at the services of healing in Christ Church, Westminster 1931-1933*. London: Methuen, 1937. This is a collection of messages preached by James Moore Hickson, revealing some of his insights into healing. It was published posthumously.

Hickson, James Moore. *Christmas Roses, Etc.: A Collection of Testimonies on Faith-Healing*. London: The Healer Press, 1930. This is a compilation of healing testimonies culled from the ministry of James Moore Hickson.

Hickson, James Moore. *Heal The Sick*. New York: EP Dutton and Company, 1924. In this work, Hickson shares his insights on healing. Hickson, along with others, launched a healing resurgence within Anglicanism.

Hickson, James Moore. *Litany and Prayers For Healing*. London: The Women's Printing Society, undated. Hickson, in this anthology, provides healing prayers and liturgical expressions.

Hickson, James Moore. *The Healing of Christ in His Church*. New York: Edwin S. Gorham Publisher, 1919. This is an overview of healing from an Anglican proponent of healing.

Hickson, James Moore. *The Revival of the Gifts of Healing: Some of the Practical Difficulties Which Hinder the Revival of Spiritual Healing*. New York: Gorham, 1919. This healing work was published by Hickson during some of his healing missions in the United States.

Howard, James Keir. *Disease and Healing in the New Testament: An Analysis and Interpretation*. Lanham, Maryland: University Press of America, 2001. Howard, a physician and Anglican rector, provides insightful work on healing in the New Testament.

Howard, James Keir. "In the Eye of the Beholder: An Approach to the Healings of Jesus" *Journeyings* 4:2. (1991): 7-13. This article is an examination of healings in the ministry of Jesus.

Howard, James Keir. *"Is Healing Ever 'Miraculous?'" Stimulus: The New Zealand Journal of Christian Thought and Practice* 4:2 (1996): 7-13. In this article, Howard considers whether biblical healing is "miraculous" or not.

Howard, James Keir. "Medicine and the Bible." *The Oxford Companion to the Bible,* Bruce M. Metzger, and Michael David Coogan, 509-510. London: Oxford University Press, 1993. This essay explores the understanding and practice of "medicine" in the ancient biblical world

Howard, James Keir. *Medicine, Miracle, And Myth in The New Testament.* Eugene, Oregon: Resource Publications, 2010. This work interprets the New Testament data about illness. Howard suggests that Jesus acted as a prophetic folk healer in the tradition of the Old Testament prophets such as Elijah and Elisha.

Howard, James Keir. "Men as Trees, Walking: Mark 8.22-26." *Scottish Journal of Theology* 37:2 (May 1984): 163-170. Howard engages a Markan passage that interprets healing as a progressive work.

Howard, James Keir. *The Healing Myth: A Critique of the Modern Healing Movement.* Eugene, Oregon: Cascade Books, 2013. Howard, in this work, dismisses the claims of modern faith healing.

Howton, Richard. *Divine Healing and Demon Possession.* London: Ward, Lock and Limited, 1909. An Anglican rector and founder of Bethrapha, a home of rest and healing in central England, wrote this book. In this work, Howton discusses the ministry of healing and other works of the Spirit.

Israel, Martin. *Healing as Sacrament.* London: Darton, Longman and Todd, 1984. Israel, a medical practitioner and Anglican rector, explores the idea of healing as a sacrament.

Jones, A.W., ed. *Resources for Christian Healing Ministry.* London: The Churches Council for Health and Healing, 1996. This is a collection of resources for Christian leaders, enabling them to deal with sickness and disease. The book is more concerned with the therapeutic than the spiritual.

Large, John Ellis. *The Ministry of Healing.* London: Arthur James, 1959. Large was an Episcopal rector and proponent of spiritual healing in the New York area. This work provides some of his insights into this ministry.

Kammer, Donald. "The Perplexing Power of John Wimber's Power Encounters." *Churchman* 106:1 (1992): 45-64. Kammer provides a well-researched overview of John Wimber's signs and wonders ministry for an Anglican journal.

Kelsey, Morton T. "Faith: Its Function in the Holistic Healing Process," *Dimensions In Holistic Healing*, eds. Herbert A. Otto and James W. Knight, 213-225. Chicago: Nelson-Hall, 1979. In this article, Kelsey shares his firsthand insights into the way that faith impacts the ministry of healing.

Kelsey, Morton T. *Healing and Christianity in Ancient Thought and Modern Times*. New York: Harper and Row Publishers, 1973. Although needlessly influenced by Jungian psychology, Kelsey's thorough work on the history and theology of healing was groundbreaking.

Kelsey, Morton T. *Psychology, Medicine and Christian Healing*. San Francisco: Harper and Row Publishers, 1988. Kelsey's later work is a revision and expansion of *Healing and Christianity*.

Maddocks, Morris. *The Supernatural in Medicine*. London: C.M.F. Publications, 1971. Morris Maddocks, an English researcher, explores divine healing and its relationship with medical practice.

Maddocks, Morris. *The Christian Healing Ministry: A New Edition of the Classic Study of Christian Healing*. London: Society For Promoting Christian Knowledge, 1981, 1990. Maddocks pens a practical treatment on the subject of healing.

Maillard, John. *Healing Faith And Practice*. Devon, United Kingdom: Healing Life Press, 1950. Maillard was an influential Anglican minister who helped revive interest in healing. This book not only delves into the foundations of faith healing, but also talks about effective practices associated with it.

Maillard, John. *Healing In The Name of Jesus*. London: Hodder & Stoughton, 1936. This work is a theological and practical analysis of healing. Maillard rightly grounds the ministry of healing in the person of Jesus Christ.

Maillard, John. *The Sacrament Of Healing.* London: Morgan & Scott, 1925. This well-researched work examines the Anglican ministry of healing through the lens of sacramentalism.

Maillard, John. *The Healing Word: A Miscellany of Healing Addresses, Instructions, and Verses.* London: Healing Life Mission, 1957. This is an inspiring collection of sermons, teachings, and reflections on healing for the purpose of devotion.

Malia, Linda M. *Healing Touch And Saving Word: Sacraments of Healing, Instruments of Grace.* Portland, Oregon: Pickwick Publications, 2013. This book thoroughly explores sacramental healing in the Anglican tradition.

Mead, Harriet. "History of the International Order of St. Luke the Physician." *Sharing* (January 1984): 8–13. This is an essay exploring the history and scope of the Order of Saint Luke.

Melinsky, Michael Arthur Hugh. *Healing Miracles: An Examination From History and Experience of the Place of Miracle in Christian Thought and Medical Practice.* London: A. R. Mowbray, 1968. This work is an objective analysis of healing and supernatural phenomena. Melinsky reflects on the philosophy of religion, demonstrating how biblical and scientific criticism influences our understanding of miracles.

Mews, Stuart. "The Revival of Spiritual Healing in the Church of England 1920-1926." *The Church and Healing*, ed. W.J. Shiels, 299-331. Blackwell: Oxford Press, 1982. This essay is a historical analysis of a healing resurgence within Anglicanism in the 1920s.

Morris, George. *Our Lord's Permanent Healing Office: A Clergyman's Testimony.* London: Stock, 1887. George Morris, an Anglican vicar, declares his belief that the church should be actively involved with healing.

Mullin, Robert Bruce. "The Debate Over Religion and Healing in the Episcopal Church: 1870 – 1930." *Anglican And Episcopal History* 60

(June 1991): 213-234. This is a well-researched article examining the mounting debate about healing in Episcopal circles.

Neal, Emily Gardiner. *A Reporter Finds God Through Spiritual Healing*. Wilton, Connecticut: Morehouse-Barlow, 1956. Neal (1911-1989), a gifted journalist, set out to expose "false healing claims" from evangelists during the 1950s. However, instead of discovering fraud, she found genuine life-change. This is her account of what transpired and how she became a Christian.

Neal, Emily Gardiner. *God Can Heal You Now*. Englewood Cliffs, New Jersey: Prentice-Hall, 1958. After experiencing healing, Neal wrote several books on the ministry of healing. This one reiterates the viability of healing.

Neal, Emily Gardiner. *The Lord is Our Healer*. Englewood Cliffs, New Jersey: Prentice-Hall, 1961. In this pragmatic work, Neal answers some of her readers' questions about the ministry of healing.

Neal, Emily Gardiner. *The Healing Power of Christ*. New York: Hawthorn Books, 1972. In this work, Neal focuses on Jesus and the models he espoused. This is the last book on healing that Gardiner wrote.

Neal, Emily Gardiner. *Where's There's Smoke: The Mystery Of Christian Healing*. New York: Morehouse-Barlow, 1967. In this book, Neal recounts some of her personal experiences ministering healing.

Ostrander, Peter E. *New Testament Healing*. Maitland, Florida: Xulon Press, 2011. This book, written by a retired Anglican priest and prominent leader in the International Order of Saint Luke the Physician, explores theology and praxis.

Owen, Henry John. *The Prayer of Faith Viewed in Connection with the Healing of the Sick*. London: Published By James Nisbet, 1821. This sermon collection was compiled to reiterate the efficacy of healing.

Parke, John H. "The Reawakening: A Brief History of the OSL." *Sharing* (March 1989): 22–29. This article examines the history of the Order of Saint Luke, a healing organization rooted in the Anglican communion.

Parratt, J.K. "The Laying On Of Hands In The New Testament: A Reexamination In The Light Of Hebrew Terminology." *The Expository Times* 80, (1969): 210-214. Parratt's article explores the practice of laying on of hands.

Parsons, Stephen. *The Challenge of Christian Healing.* London: Society For The Promotion of Christian Knowledge, 1986. This practical work on healing was penned by an Anglican leader who was impacted by the Charismatic Renewal.

Patton, William W. *Prayer And Its Remarkable Answers: Being A Statement of Facts In Light Of Reason and Revelation.* Chicago: J.D. Goodman Publishers, 1876. This is a collection of stories and testimonies. It includes accounts of people being healed.

Pearson, Mark. *Christian Healing: A Practical and Comprehensive Guide.* Lake Mary, Florida: Charisma House, 1990, 2004. This book is a practical guide to the healing ministry from an Anglican Charismatic.

Peddie, John Cameron. *The Forgotten Talent: God's Ministry of Healing.* London: Oldbourne Book Company, 1961. Peddie was a gifted English minister who began praying for the sick in the 1940s. In this noted work, he not only shares his story, but also insights into the ministry of healing.

Percy, Martyn. "Christ the Healer: Modern Healing Movements and the Imperative for the Poor." Studies in World Christianity 1:2 (1995): 111-130. Percy, a liberal Anglican scholar, explores contemporary expressions of healing through a critical, sociological lens.

Percy, Martyn. "The Gospel Miracles and Modern Healing Movements." Theology 99:793 (January-February 1997): 8-17. In this article, Percy critiques modern healing movements, exploring the original meaning of healing accounts in the gospels.

Percy, Martyn. "Some Sociological and Theological Perspectives on Christian Charismatic Healing Ministries, with Special reference to the 'Toronto Blessing,'" in *Healing and Religion,* ed. Marion Bowman, 1-21. Enfield Lock: Hisarlik Press, 2000. This is a critical socio-theological article that explores the practice of healing among participants in the Toronto Blessing.

Percy, Martyn. *Words, Wonders and Power: Understanding Contemporary Christian Fundamentalism and Revivalism.* London: SPCK, 1996. This is a study of contemporary revivalism from an Anglican theologian and anthropologist. This work focuses on the ministry and writings of John Wimber.

Pett, Douglas Ellory. *The Healing Tradition of the New Testament.* Cambridge, United Kingdom: Lutterworth Press, 2015. Pett, an Anglican chaplain, redefines Jesus's healings. He identifies them with psychotherapy.

Porter, Harry Boone. "Laying Hands on the Sick: Ancient Rite and Prayer Book Formula." *Anglican Theological Review* 36:2 (1954): 83-89. This well-researched article explores laying on of hands and other ancient liturgical practices.

Portsmouth, William. *Healing Prayer With Daily Prayers For A Month.* Eveshame, Worcs, United Kingdom: Arthur James Limited, 1954, 1963. This is an Anglican prayer book that focuses on healing prayer and petition.

Price, Alfred. *Ambassadors of God's Healing, and, An Adventure in the Church's Ministry of Healing.* Irvington, New Jersey: St. Luke's, 1945. Price was a prominent leader in the Order of Saint Luke. In this work, he shares practical insights into healing.

Pridie, James Robert. *The Churches Ministry of Healing.* London: Society For Promoting Christian Knowledge, 1926. This is a general overview of the ministry of healing from an Anglican churchman.

Pytches, David. *Come Holy Spirit: Learning How To Minister in Power.* London: Hodder and Stoughton, 1985. In this practical handbook, Anglican Rector David Pytches offers guidelines for learning to minister in the power of the Spirit. He argues that signs and wonders are a routine part of the biblical ministry.

Pytches, David. *Fully Anglican, Fully Renewed, Riding the Third Wave.* Basingstoke, United Kingdom: Marshall Pickering, 1987. In this work, Pytches describes his experiences in the burgeoning signs and wonders movement in Europe.

Pytches, David. *Healing Ministry Training: Equipping Saints for the Work of the Ministry.* Chorleywood, United Kingdom: New Wine Resources Limited, 1999. This is a practical guidebook for ministering healing.

Pytches, David. "Signs And Wonders Today." *International Review of Mission* 75:298 (April 1986): 137-142. Pytches shares some of what he learned about signs and wonders in the context of evangelism.

Richards, John. *Exorcism, Deliverance and Healing: Some Pastoral Guidelines.* Nottingham: Grove Books, 1976. This book is a practical guide for leaders to provide spiritual breakthrough in the local church.

Richards, John. "The Church's Healing Ministry And Charismatic Renewal," in *Strange Gifts? A Guide to Charismatic Renewal,* ed. David Martin and Peter Mullen, 151-158. Oxford, United Kingdom: Basil Blackwell Publisher, 1984. This is an article on healing in history, written from the point of view of an Anglican churchman.

Richards, John. *The Question of Healing Services.* London: Darton, Longman and Todd, 1989. Richard's book explores the viability of holding healing services in the local church. Richards effectively engages this subject and provides insights about practical ministry.

Smail, Tom A. *The Quest for a Theology of Healing.* London: Churches Council for Health and Healing, 1993. Smail, an Anglican scholar, explores the contours of healing theologies in the Church.

Taylor, Harold. *Sent to Heal: A Handbook On Christian Healing.* Roseville, Minnesota: Speedwell Press, 2007. This is a valuable guide to the ministry of healing from a prominent member of the Order of St. Luke.

Various. *A Handbook for Clergy of the Order of St. Luke The Physician.* San Antonio, Texas: The International Order of St. Luke the Physician, 1997. This is a practical guidebook for mainline ministers to more effectively function in the ministry of healing.

Various. *Going Deeper: Learning Resources for Nurturing Your Christian Healing Ministry, Year One.* San Antonio, Texas: The International Order of St. Luke The Physician, April 2003. This is a collection of articles from members of the Order of St. Luke, an Episcopal healing organization.

Various. *Going Deeper: Learning Resources for Nurturing Your Christian Healing Ministry, Year Two.* San Antonio, Texas: The International Order of St. Luke The Physician, 2003. This is another anthology of teaching articles for the members of the Order of St. Luke.

Various. *Spiritual Healing, A Report of a Clerical and Medical Committee of Inquiry into Spiritual, Faith and Mental Healing.* London: Macmillan, 1914. This report, from an Anglican committee, evaluates the efficacy of twentieth century healing ministries.

Various. *The Church's Ministry of Healing: The Report of the Archbishops' Commission of the Church of England.* London: The Church Information Office, 1958. This is an official statement on the ministry of healing in the Anglican Church. In many ways, this is a response to the salvation-healing revival (1946-1958).

Vogel, Arthur A. *God, Prayer, And Healing: Living with God in A World Like Ours.* Grand Rapids, Michigan: Eerdmans, 1995. A retired Episcopal bishop reflects on the nature of God as he wrestles with his son's cancer.

Waylen, Hector. *An Apostle of Healing: Studies in The Life and Work of Pastor Howton.* London: Stockwell, 1928. This is a biographical account of an early twentieth century Anglican healing proponent.

Webster, George. *Divine Healing by Faith: The Teaching of Reverend J. F. B. Tinling, B. A. Reviewed.* United Kingdom: J. Snow and Company, undated. Webster, an Anglican leader who is conservative in outlook, dismisses the values of faith healing.

Winckley, Edward. *Healing Missions Around the World.* San Diego, California: St. Luke's Press, 1959. Winckley, associated with the Order of Saint Luke, shares the ways the ministry of healing is taking root around the world.

Winckley, Edward. *The Practice of Healing Evangelism.* San Diego, California: St. Luke's Press, 1963. Winckley shares how to conduct evangelistic healing missions, pray for the sick, follow-up on people, and more.

Wilson, Henry Blauvelt. *Does Christ Still Heal? An Examination of the Christian View of Sickness and a Presentation of the Permanency of the Divine Commission to Heal.* New York: E.P. Dutton and Company, 1917. Wilson was strongly impacted by James Moore Hickson and the "Society of Emmanuel." After moving to the United States, Wilson went on to start the Society of the Nazarene, a forerunner to the Order of St. Luke. The society's purpose was "to deepen spiritual life and to impart strength and health to body and soul by prayer, laying on of hands, or anointing." In this influential book, Wilson explores the viability of healing.

Wilson, Henry Blauvelt. *Ghosts Or Gospels: The Methods Of Spiritualism In Healing Compared With The Methods Of Christ.* Booton, New Jersey: The Nazarene Press, 1922. In this unusual work, Wilson critiques spiritualism, séances, and other practices that were emerging in the early twentieth century.

Wilson, Henry Blauvelt. *God's Will For The World: A Refutation of the Popular Interpretation Of The Phrase 'Thy Will Be Done.'* New York: E. P. Dutton and Company Publishers, 1923. In Wilson's final work, he discusses methodology of prayer. He was opposed to the notion that one should always pray, "Thy will be done." He did not believe that sickness was God's will.

Wilson, Henry Blauvelt. *The A.B.C.s of Divine Health.* New York: Alliance Press Company, 1908. This book is an overview of divine healing, written to encourage others to see its viability.

Wilson, Henry Blauvelt. *The Power to Heal: A Handbook for the Practice of Healing According to the Methods of Jesus.* Ashville, North Carolina: Nazarene Press, 1923. This is a practical guide for members of the Society of the Nazarene, an early healing order organized by American Episcopalians. It provides practical strategies for ministry.

Wilson, Henry Blauvelt. *The Revival of the Gift of Healing: Including Suitable Prayers and an Office for The Anointing of the Sick.* London: A.R. Mowbray and Company, 1914. This is a reflection on liturgical rites and healing prayer.

Watson, David. *Jehovah Rapha: God Who Heals.* United Kingdom: Gilead Books, 2010. This is a collection of healing lectures from a popular Anglican rector. Watson provides an overview of the theology and practice of healing. These lectures were presented shortly before his own passing.

Watt, James. *What's Wrong with Christian Healing?* London: Latimer Trend and Company, 1993. This collection of articles, from officials from the Church of England, explores the subject of healing.

Wetherill, Francis M. *Healing in The Churches.* New York: Fleming H. Revell, 1925. Wetherill, an Episcopal rector, makes observations about the biblical foundations of healing.

Wolmer, John. *Healing and Deliverance*. London: Hodder and Stoughton, 1999. Wolmer examines the biblical foundations of healing and deliverance. He explores areas of concern such as church history, theology, and praxis.

Wyman, Frank Leonard. *Divine Healing and Healing Through Christ*. London: Bannisdale Press, 1953. Wyman, an Anglican priest from York in the United Kingdom convincingly presents how in his parish Jesus confirmed the message of the gospel with signs following.

13. FUNDAMENTALIST-EVANGELICAL

Allison Jr., Dale C. "Healing In The Wings Of His Garment: The Synoptics And Malachi 4:2," in *Word Leaps The Gap: Essays On Scripture and Theology In Honor of Richard B. Hayes*, ed. J. Ross Wagner, C. Kavin Rowe, and A. Katherine Grieb, 132-146. Grand Rapids, Michigan: Eerdmans, 2008. This essay explores the background and meaning of the afflicted woman touching Jesus' garment in the gospel accounts.

Althouse, LaVonne. "A Study Of The Introduction Of Healing Ministry Into A Congregation." Eastern Baptist Theological Seminary, 1981. In this work, an evangelical seminary student investigates the integration of healing ministries in a non-Pentecostal settings.

Althouse, Lawrence W. *Rediscovering the Gift of Healing*. Nashville, Tennessee: Abingdon Press, 1977. Althouse, a sympathetic Methodist pastor, provides an overview of the gift of healing.

Armerding, Carl. "'Is Any Among You Afflicted' A Study of James 5:13-20." *Bibliotheca Sacra* 95 *(*April-June 1938): 195-201. This is an exegetical article on James 5:13-20 that explores the meaning and scope of the passage. The cessationist bias of *Bibliotheca Sacra* is evident throughout the work.

Armstrong, Chris, general ed. "Healthcare and Hospitals in the Mission of the Church." *Christian History Magazine* 101. Worcester, Pennsylvania, 2011. This informative issue of the *Christian History* magazine was devoted to examining hospitals and health care in the early church. Although ignoring divine healing, it includes articles that are useful for the study of the church's response to disease.

Ascough, Richard. "Illness and Health." *Eerdmans Dictionary of the Bible*. Grand Rapids, Michigan: Eerdmans Publishing, 2000. This is a well-researched article examining illness and health in the Bible.

Bacon, Leonard Woolsey. "The Faith Cure Delusion." *Forum* 5 (March 1888): 691-698. Like many other articles that were published during this period, Bacon's article fiercely denounces the evangelical faith cure movement.

Bales, James D. *Miracles Or Mirages?* Austin, Texas: Firm Foundation Publishing House, 1956. Bales, a Harding College professor, wrote a biting critique of twentieth century healing ministries. This work was composed during the height of the salvation-healing revivals.

Bauermeister, Paul. "Healing, Mission, and the Ministry of the Church." *Currents in Theology and Mission* 13:4 (August 1986): 205-213. Bauermeister, an Evangelical Lutheran, explores the complexities of healing and missions.

Baxter, J. Sidlow. *Divine Healing of the Body.* Grand Rapids, Michigan: Zondervan Publishing, 1979. Baxter, a beloved mid-twentieth century itinerate minister, provided a robust reflection on the biblical dimensions of healing.

Bennett, George. "Errors of The Faith-Healers." *Methodist Review* 87 (November 21, 1905): 935-942. Bennett, a prominent Methodist, wrote a searing critique of early twentieth century healing practices.

Biederwolf, William Edward. *Whipping-Post Theology or Did Jesus Atone for Disease.* Grand Rapids, Michigan: William B. Eerdmans Company, 1934. Biederwolf, a conservative Evangelical, counteracts the teachings of Aimee Semple McPherson, F.F. Bosworth, and other Pentecostal healing evangelists.

Bingham, Rowland Victor. *The Bible and the Body, or Healing in the Scriptures.* London: Marshall, Morgan and Scott, 1921, 1924, 1934. In this work, Bingham criticizes the doctrine of healing in the atonement.

Bingham, Rowland Victor. "The Bosworth Campaign in Toronto." *The Evangelical Christian,* July 1921, 199-200, 218. This article discusses one of F.F. Bosworth's healing campaigns in Canada. Bingham reports that many were either converted or filled with the Holy Spirit, but relatively few were healed during the month-long campaign. He exploits this to critique Bosworth's belief that healing is "in the atonement."

Blackburn, B. L. "Miracles and Miracle Stories" in *Dictionary of Jesus and the Gospels*, ed. Joel B. Green, Scot McKnight, I. Howard Marshall, 529-560. Downers Gove, Illinois: Intervarsity Press, 1992. This essay, by an Evangelical scholar, examines the background and meaning of miracles in the Gospels.

Blomberg, Craig L. "Healing," in *Dictionary of Jesus and the Gospels*, eds. Joel B. Green, Scot McKnight, I. Howard Marshall, 299-307. Downers Grove: Illinois: Intervarsity Press, 1992. Blomberg examines the topic of healing in the gospels.

Bombay, Carl R. *Sin, Sickness and God.* Nairobi, Kenya: Evangel Publishing House, undated. This pamphlet, composed by an Evangelical missionary, explores what the Bible has to say about healing.

Boggs Jr., Walter H. "Bible and Modern Religions: Faith Healing Cults." *Interpretation* 11 (January 1957): 55-70. This is extended critique of mid twentieth century faith healing and its proponents.

Bosch-Heij, Deborah Van Den. *Spirit and Healing in Africa: A Reformed Pneumatological Perspective.* Bloemfontein: Sun Media, 2012. This is an insightful book about healing and the work of the Holy Spirit in Africa.

Bourgeois, Sarah L. "Mark 8:22-26: Jesus and the Use of Spittle in A Two-Stage Healing," Th.M., thesis, Dallas Theological Seminary, 1999. This is a well-researched textual analysis of the usage of spit in Jesus' healing ministry.

Boyd, Jeffrey H. "Biblical Theology of Chronic Illness: Why do sick people cling to the Bible?," paper presented at the 54th ETS Annual Meeting, Toronto, November 20, 2002. In this paper, a conservative

Evangelical skeptically examines what the Bible has to say about sickness and disease. This is a follow up to a previous paper.

Boyd, Jeffrey H. "Theology of Chronic Illness," paper presented at the 53rd Annual Meeting of the Evangelical Theological Society. Colorado Springs Colorado, November 16, 2001. In this research paper, Boyd is rather dismissive of the ministry of healing.

Brand, Paul and Phillip Yancey. "A Surgeon's View of Divine Healing." *Christianity Today* 27:18 (November 25, 1983): 14-21. This is an article on divine healing from an Evangelical doctor and journalist.

Bridge, Donald. *Signs and Wonders Today*. Leicester, United Kingdom: Intervarsity Press, 1985. This book, by a European Evangelical, examines the meaning and application of signs and wonders.

Brown, Colin. *Miracles and the Critical Mind*. Grand Rapids, Michigan: William B. Eerdmans Publishing Company, 1984. This book is an analysis of the conception of miracles in the Western mind.

Brown, Colin. *That You May Believe: Miracles and Faith Then and Now*. Grand Rapids, Michigan: Eerdmans Publishing, 1985. Brown's thorough research on miracles is noteworthy.

Bryan, W.S. Plumer. *Prayer and The Healing of Disease*. Chicago: Fleming H. Revell Publishing, 1896. Bryan reflects on the healing of Hezekiah and other biblical paradigms of healing.

Buckley, James Monroe. *An Address On Supposed Miracles Delivered Monday, September 20, 1875, before the New York Minister's Meeting of the Methodist Episcopal Church*. New York: Hurd and Loughton, 1875. Buckley was a prominent Methodist magazine editor in the late nineteenth century. In this work, he recounts his insistence that miracles no longer define the work of the church.

Buckley, James Monroe. "Faith Healing and Kindred Phenomena." *The Century Magazine* 33 (March 1887): 781-787. This is a highly critical article from Buckley that dismisses faith healing and other supernatural practices. This article was later expanded into a book.

Buckley, James Monroe. *Faith Healing, Christian Science and Kindred Phenomena.* New York: The Century Company, 1892. This work is a negative treatment of healing. In it, he associates the faith cure movement with Christian Science.

Budgen, Victor. *The Charismatics and the Word of God: A Biblical and Historical Perspective on the* Charismatic Movement. United Kingdom: Evangelical Press, 1989. This work, written from a Cessationist point of view, is an assessment of Pentecostalism and contemporary Spiritual gifts.

Caneday, Ardel B. "The Significance and Relationship of the Laying on of Hands and the Bestowal of Spiritual Gifts," M.Div. thesis, Grace Theological Seminary, 1976. This thesis is an examination of the meaning of laying on of hands in the Bible.

Chandler, Marjorie Lee. "Fuller Seminary Cancels Course on Signs and Wonders,' *Christianity Today,* (February 1986): 48-49. This news article explores the controversies of John Wimber's "Signs and Wonders" course at Fuller Theological Seminary.

Carson, D. A. *How Long, O Lord? Reflections On Suffering and Evil.* Grand Rapids: Baker, 1990, 2006. This book is a terse examination of biblical themes related to human suffering and evil. It was written by a prominent American Calvinist who sees God's hand at work in much of this.

Carter, Pat Harold. "An Evangelical Critique of the Use of the Bible in Divine Healing by Representative Protestant Groups," Ph.D., diss., Southwestern Baptist Theological Seminary, 1960. This dissertation systematically denounces the exegetical work of divine healing proponents.

Chamberlain, F. Bruce. "A Christian Teaching Concerning Bodily Healing," Ph.D., diss., Western Evangelical Seminary, 1958. Chamberlain, an Evangelical researcher, reflects on the ministry of healing.

Chantry, Walter J. *Signs of the Apostles: Observations on Pentecostalism Old and New*, 2nd ed. (Edinburgh: Banner of Truth, 1976). Chantry, a Reformed pastor, explores what the Bible has to say about apostles and the miraculous. He comes to the conclusion that the apostolic ministry of healing and the other works of the Spirit are no longer in operation.

Cheung, Vincent. *Biblical Healing*. Boston: Vincent Cheung, 2003, 2012. Cheung is a hyper-Calvinist and analytical thinker. Some find fault with his theology and tone. Yet, like any work, value can be gained.

Clapp, Rodney. "Faith Healing: A Look at What's Happening." *Christianity Today* (December 16, 1983): 12-17. This is a cautious, but open, article on the ministry of faith healing.

Clymer, Meredith. "Creed, Craft, and Cure." *Forum* 5 (April 1888): 192-206. This biting article is a critical analysis of the faith cure movement. A conservative Protestant wrote it.

Cobb, E. Howard. *Christ Healing: The Case for Divine Healing does Not depend upon the Evidence of Medically Certified Cures, but Upon the Sure and Certain Promises of God*. London: Marshall, Morgan & Scott, 1952. This book is a conservative defense of healing based on a careful reading of Scripture.

Coggins, James Robert. *Wonders and the Word: An Examination of the Issues Raised by John Wimber and the Vineyard Movement*. Hillsboro, Kansas: Kindred Press, 1989. This book is a critical assessment of John Wimber and the Vineyard Movement by a conservative Evangelical.

Cotter, Wendy J. *The Christ of the Miracle Stories: Portrait Through Encounter*. Grand Rapids, Michigan: Baker Academic, 2010. Cotter provides a fascinating analysis of the healing and miracle stories of Jesus in this well-researched book.

Cunningham, Scott. "The Healing of the Deaf and Dumb Man (Mark 7:31-37), with Application to The African Context." *African Journal of Evangelical Theology* 9 (1990): 13-26. In this article, an African Evangelical author finds ways of rooting the healing story of Mark 7:31-37 to an African context.

Culpepper, R. Alan, "Mark 10:50: Why Mention the Garment?" *Journal of Biblical Literature*, 1982. Culpepper, a Southern Baptist theologian, considers what the garment in the story of the healing of blind Bartimaeus means.

Dailey, Timothy J. *Healing Through the Power of Prayer: What The Bible Says About Healing.* Lincolnwood, Illinois: Publications International, 1998. Dailey provides a useful overview of the ministry of healing, citing several other studies.

De Haan, M. R. *Divine Healing and Divine Healers: A Scriptural Examination of the Modern Healing Movement.* Grand Rapids, Michigan: M. R. De Haan publisher, undated. This booklet, published in the 1970s, is an anthology of De Haan's radio broadcasts criticizing healing evangelists.

Derickson, Gary W. "The Cessation of the Charismata of Healing Ministries in Paul's Ministry." *Bibliotheca Sacra* 155 (July-September 1998): 299-315. This Dallas Theological Seminary article suggests that Paul's healing ministry diminished with time.

Diale, Frank N. *The Divine Antidote to Sin, Sickness, And Death,* revised edition. New York: Christian Work, 1921. Frank Diale was an advocate of healing in the Presbyterian church. His book provides an overview of the Bible's teaching on healing.

Dickinson, Robert. *God Does Heal Today: Pastoral Principles and Practice of Faith-Healing.* Carlisle, United Kingdom: Paternoster Press, 1995.

This is a study of faith healing practices from a conservative evangelical.

Dixon, Larry Edward. "The Pneumatology of John Nelson Darby (1800-1882)," Ph.D., diss., Drew University, 1985. Dixon explores Darby's understanding of Holy Spirit. Notable is his appendix: "The Church's 'Jewels;' Have They Been Found Again? A Comparative Study of Miraculous Gifts in the Writings of John Calvin, John Wesley, Edward Irving, and John Nelson Darby."

Dollar, Harold Ellis. "A Cross Cultural Theology of Healing," Ph.D., diss., Fuller Theological Seminary, 1981. In this work, Dollar explores the theology and scope of healing.

Downing, Raymond. *Death and Life in America: Biblical Healing and Bio-Medicine*. Scottsdale, Pennsylvania: Herald Press, 2008. This book is a theological and medical critique of Western biomedicine written by a Mennonite medical missionary.

Doyle, Robert, ed. *Signs and Wonders and Evangelicals: A Response to the Teaching of John Wimber*. Randburg, Australia: Fabel Distributors, 1987. This is a collection of articles written by Australian Evangelicals who are in opposition to John Wimber and his practice of "power evangelism."

Dunn, Ron. *Will God Heal Me: God's Power and Purpose in Suffering*. Colorado Springs, Colorado: David C Cook, 2007. This work examines the meaning of sickness from a conservative Evangelical perspective. It positions itself to be a corrective of the Pentecostal-Charismatic approach to healing.

Edgar, Thomas, R. *Miraculous Gifts: Are They for Today?* Neptune, New Jersey: Loizeaux, 1983. In this theological work, Thomas, an avowed cessationist, explores a number of biblical texts related to healing and the gifts of the Spirit. He comes to the conclusion that the miraculous is no longer in operation.

Edgar, Thomas R. *Satisfied by the Promise of the Spirit: Affirming the Fullness of God's Provision for Spiritual Blessing.* Grand Rapids, Michigan: Kregel Publishing, 1996. This work is a cessationist polemic against modern signs and wonders. It was written in response to Jack Deere's *Surprised by the Power of the Holy Spirit.*

Editor, "SBC President Addresses Charismatics," *Baptist Standard* (January 1, 1975): 11. In this article, there is a discussion about the Charismatic Renewal and how it is influencing Baptist Churches.

Edmunds, Vincent and C. Gordon Scorer. *Some Thoughts On Faith Healing.* London: Tyndale Press, 1979. In this work, from members of the Christian Medical Fellowship, healing is explored. Their assessment is that faith healing, as practiced by Pentecostals and Charismatics, is not an appropriate approach to alleviating sickness.

Entzminger, Louis. *The Modern 'Divine Healing' Racket: Are Bible Miracles to be Performed by the People of God Today?* Houston, Texas: Louis Entzminger Publisher, 1938. Entzminger's work is a fierce critique of the ministry of divine healing.

Evans, Craig A. "Jesus and Jewish Miracle Stories" in *Jesus and His Contemporaries: Comparative Studies,* ed. Craig Evans, 213-243. Leiden, United Kingdom: Brill, 1995. Evans points out that Jesus' miracles are similar to those attributed to the rabbis. However, they are different. Jesus doesn't pray for healing. He simply speaks a word or touches the sufferer.

Farris, William T. *How Healed Do You Want to Be? Finding Hope and Wholeness in A Sharp-Edged World.* Boise, Idaho: Ampelon Publishing, 2009. This is a practical book on healing that provides a lot of value.

Fee, Gordon D. *The Disease of the Health and Wealth Gospels.* Costa Mesa, California: The Word for Today, 1979. In this work, prominent Evangelical theologian, Gordon Fee, brings his measured critique of the Word of Faith movement.

Fisk, Samuel. *Divine Healing Under the Searchlight*. Schaumburg, Illinois: Regular Baptist Press, 1978. This hastily written book is an unsympathetic critique of the ministry of healing from a Baptist author.

Flory, J. S. *Mind Mysteries Phenomena, "Spiritism," "Christian Science," And Faith Healing: Gospel Healing A Bible Standpoint Completely Vindicated*. Mount Morris, Illinois: Published by Elder J.S. Flory, 1897. This is a denouncement of the faith cure movement and its expressions of healing; associating it with Christian Science and the other heterodox movements.

Frank, Derek. *Tough Questions about Healing*. Guildford, United Kingdom: Highland, 1993. Frank, an Evangelical author from the United Kingdom delves into some difficult questions about healing.

Frazier, Claude, compiler. *Faith Healing: Finger of God? Or, Scientific Curiosity*. Nashville: Thomas Nelson Publishing, 1973. Frazier has brought together a series of articles on healing practices.

Frost, Henry. *Miraculous Healing: Why Does God Heal Some and Not Others?* Scotland, United Kingdom: Christian Focus Publications, 1931, 2008. This is a Reformed missionary's moderating analysis of healing. Frost suggests that God grants healing to some through prayer, but to others, restoration takes place through rest or medical means.

Gaebelein, Arno Clemens. "Anointing With Oil." *Our Hope* (February 1925): 471-472. Gaebelein was a prominent Methodist leader and avowed Dispensationalist. He stood opposed to healing and other works of the Spirit. In this essay, he dismisses the practice of anointing with oil for healing.

Gaebelein, Arno Clemens. "Divine Healing." *Our Hope* (March 1925): 548-553. In this theological article, Gaebelein dismisses contemporary divine healing. He believes that it is unscriptural and unsound.

Gaebelein, Arno Clemens. "Faith Cure." *Our Hope* (August 1922): 75-76. Gaebelein, as already noted, wrote at length to undermine the practice of divine healing. This article is a denouncement of the faith cure healing approach.

Gaebelein, Arno Clemens. "Faith Healers Everywhere." *Our Hope* (December 1922): 354-355. In this article, Gaebelein complains about the abundance of healing ministries in Holiness and Pentecostal circles. He desires to lessen their influence.

Gaebelein, Arno Clemens. "The Healing Craze in A New Form." *Our Hope* (September 1923): 167-168. In this article, Gaebelein critiques the practices that were emerging in the divine healing movements.

Gaebelein, Arno Clemens. *The Healing Question: An examination of the claims of Faith-Healing and Divine Healing Systems in the light of the Scriptures and History*. New York: Our Hope, 1925. In this work, Gaebelein attempts to undermine early twentieth century healing practices.

Gaiser, Frederick J. *Healing in the Bible: Theological Insight for Christian Ministry*. Grand Rapids, Michigan: Baker Academic, 2010. Gaiser, a conservative Evangelical, provides an outstanding academic analysis of key healing scriptures.

Gaiser, Frederick J. "Healing in the Bible: A Grateful Response." *Journal of Pentecostal Theology* 21:1. (2012): 41-63. In this article, Gaiser interacts with Pentecostal scholars who were engaging his scholarship.

Gaiser, Frederick J. "The Emergence of Self in The Old Testament: A Study of Biblical Wellness." *Horizons in Biblical Theology* 14:1 (1992): 1-29. Gaiser provides a study of "self" and the meaning of wellness from the Bible.

Gaiser, Frederick J., "'Your Faith Has Made You Well:' Healing and Salvation in Luke 17:12-19," *Word and World* 16:3 (1996): 291-301.

Gaiser explores the relationship between healing and salvation in a key Lucan passage.

Garland, David E. "I Am the Lord Your Healer: Mark 1.21-2.12," *Review and Expositor* 85:2 (1988): 327-343. Garland explores the meaning of the numerous healing accounts referenced in Mark 1:21-2:12.

Geivett, R. Douglas R. and Gary R. Habermas. *In Defense of Miracles: A Comprehensive Case for God's Action in History.* Downer's Grove, Illinois: Intervarsity Press, 1997. This work advocates for the validity of miracles in scripture and history.

Gibb, David. "Look Back in Wonder? Reviewing the Power Evangelism of John Wimber." *Vox Evangelica* 26 (1996): 23-43. This article, from a European Evangelical, criticizes John Wimber and his "supernatural" approach to ministry.

Gillespie, Charles George Knox. *The Sanitary Code of the Pentateuch.* Chicago: Fleming H. Revell Company, 1894. This book is an in-depth study of the disease and the health codes in the first five books the Old Testament.

Goldingay, John. "Theology and Healing." *Churchman* 92 (1978): 23-33. In this article, noted Evangelical theologian, John Goldingay, explores the implications of healing in the Bible.

Go, Peter Kwang-Seog. "Healing Ministry in Kingdom Perspective," Ph.D., diss., Fuller Theological Seminary, Pasadena, California, 1993. This work examines the Third Wave perspective on the ministry of healing.

Gonzalez, Eliezer. "Healing in The Pauline Epistles: Why The Silence?" *Journal of Evangelical Theology Society* 56:3 (2013): 557–575. Gonzalez explores why the Apostle Paul is depicted as a prodigious worker of miracles in Acts, but not in the Epistles.

Goodwin, E. P. *Supernatural Healing*. Chicago: Advance Publishing, 1889. Goodwin, a Congregational minister from Chicago, provides his critique of orthodox and heretical healing movements.

Gordon, S.D. *Quiet Talks About the Healing Christ*. New York: Fleming H. Revell Publishing, 1924. Gordon was a popular speaker and author in the early twentieth century. In this collection, he talks about Jesus and His role in healing.

Gowan, Donald E. "Salvation as Healing." *Ex Auditu* 5 (1989): 1-19. This pastoral article argues that Christianity is for individuals who are sick and have ill health.

Gower, Christopher. *Speaking of Healing*. London: Society For Promoting Christian Knowledge, 2003. This book explores the different ways one might examine the stories of healing from the Bible—literal, liberal, metaphorical, spiritual, and social commentary. The author recommends a synthesis of all models.

Graham, Billy. *The Holy Spirit: Activating God's Power in Your Life*. Nashville: Thomas Nelson, 2011. In this pneumatological work, Bill Graham, the most recognized Evangelical in the world, shares his insights into healing.

Grayston, Kenneth. "Healing Services." *The Expository Times* 111:12 (2000): 415-417. This article, by a Methodist scholar, is a skeptical analysis of healing services conducted at church.

Griffith, R. Marie. *Born Again Bodies: Flesh and Spirit in American Christianity*. Berkley, California: University of California Press, 2004. This work examines the understanding of embodiment and physicality within American Christianity.

Grindheim, Sigurd. "Everything is possible for one who believes: Faith and Healing in the New Testament." *Trinity Journal* 26.1 (2005): 11-17. This is a fascinating article on healing in the New Testament from a prominent Evangelical journal.

Hacking, Keith J. *Signs and Wonders, Then and Now: Miracle-Working, Commissioning and Discipleship*. Nottingham, United Kingdom: Apollos, 2006. With the Third Wave's expansion into Anglicanism, Hacking examines the biblical foundations of signs and wonders. He argues that while signs and wonders are not commonplace, the church must remain open to God's sovereign activity. It "may on occasion extend to the validation of individuals and their ministries through signs and wonders."

Haldeman, I. C. *Did Our Lord Jesus Christ by His Death Atone for Bodily Sickness?* New York: I.C. Haldeman, undated. This pamphlet explores whether healing is available through the atoning work of Christ.

Hanegraaff, Hank. *Christianity in Crisis*. Eugene, Oregon: Harvest House, 1993. In this work, Hanegraaff renounces modern Christian movements and their deviation from orthodox theology. He is particularly hard on Kenneth Hagin and the Word of Faith Movement.

Harper, Michael. *The Healings of Jesus*. Downers Grove, Illinois: Intervarsity Press, 1986. This work is a sound Evangelical treatise. Harper's discussions of the Kingdom of God, a biblical view of health, as well as the healings of Jesus, are insightful.

Hedstram, C.B. *Religious Racketeering: Are Days of Miracles Over? Is There Healing in the Atonement?* Louisville, Kentucky: Reverend A.D. Muse Publisher, 1938. This dismissive early twentieth century work considers whether healing is in the atonement.

Heiser, Michael S. *The Unseen Realm: Recovering The Supernatural Worldview of the Bible*. Bellingham, Washington: Lexham Press, 2015. This is a fascinating book that enables modern readers to understand the worldview of the ancients by seriously engaging Scripture.

Hiebert, Paul G. "Healing and the Kingdom," in *Anthropological Reflections on Missiological Issues*. Grand Rapids, Michigan: Baker, 1994, 217-253.

Hiebert, a Christian apologist, examines global trends and data from cultures around the world. Among other things, he discusses the role of healing.

Hiebert, Paul G. "The Flaw of the Excluded Middle" *Missiology: An International Review* 10:1. (January 1982): 35-47. This article, from a Fuller Seminary Professor, explores the Western worldview. Hiebert talks about how we envision the world and how it affects our openness to the supernatural. This article was extremely influential in the Third Wave Movement.

Hobbs, A.G. "Have Miracles Ceased?" Fort Worth, Texas, undated. This booklet was written by a conservative evangelical criticizing the healing revival of the 1940s and 1950s.

Hollinger, Dennis. "Enjoying God Forever: An Historical/Sociological Profile Of The Health And Wealth Gospel." *Trinity Journal* 9:2 (Fall 1988), 145-148. In this article, Hollinger provides an overview of the Word of Faith Movement.

Horton, Michael. *Power Religion: The Selling Out of the Evangelical Church?* Chicago: Moody Press, 1992. This is an Evangelical critique of the purported focus on "power" in the emerging Third Wave movement. The book includes three chapters that are specifically dismissive of John Wimber and the signs and wonders movement.

Hoyt, Francis S. "Anointing The Sick for Healing." *Western Christian Advocate*. (October 25, 1882). This is the first of two editorials on anointing the sick for healing.

Hoyt, Francis S. "Anointing The Sick for Healing." *Western Christian Advocate* (November 8, 1882). This is the second editorial on the ministry of healing from Hoyt. These articles provide a window into responses that outsiders were bringing to the faith cure movement.

Huggett, John. *Healing in the Balance*. Eastbourne: United Kingdom: Kingsway, 1989. Huggett's emphasis in this work is on what the

Bible teaches about healing. He backs up his teaching with examples from his own ministry.

Hui, Edwin "Healing," in *The Complete Book of Everyday Christianity*, ed. Robert Banks and R. Paul Stevens, 478-481. Downer's Grove, Illinois: Intervarsity Press, 1997. This is an introduction to healing by a professor of medical ethics and spiritual theology. Sections include: "Healing as Curing and Caring," "Biblical Perspectives on Healing," "Healing Through Medicine," "Faith and Healing," "Miraculous Healing," and "Healing and Redemption."

Igenoza, Andrew Olu. "Medicine and Healing in African Christianity: A Biblical Critique." *African Ecclesial Review* 30 (1988): 12-25. Igenoza, an African Evangelical, explores sickness and healing in African Christianity.

Ising, Dieter. *Johann Christoph Blumhardt Life and Work: A New Biography*, tr. Monty Leford. Eugene, Oregon: Cascade Books, 2009. This is an important biography of one of the leaders of the nineteenth century faith-cure movement in Europe.

Jessel, Susie and Mary Jessel Sanderson. *Healing Hands: The Story of Susie Jessel as Told to Her Daughter, Mary Jessel Sanderson*. Ashland, Oregon: The Print Shop, undated. Jessel, a Baptist layperson, had a widely-recognized healing ministry. People from various denominations would visit her home in Ashland, Oregon in the late 1960s and 1970s.

Johnston, Phillip S. "Life, Disease and Death." *Dictionary of the Old Testament: Pentateuch*, ed. T. Desmond Alexander and David W. Baker, 535. Downers Grove, Illinois: Intervarsity Press, 2003. This is a well-researched article on the topic of health and disease in the first five books of the Old Testament.

Jones, Martyn Wendell. "Kingdom Come In California?," *Christianity Today* (May 2016): 30-37. Jones, the Presbyterian grandson of

Evangelical Martyn Lloyd-Jones, wrote a detailed reflection on Bethel Church in Redding, California.

Kallas, James. *The Significance of the Synoptic Miracles: Taking The Worldview of Jesus Seriously.* London: Society For Promoting Christian Knowledge, 1961. This book was written as a protest against Rudolf Bultmann and the demythologizing of the Bible. Kallas argued that one cannot remove miracles from Scripture without changing the meaning of the text.

Keener, Craig S. "A Reassessment of Hume's Case Against Miracles in Light of Testimony from the Majority World Today." *Perspectives in Religious Studies* 38:3 (Fall 2011): 289-310. Keener argues that numerous modern healing claims refute Hume's assertion that contemporary miracles are not viable.

Keener, Craig S. *Miracles: The Credibility of the New Testament Accounts*, 2 Volumes. Grand Rapids, Michigan: Baker Academic, 2011. This seminal two-volume work explores the philosophical, historical, and theological implications of miracles.

Keener, Craig S. "Cultural Comparisons for Healing and Exorcism Narratives in Matthew's Gospel: Original Research." HTS: *Theological Studies* 66:1 (2010): 1-7. In this article, Keener draws from interviews with people claiming first-hand experiences of healing and exorcism in the Republic of Congo. He suggests that these experiences invite a more sympathetic reading of healings and exorcisms in the Bible.

Keener, Craig S. "He Still Heals: Radical Testimonies of the Holy Spirit's Healing Power Today." *Charisma and Christian Life* 36 (August 1, 2010): 52–55. Keener, one of the most prominent New Testament scholars in America, reflects on contemporary healing.

Kinghorn, Kenneth. "Gifts of Healing," Gifts of the Spirit (Abingdon, 1976), 67-72. Kinghorn, a Church history professor, lists different ways God heals. God heals instantly and directly. God heals gradually through the processes of nature. God heals through medical science. God gives the grace to suffer redemptively by healing our attitudes. God heals in the resurrection.

Kwan, Simon S. "Clinical Efficacy of Ritual Healing and Pastoral Ministry." *Pastoral Psychology* 55:6 (2007): 741-749. Ritual healing is discussed in this article as a "phenomenon of association" between religion and healing.

Lalleman, Peter J. "Healing by a Mere Touch as a Christian Concept," *Tyndale Bulletin* 48:2 (1998): 355-362. In this academic article, Lalleman argues that healing by touch is exclusively a Christian approach. He responds to the criticism that it has Greek origins.

Lambert, J.C. *"Gifts of Healing." International* Standard Bible Encyclopedia, ed. Orr, James, John Nuelsen, Edgar Mullins, Morris Evans, and Melvin Grove Kyle, 1349-1350. Grand Rapids: Eerdmans Publishing, 1915. This is an academic article that explores the topic of the gifts of healings in the Bible.

Lambourne, R. A. *Community, Church, and Healing: A Study of Some of the Corporate Aspects of the Church's Ministry to The Sick*. London: Darton, Longman and Todd, 1963. Lambourne examines some practical approaches to healing.

Lance, Douglas G. *Holiness-Pentecostal Evangelists Maria Woodworth-Etter and John G. Lake and Their Teaching on Healing in the Atonement*, paper, Western Conservative Baptist Seminary, 1991. This is an insightful paper exploring the methodologies of two prominent Pentecostal healing evangelists.

Lawrence, Roy. *Invitation to Healing*. East Sussex, United Kingdom: Kingsway Publications, 1979. Lawrence, an insightful British Evangelical, wrote this polemic on healing.

Lawrence, Roy. *The Practice of Christian Healing: A Guide for Beginners.* Downers Grove, Illinois: Intervarsity Press, 1996. Lawrence produced an introductory guide to the healing ministry.

Lewis, David C. *Healing: Fiction, Fantasy or Fact?* London: Hodder and Stoughton, 1989. Questionnaires from two thousand participants at John Wimber's November 1985 Harrogate Conference confirmed a number of healings. Lewis concludes that genuine healing does occur, but less often than claimed.

Lewis, David C. "John Wimber and the British Church: How Different Churches and Church Leaders Have Reacted to John Wimber's Teaching," *Renewal* (August 1989): 6-10. Lewis, a noted researcher, reflects on the signs and wonders ministry of John Wimber.

Lalleman, Pieter J. "Healing by A Mere Touch as A Christian Concept." *Tyndale Bulletin* 4:2 (1997): 355-362. This insightful article by Lalleman examines the notion of divine healing through the process of touch.

Lloyd-Jones, D. Martyn. *Healing and the Scriptures.* Nashville, Tennessee: Thomas Nelson Publishers, 1988. This book is a fascinating work written by a conservative Evangelical leader. In the second chapter, Lloyd-Jones wrote about "Supernatural Medicine."

Lucas, Ernest, ed. *Christian Healing: What Can We Believe?* London: Lynx, 1997. This anthology, from a variety of European evangelicals, discusses the intersection of Christianity and health.

MaCalister, Alex. "Heal." *International Standard Bible Encyclopedia*, revised edition, ed. Geoffrey W. Bromiley, 1349. Grand Rapids, Michigan: Eerdmans Publishing, 1995. This is an insightful article on the biblical scope of healing.

MacArthur, John. *Charismatic Chaos.* Grand Rapids, Michigan: Zondervan Publishing, 1992. This is a biased assessment of the

Pentecostal-Charismatic Movement. MacArthur emphasizes the anomalies and mistakes.

MacArthur, John. *Strange Fire: The Danger of Offending the Holy Spirit with Counterfeit Worship*. Grand Rapids, Michigan: Zondervan Publishing, 2013. MacArthur, in this work, provides a stern critique of the Pentecostal-Charismatic movement.

Marr, George Simpson. *Christianity and the Cure of Disease*. London: H.R. Allenson Publisher, 1931. Drawing on an overview of Jesus' ministry, Marr argues that ministering to the sick should be a part of the normal function of the pastoral clergy.

Marta, Judith A. *The Born Again Jesus of Word-Faith Teaching*. Fullerton, California: Spirit of Truth Ministry, 1987. In this work, Marta critiques E. W. Kenton, Kenneth Hagin, and the Word of Faith Movement.

Martin, Bernard. *The Healing Ministry In the Church*. London: Lutterworth Press, 1960. Martin was the pastor of the Reformed Church in Geneva Switzerland. Along with pastoral ministry he also worked at a psychiatric clinic and led a monthly healing service.

Martin, B. N. "Faith Cures." *The Congregationalist* 47:1 (August 30, 1882): 1. Martin's critique of faith cure adherents was published in the *Congregationalist* magazine in the North East.

Marty, Martin E. and Kenneth L. Vaux, eds. *Health/Medicine and The Faith Traditions*. Philadelphia, Pennsylvania Fortress Press, 1982. This work examines healing in a variety of Christian traditions. While hesitant about the faith healing tradition, it provides a number of valuable insights. There are two insightful sections from Gary B. Ferngren and Darrel W. Amundsen: "Medicine and Religion: Pre-Christian Antiquity," 55-92. "Medicine and Religion: Early Christianity Through the Middle Ages," 93-131.

Masters, Peter. *The Healing Epidemic*. London: The Wakeman Trust, 1988. Masters, a British Evangelical, analyzes modern healing practices. Among other things, he traces the origin of Third Wave healing modalities.

Mayhue, Richard L. "Cessationism, 'The Gifts of Healings,' And Divine Healing." *The Masters Seminary Journal* 14:2 (Fall 2003): 263-286. Mayhue, an avowed cessationist, says that divine healing should not be anticipated. Instead, Christians "hould focus on the spiritual rather than the physical.

Mayhue, Richard L. *Divine Healing Today*. Chicago, Illinois: Moody Press, 1983. Making an exegetical case, Mayhue asserts that healing and the works of the Spirit are not a viable part of Christian ministry.

Mayhue, Richard L. "Does God Still Heal Today?" *Moody Monthly* (March 1989): 38, 40, 42 - 43. Mayhue acknowledges God can bring healing, but argues that it should not be expected to be the norm.

Mayhue, Richard L. "For What Did Christ Atone in Isaiah 53:4-5?" *Didaskalia* 3 (1991): 26-35. Analyzing Isaiah 53:4-5, Mayhue contends that healing is not in the atonement.

Mayhue, Richard L. "Is Healing in the Atonement?" *Moody Monthly* (April 1989): 36ff. In this essay, Mayhue continues to argue that healing is not included in the atonement.

Mayhue, Richard L. *The Biblical Pattern for Divine Healing*. The Woodlands, Texas: Kress Christian Publications, 2008. This work summarizes Mayhue's views. While he rejects contemporary healing, he provides useful charts and analysis in this booklet.

Mayhue, Richard L. *The Healing Promise: Is It Always God's Will to Heal?* Eugene, Oregon: Harvest House Publishers, 1994. Continuing to assert his cessationist perspective, Mayhue takes a critical look at the promises of healing in the New Testament.

McAlister, R.E. *God's Sovereignty in Healing.* Toronto, Canada: Full Gospel Publishing House, undated. McAlister's 1920s era tract presented a moderate stance on divine healing. It acknowledged physical deliverance, but placed it within the matrix of God's sovereignty.

McClenton, Rhonda J. *Spirits of the Lesser Gods: A Critical Examination of Reiki and Christ-Centered Healing.* Bacon Raton, Florida: Rhonda McClenton, 2005. McClenton contrasts Evangelical healing practices with new age modalities.

McClenton, Rhonda J. *Reiki and Christ-Based Healing: Differences and Dangers.* Bala Cynwyd, Pennsylvania: Ichthus Press, 2011. McClenton discusses the history of reiki, comparing it to sound biblical practices.

McConnell, D.R. *A Different Gospel: A Biblical Look at the Word of Faith Movement.* Peabody, Massachusetts: Hendrickson Publishers, 1988, 1995. This is a critical work that associates E. W. Kenyon and those that he has influenced with Christian Science and heretical ideals.

McKinney, Bethany Ann. "Disability, Healing, and Jesus: Perspectives and Practices from The Gospels," Ph.D., diss., Fuller Theological Seminary, 2014. In this work, McKinney explores disability and healing in the gospels.

McMillen, S. I. *None of These Diseases.* Westwood, New Jersey: Revell Publishing, 1953. McMillen, a graduate of University of Pennsylvania Medical School and the London School of Tropical Medicine, was a medical missionary in Africa before he established a medical practice in New York. In this work, he talks about faith, food, and health.

Meesaenig, Lee Choi, "Healing," *Encyclopedia of Christianity In the United States*, volume 3, eds. George Thomas Kurian and Mark A. Lamport (Lanham, Maryland: Rowman & Littlefield, 2016), 1062-1070. This superbly sourced article explores the history of healing in Christianity.

Miller, Duane. *Out of the Silence: A Personal Testimony of God's Healing Power.* Nashville: Thomas Nelson, 1996. Duane Miller was a Baptist minister whose voice was miraculously during a Sunday school class. This is the account of his story.

Miller, Waymon D. *Modern Divine Healing.* Rosemead, California: Old Path Book Club, 1956. Miller, in this dismissive work, argues against the viability of healing. Among other things, he denounces the work of the Voice of Healing evangelists.

Mitchell, John G. "Does God Heal Today," *Bibliotheca Sacra* 122:485 (January 1965): 41-53. Mitchell, in an article from Dallas Theological Seminary's official journal, discusses the viability of divine healing.

Montgomery, John Warwick, ed. D*emon Possession: A Medical, Historical, Anthropological and Theological Symposium.* Minneapolis, Minnesota: Bethany Fellowship, 1976. In this work, Montgomery provides an analysis of demonic activity from the perspective of doctors, psychiatrists, historians, anthropologists, and theologians. One of the questions that he explores is how demons can influence health.

Moo, Douglas. "Divine Healing in the Health and Wealth Gospel." *Trinity Journal* 9:2 (1988): 191-209. Moo, a noted Evangelical scholar, examines the theology and practice of the Word of Faith Movement.

Mooney, Sharon Fish. "Touch: Trouble with Angels." *Christian Research Journal* 28:2 (2005): 22-31. This article delves into the problems of Therapeutic Touch, Reiki, and other new age healing modalities.

Mooney, Sharon Fish. "Therapeutic Touch: Healing Science or Psychic Midwife?" *Christian Research Journal* 18:1 (1995): 28-38. In this essay, Mooney examines New Age healing modalities.

Neff, David. "Wimber's Wonders." *Christianity Today* 42:2 (February 9, 1998): 15. Neff, a conservative evangelical, writes a eulogy of John Wimber, the leader of the Third Wave movement.

Nicholas, Tim. "Baptist Charismatics Emerging From the Closets." *Baptist Standard* (July 21, 1975): 4. This article explores the influence of the Charismatic Renewal in the Baptist Church.

Ogilvie, Lloyd John, *Jesus the Healer* (Old Tappan, New Jersey: Power Books, 1985), 19–20. Ogilvie, the former pastor of First Presbyterian Church of Hollywood, California (1972-1995) and Chaplain of the United States Senate, Washington D.C. (1995-2003), wrote a biblical reflection on the doctrine of healing. In addition to reflecting on scripture, Ogilvie shares some interesting testimonies.

Onunwa, Udobara. "The Biblical Basis for Some Healing Methods in African Traditional Society." *East African Journal of Evangelical Theology* 7 (1988): 56-63. This article, from an African Evangelical, explores the intersection of biblical healing with African practices.

Onwu, Nlenanya. "'Don't Mention it:' Jesus' Instruction to Healed Persons." *African Journal of Biblical Studies* 1:1 (1986): 35-47. This article, from an African Evangelical, explores what Jesus said to individuals who were healed.

Packer, J. I. "Poor Health May Be the Best Remedy." *Christianity Today* (May 21, 1982): 14-26. Evangelical theologian, J.I. Packer, drawing from a Reformed ethos, argues that sickness and disease may be beneficial.

Patterson, Ben. "Cause for Concern" *Christianity Today* (August 8, 1986): 20. This article evaluates the ministry of John Wimber and Charismatic leaders who advocate for healing.

Pherigo, Lindsey. *The Great Physician: Healing Stories in Luke and Their Meaning Today*. Nashville, Tennessee: Abingdon Press, 1991. This is an analysis of the healing stories in the Gospel of Luke. It considers how these biblical paradigms should be applied to believers today.

Phillips, Ron. *An Essential Guide to The Gift of Healing.* Lake Mary, Florida: Charisma House, 2012. A prominent Baptist pastor from Tennessee wrote this healing work. Phillips provides some practical strategies for increased effectiveness.

Pierson, Arthur Tappan. "The Growth of Belief in Divine Healing," in *Forward Movements of the Last Half Century*, 389-408. New York: Funk & Wagnalls, 1900. Pierson, a notable early twentieth century Evangelical, examines the ministry of healing. He embraces a moderate position.

Pierson, Arthur Tappan. "What About Divine Healing? Have Supernatural Signs Ceased?" *King's Business* (March 1921): 231. In this article, A.T. Pierson, affirms a confidence in the continuing reality of healing.

Pink, Arthur Walkington. *Divine Healing: Is it Scriptural?* Swengel, Pennsylvania: Reiner Publications, 1952. Beloved Fundamentalist, A. W. Pink, offers a corrective about healing. Although criticizing healing ministers, he remained open to healing's feasibility.

Pitt, F. W. *Faith Healing Tragedies.* London: Pickering and Inglis, undated. Pitt, a prominent London pastor, dismissed the viability of divine healing. In persuading others to dismiss this approach to ministry, he recounts a number of "faith healing tragedies."

Pitts, John. *Faith Healing: Fact or Fiction?* Westwood, New Jersey: Revell Publishing, 1961. Pitts, a handicapped Presbyterian leader, composed a critical examination of the ministry of healing.

Pollock, A. J. *Modern Pentecostalism, Foursquare Gospel, "Healings," and "Tongues:" Are They of God?* London: Central Bible Truth Depot, undated. This is a critical analysis of Pentecostalism and the ministry of healing.

Pursey, Barbara A. "Healing Ministry." *The Westminster Handbook to Reformed Theology*, ed. Donald K. McKim, 99-100. Kentucky:

Westminster|John Knox Press, 2001. Pursey wrote a short essay on healing to include in this Reformed reference work.

Putnam, C. E. *Modern Religio-Healing: Man's Theories or God's Word?* Chicago: C. E. Putnam, 1924. In this critical work, Putnam renounces Pentecostalism and its claims of healing.

Reimer, Andy M. "Divine Healing Rites in the New Testament: Diversity and Unity," M.A., thesis, Regent College, 1994. Reimer explores the models of healing in the New Testament

Reisser, Paul C., Teri K. Reisser and John Weldon. *The Holistic Healers: A Christian Perspective on New-Age Health Care.* Downers Grove: InterVarsity Press, 1983. This book examines the New Age foundations of alternative medical practices.

Riley, William Bell. "Divine Healing and the Dangers Incidental to the Doctrine." *Christian Fundamentals in School and Church* 4:3 (April-June 1922): 10-11. Although critical of Pentecostalism, Riley, nevertheless, expressed openness to divine healing. He wrote, "We can find no warrant whatever for the contention that miracles were only temporary and intended to prove the deity of Christ, nor do we discover anywhere a hint of that other teaching that miracles 'were limited to apostolic days' and possibly to answers to apostles' prayers."

Ryan, Frank Jamieson. *Protestant Miracles: High orthodox and evangelical authority for the belief in divine interposition in human affairs. Compiled from the writings of men eminent in Protestant churches.* Stockton, California: Record Publishing Company, 1899. Ryan's inspiring collection of miracle stories includes accounts of divine healing.

Ryrie, Charles C. "The Cleansing of the Leper." *Bibliotheca Sacra* 113 (July 1956): 262-267. Ryrie, a prominent Dispensational teacher, analyzes a healing account from the Gospels.

Ryrie, Charles C. "An Act of Divine Healing," *Bibliotheca Sacra* 113:452 (October 1956) 353-360. Ryrie pens an exegetical article on a biblical account of healing for the official journal of Dallas Theological Seminary.

Sala, Harold J. *What You Need to Know About Healing: A Physical and Spiritual Guide*. Nashville, Tennessee: Broadman and Holman, 2013. Sala, a Baptist minister, provides a practical guide for the ministry of healing in the local church.

Sarles, Ken L. "An Appraisal of the Signs and Wonders Movement." *Bibliotheca Sacra* 145:577 (January-March 1988): 57-82. Sarles, a professor at Dallas Theological Seminary, evaluates John Wimber and the Third Wave Movement.

Saucy, Mark. "Miracles and Jesus' Proclamation of the Kingdom of God." *Bibliotheca Sacra* 153 (July-September 1996) 281-307. Saucy, an Evangelical scholar, explores how Jesus' healings and other works of power are to be associated with His proclamation of the Kingdom of God. Saucy ultimately tries to make a case for the Kingdom's delay.

Schauffer, A. F. "Faith Healing." *Century Magazine* 27 (April 27, 1882): 274-278. This essay is a fascinating reflection on faith healing practices from a conservative periodical in the late 1800s.

Schauffer, A. F. "Faith-Cures: A Study in Five Chapters." *Century Magazine* 31 (December 1885): 274-278. Schauffer shares more of his outlook on divine healing. He breaks his study down into five sections: 1. The theory. 2. The fallacy. 3. Bible Cures. 4. The Practice. 5. Questions in conclusion.

Schwarz, Ted. *Healing in The Name of God: Faith or Fraud?* Grand Rapids, Michigan: Zondervan Publishing, 1993. This is an examination of the ministry of healing by an inquiring Evangelical.

Scorer, Charles Gordon. *Healing, Biblical, Medical, and Pastoral.* United Kingdom: Christian Medical Fellowship, 1979. This book, written by a Christian physician, exams health, healing, and medicine.

Seet, Charles. "The Doctrine of Healing in the Atonement (Isaiah 53:4-6)," *The Burning Bush* 2:2 (July 1996): 93-99. Drawing on an exegetical analysis of Isaiah 53:4-6, Seet refutes the assertion that healing is provided in the atonement.

Shelhamer, Julia A. *How To Be Healed.* Atlanta, Georgia: Repairer Publishing Company, 1910. This book is a small, practical work on healing from a gifted Holiness writer. She tries to explain some strategies on how to receive healing.

Shogren, Gary S. "Will God Heal Us?" *Evangelical Quarterly* 61 (1989): 99-108. This exegetical article examines anointing with oil for healing in James 5.

Short, A.R. *The Bible and Modern Medicine: A Survey of Health and Healing in The Old and New Testaments.* London: Paternoster Press, 1953. This is an overview of what the Bible has to say about disease and health.

Short, David. "Modern Healing Miracles in Perspective." *Journal of The Christian Medical Fellowship* 33:4 (1987): 26-27. This article explores the meaning of miracles from a conservative Evangelical perspective.

Simundson, Daniel J. "Mental Health in the Bible." *Word and World* 9:2 (1989): 140-146. This article explores what the Bible has to say about mental health and other psychological issues.

Simundson, Daniel J. "Health and Healing in the Bible." *Word and World* 2:4 (1982): 330-339. Simundson carefully examines the subject of healing in the Bible.

Sipley, Richard M. *Understanding Divine Healing.* Wheaton, Illinois: Victor Books, 1986. This book is a mediocre introduction to the ministry of divine healing from a Christian and Missionary Alliance proponent.

Skinner, R. David. "Is Healing in the Atonement? or, the Question of Faith-Healing." *Mid-America Theological Journal* 9 (Fall 1985): 31-47. This is a cautious academic article on the subject of divine healing from Wesleyan-Holiness perspective.

Small, Alexander. "Divine Healing." *The Expository Times* 47:10 (1936): 471-474. This is an exegetical article that explores divine healing in the Scriptures. It provides valuable insight.

Smedes, Lewis, ed. *Ministry and the Miraculous: A Case Study at Fuller Theological Seminary.* Pasadena, California: Fuller Theological Seminary, 1987. This is an analysis of John Wimber's "Signs and Wonders" course at Fuller Seminary in the mid-1980s.

Smith, Lucius E. "Are Miracles to Be Expected?" *Bibliotheca Sacra* 48 (January 1891): 1-26. Smith, in this article from the theological journal of Dallas Theological Seminary, dismisses the possibility of miracles.

Smith, Timothy. "The Spirit's Gifts: Then and Now." *Christianity Today* 34:5 (March 19, 1990): 25-26. Smith, a history professor at John Hopkins University, explores gifts of the Spirit through the five hundred year span of the Protestant tradition.

Spence, Hubert. *Suffering and Healing.* Greenville, Pennsylvania: Tribute Press, 1950. This booklet that was written to counteract Pentecostal teaching on the function of divine healing.

Sproul, John Welsh. *Divine Healing Today: Hebrews 13:8.* Camden, New Jersey: Haddon Craftsmen Publishers, 1927. Sproul, an early twentieth century Methodist, wanted to consider the significance of divine healing.

Spurgeon, Charles Haddon. *First Healing and then Service, and Other Sermons Preached in 1885.* New York: Robert Carter and Brothers, 1885. In this sermonic collection from Spurgeon is one on the subject of divine healing. The prince of preachers practiced healing prayer to some degree.

Stafford, Tim. "Fruit of the Vineyard." *Christianity Today* 17 (November 1989): 35-36. This article examines healing and other expressions emanating from the Vineyard Movement.

Stafford, Tim. *Miracles: A Journalist Looks at Modern-Day Experiences of God's Power.* Bloomington, Minnesota: Bethany House, 2012. This is an overview of miracles and the outworking of God's power today.

Stafford, Tim. "Miracles in Mozambique: How Mama Heidi Reaches the Abandoned." *Christianity Today* 56:5 (May 2012): 18-26. This was a feature article in *Christianity Today* on Heidi and Roland Baker and their ministry in Mozambique. It is written by an evangelical journalist.

Stafford, Tim. "Testing The Wine from John Wimber's Vineyard: California's Latest Boom Church: Signs and Wonders Movement." *Christianity Today* 11 (August 8, 1986): 17-22. Stafford analyzes John Wimber and the Vineyard Movement.

Stafford, Tim. "Wimber's Last Words." *Christianity Today* (February 1998): 20. In this article, Stafford reflects on the notable life and death of John Wimber, the founder of the Vineyard Movement.

Stitzinger, James F. "Spiritual Gifts: Definitions and Kinds." *The Master's Seminary Journal* 14:2 (Fall 2003): 143-176. This article, from an associate of John Macarthur, criticizes the Pentecostal-Charismatic understanding of spiritual gifts.

Storms, C. Samuel. *Healing and Holiness, A Biblical Response to the Faith-Healing Phenomenon.* Phillipsburg, New Jersey: Presbyterian and Reformed Publishing Company, 1990. Storms explores the Pentecostal-Charismatic theology of healing, studying numerous healers from F. F. Bosworth to William Branham, Jack Coe, Oral

Roberts, Pat Robertson, Kenneth Copeland, as well as other evangelists of the Faith Healing movement. He takes an open but cautious approach to the subject.

Swartley, Willard M. *Health, Healing and The Church's Mission: Biblical Perspectives on Moral Priorities.* Downer's Grove, Illinois: Intervarsity Press Academic, 2012. This is an analysis of health, healing and mission. While allowing room for divine healing, it tends to focus on other approaches to rejuvenation.

Sweet, Leonard I. *Health and Medicine in the Evangelical Tradition.* Harrisburg, Pennsylvania: Trinity Press International, 1994. This is a well-researched article on the understanding of healing within early Evangelicalism.

Teter, Eber. *Faith Healing.* Syracuse, New York: Wesleyan Methodist Publishing Association, 1899. This work is an examination of "faith healing" from a sympathetic Methodist author.

Theissen, Gerd. *The Miracle Stories of the Early Christian Tradition.* Philadelphia: Fortress Press, 1983. This is a well-researched book that considers the syntax and structural elements of the healing and miracle stories in the gospels.

Thiselton, Anthony C. *The Holy Spirit - In Biblical Teaching, Through The Centuries and Today.* Grand Rapids, Michigan: Eerdmans Publishing, 2013. While this outstanding academic work does not focus on Spiritual gifts, it does include outstanding general references to healing in historic and theological contexts.

Thomas, Robert L. *Understanding Spiritual Gifts: A Verse-by-Verse Study of 1 Corinthians 12-14*, revised edition. Grand Rapids: Kregel, 1999. Thomas is professor of New Testament at The Master's Seminary in Sun Valley California. In this book, he applies the cessationist hermeneutic to the key Pauline periscope on spiritual gifts.

Tilley, J.A. "A Phenomenology of the Christian Healer's Experience with Faith Healing," Ph.D., diss., Fuller Theological Seminary, 1989. This is an examination of faith healing from doctoral student at Fuller Theological Seminary.

Tinling, James Forbes Bisset. *Faith Healing: Truth and Extravagance.* London: Morgan and Scott, 1884. Tinling wrote a series of articles in *The Christian* documenting concerns that he had with the faith-cure movement. The articles were later compiled and published as this work.

Tomaszewski, Mariano K. "Healing Patterns of the Hebrew Bible in the Synoptic Healing Activity of Jesus," Ph.D., diss., Claremont School of Theology, 2006. This work examines patterns of healing in the Synoptic gospels.

Torrance, Thomas Forsyth. 'The Giving of Sight to the Man Born Blind," *The Evangelical Quarterly* 9:1 (January 1937): 74-82. In this essay, Torrance examines the healing story from John 9, considering its grammar and historical framework.

Torrey, R. A. *Divine Healing.* Grand Rapids, Michigan: Baker Book House, 1974. Torrey, the prominent evangelical leader and associate of D.L. Moody in Chicago, wrote a small publication on divine healing.

Townsend, Frank S. "Faith-Cure." *Christian Advocate* 57 (October 19, 1882): 660. This essay examines the validity of the faith-cure approach to healing.

Townsend, Luther Tracy. *Faith Work, Christian Science and Other Cures.* Boston: W.A. Wilde Publishers, 1886. Townsend evaluates alternative forms of healing. He suggests that if nothing else, there is at least some psychological value of religious therapies.

Treharne, David. *Healing Via Redemption.* Swengel, Pennsylvania: Bible Truth Depot, 1913, 1925. This is a rudimentary work that examines whether healing is rooted in the atoning work of Jesus on the cross.

Trapnell, David H. "Health, Disease, and Healing." *Intervarsity Press New Bible Dictionary*, ed. I. Howard Marshall, A.E. Millard, J.I. Packer, and Donald Wiseman, 457-465. Downers Grove, Illinois: Intervarsity Press, 1982. This essay, on healing and disease in scripture, was written by a conservative Evangelical scholar.

Twelvetree, Graham H. *Jesus The Exorcist: A Contribution to The Study of the Historical Jesus.* Peabody, Massachusetts: Hendrickson Publishing, 1993. This is an analysis of Jesus' role as exorcist in the New Testament. The relationship between healing and deliverance is carefully noted.

Twelvetree, Graham H. *Jesus: The Miracle Worker.* Downers Grove, Illinois: Intervarsity Press, 1999. This book examines Jesus as a miracle worker in the New Testament.

Twelvetree, Graham H. "Healing, Illness," in *Dictionary of Paul and His Letters*, eds. Gerald F. Hawthorne, Ralph P. Martin, and Daniel G. Reid, 378-381. Downers Grove, Illinois: Intervarsity Press, 1993. Twelvetree provides an excellent analysis of the Pauline understanding of healing.

Twelvetree, Graham H. "Signs, Wonders, Miracles," in *Dictionary of Paul and His Letters*, eds. Gerald F. Hawthorne, Ralph P. Martin, and Daniel G. Reid, 875-877. Downers Grove, Illinois: Intervarsity Press, 1993. In this essay, Twelvetree considers the Pauline understanding of signs, wonders, and miracles.

Twelvetree, Graham H. "Signs and Wonders," in *New Dictionary of Biblical Theology*, eds. T. D. Alexander and Brian S. Rosner, 775-781. Downers Grove, Illinois: Intervarsity Press, 2000. In this insightful article, twelvetree reflects on signs and wonders in the New Testament.

Twelvetree, Graham H. "The Miracles of Jesus: Marginal or Mainstream?" *Journal for the Study of the Historical Jesus* 1:1 (2003): 104-124. This article examines whether Jesus' miracles should be considered normative or extraordinary.

Twelvetree, Graham H. "Miracle Story." *Encyclopedia of the Historical Jesus*, ed. Craig A. Evans, 416-420. New York and London: Routledge, 2008. Twelvetree brings his scholarly expertise to this essay on the meaning of a "miracle story" in the New Testament.

Twelvetree, Graham H. "The Message of Jesus I: Miracles, Continuing Controversies," in *Handbook for the Study of the Historical Jesus*, ed. Tom Holmen, and Stanley E. Porter, 2517-2548. Leiden: Brill, 2011. Twelvetree provides analysis on Jesus' message and miracles.

Twelvetree, Graham H. "Miracle in an Age of Diversity," In *The Cambridge Companion to Miracles*, ed. Graham H. Twelftree, 1-15. Cambridge, United Kingdom: Cambridge University Press, 2011. In this essay, Twelvetree explores the understanding and meaning of miracles.

Twelvetree, Graham H. "Miracles and Miracle Stories," in *Dictionary of Jesus and the Gospels*, ed. Joel B. Green, Jeannine K. Brown, and Nicholas Perrin, 594-604. Downers Grove: Intervarsity Press, 2013. This is an analysis of healing and miracles in the story of Jesus.

Twelvetree, Graham H. "The Miraculous in the New Testament: Current Research and Issues." *Currents in Biblical Research* 12 (2014): 321-352. Twelvetree provides scholarly analysis on the meaning and understanding of miracles.

Turner, G. "Healing in Church Services." *Journal of The Christian Medical Fellowship* 37:2 (1991): 7-9. This is a practical article on healing from a member of the Christian Medical Fellowship in the United Kingdom.

Unger, Merrill F. "Divine Healing." *Bibliotheca Sacra* 128 (1971): 234-244. Unger, a conservative Evangelical, pens a critical take on divine healing. This was published in the Dallas Theological Seminary journal.

Various. "Leadership Forum: The Church: Healing's Natural Home?" *Leadership* 6:2 (Spring 1985): 116-127. In this article, four healing practitioners from different Christian traditions (Alliance, Baptist, Presbyterian, and Vineyard) discuss their approach to ministry.

Various. "The Holy Spirit: God at Work." *Christianity Today* 34:5 (March 19, 1990): 27-35. This is an extended interview with Charles Ryrie, J.I. Packer, Stuart Briscoe, Russell Spittler, and John Wimber on their understanding of healing and the gifts of the Spirit. This interview was conducted by Kenneth S. Kantzer and published in *Christianity Today*. While Wimber and Spittler approached the conversation from Spirit-filled ethos, the rest were relatively hesitant about modern day miracles.

Waggett, J. MacPhail. *Mental, Divine, and Faith Healings: Their Explanation and Place*. Boston: Richard G. Badger Publisher, 1919. Waggett's book explores some of the healing claims in the early part of the twentieth century.

Wan, Wan Chee. *Healing: A Pastor's Reflection*. Singapore: Wan Chee Wan, 2012. Wan, a graduate of Fuller Theological Seminary, penned a pastoral analysis on the practice of healing.

Warfield, B. B. *Counterfeit Miracles*. Carlisle, Pennsylvania: Banner of Truth Trust, 1917. Warfield's noted cessationist polemic has remained influential in Fundamentalist and Evangelical circles for a century. Many who reject healing still reference this work.

Waterson, A.P. "Faith Healing and Faith Healers." *Theology* 60 (1957): 8-16. Waterson, a conservative theologian, dismissively evaluates faith healing and those who practice it.

Weaver, Edward Ebenezer. *Mind and Health: With an Examination of Some Systems of Divine Healing.* New York: Macmillan Publishing, 1913. This work is an early twentieth century analysis of Evangelical faith healing. Wevar compares it to Christian Science and other heterodox forms.

Westermann, Claus. "Salvation and Healing in the Community: The Old Testament Understanding." *International Review of Mission* 61:241 (1972): 8-19. Westermann's article examines the healing power of community in the Old Testament.

White, John. *When the Spirit Comes with Power: Signs and Wonders Among God's People.* Downers Grove, Illinois: Intervarsity Press, 1988. This work is an assessment of revival phenomena by an evangelical psychologist. White attended John Wimber's "Signs, Wonders, and Church Growth" class at Fuller and it transformed his thinking.

Williams, Roy Leonard. "William E. Boardman (1810-1886): Evangelist of the Higher Christian Life," Ph.D., diss., Calvin Theological Seminary, 1998. Williams did extensive research on the life and ministry of William Boardman, one of the late nineteenth century healing proponents.

Wilkinson, John. "A Study of Healing in The Gospel According to John." *Scottish Journal of Theology* 19 (1966): 442-461. Wilkinson, an Evangelical physician, delves into the ministry of healing in the Gospel of John.

Wilkinson, John. "Healing and Salvations: Some Theological Considerations." *Journal of the Christian Medical Association of India* 2 (1988): 14-20. In this article, Wilkinson examines the relationship of salvation and healing.

Wilkinson, John. *Healing and the Church.* Edinburg, United Kingdom: The Handsel Press, 1984. Wilkinson, an Evangelical from the United Kingdom, examines the meaning of healing in the Christian church.

Wilkinson, John. "Healing in Semantics, Creation, and Redemption." *Scottish Bulletin of Evangelical Theology* 5 (Spring 1986): 17-37. In this article, Wilkinson explores the definition and means of healing.

Wilkinson, John. "Healing in The Epistle of James." *Scottish Journal of Theology* 24 (1971): 326-345. Wilkinson delves into an exegetical analysis of James 5, determining what this central text has to say to about healing.

Wilkinson, John. *Health and Healing: Studies in New Testament Principles and Practice.* Edinburgh, Scotland: Hansel Press, 1980. This book is an analytical overview from a man who has been trained both theologically and medically. Wilkinson attempts to bring his expertise in both fields to bear on the topic of health and healing in the New Testament.

Wilkinson, John. *Making Men Whole: The Theology of Medical Missions.* London: Christian Medical Fellowship, 1990. This work examines the significance of medical missions within the Evangelical tradition. It largely sidesteps spiritual and supernatural dimensions.

Wilkinson, John. "Physical Healing and the Atonement." *The Evangelical Quarterly* 63:2 (1991): 149-167. Drawing upon exegetical processes, Wilkinson considers whether physical healing is in the atonement. His conclusion is that it is not.

Wilkinson, John. *The Bible and Healing: A Medical and Theological Commentary.* Grand Rapids, Michigan: Eerdmans, 1998. In this larger work, Wilkinson draws from his medical and theological training to consider what the Bible has to say about disease and healing.

Wilkinson, John. "The Body in the Old Testament." *Evangelical Quarterly* 63 (1991): 195-210. In this exegetically informed article, Wilkinson delves into the topic of human embodiment in the Old Testament.

Wilkinson, John. "The Theological Basis of Medicine." *Scottish Journal of Theology* 8 (1955): 142-154. This is a well-written article that explores the theological foundations of modern medicine.

Wilkinson, Michael and Peter Althouse. *Catch the Fire: Soaking Prayer and Charismatic Renewal.* DeKalb, Illinois: Northern Illinois University Press, 2014. This well-researched academic work examines some of the later developments in the Toronto Blessing. The authors explore the theology and practice of "soaking prayer."

Williams, C. Peter. "Healing and Evangelism: The Place of Medicine in Later Victorian Protestant Missionary Thinking," in *The Church and Healing: Papers Read at The Twentieth Summer Meeting and The Twenty-First Winter Meeting of the Evangelical Historical Society*, ed. W.J. Sheils, and Basil Blackwell, 271-285. United Kingdom: Oxford, 1982. Williams' well-researched article examines the thinking behind early medical missions.

Wilson, Andrew. "God Always Heals: Good News for Our Bodies - In This Life and The Next." *Christianity Today* 58:9 (November 2014): 34. This hopeful Evangelical article affirms the value of healing. It suggests that even if healing doesn't occur at this time, it will be ultimately realized in the resurrection.

Woods, Bertram Ernest. *The Healing Ministry.* London: SCM Press, 1966. Woods was an English Methodist and noted musical composer. This work examines the trajectories of the healing ministry in the local church.

Various. "Divine Healing, Pentecostalism and Mission." *International Review of Mission* 93 (July-October 2004): 370-371. This issue of *International Review of Mission* examines healing and Spirit-filled Christianity. The articles are as follows: "Faith, Healing and Mission," "Faith, Healing and Mission: Reflections on a Consultative Process," "Healing, Salvation and Mission: The Ministry of Healing in Latin American Pentecostalism," "James 5:14-18: Healing Then and Now," "Mission to 'Set the Captives

Free:' Healing, Deliverance, and Generational Curses in Ghanaian Pentecostalism," and "Pentecostals, Healing and Ecumenism."

Various. "Health and Healing in Mission." *International Review of Mission* 83 (April 1994): 223-311. In this issue of the *International Review of Mission*, several researchers reflect on issues of health, healing, and the mission of the church. The standout essays are: Martin Marty, "The Tradition of the Church in Health and Healing" and John S. Pobee, "Healing—An African Christian Theologian's Perspective."

Various. *Signs and Wonders Today: The Remarkable Story of Experimental Course MC510-Signs Wonders and Church Growth at Fuller Theological Seminary*. Wheaton, Illinois: Christian Life Magazine Publications, 1983. Christian Life Magazine produced a special account of John Wimber's influential Signs and Wonders class at Fuller Theological Seminary. In addition to interviews and articles, there are a number of photographs.

Various. "The Healing Ministry" *The International Review of Mission* 57 (April 1968): 151-270. This entire issue of *The International Review of Mission* explores health and healing. Some of the articles include: "Salvation's Message About Health," "Sacraments in the Church in Relation to Healing," "Health and the Congregation," and more.

Vaux, Kenneth L. *Health and Medicine in the Reformed Tradition: Promise, Providence, and Care*. New York: Crossroad, 1984. This thoroughly researched work explores medicine, health, and healing within the Reformed Protestant tradition.

Wallis, Ian G. "Christ's Continuing Ministry of Healing." *The Expository Times* 104:2 (1996): 42-45. This exegetical article explores what scripture has to say about Jesus and the ministry of healing.

Witherington III, Ben. "Salvation and Health in Christian Antiquity: The Soteriology of Luke-Acts in Its First Century Setting." *Witness to The Gospel: The Theology of Acts*. Grand Rapids, Michigan: Eerdmans, 1998. Witherington, a noted New Testament scholar, examines the theology of Luke and Acts. He focuses on the understanding of salvation and healing.

Witty, Robert Gee. *Divine Healing: A Balanced Biblical View.* Nashville, Tennessee: Broadman Press, 1989. Witty, a Southern Baptist, attempts to articulate a moderate view of the healing ministry.

Workman, George Coulson. *Divine Healing or True Science Versus Christian Science and Faith-Cure.* Toronto: Ryerson Press, 1923. Like many conservatives at this time, Workman conflated Evangelical healing practices with Christian Science.

Wright, F. J. "Healing: An Interpretation of James 5:13-20." *Journal of The Christian Medical Fellowship* 37:1 (1991): 20-21. This article, in a medical missions journal, attempts to interpret James 5:13-20 exegetically.

Yancey, Phillip, and Paul Brand. *Fearfully and Wonderfully Made.* Grand Rapids, Michigan: Zondervan Publishing, 1987. In Fearfully and Wonderfully Made, renowned surgeon, Paul Brand, and bestselling writer, Philip Yancey, examine the human body. The authors suggest that cells, systems, and chemistry bears the impress of a deeper, unseen reality.

Yancey, Phillip, and Paul Brand. *In His Image.* Grand Rapids, Michigan: Zondervan Publishing, 1987. In this follow up work, Yancey and Brand argue that God's voice is encoded in the structure of human bodies.

Yancey, Phillip, and Paul Brand. *The Gift of Pain.* Grand Rapids, Michigan: Zondervan Publishing, 1997. Yancey and Brand, in their multi-volume medical series, turn to the meaning and scope of pain. Many of the conclusions are based on Brand's fifty-year career working with lepers in India.

Yancey, Phillip. *Where is God When It Hurts?* Grand Rapids: Zondervan, 1979. Using examples from the Bible and his own experiences,

Yancey evaluates the meaning of physical, emotional, and spiritual pain.

Yarbrough, Mark M. "When God Doesn't Heal: Why doesn't God cure everyone who prays fervently for healing?" *Christianity Today* 48:9 (September 2004): 80. Yarbrough, the pastor of Eastfield Bible Chapel and executive director of communications at Dallas Theological Seminary, shares his insights about suffering.

Yates, K.M. "The Theological Significance of Healing in the Old Testament," Ph.D., diss., Southern Baptist Theological Seminary, 1955. Yates provides a serious examination of healing in the Old Testament.

Zuck, Roy. "Review of *Power Healing*, by John Wimber with Kevin Springer." *Bibliotheca Sacra* 145 (January-March 1988): 102-104. Zuck (1932-2013), a Dallas Theological Seminary Professor, examines John Wimber's book on divine healing.

14. MAINLINE AND LITURGICAL

Achtemeier, Paul J., "'And He Followed Him:' Miracles and Discipleship in Mark 10:46-52," *Semeia* 11 (1978): 115-145. In this article, Achtemeier explores the relationship between discipleship and healing.

Achtemeir, Paul. "Toward The Isolation of Pre-Markan Miracle Catenae." *Journal of Biblical Literature* 89 (1970): 265-291. Achtemeir examines textual issues in the Gospels and what the miracle stories reveal about the movement and flow of the text.

Achtemeir, Paul. "The Origin and Function of the Pre-Markan Miracle Catenae." *Journal of Biblical Literature* 91 (1972): 198-221. In this article, Achtemeir examines Jesus' early miracles.

Achtemeir, Paul. "The Lukan Perspective on the Miracles of Jesus: A Preliminary Sketch." *Journal of Biblical Literature* 94 (1975): 547-562. Achtemeir continues his reflections on supernatural signs. This time he focuses on the Lukan texts.

Aikman, David. *Jesus in Beijing: How Christianity is Transforming China and Changing the Global Balance of Power.* Washington D.C.: Regnery, 2006. This work, from a former *Time Magazine* correspondent, documents Christianity's emergence in China. It includes a number of references to healing and spiritual gifts.

Adams, Damon S. "Divine Healing in Australian Protestantism, 1870-1940," *Journal of Religious History* 40:3 (September 2016): 1-18. This well-researched article examines the ministry of John Alexander Dowie. It also references other healing figures emerging out of Australia.

Alexander, William M. *Demonic Possession in The New Testament: its Historical, Medical, and Theological Aspects.* Edinburgh, Scotland: T&T Clark, 1902. This book is an early twentieth century analysis of demonic activity and its influence on health.

Allen, E. Anthony. "What is the Church's Healing Ministry? Biblical and Global Perspectives." *International Review of Mission* 90:356-357 (January-April 2001): 46-54. Allen, a Jamaican psychologist, wrote a missiologically-themed article that considers the ministry of healing.

Andrews, E. "Healing, Health." *Interpreter's Dictionary of the Bible*, ed. George Arthur Buttrich, 541-549. New York: Abingdon. 1962. Andrews provides an insightful essay on healing and health in Scripture.

Avalos, Hector, Sarah J. Melcher, and Jeremy Schipper, eds. *This Abled Body: Rethinking Disabilities in Biblical Studies*. Atlanta: Society of Biblical Literature, 2007. This book explores what health and embodiment might mean to those who are handicapped and diseased.

Baer, Jonathan Richard. "Health, Disease, and Medicine," in *The Encyclopedia of Religion in America*, ed. Peter W. Williams, and Charles H. Lippy, 954-965. Thousand Oaks, California: CQ Press, 2010. This is a well-researched article on disease and health in American religion.

Baer, Jonathan Richard. "Perfectly Empowered Bodies: Divine Healing in Modernizing America," Ph.D. diss., Graduate School of Yale University, 2002. This ground-breaking dissertation analyzes healing practices from the late nineteenth to the early twentieth centuries.

Bartach, Hans Werner, editor. *Kerygma and Myth: A Theological Debate*, tr. Reginald H. Fuller. London: Society For Promoting Christian Knowledge, 1957. At the center of this book is the perspective of Rudolf Bultmann (1884-1976), a German theologian and professor of New Testament at the University of Marburg. Bultmann suggests that the healings and miracles of the New Testament are simply myths.

Bastin, Marcel. "Jesus Worked Miracles: Texts from Matthew 8." *Lumen Vitae* 39 (1984): 131-139. This article explores the underlying meaning and scope of miracles.

Baxter, Wayne. "Healing and The Son of David: Matthew's Warrant." *Novum Testamentum* 48 (2006): 36-50. This article explores the relationship between Jesus' title of "Son of David" and his role as a healer.

Betz, Hans Dieter. "The Early Christian Miracle Story: Some Observations on the Form Critical Problem." *Semeia* 11 (1978): 69-81. In this article, Betz critically examines the form and structure of the New Testament miracle stories.

Beuoy, Herbert J. "The Place of Faith in the Healing of Persons at Central United Methodist Church, Decatur, Illinois," D.Min., thesis, Asbury Theological Seminary, Wilmore, Kentucky, 1983. This case study explores healing practices in a United Methodist Church.

Blanton, Anderson. *Hittin' the Prayer Bones: Materiality of Spirit in the Pentecostal South*. Chapel Hill, North Carolina: University of North Carolina Press Books, 2015. From the radios used to broadcast prayer to the curative faith cloths circulated through the postal system, material objects have been used to 'transmit" the anointing of the Holy Spirit since the 1940s. Blanton argues that this has been vital to the Pentecostal community's understanding and performances of faith.

Boggs, Wade H. *Faith Healing and The Christian Faith*. Richmond, Virginia: John Knox Press, 1956. Boggs, writing from a Reformed ethos, explores the efficacy of faith healing.

Bonnell, John Suntherland. *Do You Want To Be Healed? How Religion and Science Combine to Work the Miracles of Healing*. New York: Harper. 1968. Bonnell writes about healing prayer, framing it as a therapeutic process unifying body, soul, and spirit.

Bonner, Campbell. "Traces of Thaumaturgic Technique in the Miracles." *Harvard Theological Review* 20:3 (July 1927): 171-181. In this article, Bonner argues that there was a stock "wonderworking" story that was utilized over and over in the ancient world. It would differ in terms of characters, time, and setting, but would carry other commonalities. Bonner believes that the New Testament accounts of miracles were largely a rhetorical device. They were not recounting actual events.

Booth, Howard. *Healing Experiences: A Devotional And Study Guide*. London: Bible Reading Fellowship, 1985. Howard Booth, a European mainline leader, delves into the foundations of healing, inviting people to reflect on it biblically.

Booth, Howard. *Health, Healing, And Wholeness: The Ongoing Quest*. United Kingdom: Arthur James Limited, 1998. Booth's practical study was written to help people gain a better grasp of healing.

Booth, Howard. *Healing Is Wholeness: A Resource Book to Encourage Healing Ministry Initiatives in the Local Church*. London: The Methodist Church and The Churches' Council for Health and Healing, 1987. This is a practical guide to encourage the healing ministry in the Methodist Church.

Booth, Howard. *Prayer Tools for Health and Healing*. United Kingdom: Grail Publications, 1980. This is the first work that Howard Booth wrote on healing. He wants to help Christians learn how to pray for healing.

Borgen, Peder. "Miracles of Healing in the New Testament." *Studia Theologica: Nordic Journal of Theology* 35:1 (1981): 91-106. Borgen, a European scholar from the Reformed tradition, explores healing prayer as a theological question.

Brown, Candy Gunther. "Feeling is Believing: Pentecostal Prayer and Complementary and Alternative Medicine." *Spiritus: A Journal of*

Christian Spirituality 14.1 (2014): 60-67. Brown explores Pentecostal-Charismatic prayer and its effectiveness as "alternative medicine."

Brown, Candy Gunther. "From Tent Meetings and Store-Front Healing Rooms to Walmarts and the Internet: Healing Spaces in the United States, the Americas, and the World, 1906-2006." *Church History* 75 (2006): 631-47. In this article, Brown examines "healing rooms" and the "spaces" where Christians pray for the sick.

Brown, Cathy Gunther, ed. *Global Pentecostal and Charismatic Healing*. New York: Oxford University Press, 2011. These essays consider the history, doctrine, and practice of healing among Spirit-filled believers around the world.

Brown, Candy Gunther. "Healing." *Cambridge Companion to American Methodism*, ed. Jason Vickers, 227-242. Cambridge: Cambridge University Press, 2013. Brown provides a thoroughly researched article on healing's intersection with Methodism in the United States.

Brown, Candy Gunther. "Healing Words: Narratives of Spiritual Healing and Kathryn Kuhlman's Uses of Print Culture, 1947-1976," in *Religion and the Culture of Print in Modern America*, ed. Charles L. Cohen and Paul S. Boyer, 271-297. Madison: University of Wisconsin Press, 2008. This article explores Kathryn Kuhlman's utilization of print medium to disseminate her message of healing.

Brown, Cathy Gunther. "Living On a Prayer: Is There Scientific Evidence That Talking to God Is Good for Your Health?" The Daily, April 22, 2012. Brown's op-ed piece on healing prayer was published by an internet news service.

Brown, Candy Gunther. "Pentecostal Healing Prayer in an Age of Evidence-Based Medicine." *Transformation: An International Journal of Holistic Mission Studies* 32:1 (2015): 1-16. Brown examines the Pentecostal-Charismatic resistance to empirical investigations of healings. Since the general public insists on medical corroboration before giving claims credence, the Charismatic resistance to medical validation comes at a price of reduced missionary impact.

Brown, Candy Gunther. "Pentecostal Power: The Politics of Divine Healing Practices." *PentecoStudies: An Interdisciplinary Journal for Research on the Pentecostal and Charismatic Movements* 13.1 (2013): 35-57. This article interprets Pentecostal healing practices as a strategy for mobilizing spiritual power, and as a complement to or replacement of political power. Although sometimes engaging in political activism to remedy the causes and symptoms of social and physical ills, Pentecostals prioritize spiritual approaches to addressing ailments that are envisioned as spiritual in causation, and hence uniquely ameliorated by spiritual means.

Brown, Candy Gunther. "Spirits of Protestantism: Medicine, Healing, and Liberal Christianity." *Church History* 82:1 (March 2013): 245-247. This is an insightful academic article exploring the understanding of sickness and healing in the mainline tradition.

Brown, Candy Gunther. "Studying Divine Healing Practices: Empirical and Theological Lenses and the Theory of Godly Love." *PentecoStudies: An Interdisciplinary Journal for Research on the Pentecostal and Charismatic Movements* 11.1 (2012): 48-66. Brown considers approaches to studying healing prayer in the Christian tradition in a clinically acceptable way.

Brown, Candy Gunther. *Testing Prayer: Science and Healing*. Cambridge, Massachusetts: Harvard University Press, 2012. This is an important work that analyzes the intersection of healing and scientific analysis. The work primarily centers on Missionary Evangelist, Randy Clark, and his ministry associates.

Brown, Candy Gunther. "Touch and American Religions." *Religion Compass* 3.4 (2009): 770-783. This essay engages theories of philosophical phenomenologists, students of ritual and performance studies, historians and anthropologists of art and architecture, neuroscientists, and feminist scholars that envision touch as a unique mode of gaining knowledge about the world and oneself. Apparently, touch stimulates ethical behavior by working directly on the emotions to motivate empathetic, compassionate concern for others.

Bruce, A. B. *The Miraculous Element in the Gospels.* London: Hodder & Stoughton, 1886. Bruce, a popular Scottish expositor, discusses the philosophical nature of miracles and the way they fit into various worldviews.

Bruce, Patricia. "John 5:1-18: The Healing at the Pool: Some Narrative, Socio-Historical and Ethical Issues," *Neotestamentica* 39:1 (2005): 39-36. Bruce's reading of John 5:1-18 considers the socio-historical and religious aspects of disability in the Jewish world. She suggests that it is necessary to locate people with disabilities in the biblical narratives in positive and empowering ways.

Bryan, Steven M. "Power in the Pool: The Healing of the Man at Bethesda and Jesus' Violation of the Sabbath (John 5.1-18)." *Tyndale Bulletin* 54:2 (2003): 7-22. In this article, Bryan argues that Jesus demonstrated unity with the Father through healing acts. He was not operating in magic or in an unauthorized way.

Bultmann, Rudolf. *Jesus Christ and Mythology.* New York: Charles Scribner's Sons, 1958. Bultmann argues that the biblical accounts of Jesus are clouded in myth. Since the New Testament asserts a primitive worldview, readers must engage in demythologization to discover who Jesus truly was.

Bultmann, Rudolf. "The New Testament and Mythology," in Kergyma and Myth, ed. H. W. Bartsch, 1–44. London: Society For Promoting Christian Knowledge, 1953. Bultmann, in this essay, articulates anti-supernatural theological formations.

Bushnell, Horace. *Nature and the Supernatural, as Together Constituting the One System of God.* New York: Scribner and Sons, 1860. Although liberal in his leanings, Bushnell expressed openness to healing.

Chapter 14 of *Nature and the Supernatural* was titled, "Miracles and Spiritual Gifts Not Discontinued." By affirming a belief in contemporary miracles, he was sparking controversy in the academy.

Capps, Donald. *Jesus The Village Psychiatrist*. Louisville: Westminster/John Knox Press, 2008. Capps reduces disease in the Bible to merely psychosomatic disorders. He thinks of Jesus, as a "psychiatrist." This work is largely reductionistic, demonstrating a skepticsm about Jesus' healing prowess.

Caroll, John T. "Sickness and Healing in the New Testament Gospels." *Interpretation* 49:2 (April 1995): 130-142. Caroll, a professor at Union Theological Seminary, examines healing accounts in the gospels.

Case, Julia Riley. *An Unpredictable Gospel: American Evangelicals and World Christianity, 1812 - 1920*. New York: Oxford University Press, 2012. Case analyzes the currents of Western Protestantism in the nineteenth and early twentieth centuries.

Cave, Cyril H. "The Leper: Mark 1:40-45." *New Testament Studies* 25:2 (1978): 245-250. Cave explores the theological contours of Mark 1:40-45, an account of the healing of lepers.

Chappell, Paul G. "Oral Roberts." *Dictionary of Pentecostal Charismatic Christianity*, ed. Gary McGee, Stanley Burgess, and Patrick Alexander, 759-760. Grand Rapids, Michigan: Zondervan Publishing, 1988. Chappell provides an ample biographical sketch of Oral Roberts.

Chappell, Paul G. "Origins of the Divine Healing Movement in America." *Spiritus* 1 (Winter 1985): 5-18. This is a well-researched article that focuses on the contributions of R. Kelso Carter, Ethan O. Allen, and Charles Cullis.

Chappell, Paul G. "The Birth of the Divine Healing Movement in America," in *Healing in the Name of God*, ed. Pieter G.R. de Villiers,

60-77. Pretoria: Powell Bible Centre, University of South Africa, 1986. This is a thoroughly researched article recounting the history of healing in the United States.

Chappell, Paul G. "The Divine Healing Movement in America," Ph.D., diss., Drew University, 1983. Chappell's research on the Faith Cure and subsequent healing movements was groundbreaking when it submitted in the early 1980s.

Chilton, Bruce. *Jesus' Baptism and Jesus' Healing: His Personal Practice of Spirituality*. Harrisburg, Pennsylvania: Trinity Press International, 1998. This work is a scholarly exploration of healing in Jesus' ministry. Of particular interest is the chapter titled, "Purification and Healing in the Ministry of Yeshua."

Chirban, John T. "Healing and Spirituality." *Pastoral Psychology* 40:4 (1992): 235-244. Chirban believes that the topic of healing provides a natural link to the disciplines of medicine, psychology, and religion.

Clark, Glenn. *Be Thou Made Whole*. St. Paul, Minnesota: Macalester Park, 1953. Clark, a Presbyterian layman, became the founder of the Camps Farthest Out. These gatherings became laboratories for experimentation in the art of praying, Healing became an emphasis in these gatherings.

Clark, Glenn. *How to Find Health Through Prayer*. New York: Harper, 1940. In this practical book, Clark makes the case that prayer combined with faith elicits cures. Clark uses many scriptural and practical examples.

Collins, Nina L. *Jesus, the Sabbath and the Jewish Debate: Healing on the Sabbath in the 1st and 2nd Centuries CE*. New York: Bloomsbury T&T Clark 2014. Collins argues that first-century criticisms of Jesus healing on the Sabbath needs to be revisited in light of recent insights into the biblical text.

Comber, Joseph A., "The verb 'therapeuo' in Matthew's Gospel," *Journal of Biblical Literature* 97:3 (September 1978): 431- 434. Comber provides an exegetical understanding of the Greek word "therapeuo," considering what it might mean for modern healing practice.

Crowlesmith, John, ed. *Religion and Healing: Essays by Members of the Methodist Society for Medical and Pastoral Psychology*. London: Epworth Press, 1962. This is an anthology on disease, health, and healing from Methodist leaders in England.

Cunningham, Raymond J. "From Holiness to Healing: The Faith Cure in America 1872-1892." *Church History* 43:4 (1974): 499-513. In this article, Cunningham explores the faith cure movement and its influence on twentieth century Protestantism.

Cunningham, Raymond J. "Ministry of Healing: The Origins of Psychotherapeutic Role of the American Churches," Ph.D., diss., John Hopkins University, 1965. Although dealing with heterodox expressions of healing in this dissertation, Cunningham begins this work looking at healing's emergence within the Holiness movement in the late 1800s and 1900s.

Curtis, Heather D. "A Thorn in the Flesh: Pain, Illness and Sanctification in Late-19th-Century Protestantism," paper submitted to the American Society of Church History Annual Meeting, Washington, DC, January 2004. Curtis explores disease, suffering, and healing within the Evangelical faith cure movement.

Curtis, Heather D. "'Acting Faith:' Divine Healing as Devotional Practice in Late-Nineteenth-Century Protestantism," in *Practicing Protestants: Histories of the Christian Life in America*, eds. Laurie Maffly-Kipp, Leigh Schmidt, and Mark Valeri, 137-158. Baltimore: Johns Hopkins University Press, 2006. This essay explores how evangelicals participated in the divine healing movement of the late-nineteenth century. It talks about how human action and religious ritual played a role in the pursuit of physical and spiritual healing.

Curtis, Heather D. "Faith Healing, Christian Science and Kindred Phenomena: Women and Healing in Late Nineteenth Century Boston," in *Religious Healing in Boston: First Findings*, ed. Susan Sered and Linda L. Barnes, 21-24. Cambridge, Massachusetts: Center for the Study of World Religions, 2005. This article explores the reality of the ministry of healing in Boston in the late 1800s.

Curtis, Heather D. "Faith Homes: Sacred Space and Spiritual Practice in the Divine Healing Movement, 1870-1890," paper submitted to the American Society of Church History annual meeting, Philadelphia, Pennsylvania, January 2006. Curtis examines how the physical arrangement of faith homes helped define the experience of healing.

Curtis, Heather D. "Faith in the Great Physician: Suffering and Divine Healing in American Culture 1860-1900," Ph.D., diss., John Hopkins University, 2007. Curtis' well-researched dissertation considers the background and sociological patterns of the faith cure movement.

Curtis, Heather D., Brandon Bayne, and Candy Gunther Brown. "Forum on Sacred Spaces of Healing in Modern American Christianity." *Church History* 7:3 (2006): 594 - 647. This essay considers how physical environments can be utilized to shape Christian practice.

Curtis, Heather D. "Healing," in *Encyclopedia of Religion in America*, ed. Charles Lippy and Peter Williams, 948-954. Thousand Oaks, California: CQ Press, 2010. This is a general article on the subject of healing from Heather Curtis, a noted Harvard scholar.

Curtis, Heather D. "Houses of Healing: Sacred Space, Spiritual Practice, and the Transformation of Female Suffering in the Faith Cure Movement, 1870-1890." *Church History* 75:3 (September 2006): 598-611. In this essay, Curtis explores nineteenth century healing homes and the Protestant theology of space.

Curtis, Heather D. "Piety, Practice, Performance: Action and Embodiment in American Christianity," paper submitted to the American Academy of Religion Annual Meeting, Washington DC, November 2006. In this paper, Curtis continues to examine key areas of study in the faith cure movement of the late 1800s.

Curtis, Heather D. "Religion, Suffering and Healing in American History and Culture." Visiting Scholar Lecture, Center for Spirituality, Theology and Health, Duke University Medical Center, December 2008. Curtis explores the antebellum understanding of suffering and what it meant for the emerging healing movement.

Curtis, Heather D. "The Lord for the Body:" Sickness, Health and Divine Healing in Nineteenth-Century Protestantism," Ph.D., diss., Harvard University, 2005. Curtis' doctoral project work traces "the emergence of the divine healing movement among evangelical Protestants through the testimonies of "faith cures" published in popular periodicals and pamphlets.

Curtis, Heather D. "Women as Healers within the Evangelical Movement of the 19th Century," Religion, Health, and Healing Initiative Presentation, Center for the Study of World Religions, Harvard University, October 2002. In this work, Curtis explores the heightened role of women in the faith cure movement.

Dale, David. *In His Hands: Towards A Theology of Healing*. London: Darton, Longman and Todd, 1989. Dale was the moderator of United Reformed Church's General Assembly and the Chairman of the Churches Council of Health and Healing. This is his reflection on healing.

Dalley, Stephanie. "Anointing in Ancient Mesopotamia," in *Oil of Gladness: Anointing in The Christian Tradition*, ed. M. Dudley and G. Rowell, 19-25. London: Society For Promoting Christian Knowledge, 1993. In this essay, Dalley examines the meaning of anointing in the ancient Mediterranean world.

Davey, F. N. "Healing in The New Testament," in *Miracles and The Resurrection*, ed. I. Ramsey, 50-63. London: Society for Promoting Christian Knowledge, 1964. Davey provides a penetrating analysis of divine healing from the pages of the New Testament.

Davies, Steven L. *Jesus the Healer: Possession, Trance, and the Origins of Christianity*. New York: Continuum Publishers, 1995. Davies shows how contemporary anthropological findings confirm that Jesus was a healer and exorcist.

Dawson, Audrey. *Healing, Weakness, and Power: Perspectives on Healing in the Writing Of Mark, Luke, and Paul*. Eugene, Oregon: Wipf and Stock, 2008. In this thoroughly researched work, Dawson delves into the first century understanding of healing.

Dawson, George Gordon. *Healing: Pagan and Christian*. London: Society For Promoting Christian Knowledge, 1935. In this work, Dawson contrasts ancient pagan medicine with early Christian healing modalities.

Dods, Marcus. "Jesus as Healer." *The Biblical World* 15:3 (1900): 169-177. This article explores the idea of Jesus as a healer and how that was worked out in the broader Christian tradition. Dods expresses openness to the viability of healing.

Droege, Thomas A. "Congregations as Communities of Health and Healing." *Interpretation* 49:2 (1995): 1 17-129. This article focuses on practical ways that Christian congregations can foster health and betterment in the lives of people.

Duling, Dennis C, "The Therapeutic Son of David: An Element in Matthew's Christological Apologetic," *New Testament Studies* 24:3 (April 1978): 392-410. This article carefully examines the "son of David" language in a healing account from the Gospel of Matthew.

Duncan, Denis. *Health and Healing: A Ministry to Wholeness*. Edinburgh, Scotland: Saint Andrew Press, 1988. This work, based on a report given to the Church of Scotland General Assembly, tries to wrestle with some of the difficulties of healing in the local church.

Editor. "Well-Meant Wrong." *The Congregationist* 67 (August 24, 1882): 266. This essay is a critique of the theology and praxis of faith healing adherents.

Elliott, James Keith. "The Conclusion of the Pericope of the Healing of the Leper and Mark 1:45," *Journal of Theological Studies* 22:1 (April 1971): 153-157. This article considers the linguistics and literary structure of the healing account in Mark 1:45.

Elliott, James Keith. "The Healing of the Leper in the Synoptic Parallels," *Theologische Zeitschrift* Z 34 (1978): 175-81. Elliot, professor of New Testament Textual Criticism at the University of Leeds, argues that Mark 1:45 is not part of Mark's account, but a separate summary statement.

Epperly, Bruce G. *God's Touch: Faith Wholeness, And The Healing Miracles of Jesus.* Louisville: Westminster, John Knox, 2001. This work considers continuities between the restoration of the mind, body, and spirit in Jesus' ministry and the practices of alternative medicine today.

Evans, Abigail Rian. *Healing Liturgies for the Seasons of Life.* London: Westminster John Knox Press, 2004. This book is a collection of prayers and healing liturgies for the usage of mainline congregations.

Evans, Abigail Rian. *The Healing Church: Practical Programs for Health Ministries.* Cleveland, Ohio: United Church Press, 1999. Utilizing historical, medical, and theological insights, Evans has attempted to compose a program for healthcare in the local church.

Eve, Eric. "Spit in Your Eye: The Blind Man of Bethsaida and The Blind Man of Alexandria." *New Testament Studies* 54:1 (2008): 1-17. This article explores the use of saliva in the gospel stories. It clarifies spit's relationship to Roman history and Jewish Messianic expectations.

Eve, Eric. *The Healer from Nazareth: Jesus' Miracles in Their Historical Context*. London: Society For Promoting Christian Knowledge, 2009. Eve, a research fellow at Oxford University, researches the cultural and theological context of Jesus' miracles.

Eve, Eric. *The Jewish Context of Jesus' Miracles*. London: Sheffield, 2002. In this groundbreaking book, Eve explores early Jewish and Greco-Roman conceptions of miracle. Among other observations, Eve believes that Jesus associates sickness with demons—not God or humanity.

Foster, John, "Healing the Sick in the Early Church," *London Quarterly and Holborn Review*, 182 (July-October, 1957): 217-222, 299-304. This brief critique is Foster's measured response to Henry C. Robin's "Spiritual Healing in the History of the Church," published in the same journal the previous year.

Frayer-Griggs, Daniel. "Spittle, Clay, and Creation in John 9:6 and Some Dead Sea Scrolls," *Journal of Biblical Literature* 132:2 (2013): 659-670. In the scholarly community, there is debate over the meaning of Jesus' use of saliva. Frayer-Griggs explores this, drawing insights from the Dead Sea Scrolls.

Fridrichsen, Anton. *The Problem of Miracle in Primitive Christianity*, tr. Roy A. Harrisville. Minneapolis: Augsburg, 1972. This work, originally published in French, uses form criticism to consider the explanation of miracles. Fridrichsen believes that miracles were intimately bound with the origin of the church, but they were subordinate to the moral character of Christianity.

Fuller, Reginald H. *Interpreting the Miracles*. London: SCM, 1963. In this work, Fuller approaches the subject of healing and miracles from the same skeptical outlook as Rudolph Bultmann.

Funk, Robert W. "The Form of the New Testament Healing Miracle Story." *Semia* 12 (1978): 57-96. This is an academic analysis of the structure and form of New Testament miracle stories.

Furness, George M. "Healing Prayer and Pastoral Care." *The Journal of Pastoral Care* 38:2. (June 1984): 107-119. In this essay, Furness advocates for a functional approach to healing prayer for pastors and ministry leaders

Germany, Charles H. "The Healing Ministry: A Report On the Tubigen Consultation." *International Review of Mission* 53 (October 1964): 467-475. This article is the deliberations of a group of missionaries, pastors, and medical officials who met to discuss the role of healing in the church.

Glidon, Aurelius J.L. *Faith Cures: Their History and Mystery*. London: The Christian Commonwealth Publishing Company, 1890. Gliddon examines the claims of faith-cure proponents and those from heterodox groups. Most of this book came from a series of articles previously published in the *Christian Commonwealth*.

Goldsmith, Harry. "Anatomy of a Healing." *Sharing* 57:3 (1989): 30–36. Goldsmith experienced healing while receiving prayer from Agnes Sandford. He later became involved with the healing ministry as well. This article recounts some of his insights.

Graebner, Theodore. *Faith-Cure: The Practice Sometimes Miscalled "Divine Healing." A Study of its Methods and an Appraisal of its Claims*. Adelaide: Lutheran Publishing Company, 1921. This work is a critical reflection of the history, theology, and methodology of the faith cure movement.

Grant, Robert M. *Miracle and Natural Law in Graeco-Roman and Early Christian Thought*, Amsterdam: North Holland Publishing Company, 1952. Robert M. Grant was the Professor Emeritus of New Testament and Early Christianity at the University of Chicago Divinity School in Chicago, Illinois. He was a renowned authority on the history of early Christianity. In this work, he examines early Roman and Christian worldviews.

Green, Joel B. "Healing." *The New Interpreter's Dictionary of the Bible*, volume 2, ed. Katharine Doob Sakenfeld, 755-759. Nashville: Abingdon, 2007. This is a well-researched essay on Christian healing from a gifted mainline scholar.

Grundmann, Christoffer H. "Faith and Healing–What Faith-Healing is About, with Special Reference to the Christian Tradition." *Irish Theological Quarterly* 80.3 (2015): 233-247. This essay provides an analysis of faith-healing in the Bible and across other cultures. It also considers how medical professionals interpret healings.

Guijarro, Santiago. "Healing Stories and Medical Anthropology: A Reading of Mark 10:46-52." *Biblical Theology Bulletin*: Journal of Bible and Culture 30:3 (August 2000): 102-112. This article utilizes cross-cultural models from medical anthropology to imagine how Jesus and his contemporaries understood illness and healing.

Hamilton, Kenneth. *Revolt Against Heaven: An Enquiry Into Anti-Supernaturalism.* Grand Rapids: Eerdmans, 1965. This book critiques demythologization and anti-supernaturalism in mid twentieth century mainline Christianity. Hamilton seeks to counteract the reductionism of Bultmann and Schleiermacher.

Hamlyn, Thomas Frederick Piers. "Healing Teaching and Practice in the Word of Faith: An Appraisal," M.Div. thesis, University of Birmingham, 2015. This is a thoroughly researched critique of the Word of Faith movement. One of the correctives that Hamlyn recommends is that the followers of Kenneth Hagin place a greater focus on helping the poor.

Hamm, M. Dennis. "Acts 3:1-10: The Healing of the Temple Beggar as Lucan Theology." *Biblica* 67 (1986): 305-309. Hamm's essay examines one of the pivotal healing stories in Acts.

Hamm, M. Dennis. "Acts 3:12-26: Peter's Speech and the Healing of the Man Born Lame." *Perspectives in Religious Studies* 11 (1984): 199 - 217. In this essay, Hamm delves exegetically into one of the healing stories from Acts.

Hamm, M. Dennis. "Gifts of Healing." *Anchor Bible Dictionary*, David Noel Freedman, 89-90. New York: Doubleday Publishing, 1992. This succinct essay is a scholarly overview of gifts of healing in the New Testament.

Hamm, M. Dennis. "Paul's Blindness and Its Healing: Clues to Symbolic Intent (Acts 9, 22, and 26)." *Biblica* 71 (1990): 63-72. This article is an exegetical examination of the blindness and subsequent healing of the Apostle Paul.

Hamm, M. Dennis. "Sight to The Blind: Vision as Metaphor in Luke." *Biblica* 67 (1986): 457-477. Hamm mines the theological implications of healing the blind in the Gospel of Luke.

Hammell, George M. "Religion and Fanaticism," *Methodist Review* 70 (July 1888), 530-538. Critiquing the rise of the faith cure movement, Hammell pontificates on the problem of fanaticism.

Hardesty, Nancy. *The Faith Cure: Divine Healing in the Holiness and Pentecostal Movements*. Peabody, Massachusetts: Hendrickson Publishers, 2003. In this notable work, Hardesty explores the history and praxis of the faith cure movement

Hardesty, Nancy A. "Transatlantic Roots of the Holiness-Pentecostal Healing Movement," papers for The American Society of Church History. Clemson University, Seattle, Washington, January 10, 1998. In this thoroughly researched paper, Hardesty provides an overview of the history and challenges of the faith cure movement.

Harnack, Adolf von. "What Is Christianity? The Miraculous Element," in *Lectures Delivered in The University of Berlin During the Winter Term 1899-1900*, tr. Thomas Baley Saunders. New York: G.P. Putnam's

Sons, 1903. In this influential work, Harnack outlines what he considers the core precepts of the Christian faith. He makes interesting observations about the significance of health and healing in the Christian ethos.

Harnack, Adolf von. *The Mission and Expansion of Christianity in the First Three Centuries*, tr. James Moffatt. London: William and Norgate, 1908. This work traces the history of Christianity from the first century to the early church councils. Harnack had a relative openness to the ministry of healing.

Harrell Jr., David Edwin. *All Things Are Possible: The Healing and Charismatic Revivals in Modern America*. Bloomington, Indiana: Indiana University Press, 1975. Harrell's book is the definitive work on the salvation healing revival of the 1940s and 50s. Harrell won the trust of his subjects with his objective approach. No study of healing would be complete without this work.

Harrell Jr., David Edwin. "*Divine Healing in Modern American Protestantism,*" in *Other Healers: Unorthodox Medicine in America*, ed. Norman Gevitz, 215-227. Baltimore, Maryland: John Hopkins University Press, 1988. In this well-researched article, Harrell examines some of the other trajectories of the divine healing movement.

Harrell Jr., David Edwin. *Oral Roberts: An American Life*. Bloomington, Indiana: Indiana University Press, 1985. This book is, arguably, the definitive biography of healing evangelist Oral Roberts.

Harrell Jr., David Edwin. "The Disciples of Christ-Church of Christ Tradition," in *Caring and Curing: Health and Medicine in the Western Religious Traditions*, ed. R. L. Numbers, and D. Amundsen, 376-396. Baltimore and London: The Johns Hopkins University Press, 1986. This insightful essay, by Harrell, explores responses to sickness in the Disciples of Christ/Christian tradition.

Harrison, Peter. "Miracles, Early Modern Science, And Rational Religion." *Church History* 75:3 (September 2006): 493-510. This is a well–researched article examining the conception of miracles in scientific and religious communities of the late nineteenth and early twentieth centuries.

Hassel, Gerhard. "Health and Healing in The Old Testament." *Andrews University Seminary Studies* 21:3. (Autumn 1983): 191-202. This article analyzes the health and healing practices depicted in the Old Testament.

Hauerwas, Stanley. *Naming The Silences: God, Medicine, and the Problem of Suffering*. Grand Rapids, Michigan: Eerdmans, 1991. Hauerwas, a noted Evangelical theologian, explores the meaning of suffering and pain.

Heidenreich, Alfred. *Healings in the Gospels*. Edinburgh, Scotland: Floris Books, 1936, 1980. Heidenreich explores healing stories in the gospels, interpreting them in a therapeutic and liturgical sense.

Hendrickx, Herman. *The Miracle Stories of the Synoptic Gospels*, San Francisco: Harper and Row, 1987. This is a relatively sympathetic examination of signs and wonders in Matthew, Mark, and Luke.

Henriksen, Jan-Olav and Karl Olav Sandnes, *Jesus as Healer: A Gospel for the Body*. Grand Rapids, Michigan: William B. Eerdmans Publishing Company, 2016. Although the ministry of healing was prominent in Jesus' life and ministry, it is often downplayed in the Western tradition. Jan-Olav Henriksen and Karl Olav Sandnes draw upon New Testament studies and philosophical theology to challenge and investigate the reasons for that oversight. This is one of the most proficient modern academic works on healing.

Hillman, Robert J., Coral Chamberlain, and Linda Harding. *Healing and Wholeness: Reflections on the Healing Ministry*. Oxford, United Kingdom: Regnum International, 2002. This work is a reflection on health and healing from a relatively conservative outlook. It culls insights from three different scholars.

Hiltner, Seward. "A Selected Bibliography On Christian Faith and Health." *Pastoral Psychology* 12:10 (1962): 27-38. This bibliography is associated with a 1956 report from the General Assembly of the Presbyterian Church in the United States—"The Relation of Christian Faith to Health." The entries highlight therapeutic approaches and lean away from divine healing modalities.

Hoch, Dorothee. *Healing and Salvation: An investigation of Healing Miracles in The Present Day.* London: SCM Press LTD., 1955, 1958. Hoch's work, translated from German, provides an excellent scholarly overview of healing.

Horsley, Richard. *Jesus and Magic: Freeing the Gospel Stories from Modern Misconceptions.* Portland, Oregon: Cascade Books, 2014. Horsley carefully examines healing and exorcism accounts from the Gospels.

Hull, William E. "Effects of Mind On Body as Evidenced by Faith-Healing." *Lutheran Quarterly* 37 (1907): 263. This article, examining faith healing effects, is a critique from a leading Lutheran journal.

Hull, William E. "Divine Healing or Faith Cure." *Lutheran Quarterly* 27 (April 1897): 263-276. In this article, Hull is fairly dismissive of the faith cure approach to healing prayer.

Hultgren, Artland. "The Miracle Stories of the Gospels: The Continuing Challenge for Interpreters." *Word and World* 29:2 (Spring 2009): 129-135. In this engaging essay, Hultgren considers recent literature about miracles in the New Testament.

Jefferson, Lee M. *Christ Miracle Worker in Early Christian Art.* Minneapolis, Minnesota: Fortress Press 2014. This fascinating work considers some of the etchings, sculptures, and paintings associated with the early Christianity. The scenes depicted in these renderings typically reflect a biblical account of healing.

Jenkins, Philip. *The Next Christendom: The Coming of Global Christianity.* New York, Oxford University Press, 2002. In this thoroughly researched work, Jenkins explores how Christianity is growing in Africa, Asia, and Latin America. He suggests that healing and charismatic activity is driving some of this growth.

Johnson, E.S. "Mark 8:22-26: The Blind Man from Bethsaida," *New Testament Studies* 25 (1979): 370-383. In this essay, Johnson provides a critical examination of the healing of the blind man in Mark 8.

Johnson, E. S. "Mark 10.46-52: Blind Bartimaeus," *Catholic Biblical Quarterly* 40:2 (1978): 191-204. Writing for Catholic researchers, Johnson provides an exegetical examination of the account of blind Bartimaeus.

Johnson, Luke Timothy. *The Revelatory Body: Theology as an Inductive Art.* Grand Rapids, Michigan: Eerdmans, 2015. This fascinating book explores how the human body contributes to our development of theology. While not specifically about healing, the work enables better understanding of human embodiment.

Kahl, Werner. *New Testament Miracle Stories in their Religious-Historical Setting: A Religionsgeschichtliche Comparison from a Structural Perspective.* Göttingen: Vandenhoeck and Ruprecht, 1994. In this work, Kahl explores the language and form of New Testament Miracles stories.

Kallas, James. *The Significance of the Synoptic Miracles: Taking The Worldview of Jesus Seriously.* Woodinville, Washington, Sunrise Imprints, 1961, 2010. In this notable work, Kallas challenges Rudolph Bultmann's theological formations. He argues, "Demythologizing is a dead end. It does not rephrase Scripture. It reverses it. It repudiates it."

Kaye, Bruce N., *The Supernatural in the New Testament.* London: Lutterworth Press, 1977. This reductionistic work seeks to redefine healing and miracles in a way that is more readily received by Westerners today.

Kee, Howard Clark. "Aretalogy and Gospel." *Journal of Biblical Literature* 92:3 (September 1973): 402-422. Kee, in this scholarly article, examines the role of "aretalogy," or ancient miracle stories in shaping the gospels.

Kee, Howard Clark. "Medicine and Healing," in *Anchor Bible Dictionary*, ed. David Noel Freedman, 659-664. New York: Doubleday, 1992. This is an important essay from a noted New Testament scholar, exploring medicine and disease.

Kee, Howard Clark. *Miracle in The Early Christian World: A Study in Sociohistorical Method.* New Haven Connecticut: Yale University Press, 1983. In this work, Kee explores the understanding of miracles in the early centuries of the church.

Kelhoffer, James A. "Ordinary Christians as Miracle Workers in the New Testament and the Second and Third Century Christian Apologists." *Biblical Research* 44 (1999): 23–34. Mark 16:9-20 promises that "those who believe" will perform miraculous signs. This essay considers whether ordinary Christians functioned as miracle workers in the second and third centuries.

Kester, Aaron. "The Charismata in Crisis: The Gifts of the Holy Spirit in the Reformation Church of England," Ph.D., diss., Miami University, 1990. This well-researched work explores the understanding of "charismata" in the history of the Anglican church.

Kilgallen, John J. "The Obligation to Heal (Luke 13.10-17)," *Biblica* 82:3 (2001): 402-409. This essay carefully contrasts Luke 13:10-17 with Luke 14:1-6, two notable examples of Sabbath cures.

Klassen, Pamela E. "Radio Mind, Experiments on the Frontiers of Healing." *Journal of the American Academy of Religion* 75 (September

2007): 651-683. This is a well-researched article that explores the unusual ways that healing was being administered by mainline ministers at the beginning of the twentieth century.

Klassen, Pamela E. *Spirits of Protestantism: Medicine, Healing, And Liberal Christianity*. Los Angeles: University of California Press, 2011. Klassen explores the unorthodox approach of Mainline Christians to medicine, health, and the ministry of healing.

Klassen, Pamela E. "Textual Healing: Mainstream Protestants and the Therapeutic Text, 1900-1925." *Church History* 75:4 (2006): 809-848. In this essay, Klassen points out that Western Protestantism has found a ritual and therapeutic dimension to scripture and other texts.

Klassen, Pamela. "The Politics of Protestant Healing: Theoretical Tools for the Study of Spiritual Bodies and The Body Politic." *Spiritus: A Journal of Christian Spirituality* 14.1 (2014): 68-75. Klassen examines anthropological and sociopolitical issues intersecting with embodiment and healing.

Knight III, Henry H. "Holiness and Healing," in *Anticipating Heaven Below: Optimism of Grace from Wesley to the Pentecostals*, 157-182. Eugene Oregon: Cascade Books, 2014. Knight examines nineteenth and early twentieth century healing modalities through the lens of Wesleyan theology.

Krüger, Günter. "Johann Christoph Blumhardt (1805–1880): A Man for the Kingdom." *Currents in Theology and Missions* 23:6 (December 1996): 427–441. This is a well-researched article on noted German healing proponent, Johann Christoph Blumhardt.

Larson, E. L. and S. M. Larson. "A Philosophy of Healing from the Ministry of Jesus," *Faith & Thought* 112:1 (1986): 67-75. This article examines Jesus' healing ministry through the lens of science.

Love, Stuart L. "Jesus, Healer of the Canaanite Woman's Daughter in Matthew's Gospel: A Social-Scientific Inquiry." *Biblical Theology Bulletin: Journal of Bible and Culture* 32:1 (February 2002) 11-20. Love examines a healing account from Matthew through the lens of sociology.

Ludwig, Garth D. *Order Restored: A Biblical Interpretation of Health, Medicine, and Healing.* St. Louis: Concordia Academic Press, 1999. Ludwig, a Lutheran pastor and anthropologist, examines biblical models of healing placing them in tension with contemporary medical practice.

Martin, Trevor. *Kingdom Healing: A New Look at What the Bible Says About Healing.* London: Marshall Morgan and Scott, 1981. Martin, an English churchman, carefully frames the doctrine of healing in terms of the Kingdom of God. John Wimber later claimed that this book helped him in his theological formation.

Morton, John G. "Christ's Diagnosis of Disease at Bethesda," *Expository Times* 33:9 (June 1922): 424-425. This essay briefly engages the linguistics and form of this healing account from the gospels.

McClymond, Michael J. "Charismatic Gifts: Healing, Tongue Speaking, Prophecy, and Exorcism," in *The Wiley-Blackwell Companion to World Christianity*, eds. Lamin Sanneh and Michael J. McClymond, 399-418. West Sussex, United Kingdom: John Wiley and Sons, 2016. McClymond navigates the historical, theological, and practical dimensions of spiritual gifts.

McClymond, Michael J. "Charismatic Renewal and Neo-Pentecostalism: From North American Origins to Global Permutations," in *The Cambridge Companion To Pentecostalism*, eds. Cecil M. Robeck, Jr., and Amos Young, 31-51. New York, Cambridge University Press, 2014. In this essay, McClymond considers the expanding trajectories of Spirit-filled Christianity.

McClymond, Michael J. "Protestantism, Evangelicalism, Pentecostalism: Changing Contours of Christianity in the Modern Era," in *Theological*

Foundations, ed. J. J. Mueller, 121-143. Winona, Minnesota: Anselm Academic, 2011. McClymond examines the intersection of Evangelicalism and Spirit-filled Christianity in the twenty-first century.

Michael McClymond, "After Toronto: Randy Clark's Global Awakening, Heidi and Rolland Baker's Iris Ministries, and the Post-1990s Global Charismatic Networks," *Pneuma Journal* (2016): 38. McClymond examines Post-Toronto ministries redefining the Third Wave Movement.

McEwen, J. S. "The Ministry of Healing." *Scottish Journal of Theology* 7 (1954): 133-152. In responding to claims by healing evangelists in the United States and Europe, McEwen explores the history and scope of physical deliverance.

McGinley, Lawrence J. *Form Criticism of the Synoptic Healing Narratives: A Study Theories of Martin Dibelius and Rudolf Bultmann.* Woodstock, Maryland: Woodstock College Press, 1944. Responding to Bultmann's "demythologizing" approach, McGinley explores the healing narratives in the synoptic gospels.

McGinley, Lawrence J. "Form Criticism of the Synoptic Healing Narratives." *Theological Studies* 4 (1943): 53-99, 385-419. This well-researched article examines the syntax and linguistics of healing passages from the synoptic gospels.

McGilvray, J.C., ed. *Health: Medical -Theological Perspectives: The Report of the Second Tubingen Consultation.* Geneva: World Council of Churches, 1967. This work, from the World Council of Churches, examines the merits and challenges of the ministry of healing.

McGuire, Meredith B. *Lived Religion: Faith and Practice in Everyday Life.* New York: Oxford University Press, 2008. In this eclectic work, McGuire argues that religion should not be overly defined by religious organizations. It should also gain its meaning by how it is practiced in everyday lives.

McKay, Bobbie, and Lewis A. Musil, *Healing The Spirit: Stories of Transformation*. Allen, Texas: Thomas More, 2000. McKay and Musil interact with United Church of Christ and other mainline adherents, exploring experiences of spiritual healing.

Mead, Richard T. 'The Healing of the Paralytic: A Unit?" *Journal of Biblical Literature* 80:4 (1961): 348-354. In this well-researched essay, Mead provides an insightful exegetical study of Mark 2:1-12.

Meier, John P. *A Marginal Jew: Mentor, Message, and Miracles*, volume two. New Haven Connecticut: Yale University Press, 1994. In this expansive, well-researched volume on the historical Jesus, Meier focuses his attention on Jesus' miracles.

Menken, Maarten J. J. "The Source of the Quotation from Isaiah 53:4 in Matthew 8:17." *Novum Testamentum* 39 (1997): 313-327. This article examines Isaiah's suffering servant and how the role of healing is affirmed in the Gospel of Matthew.

Mills, Mary E. *Human Agents of Cosmic Power in Hellenistic Judaism and the Synoptic Tradition*. Sheffield, England: Sheffield Academic Press, 1990. Mills suggests that the ancients believed that the universe was made up of spiritual and material elements. These elemental forces affected human life positively or negatively. Mills suggests that this was what shaped the life and ministry of Jesus of Nazareth.

Moltmann, Jürgen. *The Spirit of Life: A Universal Affirmation*. Minneapolis, Minnesota: Fortress Press, 1992. In this notable work, Moltmann articulates how his pneumatology has been shaped by the ethos of Johann Christoph Blumhardt and his son. In this notable work, Moltmann affirms Charismatic Christianity and acknowledges divine healing's validity.

Moltmann, Jürgen. "The Hope for the Kingdom of God and Signs of Hope in the World: The Relevance of Blumhardt's Theology Today." *Pneuma: A Journal for Pentecostal Studies* 26:1 (Spring 2004): 4

– 16. This essay considers the implications of Johann Christoph Blumhardt's victorious theology.

Morgan, Edmund R. *The Ordeal of Wonder: Thoughts on Healing*. London: Oxford University Press, 1964. A man who spent forty-five years in practical ministry wrote this book. He addresses clergy, hospital chaplains, and those interested in the relationship between bodily and spiritual health.

Morris, Russell A., and Daniel T. Lioy. "A Historical and Theological Framework for Understanding Word of Faith Theology." *Conspectus* 13 (2012): 73-115. This journal article considers the historical origins, contextual influences, and key components in the development of the Word of Faith message.

Muir, Steven C. "Healing, Initiation, and Community in Luke-Acts: A Comparative Analysis," Ph.D., diss., University of Ottawa, 1998. This work explores healing and related elements in the Gospel of Luke and Acts.

Neyrey, Jerome H. "Miracles in Other Words: Social Science Perspectives On Healing," in *Miracles in Jewish and Christian Antiquity*, ed. John C. Cavadini, 19-55. Notre Dame, Indiana: University of Notre Dame Press, 1999. Some of the underlying sociological dynamics of healing are examined in this is a well-researched work.

Norberg, Tilda and Robert D. Webber. *Stretch Out Your Hand: Exploring Healing Prayer*. Nashville, Tennessee: Upper Room, 1998. Norberg, a pastor and psychotherapist, joins Webber, a New Testament professor. They discuss healing practices in the local church and wrestle with the difficulties that ensue. In a typical mainline approach, they focus more on psychological, emotional, and relational healing, somewhat minimizing charismatic approaches to healing.

Novakovic, Lidija. *Messiah, the Healer of the Sick: A Study of Jesus as the Son of David in the Gospel of Matthew*. Tübingen: Mohr Siebeck, 2003. This in-depth analysis explores how Jesus' role as a healer is grounded in His role as the Davidic king. Many studies have found no connections between David and miracles, but Novakovic offers a different outlook.

Novakovic, Lidija. "The Healer of the Sick: A Study of the Origins of Matthew's Portrayal of Jesus as the Son of David," Ph.D., diss., Princeton Theological Seminary, 2002. Novakovic ties Jesus' role as a Davidic king with His function as a healer.

Numbers, Ronald L., and Darrel W. Amundsen, eds. *Caring and Curing: Health and Medicine in the Western Religious Traditions.* New York: Macmillan Publishing Company, 1986. This well-researched anthology explores health and healing traditions in several religious movements in the West.

Olsen, Peder. *Healing Through Prayer*, tr. John Jensen. Minneapolis: Augsburg, 1962. Olsen, a Norwegian chaplain, argues that healing prayer is still efficacious and encourages ministers to pray for the sick.

Opp, James W. "Healing Hands, Healthy Bodies: Protestant Women and Faith Healing in Canada and the United States, 1880 – 1930," in *Women and Twentieth-Century Protestantism*, eds. Margaret Lamberts Bendroth and Virginia Lieson Brereton, 236-256. Urbana, Illinois: University of Illinois Press, 2002. This well-researched article explores the pivotal role of women in the faith cure movement.

Opp, James W. *Lord for the Body: Religion, Medicine, and Protestant Faith Healing in Canada, 1880-1930.* Montreal: McGill-Queens University Press, 2005. In this notable work, Opp explores the faith cure movement and early Pentecostalism in Canada.

Opp, James W. "The Word and the Flesh: Religion, Medicine, and Protestant Faith Healing Narratives in North America, 1880-1910." *Social History/Histoire Sociale* 36:71 (2003): 205-224. Opp explores healing practices associated with the antebellum faith cure movement.

Ostrander, Rick. *The Life of Prayer in A World of Science: Protestants, Prayer and American Culture 1870-1930.* New York: Oxford University Press, 2000. This work examines American intercessory practices against the backdrop of Darwinism, urbanization, and the industrial revolution.

Palmer, Paul F. "The Purpose of Anointing the Sick: A Reappraisal." *Theological Studies* 19:3 (September 1958): 309-344. Palmer effectively argues that the sacrament of Extreme Unction was associated with anointing the sick before it became a rite for purifying the dying.

Pattison, Stephen. *Alive and Kicking: Toward A Practical Theology of Illness and Healing.* London: SCM Press, 1989. This is an examination of the theology of illness, written by a mainline leader with concerns about social organization and justice.

Peter, Theodore. "Wholeness in Salvation and Healing." *Lutheran Quarterly* 5:3 (1991): 297-314. Peters' insightful essay examines the scope of the salvific work of Jesus.

Pilch, John J. "Biblical Leprosy and Bodily Symbolism." *Biblical Theology Bulletin* 11 (1981): 119-133. This fascinating engagement with scripture considers the sociological dimensions of human embodiment and suffering.

Pilch, John J. "Deafness, disease, dropsy, dumb, dysentery, ecstasy, epilepsy, and fever," in *New Interpreter's Dictionary of the Bible.* vol. 2: D-H. Nashville: Abingdon Press, 2007. Pilch, recognized for his anthropological and sociological studies, wrote essays on some of the major illnesses of the Bible. These were included in the *New Interpreter's Dictionary of the Bible.*

Pilch, John J. "Heal, health, ill, illness, sick, and sickness," in *The Westminster Theological Wordbook of the Bible.* Donald E. Gowan, ed.

Louisville: Westminster John Knox Press, 2003. Pilch examines the cultural and social background of disease and healing in the Bible.

Pilch, John J. "Healing in Mark: A Social Science Analysis." *Biblical Theology Bulletin Journal of Bible and Culture* 15:4 (November 1985): 142-150. This essay is a fascinating sociological excursus on healing in the Gospel of Mark.

Pilch, John J. *Healing in the New Testament: Insights from Medical and Mediterranean Anthropology*. Minneapolis: Augsburg Fortress Press, 2000. Pilch examines some of the Hebraic customs and culture pertaining to health.

Pilch, John J. "Improving Bible Translations: The Example of Sickness and Healing." *Biblical Theology Bulletin* 30 (2000): 129-134. In this essay, Pilch demonstrates how a better understanding of first century conceptions of sickness and healing could improve modern biblical translations.

Pilch, John J. "Insights and Models for Understanding the Healing Activity of the Historical Jesus," in *Society of Biblical Literature Seminar Papers*, Atlanta: Scholars Press, 1993, 154-77. Pilch brings further sociological and anthropological insights into New Testament healing studies.

Pilch, John J. "Jesus' Healing Activity: Political Acts?" in *Understanding the Social World of the New Testament*, ed. Dietmar Neufeld and Richard E. DeMaris, 147-155. London and New York: Routledge, 2009. This article explores the political and social implications of Jesus' healing acts.

Pilch, John J. "Sickness and Healing in Luke – Acts." In *The Social World of Luke – Acts: Models for Interpretation*, ed. Jerome H. Neyrey, 181-210. Peabody, Massachusetts: Hendrickson Publishers, 1991. Pilch examines the sociological implications of disease and healing in the Book of Acts.

Pilch, John J. "Sickness and Long Life." *Biblical Theology Bulletin* 33 (February 1995): 94-98. In this essay, Pilch delves into ancient Mediterranean notions of lifespan, death, and disease.

Pilch, John J. "The Health Care System in Matthew: A Social Science Analysis." *Biblical Theology Bulletin: Journal of Bible and Culture* 16:3 (August 1986): 102-106. Pilch considers the treatment of illness in the first century and how it informs one's reading of the gospel of Matthew.

Pilch, John J. "Understanding Biblical Healing: Selecting the Appropriate Model." *Biblical Theology Bulletin: Journal of Bible and Culture* 18: 2 (May 1988): 60-66. Pilch argues that the expositors of biblical healing stories must clarify the models behind their interpretations. Biblical cures of lepers are typically considered through two models: the biomedical/empiricist and the hermeneutic/cultural.

Pilch, John J. "Understanding Healing in the Social World of Early Christianity." *Biblical Theology Bulletin: A Journal of Bible and Theology* 22:1 (February 1, 1992) 26-33. Pilch discusses two culturally diverse healing definitions and presents a select list of books that aid in cross-cultural efforts in interpreting ancient Mediterranean texts.

Pilch, John J. *Visions and Healing in the Acts of the Apostles: How the Early Believers Experienced God.* Collegeville, Minnesota: Liturgical Press, 2004. Pilch offers anthropological and sociological insights on some of the healings depicted in the Book of Acts.

Pinnock, Clark and Robert Brow. "Healing: Transforming Love," in *Unbounded Love.* Downer's Grove, Illinois: Intervarsity Press, 1994, 151-159. Pinnock, a noted professor of theology, and Brow, a local pastor, provide an introduction to the theology of healing. The book begins with the following line: "Salvation is the healing of persons."

Poloma, Margaret M. "An Apostle of Love: Heidi Baker, the 'Toronto Blessing,' and the New Apostolic Reformation," paper presented at the Society for Pentecostal Studies Annual Meeting at Regent University, February 29-March 3, 2012. Against the backdrop of the Toronto Blessing and a splintering of twenty first century revivalism, Poloma examines the extraordinary ministry of Heidi Baker, missionary to Mozambique.

Poloma, Margaret M. "A Comparison of Christian Science and Mainline Christian Healing Ideologies and Practices." *Review of Religious Research* 32:4 (1991): 337-350. In this article, Poloma compares the healing practices between orthodox and heterodox groups.

Poloma, Margaret M. "An Empirical Study of Perceptions of Healing Among Assemblies of God Members." *Pneuma: The Journal For The Society of Pentecostal Studies* 7:1 (Spring 1985): 61-78. This article explores conceptions of healing within the General Council of the Assemblies of God. Poloma is a gifted sociologist and presents some fascinating findings.

Poloma, Margaret M. " Divine Healing, Religious Revivals, and Contemporary Pentecostalism: A North American Perspective," in *The Spirit in the World: Emerging Pentecostal Theologies in Global Contexts*, ed. Veli-Matti Karkkainen, 21-39. Grand Rapids, Michigan: Eerdmans, 2009. Poloma explores contemporary Charismatic movements and their involvement with divine healing.

Poloma, Margaret M. *Main Street Mystics: The Toronto Blessing and Reviving Pentecostalism*. Lanham, Maryland: Altamira Press, 2004. In this work, Poloma explores late nineteenth and early twentieth century revival ministries.

Poloma, Margaret M. "Old Wine, New Wineskins: The Rise of Healing Rooms in Revival Pentecostalism." *Pneuma: The Journal of the Society of Pentecostal Studies* 28:1 (Spring 2006): 59-71. This is a well-researched article on the reemergence of healing rooms in the early twenty-first century.

Poloma, Margaret M. "The Spirit Movement in North America at the Millennium: From Azusa Street to Toronto, Pensacola and Beyond." *Journal of Pentecostal Theology* 12 (1998): 83-107. Poloma explores dynamics related to late twentieth century revivalism.

Poloma, Margaret M., and Lynette F. Hoelter. "The 'Toronto Blessing': A Holistic Model of Healing." *Journal for the Scientific Study of Religion* (1998): 257-272. This is a fascinating sociological study of healing in the Toronto Blessing.

Porterfield, Amanda. *Healing in the History of Christianity*. New York: Oxford University Press, 2005. Porterfield's notable work examines the history of healing within Christianity.

Porterfield, Amanda. "Healing in The History of Christianity, Presidential Address, January 2002, American Society of Church History." *Church History* 71:2 (June 2002): 227-242. In this article, Porterfield argues for healing's significance in the history of Christianity.

Porterfield, Amanda. "Introduction: Forum on Sacred Spaces of Healing in Modern American Christianity." *Church History* 75:3 (2006): 594 – 611. Porterfield introduces the idea of sacred space and how it shapes one's understanding and application of healing.

Pretorius, Stephan P. "Is 'Divine healing' in the 'Faith Movement' Founded on the Principles of Healing in the Bible or Based on the Power of the Mind?" *HTS Theological Studies* 65.1 (2009): 399-405. This article suggests that the healing practices espoused by Pentecostal and Charismatic ministers are nothing more than "mind-over-matter." Pretorius suggests that, in this methodology, there is no indication of Godly intervention. He also believes that in this modality, there is also no submission to the will of God.

Price, Robert M. "Illness Theodicies in the New Testament," *Journal of Religion and Health* 25:4 (Winter 1986): 309-315. Price discusses the different explanations for the origin of sickness in the New

Testament. He points out the notion that Satan victimizes the innocent as well as the idea that punishment may come from God due to sin.

Ramsey, Ian T., G.H. Boobyer, F.N. Davey, M.C. Perry, and Henry J. Cadbury. *The Miracles and The Resurrection*. Eugene, Oregon: Wipf and Stock Publishers, 1964, 2010. A group of liberal scholars reflect on the meaning and legitimacy of miracles.

Ramshaw, Elaine. "Rites of Healing," in *Ritual and Pastoral Care*. Philadelphia: Fortress, 1987, 64-67. Ramshaw provides guidance for the usage of healing rites and liturgical forms in a mainline congregation.

Remus, Harold. *Jesus as Healer, Understanding Jesus Today Series*. Cambridge, United Kingdom: Cambridge University Press, 1997. This book is a brief compendium on the "historic Jesus," examining His function and role as a healer. Remus was a professor of religion and culture at Wilfrid Laurier University in Aterloo, Ontario, Canada.

Riale, Frank N. *The Sinless, Sickless, Deathless Life: God's Glory Goal For All*. New York: L.J. Walker and Company, 1913. Riale, a secretary of the Presbyterian Board of Education of New York, writes about the overcoming life. He was convinced that believers could triumph in matters of health.

Riale, Frank N. *The Divine Antidote to Sin, Sickness, And Death*. New York: The Christian Work, 1921. In this practical work, Riale emphasizes an overcoming life through the appropriation of the gospel.

Riale, Frank N. *The Healing Ministry of Jesus: A Healing Handbook for Believers*. New York: Christian Literature Publishing Company, 1930. Riale provides some practical guidance for those who want to receive healing.

Risdon, Bennett. *Diseases of The Bible*. London: Religious Tract Society, 1887. Risdon carefully examines each of the diseases depicted in Scripture.

Riss, Richard. *A Survey of Twentieth Century Revival Movements in North America*. Peabody, Massachusetts, Hendrickson, 1988. In this work, Riss explores several different revival movements in the United States and Canada. Among other observations, there are some fascinating insights on the ministry of healing.

Riss, Richard. "Charles Sydney Price." *Dictionary of Pentecostal Charismatic Movements*, eds. Gary McGee, Stanley Burgess, and Patrick Alexander, 726-727. Grand Rapids, Michigan: Zondervan Publishing, 1988. In this essay, Riss provides a short biographical sketch of Charles S. Price, a notable Pentecostal healing evangelist.

Riss, Richard. "Faith Homes." *Dictionary of Pentecostal Charismatic Movements*, eds. Gary McGee, Stanley Burgess, and Patrick Alexander, 298-300. Grand Rapids, Michigan: Zondervan Publishing, 1988. Grand Rapids, Michigan: Zondervan, 1988. In this work, Richard Riss examines the history of North American faith healing homes.

Riss, Richard. "Raymond Theodore Richey." *Dictionary of Pentecostal Charismatic Movements*, eds. Gary McGee, Stanley Burgess, and Patrick Alexander, 758. Grand Rapids, Michigan: Zondervan Publishing, 1988. Grand Rapids, Michigan: Zondervan, 1988. Riss, in this biographical sketch, provides an overview of the life of 1950s Voice of Healing evangelist Raymond Richey.

Robins, Henry C. "Spiritual Healing in the History of the Church," *London Quarterly and Holborn Review*, 181 (July 1956): 171-174. This polemical article explores Christian healing from a historical perspective, examining liturgy and other dynamics.

Robbins, Vernon K. "The Healing of Bartimaeus (10:46-52) in Marcan Theology." *Journal of Biblical Literature* 92:2 (June 1973): 224-243.

This is an exegetical article on the account of healing in Mark 10:46-52.

Robbins, Vernon K. "The Woman Who Touched Jesus' Garment: Socio-Rhetorical Analysis of the Synoptic Account." *New Testament Studies* 33 (1987): 502-515. This is an analysis of one of the key healing stories in the New Testament.

Salmon, Elsie H. *He Heals Today*. Evesham, United Kingdom: Arthur James, 1951. Salmon, a South African minister's wife, actively operates in the ministry of healing. This work includes testimonies and biblical reflections.

Sandford, Edgar L. *God's Healing Power*. New York: Prentice Hall, 1959. Edgar "Ted" Sandford was the husband of Agnes Sandford. This work shares his insights into the doctrine of healing.

Schattauer, Thomas H. "Healing Rites and the Transformation of Life: Observations and Insights from within the Evangelical Lutheran Church in America." *Liturgy* 22:3 (July 2007): 32. This article explores liturgical healing practices within Evangelical Lutheranism.

Scherzer, Carl. *The Church and Healing*. Philadelphia: Westminster Press, 1950. Scherzer's work carefully explores early Christianity's attitude toward sickness and healing.

Schiefelbein, Kyle K. "'Receive This Oil as a Sign of Forgiveness and Healing:' A Brief History of the Anointing of the Sick and Its Use in Lutheran Worship." *Word and World* 30:1 (Winter 2010): 51-62. This is a fascinating essay on the liturgy of healing in the mainline tradition.

Seybold, Klaus and Ulrich B. Mueller. *Sickness and Healing*. Nashville, Tennessee: Abingdon Publishing, 1981. Two outstanding German scholars review biblical passages on sickness and healing, the miracles of Jesus, and the relation of faith to healing.

Sheldon, Michael G. *Health, Healing, and Medicine.* Edinburgh, Scotland, United Kingdom: The Handsel Press, 1987. This work examines contemporary issues that intersect with health and disease.

Smith, Morton. "Prolegomena to a Discussion of Aretalogies, Divine Men, the Gospels and Jesus." *Journal of Biblical Literature* 90:2 (June 1971): 174-199. In this scholarly essay, Smith reflects on the conception of God in first century Greco-Roman culture.

Stanger, Frank Bateman. *God's Healing Community.* Nappenee, Indiana: Francis Asbury Press, 1985, 2000. Stanger, a United Methodist minister, discusses definitions, theology, and practical approaches to healing.

Stoffel, Ernest Lee. "An Exposition of Mark 10:46-52." *Interpretation* 30:3 (July 1976): 288-292. Stoffel, of Riverside Presbyterian Church in Jacksonville, Florida, carefully examines the story of blind Bartimaeus' healing.

Stunt, Timothy. *From Awakening to Secession: Radical Evangelicals in Switzerland and Britain, 1815-35.* Edinburgh, Scotland: Bloomsbury T&T Clark, 2000. In this volume, Stunt has arguably produced the definitive study of radical sects in Switzerland, Scotland, Ireland, Oxford, and Plymouth. He adds new dimensions to the knowledge of nineteenth century ecclesiastical history.

Sullivan, Francis A. *The Laying on of Hands in the Christian Tradition.* Sheffield, United Kingdom: Sheffield Academic Press, 1994. This work examines the tradition of laying on of hands, reflecting on healing and other Christian practices.

Surgitharajah, R. S. "Men, Trees and Walking: A Conjectural Solution to Mark 8:24." *Expository Times* 103 (1992): 172-173. This exegetical article examines Jesus' healing interaction with a blind man in Mark 8:24.

Thiessen, Gerd. *The Miracle Stories of the Early Christian Tradition*, tr. Francis McDonagh. Edinburgh: T&T Clark, 1983. This is a study of the synoptic miracle stories, considering their linguistics, structure, and function.

Thomas, Zach. *Healing Touch: The Church's Forgotten Language*. Louisville, Kentucky: Westminster, John Knox Press, 1994. This work, by a hospital chaplain and parish minister, considers the viability of "touch" in healing engagements. While this work does not emphasize charisms, it does leave an opening for deeper works.

Tillich, Paul. "Heal the Sick, Cast Out Demons." *Union Seminary Quarterly* 11:1 (November 1955): 6–9. Tillich, one of the most noted theologians of the twentieth century, takes a skeptical approach to healing and miracles.

Tillich, Paul. "The Relation of Religion and Health," in *Religion and Health: A Symposium*, ed. Simon Daniger, 185–205. New York: Association Press, 1958. Tillich, a prominent New Testament theologian, explores how faith relates to health.

Tomlinson, John W. B. "The Magic Methodists," in *Signs, Wonders, Miracles, Representations of Divine Power in the Life of the Church*, ed. Kate Cooper and Jeremy Gregory, 389–99. Woodbridge, United Kingdom: Boydell, 2005. This work explores what early Methodists understood about healing and other works of power.

Van Buskirk, James D. *Religion, Healing, and Health*. New York: Macmillan Publishing Company, 1953. This is a work on healing from a mainline scholar that was published during the height of the salvation healing revivals.

Van Der Loos, Hendrik. *The Miracles of Jesus*. Leiden, Netherlands: Brill, 1968. This work is an in-depth study of the miracles of Jesus from a gifted European scholar.

Vledder, Evert-Jan. *Conflict in The Miracle Stories: A Socio-Exegetical Study of Matthew 8 and 9*. Sheffield, United Kingdom: Sheffield Academic Press, 1997. In this stimulating sociological study, Vledder points out that Matthew's community was called to act in the interests of the marginalized.

Wilson, Walter T. *Healing in the Gospel of Matthew: Reflections on Method and Ministry*. Minneapolis, Minnesota: Fortress Press, 2014. In this work, Wilson utilizes an interdisciplinary approach in examining the healing narratives in the Gospel of Matthew.

Various. *Anointing and Healing*. New York: United Lutheran Church in America, 1962. This is the United Lutheran Church in America's official report on healing practices in local churches. This document was written in response to the salvation healing revival of the 1950s.

Various. *Divine Healing and Co-operation Between Doctors and Clergy*. London: British Medical Association, 1956. This book focuses on ways that doctors and physicians can work together to bring healing.

Various. *Healing and Wholeness: The Churches' Role in Health*. Geneva: World Council of Churches, 1990. This is a report on the church's role in healing presented by the Christian Medical Commission. The emphasis is on medical missions, but this document allows room for additional applications.

Various. *Relation of Christian Faith to Health*. Philadelphia: United Presbyterian Church (USA), General Assembly paper, May 1960. This is an official paper on the ministry of healing from the United Presbyterian Church.

Various. *Sickness and Health*. Toronto, Ontario: United Church of Canada Board of Evangelism and Social Service, 1967. This is an assessment of health and disease from the United Church of Canada.

Various. *Spiritual Healing: A Report of a Clerical and Medical Committee of Inquiry into Spiritual, Faith, and Mental Healing*. London: Macmillan,

1914. This is a report on the efficacy of spiritual healing from pastors and medical professionals.

Various. *Spiritual Healing: The Report of the Church of Scotland Commission.* Edinburgh: St. Andrews Press, 1958. This is an official report on the ministry of healing from the Church of Scotland. Like other denominations, they are responding to the salvation–healing revival.

Various. *The Ministry of Healing in the Church: A Handbook of Principles and Practice. Presbyterian Church of England.* London: Independent Press, 1963. These are guidelines for ministering healing in Presbyterian churches in England.

Various. *The Relation of Christian Faith to Health, Adopted by The 172nd General Assembly May 1960.* Philadelphia, Pennsylvania: The United Presbyterian Church in the United States of America, 1960. This document provides reflections on healing for participants in the United Presbyterian Church.

Vincent, Marvin R. "Dr. Stanton On 'Healing Through Faith.'" *Presbyterian Review* 5 (April 1884): 305-329. This article is Vincent's rebuttal of Robert L. Stanton's article, "Healing Through Faith."

Vincent, Marvin R. "Modern Miracles." *Presbyterian Review* 4 (July 1883): 473-502. Through this article, Vincent instigates a theological dialogue with Robert L. Stanton on the viability of modern expressions of divine healing.

Vogtle, Anton. "The Miracles of Jesus Against Their Contemporary Background," in *Jesus in His Time*, ed. H.J. Schultz, tr. Brian Watchorn, 96-105. London: Society For Promoting Christian Knowledge, 1971. This study explores Jesus' healings against the broader backdrop of first century assumptions.

Waddle, Charles W. "Miracles of Healing." *The American Journal of Psychology* 20 (1909): 219-268. In this early twentieth century article, Waddle examines healing assertions throughout history.

Ware, Stephen L. *Restorationism in the Holiness Movement in the Late Nineteenth and Early Twentieth Centuries.* Lewiston, New York: Mellen Press, 2005. This well-researched work explores the history and practices of radical holiness adherents.

Webber, Robert E. "Anointing of the Sick," in *The Complete Library of Christian Worship 6*: The Sacred Actions of Christian Worship. Peabody, Massachusetts: Hendrickson, 1994, 331-340. Webber, a worship specialist, compiles history, theology, and liturgical elements in his discussion of healing.

Webber, Robert E. "A Christian View of Healing," *The Complete Library of Christian Worship 7*: The Ministries of Christian Worship Peabody, Massachusetts: Hendrickson, 1994, 239-242. In this work, Weber provides an introduction to a contemporary Protestant theology of healing.

Webber, Robert E. ed. "Worship and Pastoral Care: A Charismatic Approach," *The Complete Library of Christian Worship 7*: The Ministries of Christian Worship. Peabody, Massachusetts: Hendrickson, 1994, 305-316. Weber culls together a number of essays that cover things like: "Pastoral Care and Direct Divine Healing," "Four Basic Types of Healing," "Healing of Sin," "Inner Healing of Emotions," "Physical Healing," "Deliverance and Exorcism."

Wenham, G.J. "Christ's Healing Ministry and His Attitude to The Law" in *Christ the Lord: Studies in Christology Presented to David Gunthry*, ed. H.H. Rowden, 115-126. Leicester, United Kingdom: Intervarsity Press, 1982. This is an academic look at Jesus' healing ministry against the context of Jewish law.

Williams, Tammy R. "Is There a Doctor in The House? Reflections On the Presence of Healing in African American Churches," in *Practicing Theology: Beliefs and Practices in Christian Life*, eds. Volf, Miroslav and Dorothy C. Bass, 94-120. Grand Rapids, Michigan: William B. Eerdmans Publishing Company, 2002. This is a fascinating examination of healing practices within black Pentecostal congregations.

Wink, Walter. "Mark 2:1-12." *Interpretation* 36:1 (1982): 58-63. Wink, a noted liberal theologian, provides an exegetical examination of divine healing accounts in the second chapter of Mark.

Wink, Walter. "Write What You See: An Odyssey by Walter Wink," *The Fourth R Journal* 7:3 (May-June 1994), 3-9. Wink, noted for associating "the powers" in the Pauline epistles with systemic evil, shares some of his personal experiences with Pentecostalism and divine healing.

Yamauchi, Edwin. "Magic or Miracle? Diseases, Demons, And Exorcisms," in *Gospel Perspectives, Volume 6: The Miracles of Jesus*, eds. Wenham, David and Craig Blomberg, 89-183. Sheffield: JOST Press, 1986. Clarifying the operation of magic in the ancient world, Yamauchi rebuffs claims by scholars that Jesus was a magician.

15. ROMAN CATHOLIC

Baldwin, Robert. *Healing and Wholeness.* United Kingdom: Paternoster Press, 1988. Drawing on his medical background and teaching acumen, Baldwin examines the biblical foundations of healing.

Baldwin, Robert. *The Healers.* Huntington, Indiana: Our Sunday Visitor Publishing Society, 1986. This book compiles biographical sketches of prominent Roman Catholic healers in history.

Borobio, Dionisio. "An Inquiry into Healing Anointing in the Early Church." *Concilium* 2 (April 1991): 37-49. This essay discusses the early history of anointing the sick.

Buckley, Michael. *Christian Healing: A Catholic Approach to God's Healing Love.* London: Catholic Truth Society Publications, 1990. This booklet discusses relational and pastoral strategies for healing in a Roman Catholic context.

Buckley, Michael. *His Healing Touch: Freedom Through Good Relationships.* Mineola, New York: Resurrection Press, 1987. This book explores links between repentance, sin, suffering, and forgiveness. It offers pointers to congregations about healing broken relationships and growing in wholeness.

Buckley, Michael, *More Stories that Heal.* London: Darton, Longman and Todd, 1992. This heartfelt work is a continuation of "Stories That Heal." In it, Buckley recounts inspiring healing testimonies.

Buckley, Michael. *Stories That Heal.* London: Darton, Longman & Todd/Daybreak, 1989. This work, from a noted Catholic minister, includes a number of inspiring healing accounts from history and modern experiences.

Cranston, Ruth. *The Miracle of Lourdes, Updated and Expanded Edition.* New York: Image Books, 1955, 1988. This book has been one of the major works on Lourdes, a notable Catholic pilgrimage site in France. Since 1858, multitudes have traveled there to receive healing.

Cuschieri, Andrew. *Anointing The Sick: A Theological and Canonical Study.* Lanham, Massachusetts: University Press of America, 1993. Cuschieri provides a concentrated study on anointing with oil and interceding for healing.

Davis, Frank Stafford. "Charismatic Christian Spiritual Healing in Two Cultural Contexts: Existential-Phenomenological Approach," M.A. thesis, Duquesne University, 1990. This thesis explores the meaning of healing, trying to avoid the typical reductionistic analysis of the academy.

DeGrandis, Robert. *The Gift of Miracles: Experiencing God's Extraordinary Power in Your Life.* Mercier Press, 1992. DeGrandis shares a number of healing testimonies. He included those who encountered breakthrough through the sacraments as well as everyday life.

DeGrandis, Robert, with Linda Schubert. *Healing Through the Mass, revised and expanded edition.* New York: Resurrection Press, 1992, 1997. This book focuses on healing encounters that are mediated through the Eucharist.

DiOrio, Ralph A. *A Miracle to Proclaim: Firsthand Experiences of Healing.* New York: Doubleday, 1984. DiOrio was a prominent Catholic Charismatic priest who prayed for the sick in Northeastern United States. This is a fascinating collection of testimonies.

DiOrio, Ralph A. *Signs and Wonders: Firsthand Experiences of Healing.* New York: Doubleday, 1987. This follow-up to his first book provides thirty additional testimonies of healing. Some of the accounts refer to the alleviation of heart disease and infertility.

Duffin, Jacalyn. *Medical Miracles: Doctors, Saints and Healing in the Modern World.* New York: Oxford University Press, 2009. This work surveys Vatican records, exploring the complicated relationship between miracles and medical practice. Duffin writes, "Overwhelmingly the miracles cited in canonizations between 1588 and 1999 are healings, and the majority entail medical care and physician testimony."

Feider, Paul A. *Healing and Suffering: The Christian Paradox*. London: Darton, Longman and Todd, 1988. This work explores issues of healing and suffering. Feider frames up Jesus as a psychologist and psychotherapist. He goes on to affirm the value of suffering and pain to produce humility.

Geddes, Francis. *Contemplative Healing: The Congregation as Healing Community*. Bloomington, Indiana: iUniverse, 2011. This practical work deals with healing as a contemplative and spiritual practice. Geddes argues: Everyone can be a healer. Science and healing need not be at odds. Jesus introduced healing as a transforming spiritual practice. Healing is grounded in love.

Hacker, George. *The Healing Stream: Catholic Insights into the Ministry of Healing*. London: Darton, Longman and Todd, 2008. Hacker explores the trajectories of modern healing ministries, asking, "What happens when one person is healed and not another. What dimension does faith play? While Catholic in orientation, Hacker's approach is broad and useful for other traditions.

Hampsch, John H. *The Healing Power of the Eucharist*. Ann Arbor, Michigan: Servant Publications, 1999. This work explores how healing can come through the sacrament of communion.

Häring, Bernhard. *Healing and Revealing: Wounded Healers Sharing Christ's Mission*. Slough, United Kingdom: Saint Paul Publications, 1984. Häring (1912 –1998) was a Redemptorist priest and a theologian within German Catholicism. This work explores broader theological themes that intersect with healing.

Harris, Ruth. *Lourdes: Body and Spirit in the Secular Age*. New York: Penguin Press, 1999. Harris, in this well-researched treatise, carefully explores Lourdes, the principal site of Catholic pilgrimage and healing prayer.

Heil. John Paul. "Significant Aspects of the Healing Miracles in Matthew," *Catholic Biblical Quarterly* 41:2 (April 1979): 274-287. Heil, a gifted Catholic scholar, examines the healing accounts in Matthew. He concludes, "The message of Jesus' healing events is not a mere appendage to the gospel kerygma but an essential part of it."

Helman, Charles Jeffrey. "The Emerging Revival of Sacramental Healing: An Incarnational Theology," Ph.D., diss., Notre Dame University, October 18, 2007. This work examines the viability and growth of sacramental healing practices in Protestant, Anglican, and Catholic traditions.

Heron, Benedict M. *Channels of Healing Prayer.* Notre Dame, Indiana: Ave Maria Press, 1992. Heron, a member of the Benedictine Community in London, talks about approaches to healing prayer.

Heron, Benedict M. *Praying for Healing: The Challenge, 2nd Edition.* Leicester, United Kingdom: New Life Publishing, 1998. In this book, Heron encourages healing, but not by mastering a technique, learning formulas, or following a set of rules. Heron clarifies that it is Jesus who heals us.

Hocken, Peter. "John Salmon." *Dictionary of Pentecostal Charismatic Movements,* eds. Gary McGee, Stanley Burgess, and Patrick Alexander, 766. Grand Rapids, Michigan: Zondervan Publishing, 1988. Hocken, a Catholic Charismatic, shares a biographical sketch of John Salmon, a healing evangelist associated with the Christian and Missionary Alliance.

Hocken, Peter. *Prayer for Healing: Reflections from an Ecumenical Perspective.* Rome, Italy: International Theological Commission for Catholic Charismatic Renewal, September 2003. This is an examination of the ministry of healing from a prominent Catholic Charismatic.

Jaki, Stanley L. *Miracles and Physics.* Front Royal, Virginia: Christendom Press, 2004. Jaki (1924-2009), a brilliant Catholic physicist, mathematician, and astronomer, argues that one must avoid the naïveté that places shallow constraints on scientific disciplines and also the irreligious spirit that empties the world of wonder.

Johnson, Earl S., Jr., "Mark 10:46-52: Blind Bartimaeus." *The Catholic Biblical Quarterly* 40:2 (1978): 191-204. This essay is an exegetical examination of the healing of blind Bartimaeus.

Kasza, John. *Understanding Sacramental Healing: Anointing and Viaticum.* Chicago: Liturgy Training Publications, 2005. This book provides a theological basis for the history of the Catholic practice of the sacrament of the sick. Kasza offers a cohesive synthesis of theology, canon law, medicine, anthropology, and liturgy.

Kingsbury, Jack Dean. "Observations on the 'Miracle Chapters' of Matthew 8-9," *Catholic Biblical Quarterly* 40:4 (1978): 559-573. Kingsbury, dealing with the particularities of this pericope, examines recent scholarly discourse.

Kuuliala, Jenni. "Heavenly Healing or Failure of Faith? Partial Cures in Later Medieval Canonization," in *Processes, Church and Belief in the Middle Ages. Popes, Saints, and Crusaders,* eds. Kirsi Salonen and Sari Katajala-Peltomaa. Amsterdam, Netherlands: Amsterdam University Press, 2016. This work explores some of the healings in the later middle ages. It examines the reality of partial healings.

Larson-Miller, Lizette. "A Christian Perspective on the the Relationship Between Medicine and Religion." *Journal of the San Francisco Medical Society* 80:4 (May 2007) 10-11. In this article, a Catholic academician looks at faith and modern health care.

Larson-Miller, Lizette. "Anointing of the Sick: A Historical Overview." *Liturgical Ministry* 7 (1998): 23-35. This article explores the history of anointing the sick and praying for healing.

Larson-Miller, Lizette. "Anointing of the Sick," in *Cambridge Dictionary of Christianity,* ed. Daniel Patte, New York: Cambridge University Press, 2010. This is an insightful article on the rite of healing in the liturgical tradition.

Larson-Miller, Lizette. "Caring for the Sick: A Historical Overview of a Central Ministry of the Church" *Liturgical Ministry* 16 (Fall 2007) 172-180. This essay considers the different ways that the Roman Catholic Church has responded to the needs of the sick.

Larson-Miller, Lizette. "Healed to Life: The Historical Development of Anointing of the Sick at the Heart of the Church's Healing Ministry" *Liturgy* 22:3 (2007) 3-12. This article considers the turbulent history of the healing sacrament within the Roman Catholic tradition.

Larson-Miller, Lizette. "Healing: Sacrament or Prayer?" *Anglican Theological Review* 88:3. (Summer 2006): 361-374. In this article, Larson-Miller asks whether healing should be understood as a sacrament or a form of intercession.

Larson-Miller, Lizette. "Healing Rituals," in *Cambridge Dictionary of Christianity*, ed. Daniel Patte. New York: Cambridge University Press, 2010. This essay provides a general overview of healing practices in the liturgical tradition.

Larson-Miller, Lizette. "Healed to Life: The Historical Development of Anointing of the Sick at the Heart of the Church's Healing Ministry," *Liturgy* 22:3 (2007) 3-12. This article explores how the healing sacrament developed and expanded.

Larson-Miller, Lizette. *Pastoral Care of the Sick and Dying. Liturgical Ministry* 16, *Fall 2007*. In this practical article, the role of the church in caring for the sick and dying is explored.

Larson-Miller, Lizette. *The Sacrament of Anointing of the Sick*. Collegeville, Minnesota: Liturgical Press, 2005. In this book, Larson-Miller explores the rite of healing prayer by looking at three primary actions: the prayer of faith, the laying on of hands, and the anointing with the blessed oil. This book provides an overview of the current healing sacrament, looking at it through the lens of contemporary liturgical, theological, pastoral and cultural issues.

Larson-Miller, Lizette. "Women and the Anointing of the Sick." *Coptic Church Review* 12 (1991) 37-48. Larson-Miller considers women's role in the ministry of the sick in the Roman Catholic Church.

Latourelle, René. *The Miracles of Jesus and The Theology of Miracles*, tr. Matthew J. O'Connell. New York: Paulist, 1988. This is an insightful reflection on Jesus' miracles and what they mean for Catholic believers today.

Laurentin, René. *Catholic Pentecostalism*, tr. Matthew J. O'Connell. Garden City, New York: Doubleday and Company, 1977. This is a well-researched work that examines the history and scope of the Catholic Charismatic Renewal.

Leuret, Francois, and Henri Bon. *Modern Miraculous Cures: A Documented Account of Miracles and Medicine in the Twentieth Century*, translated A.T. Macqueen and John C. Barry. New York: Farrar Straus and Cudahy Publishers, 1957. This work is a compendium of twentieth century Catholic miracle accounts.

Linn, Matthew, Dennis Linn, and Sheila Fabricant. *Praying with Another for Healing*. Mahwah, New Jersey: Paulist Press, 1994. These Catholic authors present a practical approach to ministering to the needy.

Linn, Matthew, Dennis Linn, and Sheila Fabricant. *Simple Ways to Pray for Healing*. Paulist Press, 1998. This book is a practical guide to help Catholics in their ministry to one another.

Linn, Matthew, Dennis Linn, and Barbara Ryan Shlemon. *To Heal as Jesus Healed*. Totowa, New Jersey: Resurrection Press, 1997. The Linn brothers, who are actively involved with the healing ministry, wrote this work. They are joined in their writing by Barbara Ryan, a nurse who has also ministered to the sick.

Loader, W. R. G. "Son of David, Blindness, Possession, and Duality in Matthew." *Catholic Biblical Quarterly* 44 (1982): 570-585. This is an essay from a Catholic journal that considers Jesus' role as a healer in the Gospel of Matthew.

MacNutt, Francis, and Judith MacNutt. *School of Healing Prayer*, level 1. Jacksonville, Florida: Christian Healing Ministries, 2007. This is a practical training manual describing some foundational approaches to the ministry of healing. The MacNutts actively share their extensive experience and insight with anyone who desires to function in the ministry of healing.

MacNutt, Francis, and Judith MacNutt. *School of Healing Prayer*, level 2. Jacksonville, Florida: Christian Healing Ministries, 2007. This is the second in a series of practical ministry manuals. They share additional strategies for praying for the sick.

MacNutt, Francis, and Judith MacNutt. *School of Healing Prayer*, level 3. Jacksonville, Florida: Christian Healing Ministries, 2007. This publication is the third in a series of functional healing manuals by the MacNutts. In this work, they deal with inner healing and demonic deliverance.

MacNutt, Francis. *Healing*, revised and expanded. Notre Dame, Indiana: Ava Maria Press, 1974, 1999. This is an influential work on the ministry of healing that has influenced many practitioners.

MacNutt, Francis. "The Mystery Why Some Are Healed and Others Are Not." HW 7 (July-September 1992): 10. In this article, MacNutt shares some of his insights into the reasons why some are not healed.

MacNutt, Francis. *The Practice of Healing Prayer: A How-To Guide for Catholics*. Frederick, Maryland: The Word Among Us Press, 2010. This is a practical guide to healing for Catholics. As always, MacNutt's insights are helpful for Protestants as well.

MacNutt, Francis. *The Prayer That Heals: Praying for Healing in the Family.* Notre Dame, Indiana: Ava Maria Press, 1981, 2005. This is a practical guide to pray for members of one's family.

MacNutt, Francis. *The Power to Heal.* Notre Dame, Indiana: Ava Maria Press, 1977. This well-researched book is a foundational work on the ministry of healing from one of the leading figures of the Catholic Charismatic Renewal.

MacNutt, Francis. *The Nearly Perfect Crime: How the Church Almost Killed the Ministry of Healing.* Grand Rapids, Michigan: Chosen Books, 2005. This is a well-researched book on how the ministry of healing was almost silenced in Christian tradition. This book was later re-released in paperback with a new title "The Healing Reawakening."

Marsh, Michael. *Healing Through the Sacraments.* Collegeville, Minnesota: Liturgical Press, 1987. This work discusses breakthrough and regenerative life through the sacraments and rites of the Church. Marsh writes, "Sacraments are visible signs of an invisible healing, 'medicine for immortality,' according to St. Ignatius of Antioch. The sacraments are meant to be experienced as personal encounters with Christ in His Church, so that the healing we so urgently need can go forth from them. The purpose of this book is to contribute to that experience."

McAlear, Richard. *Healing.* Rochester, New York: Richard McAlear OMI, 2010. McAlear is a scholar and priest who was impacted in the Charismatic Renewal in 1976. In this small book, he presents a series of essays on the theology of healing.

McAlear, Richard. *The Power of Healing Prayer: Overcoming Emotional and Psychological Blocks.* Huntington, Indiana: Our Sunday Visitor, 2013. This is a practical guide to holistic healing from a gifted Catholic scholar and practitioner.

McKenna, Briege with Henry Libersat. *Miracles Do Happen.* Cincinnati, Ohio: St. Anthony Messenger Press, 2002. This book tells the story of Sister Briege McKenna O.S.C., a member of the Sisters of Saint Clare and noted healing proponent. It also shares her insights about faith, the power of the Eucharist, and the importance of prayer.

McManus, Jim. *The Healing Power of the Sacraments*. Alton Hants, United Kingdom: Redemptorist Publications, 1984, 2005. Jim McManus, a Roman Catholic Priest, impacted by the Charismatic Renewal, has been active in the healing ministry for many years. Father McManus explores how lives are healed, changed, and enriched through the sacraments.

Midelfort, H. C. Erik. *Exorcism and Enlightenment: Johann Joseph Gassner and the Demons of the Eighteenth Century*. New Haven, Connecticut: Yale University Press, 2005. This work explores the controversial life and ministry of Gassner, an eighteenth century Catholic priest who brought healing to the masses of Germany through deliverance.

Milingo, Emmanuel. *The World in Between: Christian Healing and The Struggle for Spiritual Survival*. New York: Orbis Books, 1984. This work was written by a native African bishop in Zambia. In contrast to the others, he actively ministered in healing and deliverance. However, some of his views border on syncretism and should be read with caution.

Morrill, Bruce T. *Divine Worship and Human Healing: Liturgical Theology at the Margins of Life and Death*. Collegeville, Minnesota: Liturgical Press, 2009. This is a work from a Catholic researcher that explores the history of sacramentalism and healing rites in Catholicism.

Mouden, Louis. *Signs and Wonders: A Study of the Miraculous Element in Religion*. New York: Desclee Company, 1966. This work, by a gifted Catholic Scholar, explores the biblical and historical understanding of miracles.

Mumford, Nigel W.D. *The Forgotten Touch: More Stories of Healing*. New York: Seabury Books, 2007. Mumford is the director of the healing center, the Oratory of the Little Way, a Catholic Charismatic healing ministry. He formerly served as a Royal Marine Commando in the British military.

Mumford, Nigel W.D. *Hand to Hand: From Combat to Healing.* New York: Seabury Books, 2006. Mumford summarizes his extraordinary spiritual journey. He shares his personal story, stories from his healing ministry, and healing prayers, giving the reader insight into a little-known world of modern miracles. He writes, "My journey has transformed me from Royal Marine Commando to Lay Minister of Healing. Twenty-five years ago, I was trained to kill or be killed; now it is my privilege to teach people to heal and be healed."

Mussner, Franz. *The Miracles of Jesus: An Introduction*, tr. Albert Wimmer. Notre Dame, Indiana: University Notre Dame Press, 1968. Mussner, a gifted German scholar, argues that the miracles in the gospels portray the "ipsissima facta Jesu." It reflects who He really is.

O'Neill, Andy. *Charismatic Healing in Everyday Life.* Dublin, Ireland: Mercier Press, 1991. This book is a collection of healing stories and testimonies from the ministry of a Roman Catholic businessman with a burden for healing.

O'Neill, Andy. *The Miracle of Charismatic Healing.* Dublin, Ireland: Mercier Press, 1995. This book, written by an Irish insurance salesman, talks about the fuller reality of experiencing "Charismatic healing."

Palmer, Paul F. "The Purpose of Anointing the Sick: A Reappraisal." *Theological Studies* 19 (1958): 309-344. This is an article that explores the lengthy history and scope of the sacrament of healing.

Price, Alfred W. *Ambassadors of God's Healing: Handbook for The Practice of the Church's Ministry of Healing.* Philadelphia, Pennsylvania: Saint Stephen's Episcopal Church, 1945. Price was an Episcopalian healing proponent and a leader in the Order of Saint Luke.

Price, Alfred W. *Healing, The Gift of God.* Philadelphia, Pennsylvania: Saint Stephen's Episcopal Church, 1955. In this pamphlet, Price provides a practical discussion on the virtue of healing.

Ratzinger, Joseph. "Congregation for The Doctrine of the Faith: Instruction On Prayers for Healing." Rome: The Offices of the Congregation for the Doctrine of the Faith, September 14, 2000. Ratzinger, who later became Pope Benedict XVI, composed a major doctrinal reflection on healing prayer in the Roman Catholic Church.

Rogge, Louis P. "The Anointing of the Sick in Historical Perspective," *The Linacre Quarterly* 42:3 (1975): 205-215. This is an outstanding article explaining the changes in Roman Catholicism that enable a greater openness to healing.

Rogge, Louis P. "The Relationship Between the Sacrament/Anointing the sick and the Charism of Healing within the Catholic Charismatic Renewal," Ph.D., diss., Union Theological Seminary, 1984. This is an outstanding work, exploring the history and theological foundations of anointing the sick in Roman Catholicism.

Rosage, David E. *What Scripture Says About Healing: A Guide to Scriptural Prayer and Meditation.* Ann Arbor, Michigan: Servant Publications, 1988. Rosage, an Evangelical Catholic, shares some of his insights into the ministry of healing.

Ryan, Barbara Shlemon. "Restoring the Gifts of Healing: Reflections on 35 years of healing ministry," *Pentecost Today* 28:4 (October-December 2003). In this essay, Ryan provides some of her personal reflections on the ministry of healing within the Catholic Charismatic Renewal.

Ryan, Barbara, Dennis Linn and Matthew Linn. *To Heal as Jesus Healed.* Totowa, New Jersey: Resurrection Press, 1986, 1997. This is a practical guidebook for rank and file Catholics to pray for the sick.

Sanders, Peter. *Healing in the Spirit of Jesus: A Practical Guide to the Ministry.* Enumclaw, Washington: Winepress Publishing, 2003. Sanders has written an engaging overview of the ministry of healing.

Schroer, Silvia, and Thomas Staubli. *Body Symbolism in the Bible.* Collegeville, Minnesota: Liturgical Press, 2001. This book explores questions of embodiment and what body parts seem to communicate in the pages of the Bible. While not specifically dealing with "healing," this book provides wonderful insights on the biblical understanding of the human body.

Schuchts, Bob. *Be Healed: A Guide to Encountering the Powerful Love of Jesus in Your Life.* Notre Dame, Indiana: Ave Maria Press, 2014. In this practical guide, Catholic therapist, Bob Schuchts shares principles for appropriating physical and inner healing.

Sullivan, F.A. "Sacraments," *Dictionary of Pentecostal Charismatic Movements,* eds. Gary McGee, Stanley Burgess, and Patrick Alexander, 765-766. Grand Rapids, Michigan: Zondervan Publishing, 1988. Sullivan provides a fascinating foray into the meaning and scope of the sacraments.

Thomas, Leo, with Jan Alkire, *Healing as a Parish Ministry.* Notre Dame, Indiana: Ave Maria Press, 1992. This book is a practical guide to establishing a healing ministry in a local parish.

Thomas, Leo, with Jan Alkire. *Healing Ministry: A Practical Guide.* Kansas City, Missouri: Sheed and Ward, 1994. Dominican priest Leo Thomas shares principals of pastoral care and how they can be applied to the ministry of healing. The book's goal is to show Protestant and Catholic Christians how they can share the love of Jesus and impact people's lives.

Tripp, Kevin, Susan Wood, Peter Fink, Michael Drumm, Kevin Irwin, John M. Huels, and Genevieve Glen. *Recovering the Riches of Anointing: A Study of the Sacrament of the Sick.* Collegeville, Minnesota: Liturgical Press, 2002. This is an anthology of the papers presented at a symposium of the National Association of Catholic Chaplains (NACC). Anointing of the sick is considered from the vantage point of theology, history, and canon law.

Various. *Pastoral Care of the Sick: Rites of Anointing and Vaticum.* Tolowa, New Jersey: Catholic Book Publishing Corp, 1983. This is the second English translation of pastoral care rites released for liturgical and pastoral ministry. They deal with those who are sick or dying, and their loved ones.

Walsh, James Joseph. *The Catholic Church and Healing.* New York: MacMillan Company, 1928. James Joseph Walsh, M.D., LL.D., Sc.D. (1865-1942) was a Catholic physician and author. In this book, he argues that the Catholic Church has been "in intimate relation with the healing of mankind, body, and soul." He argues that the Church has continually affirmed natural and spiritual means of healing.

Ward, Charles F. "Two Recent Theories on the Finality of Extreme Unction," *The Catholic University of American Studies in Sacred Theology (Second Series)* 144 (1963): 57-63. This article explores the history and meaning of the sacrament of Extreme Unction.

16. CHARISMATIC RENEWAL

Allen, David. *The Unfailing Stream: A Charismatic Church History in Outline.* United Kingdom: Sovereign World, 1994. This is a overview of church history emphasizing renewal and charismata. Allen provides many valuable insights.

Arbuthnot, Andy, and Audrey Arbuthnot. *Love That Heals: God Works in Power at The London Healing Mission.* Basingstoke, Hants, United Kingdom: Marshall Pickering, 1986. This is a collection of healing testimonies and stories from a London healing mission.

Baker, John Patrick. *Salvation and Wholeness: The Biblical Perspectives of Healing.* London: Fountain Trust, 1973. This book is an overview of the biblical foundations of healing from an insightful British author.

Banks, Bill. *Alive Again! Terminal Cancer. 48 Hours to Live. Miraculously Healed.* Kirkwood, Missouri: Impact Christian Books, 1977. Banks was supernaturally healed of cancer after doctors had given him only 48 hours to live. In this book, he shares his testimony.

Banks, Bill. *Overcoming Blocks to Healing.* Kirkwood, Missouri: Impact Christian Books, 2002, 2014. This book is a practical guide to overcoming obstacles to healing.

Banks, Bill. *Three Kinds of Faith for Healing.* Kirkwood, Missouri: Impact Christian Books, 1992, 2012. Banks, a cancer survivor, seeks to provide a clearer understanding of faith for healing.

Bartow, Donald W. *Adventures of Healing: How to Use New Testament Practices and Receive New Testament Results.* Canton, Ohio: Life Enrichment Publishers, 1981. This is a collection of one hundred healing "adventures" written by the former pastor of Westminster Presbyterian Church in Canton, Ohio. It covers such diverse topics as: "The Bible and Healing," "Obstacles to Health," "The Laying on of Hands," and "Introducing A Healing Service."

Bartow, Donald W. *Yes, Virginia, There Is a God Who Heals Today! Email Conversations Presenting the Biblical Basis for Spiritual Healing, Repentance,*

Being Born Again, The Power of Prayer and Helping the Poor. Canton, Ohio: Wholeness Publications, 2000. In this work, Bartow has created a healing study guide, presenting it as a series of email interchanges.

Baxter, Ern. *I Almost Died: This Book Can Save Your Life.* Mobile, Alabama: Integrity Publications, 1983. This book is testimonial as well as a reflection on healing from one of the gifted teachers of the Discipleship Movement.

Bennett, Dennis. "Does God Want to Heal Everybody?" *Charisma* (September 1983): 54, 59-61. Bennett, an Episcopalian and father of the Charismatic Renewal, reflects on the ministry of healing in Spirit-filled churches.

Bennett, Dennis and Rita Bennett. "Inner Healing: Letting Jesus Heal The Hurts," *Charisma* (June 1981): 50-52, 54-55. Bennett shares insights about the ministry of inner healing.

Bennett, Dennis. *Nine O'clock in the Morning.* Alachua, Florida: Bridge-Logos Publishers 1970. In addition to recounting his own story of the beginning of the Charismatic Renewal, Bennett shares accounts of healing that transpired in his congregation.

Bennett, Dennis. *Moving Right Along In The Spirit: The Balanced Path To Maturity.* Old Tappan, New Jersey: Fleming H. Revell Company, 1983. In this notable work, Bennett shares a mature understanding of Charismatic practices. He includes several valuable insights on healing.

Benson, Carmen. *What About Us Who Are Not Healed.* Plainfield, New Jersey Logos, 1975. In this heartfelt book, a Charismatic woman wrestles with the fact that she has not yet received her healing.

Bonnke, Reinhard. *Mighty Manifestations: The Gifts and Power of the Holy Spirit.* Orlando, Florida: Creation House, 1994. This is a reflection on the gifts and work of the Holy Spirit by evangelist Reinhard Bonnke.

Buckingham, Jamie. *Daughter of Destiny: Kathryn Kuhlman, Her Story.* New York: Pocket Books, 1978. Buckingham, in this work, penned the definitive biography of evangelist Kathryn Kuhlman.

Burge, G. M. "Problems in Healing Ministries Within the Charismatic Context," paper presented at the annual meeting of the Society for Pentecostal Studies, Cleveland, Tennessee, 1983. This is an analysis of the meaning of suffering and the challenges of Charismatic healing ministry.

Casdorph, Richard. *Real Miracles: Indisputable Medical Evidence that God Heals.* Gainsville, Florida: Bridge-Logos, 1976, 2003. This book is a collection of testimonies from Kathryn Kuhlman's healing crusades. What is unique about this work is that a doctor who worked alongside Kuhlman wrote it. He was able to confirm all of these healings clinically.

Cherry, Reginald. *Healing Prayer: God's Divine Intervention in Medicine, Faith, and Prayer.* Nashville: Thomas Nelson Publishing, 1999. This is a fascinating examination of the intersection of medical therapies and intercessory prayer from a Charismatic physician.

Cherry, Reginald. *The Bible Cure: A Renowned Physician Uncovers the Bible's Hidden Health Secrets.* Lake Mary, Florida: Creation House, 1998. Cherry not only explores God's desire to bring healing, but also discusses the restorative dietary and health practices of the ancient Mediterranean world.

Cherry, Reginald. *The Doctor and The Word: Discover God's Pathway to healing for You and Your Family.* Lake Mary, Florida: Creation House, 1998. Cherry shares his testimony and talks about combining the miraculous with modern medicine to receive a breakthrough in healing.

Christenson, Larry. *Welcome, Holy Spirit: A Study of Charismatic Renewal in the Church*. Minneapolis, Minnesota: Augsburg Publishing, 1987. Christenson, a Lutheran Charismatic leader, shares some of his reflections on the movement.

Colbert, Don. *Deadly Emotions: Understand the Mind-Body-Spirit Connection That Can Heal or Destroy You*. Nashville: Thomas Nelson Publishers, 2003. Spirit-filled physician, Don Colbert, talks about the connection between emotions and health.

Crosby, Stephen R. *Healing Hope or Hype? Why Genuine Physical Healings Are Rare in The Church and What We Must Do About It*. New York: Eloquent Books, 2008. Crosby argues that understanding what the Bible has to say about community, disease, and health is key to the appropriation of healing.

Dearing, Trevor. *Supernatural Healing Today*. Plainfield, New Jersey: Logos, 1979. Episcopalian Vicar, Trevor Dearing, became a prominent Charismatic leader, actively praying for the sick. This book reflects his understanding of healing.

DeArteaga, William L. "Agnes Sanford: Apostle of Healing, and First Theologian of the Charismatic Renewal, part I." *The Pneuma Review* 9:2 (2006): 6-17. This is the first of two-part historical reflection on the life and ministry of Agnes Sandford (1897-1982).

DeArteaga, William L "Agnes Sanford: Apostle of Healing, and First Theologian of the Charismatic Renewal, part II." *The Pneuma Review* 9:3 (2006): 4-17. DeArteaga continues his reflection on the contributions of Agnes Sandford.

DeArteaga, William. *Quenching the Spirit: Discover The Real Spirit Behind the Charismatic Controversy*. Lake Mary, Florida: Creation House Publishing, 1992, 1996. In this historical overview, DeArteaga examines the conflict between cessationism and the gifts of the Spirit in the life of the church.

Dickens, Glynn R. "Developing A Model for The Training of Believers to Practice the Healing Ministry of Christ," D.Min., thesis, Oral Roberts University, 2007. This work considers the practical implications of training and education in matters of healing.

Dunkerley, Don. *Healing Evangelism: Strengthening Your Witnessing with Effective Prayer for the Sick*. Grand Rapids, Michigan: Chosen Books, 1995. This is a guide for utilizing healing as a means of evangelism.

Editor. "Interview: Healing in the Spirit: A Wide-Ranging, Exclusive Interview with Kathryn Kuhlman." *Christianity Today* (July 20, 1973): 4-10. In this reprint of a 1966 interview, an Evangelical asks Kuhlman about her understanding of healing and other topics.

Ellis, Junior and Marilyn Ellis. *Heal The Sick: A Command of Obedience*. Lake Mary, Florida: Creation House, 2010. This is practical teaching on healing from a couple who were influenced by Charles and Francis Hunter.

Ervin, Howard M. *Healing: Sign of the Kingdom*. Peabody, Massachusetts: Hendrickson Publishers, 2002. This is a scholarly treatment of the theology of healing from a gifted Charismatic scholar.

Estes, Ted B. "Passing On the Healing Ministry of Jesus at Claremore Christian Fellowship Through Training Believers to Pray for the Sick," D.Min., thesis, Oral Roberts University, 1996. This work takes a look at practical healing practices in a local congregation in Oklahoma.

Gills, James P. *God's Prescription for Healing: Five Divine Gifts of Healing*. Lake Mary, Florida: Charisma Media, 2004. In this work, a Christian medical doctor documents what he considers to be expressions of healing. He describes them as: natural, assisted, inner, improbable, and ultimate.

Goff, Daniel B. "Revisiting The Issue of Divine Healing with Implications for Ministry: Is Physical Healing a Provision of the

Atonement," Ph.D., diss., Regent University, 2004. This well-researched work evaluates the theological implications of healing.

Grazier, Jack. *The Power Beyond: In Search of Miraculous Healing.* New York: Macmillan, 1989. Grazier, a journalist for Pennsylvania's Erie Daily Times, describes his encounters with the ministry of healing. His interest sparked in 1985 when his infertile wife conceived after attending a Charles and Frances Hunter meeting.

Heinrich, Bill. *Divine Healing: A Biblical and Practical Study Guide.* Witmer, Pennsylvania: Evidence of Truth Ministries, Inc., 2004, 2011. This work is a study guide and overview of healing within the pages of scripture.

Hejzlar, Pavel. "Two Paradigms for Divine Healing: Fred F. Bosworth, Kenneth E. Hagin, Agnes Sandford, and Francis MacNutt in Dialogue," Ph.D., diss., Fuller Theological Seminary, 2009. This work adroitly compares Pentecostal healing evangelism with pastorally oriented healing ministry.

Hinn, Benny. *Kathryn Kuhlman: Her Spiritual Legacy and Its Impact On My Life.* Nashville, Tennessee: Thomas Nelson Publishers, 1998. This is Benny Hinn's personal account of Kathryn Kuhlman's life and ministry. Her methodology and approach greatly influenced Hinn.

Hwang, Seung Hwan. "Experiencing Divine Healing Through Spiritual Training," Ph.D., diss., Oral Roberts University, 2000. This work, one of several coming out of Oral Roberts University, explores theological and practical implications of healing. In this work, the author explores how more effective ministry can be manifest through training.

Hunter, Charles and Frances. *God's Healing Promises.* New Kensington, Pennsylvania: Whitaker House Publishers, 2000. This is a compilation of healing scriptures and inspirational insights from Charles and Frances Hunter.

Hunter, Charles and Frances. *Handbook for Healing*, revised version. New Kensington, Pennsylvania: Whitaker House, 1987, 2001. In this book, the Hunters share tips and practical strategies for operating in the ministry of healing.

Hunter, Charles and Frances. *How to Heal the Sick*. New Kensington, Pennsylvania: Whitaker House, 1981. This is a practical look at the ministry of healing from Charles and Frances Hunter.

Hunter, Charles and Frances. *How to Receive and Maintain Healing*. Kingwood, Texas: Hunter Books, undated. This work draws on the miracles of Jesus, seeking to apply them to modern day circumstances.

Khoo, Oon Cnor. *Divine Healing: A Bibliography*. Tulsa, Oklahoma: Oral Roberts University Pentecostal Research, 1979. This is a bibliography of healing works from seventies era holdings at Oral Roberts University.

Kuhlman, Kathryn with Buckingham, Jamie. *A Glimpse into Glory*. Plainfield, New Jersey: Logos International, 1979. This is an autobiographical account of one of the leading healing evangelists of the Charismatic Renewal.

Kuhlman, Kathryn. *God Can Do It Again*. Englewood Cliffs, New Jersey: Prentice-Hall, 1969. This is a collection of miracle stories from Kathryn Kuhlman's crusades that she was able to verify and disseminate.

Kuhlman, Kathryn. *How Big Is God?* Minneapolis, Minnesota: Dimension Books, 1974. This short Kuhlman teaching was composed to encourage people to have faith in the works of God.

Kuhlman, Kathryn. *I Believe in Miracles*. Englewood Cliffs, New Jersey: Prentice-Hall, 1962. This book is a well-written polemical work from the Kuhlman on the validity of miracles.

Kuhlman, Kathryn. *Never Too Late: The Journey of a Catholic Woman from Despair to Deliverance*. South Plainfield, New Jersey: Bridge-Logos, 1994. This is the testimony of Marion Burgio, a middle–aged Catholic woman who developed a debilitating form of multiple sclerosis. After several operations and invasive medical procedures, she could not walk and nearly blind. Burgio received an invitation to attend Kathryn Kuhlman's Miracle Crusade and experienced healing.

Kuhlman, Kathryn. *Nothing is Impossible with God*. Englewood Cliffs, New Jersey: Prentice-Hall, 1974. This is a wonderful polemic on the miracle power of God by one of the leading evangelists of the Charismatic Renewal.

Kuhlman, Kathryn. *Victory in Jesus and the Lord's Healing Touch*. Pittsburgh, Pennsylvania: Kathryn Kuhlman Foundation, undated. This is a compilation of two of Kathryn Kuhlman's messages on healing.

Kylstra, Chester and Betsy. *An Integrated Approach to Biblical Healing Ministry: A Guide to Receiving Healing and Deliverance from Past Sins, Hurts, Ungodly Mindsets, And Demonic Oppression*. United Kingdom: Sovereign World International, 2003. This practical work explores how inner healing affects one's physical health.

Liardon, Roberts. *Kathryn Kuhlman: A Spiritual Biography of God's Miracle Working Power*. Tulsa, Oklahoma: Albury Publishing, 1990. This is a biography of Kathryn Kuhlman, a prominent Charismatic healing evangelist.

Malkmus, George. *Why Christians Get Sick*. Shippensburg, Pennsylvania: Destiny Image Publishers, 2005. George Malkmus, a Christian minister, was diagnosed with colon cancer at 42. He wondered why Christians get sick. This book recounts the answers that he found.

Malkmus, George H. *You Don't Have to Be Sick! A Christian Primer*. Shelby, North Carolina: Hallelujah Acres, 1999. This book is a reflection on health with a concentrated focus on diet and nutrition.

Martin, David. *Strange Gifts? A Guide to Charismatic Renewal.* New York: Wiley, John & Sons, 1984. This is a collection of articles from supports as well as opponents of Charismatic gifts.

McDonnell, Killian, ed. *Presence, Power, Praise: Documents On The Charismatic Renewal*, volume 1. Collegeville, Minnesota: The Liturgical Press, 1980. This is an anthology of doctrinal statements and denominational documents that pertain to the Charismatic Renewal.

McDonnell, Killian, ed. *Presence, Power, Praise: Documents On The Charismatic Renewal*, volume 2. Collegeville, Minnesota: The Liturgical Press, 1980. McDonnell compiles more of the official statements on the Charismatic Renewal.

McDonnell, Killian, ed. *Presence, Power, Praise: Documents On The Charismatic Renewal*, volume 3. Collegeville, Minnesota: The Liturgical Press, 1980. This is the final volume of denominational assessments of the Charismatic Renewal.

McGuire, Meredith B., with Debra Kantor. *Ritual Healing in Suburban America.* Piscataway, New Jersey: Rutgers University Press, 1988. This is an academic analysis of a "healing ritual" in a suburban Charismatic church. It includes valuable sociological and anthropological insights.

Murphey, Cecil and Twila Belk. *I Believe in Healing: Real Stories from The Bible, History and Today.* Ventura, California: Regal Publishing, 2013. This is a collection of healing stories from Scripture, history, and contemporary experience.

O'Neill, Andy. *The Power of Charismatic Healing: A Personal Account.* Dublin, Ireland: Mercier Press Limited, 1985. This book, written by a lay participant in the Charismatic Renewal, focuses on healing through the laying on of hands.

Prince, Derek. *God's Medicine Bottle.* Charlotte, North Carolina: Whitaker House, 1995. This is practical work explores that idea of healing coming from the Word of God.

Prince, Derek. *God's Word Heals.* New Kensington, Pennsylvania: Whitaker House, 2010. This work is a compilation of unpublished Derek Prince articles on healing.

Raudszus, S. Juanita. *Divine Healing: A Bibliography.* Tulsa, Oklahoma: Oral Roberts University Research Center, 1973. This bibliography represents many of the holdings at Oral Roberts University.

Renner, Gerald. "Faith Healing Moves Into Mainstream Holy Rollers Moving Into Religious Mainstream," *Hartford Courant,* Religious Section (April 19, 1992). This is a news story that explores the penetration of the Charismatic Renewal in the Northeast.

Roberts, Dennis. "Time Didn't Stop At Nine O'clock in the Morning," *Charisma* (May 1980), 22-27, 60. This news article explores the life and ministry of Dennis Bennett.

Sandford, Agnes. *The Healing Light.* New York: Random House Publishing, 1947, 1972. This is a controversial healing work that influenced many within the Charismatic Renewal.

Sandford, Agnes. *The Healing Power of the Bible.* Philadelphia: J.B. Lippincott Company, 1969. In this work, Sandford suggests that healing can be connected to our reading and engagement with Scripture.

Sandford, Agnes. *The Healing Touch of God.* New York: The Ballantine Books, 1983. This is another work where Sandford approaches recuperation from the position of soul care or inner healing.

Sandford, John. *Healing Body and Soul: The Meaning of Illness in the New Testament and in Psychotherapy.* Louisville, Kentucky: Westminster - John Knox Press, 1992. This book discusses the meaning of illness in the Gospels and what that might reveal about modern day recovery.

Scarborough, Peggy. *Healing Through Spiritual Warfare*. Shippensburg, Pennsylvania: Destiny Image, 2012. This healing work, from a woman who experienced recovery from breast cancer, focuses on healing through spiritual warfare.

Spraggett, Allen. *Kathryn Kuhlman: The Woman Who Believes in Miracles*, New York: Thomas Y. Crowell Company, 1970. This is a major biographical account of evangelist Kathryn Kuhlman

Stapleton, Ruth Carter. In His Footsteps: The Healing Ministry of Jesus - Then and Now. San Francisco, California: Harper & Row, 1979. Stapleton was the sister of President Jimmy Carter and involved with the Charismatic Renewal. She emphasized "inner healing" and expressions of spiritual breakthrough.

Sumrall, Lester. *Seven Ways Jesus Healed The People*. South Bend, Indiana: Lester Sumrall Evangelistic Association, 1971. In this work, Lester Sumrall discusses seven ways that Jesus operated in healing.

Sumrall, Lester. *The Life Story of Lester Sumrall*. Green Forest, Arkansas: New Leaf Publishing, 1993. This is an autobiographical account of Sumrall, a man who knew Smith Wigglesworth and ministered around the world.

Tavoacci, Scott, *Understanding Divine Healing Through the Ministry of Jesus*, 5-Fold Media, 2012. This is a book on the biblical foundations of healing from emerging Charismatic teacher.

Various. *A Sure Cure: The Acts of the Holy Spirit in The Medical Profession Today*. Costa Mesa, California: Full Gospel Business Men's Fellowship International, 1976. This book is a collection of healing testimonies from doctors and physicians.

Waugh, Geoff, ed. *Healing: Renewal Journal* 4. Brisbane, Australia: *Renewal Journal Publications*, 1994. In this issue of the *Renewal Journal*, contributors focus on various theological and practical dimensions of healing.

Warner, Wayne E. *Kathryn Kuhlman: The Woman Behind the Miracles.* Ann Arbor, Michigan: Vine Books, 1993. This is a well-researched biographical account of Kathryn Kuhlman, a prominent Charismatic healer.

White, Anne. *Healing Adventure: The Real Meaning of Divine Healing.* Plainfield, New Jersey: Bridge-Logos Foundation, 1969, 1972. This is a practical book on healing from a woman that instituted an international prayer ministry.

Yeoh, Jai Chang. "The Influence of 'The Prayer of Faith' Upon the Divine Healing," Ph.D., diss., Oral Roberts University, 2008. This dissertation examines the "prayer of faith" from the Book of James and its influence on the ministry practice of divine healing.

Young, Richard and Brenda. *Messengers of Healing: Charles and Francis Hunter.* New Kensington, Pennsylvania: Whitaker House, 2009. This is an outstanding biographical account of healing evangelists, Charles and Francis Hunter.

17. WORD OF FAITH

Andrews, Sherry. "Keeping The Faith," *Charisma Magazine* (October 1981): 24-31. This is a feature article on the ministry of Kenneth Hagin from the early 1980s.

Barron, Bruce. *The Health and Wealth Gospel*. Downers Grove, Illinois: Intervarsity Press, 1987. This book analyzes the Word of Faith Movement and its conception of prosperity and healing.

Bowman, Robert M. *The Word-Faith Controversy: Understanding the Health and Wealth Gospel*. Grand Rapids, Michigan: Baker Book House, 2001. This well-researched book is a scholarly assessment of the Word of Faith movement.

Caldwell, E. S. "Kenneth Hagin Sr: Acknowledged as the Father of the Faith Movement," *Charisma* (August 1985), 116. This is an article from Charisma magazine examining the influence of Kenneth Hagin.

Copeland, Gloria. *And Jesus Healed Them All*. Fort Worth, Texas: Kenneth Copeland Publications, 1984. This work is a practical Bible study on healing from one of the prominent Word of Faith leaders.

Copeland, Gloria. *God's Prescription for Divine Health*. Tulsa: Harrison House Publishing, 1995. This book focuses on the importance of reading and applying the Word of God for healing.

Copeland, Gloria. *God's Will for Your Healing*. Fort Worth, Texas: Kenneth Copeland Publications, 1972. This is a practical book that discusses the Scriptural foundations and the application of healing.

Copeland, Kenneth and Gloria. *Healing Promises*. Tulsa: Harrison House Publishing, 2012. This book is a collection of Scriptures and healing promises for people to apply in their day-to-day lives.

Copeland, Kenneth and Gloria. *Healing and Wellness: Your 10-Day Spiritual Action Plan*. Tulsa: Harrison House Publishing, 2008. This is an interactive study guide with audio discs and supplemental material.

Copeland, Kenneth. *Healing, It Is Always God's Will, Study Guide.* Fort Worth, Texas: Kenneth Copeland Ministries, 1983. Kenneth Copeland has constructed a Bible study on the topic of healing.

Copeland, Kenneth. "Healing, Kenneth Copeland Study Notes." *New Testament: Kenneth Copeland Personal Notes Edition.* Fort Worth, Texas: Kenneth Copeland Ministries, 1991, 2013, 62-66. This is a collection of healing notes and teaching outlines that has been utilized by Kenneth Copeland in his ministry.

Copeland, Kenneth and Gloria. *The First 30 Years: A Legacy of Faith* (Fort Worth, Texas: Kenneth Copeland Publications, 1997. This is an autobiography of Kenneth and Gloria Copeland. It recounts their life story and elaborates on their connections with Oral Roberts and Kenneth Hagin.

Copeland, Kenneth. *You Are Healed!* Tulsa, Oklahoma: Harrison House Publishing, 1979. In this practical booklet, Copeland considers the biblical foundations of healing.

Daughtery, Billy Joe. *You Can Be Healed: How to Believe God for Your Healing.* Shippensburg, Pennsylvania: Destiny Image Publishers, 2006. Billy Joe Daughtery, pastor of Victory Christian Center in Tulsa, Oklahoma, shares some of his insights on healing.

Fleischer, Richard S. *The Word On Healing: An Inclusive Reference Guide to Biblical Passages on Healing.* Lake Mary, Florida: Creation House Press, 2002. This book is an overview of every biblical passage on healing.

Hagin, Kenneth E. *Biblical Ways to Receive Healing.* Tulsa, Oklahoma: Faith Library Publications, 1999. This is a practical Bible study on the ways an individual receives healing. Hagin, the founder of the Word of Faith Movement, takes his readers through several biblical models.

Hagin, Kenneth E. *Bible Healing Study Course*. Tulsa, Oklahoma: Faith Library Publications, 1999. Hagin takes a practical biblical approach in this work. He encourages his readers to learn from Scripture and believe God for healing breakthrough.

Hagin, Kenneth E. *Healing Belongs to Us*. Tulsa, Oklahoma: Kenneth Hagin Ministries, 1969, 1984. This booklet, derived from a Hagin sermon, encourages faith in healing.

Hagin, Kenneth E. *How to Keep Your Healing*. Tulsa, Oklahoma: Faith Library Publications, 1998. This booklet provides advice about how one holds on to healing after receiving it. Hagin, in his experience, found that some "lose" their healings. He sought to share a strategy of preservation.

Hagin, Kenneth E. *Redeemed from Poverty, Sickness, And Spiritual Death*. Tulsa, Oklahoma: Kenneth Hagin Ministries, 1995. In this booklet, Hagin wants his readers to understand the full position that they are walking in.

Hagin, Kenneth E. *Seven Things You Should Know About Divine Healing*. Tulsa, Oklahoma: Faith Library Publications, 1979. In this work, Hagin shares seven insights about healing that he has learned.

Hagin, Kenneth E. *Seven Hindrances to Healing*. Tulsa, Oklahoma: Kenneth Hagin Ministries, 1980. In this booklet, Hagin talks about hindrances to healing that should be avoided.

Hagin, Kenneth E. *The Key to Scriptural Healing*. Faith Library Publications. Tulsa, Oklahoma: Kenneth Hagin Ministries, 1995. This is another practical teaching on how to receive healing.

Hagin, Kenneth W. *Executing The Basics of Healing*. Tulsa, Oklahoma: Faith Library Publications, 2014. Kenneth Hagin, Jr. discusses strategies for healing. He wrestles with some of the following questions: Should Christians suffer? Who is to blame for sickness? What are the terms of our covenant of healing?

Hagin, Kenneth W. *Healing Forever Settled.* Tulsa, Oklahoma: Faith Library Publications, 1989. In this practical book, Kenneth Hagin Jr. explores the question of whether it's God's will to heal people today.

Hagin, Kenneth W. "Trend Toward Faith Movement," *Charisma* (August 1985), 67-70. In this insightful article, Kenneth Hagin Jr. provides a reasoned defense of the Word of Faith Movement.

Hammon, Lynne. *When Healing Doesn't Come Easily.* Tulsa, Oklahoma: Word and Spirit Resources, 2010. This book provides guidance for those who are struggling with healing.

Harrison, Buddy. *Understanding Spiritual Gifts: The Operation and Administration of the Gifts of the Holy Spirit in Your Life.* Tulsa, Oklahoma: Harrison House, 1998. Harrison reveals some of the dynamics of operating and administrating the gifts of the Spirit.

Hayes, Norvel. *Divine Healing: God's Recipe for Life and Healing.* Tulsa, Oklahoma: Harrison House, 1995. This is a collection of healing insights from a beloved Word of Faith evangelist and businessman.

Hayes, Norvel. *Faith Has No Feelings: Receiving Your Healing Through James 5:14-15.* Tulsa, Oklahoma: Harrison House Publishers, 1997. In this booklet, Hayes talks about a service where God told him that faith was not dependent on feelings. He was to proclaim that and share from James 5:14-15. He told the people who weren't feeling anything that they were to receive this word for themselves. One man with clubbed feet got healed.

Hayes, Norvel. *God's Power Through the Laying On of Hands.* Tulsa, Oklahoma: Harrison House Publishers, 1982. In this booklet, Hayes explores what the Bible teaches about the laying on of hands.

Hayes, Norvel. *How to Live and Not Die.* Tulsa, Oklahoma: Harrison House Publishers, 1986. This is a practical guide for the reception of healing from a prominent twentieth century Word of Faith teacher.

Hayes, Norvel. *The Healing Handbook*. Tulsa: Harrison House Publishers, 1982. In this work, Hayes takes the reader through some practical steps to receive healing.

Hayes, Norvel. *What to Do for Healing: The Same Healing Power That Flowed Through Jesus to Open Blind Eyes and Deaf Ears Is Available for You Today*. Tulsa, Oklahoma: Harrison House Publishers, 1981. In this book, Hayes explores some practical aspects of healing from the gospels.

Hickey, Marilyn, and Sara Bowling. *30 Meditations On Healing*. New Kensington, Pennsylvania: Whitaker House, 2014. This is a collection of exhortations and scriptural reflections on healing from evangelist Marilyn Hickey and her daughter.

Hickey, Marilyn. *God's Benefit: Healing*. Tulsa, Oklahoma: Harrison House Publishers, 1981. In this booklet, Hickey explores the causes of sickness and provides a sketch of God's healing work throughout the Bible.

Hickey, Marilyn. *Total Healing: You Can Walk in Perfect Health*. New Kensington, Pennsylvania: Whitaker House Publishers, 2011. Using personal testimonies, practical suggestions, and useful reflections on the scriptures, evangelist Marilyn Hickey shares many of her insights on the ministry of healing.

Hinn, Benny. *Miracle of Healing: Promises of Healing from Every Book of the Bible*. Nashville, Tennessee: Thomas Nelson, 1998. Hinn draws out healing truths from each of the books of the Bible and shares additional notes of personal commentary.

Jones, Doug. *Positioning Yourself to Receive Healing*. Tulsa, Oklahoma: Faith Library Publications, 2001. This book is a practical approach to healing from a Rhema Bible College instructor.

Jones, Doug. *Understanding The Healing Power of God.* Tulsa, Oklahoma: Faith Library Publications, 2002. This book was written as a practical guide to operating in God's healing power.

Jones, Doyle. *Divine Healing: Giving God an Opportunity.* Mustang, Oklahoma: Tate Publishing, 2011. This work is a practical overview of healing from a Word of Faith minister.

Kenyon, E. W. *Jesus The Healer.* Lynewood, Washington: Kenyon Gospel Publishing, 1968. Kenyon's ideas influenced the Word of Faith Movement and colored Kenneth Hagin's understanding of healing.

King, Daniel. *Healing Power: Experiencing the Miracle Touch of Jesus.* Tulsa, Oklahoma: King Ministries International, 2003. King, a graduate of Oral Roberts University, shares some of his practical insights on healing.

Liardon, Roberts. *God's Generals: The Healing Evangelists.* New Kensington, Pennsylvania: Whitaker House Publishing, 2011. In this work, Liardon reflects on the ministries of Oral Roberts, F.F. Bosworth, Lester Sumrall, George Jeffreys, and Charles and Francis Hunter.

Liardon, Roberts. *God's Generals: Why They Succeeded and Why Some Failed.* Tulsa, Oklahoma: Albury Publishing, 1996. Liardon's widely-circulated work is an inspirational overview of prominent healing evangelists.

Lie, Geir. *E. W. Kenyon: Cult Founder or Evangelical Minister?* Olso, Norway: The REFLEKS, 2003. This work is a scholarly analysis of E.W. Kenyon and his theological influence on Spirit-filled movements in the United States.

McCrossan, T.J. *Bodily Healing and the Atonement.* Broken Arrow, Oklahoma: Rhema Bible Church, 1982, 1996. Noted Presbyterian, T.J. McCrossan, examines the grammatical structure of James 5. He affirms that healing is in the atonement.

McIntyre, Joe. *E. W. Kenyon: The True Story*. Orlando, Florida: Creation House Publishers, 1997. Drawing upon original sources, McIntyre corrects misunderstandings about E.W. Kenyon. This book is, in many ways, a response to D.R. McConnell's work, "A Different Gospel."

McIntyre, Joe. *Healing By Faith: Evangelical Christendom's Lost Heritage*, Bothell, Washington Empowering Grace Ministries, 2014. In this work, McIntyre explores the history of the faith cure movement.

McIntyre, Joe. "Healing in Redemption." *Reflekx* 2 (2002): 3-19. In this article, McIntyre demonstrates how the ministry of healing is tied to the atoning work of Jesus. McIntyre shares many valuable insights.

Meyer, Joyce. *Be Healed in Jesus' Name*. New York: Warner Faith, 2000. In this practical book, Meyer shares some of her insights on the biblical foundations of healing.

Meyer, Joyce. "The Believer's Attitude Toward Healing." *Life in the Word* 15:12 (2001): 12-13. In this article, Meyer shares some of her insights into the ministry of healing.

Osteen, John H. *How to Be Healed*. Houston, Texas: John H. Osteen Association, 1961. John Osteen, father of Joel Osteen, presents concrete strategies for receiving healing.

Phipps, Steven. *A. A. Allen & Miracle Valley*. Tulsa: Harrison House, 2017. Phipps has written an insightful biographical account of evangelist A. A. Allen. He explores many of the controversies of his life and ministry.

Phipps, Steven. *Maria Woodworth Etter: The Evangelist*. Tulsa: Harrison House, 2017. In this work, Phipps provides a well-researched biographical account of Maria Woodworth Etter. Phipps uses a number of original newspaper accounts to buttress his narrative.

Price, Frederick K. *Is Healing for All?* Tulsa, Oklahoma: Harrison House Publishing, 1976. This book is a practical guide to the foundations of healing from a prominent Word of Faith leader. He makes the case that healing is something that everyone can receive.

Savelle, Jerry. *God's Provision for Healing.* Tulsa, Oklahoma: Harrison House Publishers, 1981. This is a practical booklet on the biblical foundations of healing from a close associate of Kenneth Copeland.

Scheer, Bill. *Healed: God's Promise to Heal.* Tulsa, Oklahoma: Harrison House Publishers, 2007. This is an anthology of healing vignettes from the pastor of Guts Church in Tulsa, Oklahoma.

Simmons, Dale. *E. W. Kenyon and the Postbellum Pursuit of Peace, Power, and Plenty.* Lanham, Maryland: The Scarecrow Press, 1997. This is an important scholarly work on the life and doctrine of E.W. Kenyon.

Sumrall, Lester. *Healing in Every Book of the Bible.* South Bend, Indiana: Lesea Publishing, 2002. This is a collection of messages on healing from noted evangelist and statesman, Lester Sumrall.

Wommack, Andrew. *God Wants You Well: What the Bible Really Says About Walking in Divine Health.* Tulsa: Harrison House, 2010. Popular Bible teacher, Andrew Wommack, expounds on what the Bible has to say about healing.

Yandian, Bob. *Healing: How Deep Are The Stripes?* Broken Arrow, Oklahoma: Bob Yandian Ministries, 2011. Yandian, a prominent Word of Faith teacher in Tulsa, compiles some of his best insights on healing into one volume.

18. THIRD WAVE

Abildness, Abby. *Healing Prayer and Medical Care.* Shippensburg, Pennsylvania: Destiny Image Publishing, 2010. This is a practical healing work from a medical doctor who has been involved in missions. The fact that Abildness is both a minister and a doctor positions him to provide unique insights.

Ahn, Chè. *The Authority of the Believer and Healing.* Colorado Springs, Colorado: Wagner Publications, 1999. This small book is a practical guide to healing from a high profile Charismatic leader on the West Coast. Ahn was impacted through the Toronto Blessing and has an international reputation as a high profile leader.

Ahn, Chè. *How to Pray for Healing: Understanding and Releasing the Healing Power Available to Every Christian.* Ventura, California: Regal Books, 2004. In this practical guide, Ahn explains practical insights he has learned about healing.

Alter, Alexandra. "Healing Rooms Prescribe Faith for What Ails People." *Miami Herald,* May 24, 2006. This is a newspaper article that examines the modern phenomenon of faith healing rooms.

Anderson, Mark R. *Overcoming Roadblocks to Healing.* Mechanicsburg, Pennsylvania: The Apostolic Network of Global Awakening, 2012. This insightful work provides strategies for overcoming obstacles to healing.

Anderson, Mark R. *You Can Tap into Christ's Healing Power.* Cody, Wisconsin: Mark Anderson Ministries, 2004. This is a practical book on the ministry of healing from an evangelist associated with Global Awakening.

Andreas, Anita. *Breakthrough: Miraculous Stories of Healing and Hope – True Accounts from A Medical Professional.* Kansas City, Missouri: Anita Andreas, 2014. Andreas is an occupational therapist who incorporates prayer in her medical practice. In this hands-on work, she shares many of her personal observations.

Baker, Rolland, *Keeping The Fire: Discovering The Heart of True Revival.* Bloomington, Minnesota: Chosen Books, 2016. Rolland Baker, who serves alongside his wife in Mozambique, shares insights about revival and the deeper stirrings of God.

Baker, Rolland and Heidi Baker. *There Is Always Enough: The Story of Rolland and Heidi Baker's Miraculous Ministry among the Poor.* Kent, England: Sovereign World, 2001. Heidi and Rolland Baker share a number of powerful encounters that they have experienced through their mission work in Mozambique.

Baker, Trevor. *Supernatural Living: Healing Study Manual.* Dudley, England: Revival Fires Publishing, undated. Baker is a prominent pastor and revival leader in England. He compiled this ministry manual to assist people who desire to operate in the ministry of healing.

Balcombe, Dennis. *China's Opening Door: Incredible Stories of the Holy Spirit at Work in One of the Greatest Revivals in History.* Lake Mary, Florida: Charisma House, 2014. This is an excellent first-hand account of the revival that is taking place in China. It shares a number of stories about how the ministry of healing has propelled church growth throughout Asia.

Bentley, Todd. *Christ's Healing Touch: Understanding How to Take God's Healing Power to The World.* Abbotsford, British Columbia, Canada: Fresh Fire Ministries, 2004. Bentley, a controversial Canadian evangelist, shares some of his insights about the ministry of healing.

Best, Gary. *Naturally Supernatural: Joining God in His Work.* Cape Town, South Africa: Vineyard International Publishing, 2005. This book is a practical guide to operating in the power of God reasonably. Best is encouraging people to be naturally supernatural.

Blake, Curry. *Divine Healing Technician Training Manual.* Dallas: John G. Lake Ministries, 1997. This is a practical training manual describing methods of operating in healing.

Blue, Ken. *Authority to Heal: Answers for Everyone Who Has Prayed for a Sick Friend.* Downers Grove, Illinois: Intervarsity Press, 1987. An insightful Vineyard leader provides a carefully reasoned defense of healing.

Bremner, Steve. *Six Lies People Believe About Divine Healing: The Truth About God's Will to Heal the Sick.* Fire Press Publications, 2013. Bremner, a veteran missionary to Peru, provides a corrective for wrong assumptions about healing.

Bridges, Kynan T. *Possessing Your Healing: Taking Authority Over Sickness in Your Life.* Shippensburg, Pennsylvania: Destiny Image Publishing, 2013. This is a practical work on healing from a gifted Florida pastor.

Carter, Pete. *Unwrapping Lazarus: Freeing The Supernatural in Your Life.* Bloomington, Minnesota: Chosen Books, 2014. This is a well-edited collection of insights from an English physician who has learned to walk in healing.

Chavda, Mahesh. *The Hidden Power of Healing Prayer: The Healing Anointing of the Laying On of Hands.* Shippensburg, Pennsylvania: Destiny Image Publishing, 2001. This is a practical overview of healing from a prominent Charismatic prayer leader.

Clark, Dennis and Jen Clark. *Releasing The Divine Healer Within: The Biology of Belief and Healing.* Charlotte, North Carolina: Its Supernatural Press, 2015. This practical guide explains the connection between emotions, thoughts, and the physical body.

Clark, Randy. "A Study of the Effects of Christian Prayer On Pain or Mobility Restrictions from Surgeries Involving Implanted Materials," D.Min., thesis, United Theological Seminary, 2013. This dissertation explores healing's effects on individuals who have been immobilized through the surgical insertion of metal in their bodies.

Clark, Randy. *Awed by His Grace/Out of the Bunkhouse*. Mechanicsburg, Pennsylvania: Global Awakening, 2010. Clark talks about establishing a right identity in Christ and learning about the benevolent reality of grace. This is how one is positioned to minister effectively.

Clark, Randy. *Biblical Basis for Healing*. Mechanicsburg, Pennsylvania: Global Awakening, 2004. This booklet is an overview of the biblical foundations of the ministry of healing.

Clark, Randy. *Christ in You the Hope of Glory/Healing and The Glory*. Mechanicsburg, Pennsylvania: Global Awakening, 2014. In this work, Randy talks about the relationship of glory to the ministry of healing.

Clark, Randy. *Empowered: A School of Healing and Impartation Workbook*. Mechanicsburg, Pennsylvania: Global Awakening, 2005, 2006, 2009. This detailed training manual explores the history and biblical foundations of healing.

Clark, Randy, and Craig Miller. *Finding Victory: When Healing Doesn't Happen – Breaking Through with Healing Power*. Mechanicsburg, Pennsylvania: Global Awakening, 2015. In this practical guide, evangelist Randy Clark and therapist Craig Miller talk about some of the challenges associated with healing. They offer viable solutions.

Clark, Randy and Sue Thompson. *Healing Energy: Whose Is it?* Mechanicsburg, Pennsylvania: Global Awakening, 2013. Clark and Thompson explore the problem of new age healing modalities and how they differ from sound biblical approaches.

Clark, Randy. *Healing, Spiritual and Medical Perspectives: A School of Healing and Impartation Workbook*. Mechanicsburg, Pennsylvania: Global Awakening, 2009, 2011. This well-researched training manual explores medical perspectives in divine healing.

Clark, Randy. *Healing Is in The Atonement and The Power of the Lord's Supper*. Mechanicsburg, Pennsylvania: Global Awakening, 2012. This practical work examines how healing is in the atonement and how it can be expressed through communion.

Clark, Randy. *Healing Out of Intimacy/Acts of Obedience*. Mechanicsburg, Pennsylvania: Global Awakening, 2014. In this work, Clark explores insights from the Gospel of John. He focuses on healing out of intimacy and faithfulness.

Clark, Randy, Phill Olson Baynard, and Lisa Lindle. *Kingdom Foundations: A School of Healing and Impartation Workbook*. Mechanicsburg, Pennsylvania: Global Awakening, 2011. This manual is an overview of healing, words of knowledge, and other areas of supernatural ministry.

Clark, Randy. *Learning to Minister Under the Anointing/Healing Ministry in Your Church*. Mechanicsburg, Pennsylvania: Global Awakening 2011. Randy talks about operating in the anointing and developing a healing ministry in a local church.

Clark, Randy. *Ministry Training Manual*. Mechanicsburg, Pennsylvania: Global Awakening, 2004. In this well-crafted training guide, Clark equips prayer warriors to function in the ministry of healing.

Clark, Randy. *Power to Heal: Keys to Activating God's Healing Power in Your Life*. Shippensburg, Pennsylvania: Destiny Image, 2015. In this work, Clark shares eight Bible-based tools to enable people to pray for the sick.

Clark, Randy. *Pressing In/Spend and Be Spent*. Mechanicsburg, Pennsylvania: Global Awakening, 2009, 2011. In this work, Clark shares personal stories and practical guidance for those who want to press into the deeper things of God.

Clark, Randy, compiler. *Supernatural Missions: The Impact of the Supernatural On World Missions*. Mechanicsburg, Pennsylvania: Global

Awakening, 2011. This book discusses strategies for incorporating healing, deliverance, and works of power in missions. In addition to Randy Clark, the contributors include Heidi and Roland Baker, Leif Hetland, and others.

Clark, Randy. *The Battle Has Been Won: A Practical Guide for Healing and Deliverance*. Lake Mary, Florida: Charisma House, 2015. Clark discusses what the Bible has to say about the ministry of deliverance and how it can be used to bring healing.

Clark, Randy. *The Essential Guide to The Power of the Holy Spirit: God's Miraculous Gifts at Work Today*. Shippensburg, Pennsylvania: Destiny Image, 2015. In this useful work, Clark discusses healing and the gifts of the Holy Spirit.

Clark, Randy. *The Healing Breakthrough: Creating An Atmosphere Of Faith For Healing*. Bloomington, Minnesota: Chosen Books, 2016. In this outstanding book, Clark provides practical insights and biblical reflections on the ministry of healing.

Clark, Randy. *The Healing River and Its Contributing Streams*. Mechanicsburg, Pennsylvania: Global Awakening, 2013. This book is an excellent abbreviated overview of the ministry of healing in history.

Clark, Randy. "The Revivalists: Fanning The Flames of the Holy Spirit." *Charisma* 37:8 (March 2012): 34-38. This is an insightful article, from Clark, on how various revivalists are emerging with expressions of healing and signs and wonders.

Clark, Randy. *The Thrill of Victory and The Agony of Defeat*. Mechanicsburg, Pennsylvania: Global Awakening, 2009. In this heart-felt work, Randy wrestles with the victories and disappointments encountered through the ministry of healing.

Clark, Randy. *Words of Knowledge*. Mechanicsburg, Pennsylvania: Global Awakening, 2009. This is a practical guide to understanding and operating in "words of knowledge" to extend the ministry of healing.

Daniels, Marcia B. *Jesus Heals Today*. Enumclaw, Washington: Wine Press Publishing, 2013. Marcia Daniels writes from her personal experience about the modern-day availability of God's healing power.

Dawkins, Robby. *Do What Jesus Did: A Real-Life Field Guide to Healing the Sick, Routing Demons, And Changing Lives Forever*. Minneapolis: Chosen Publishing, 2013. This book, by a Vineyard evangelist, talks about touching the lives of others through healing and other works of the Spirit.

Deere, Jack. *Surprised by the Power of the Holy Spirit: A Former Dallas Theological Seminary Professor Discovers that God Speaks and Heals Today*. Grand Rapids, Michigan: Zondervan Publishing, 1993. Deere, a former conservative, talks about how he encountered the presence of God.

Deleon, Virginia. "Healing Rooms Offers Hope for Body and Soul: Ministry Draws On the Power of Prayer." *The Spokane-Review Newspaper*. (January 29, 2006). This is a newspaper article that recounts the outworking of the ministry of healing in Spokane, Washington.

Doles, Jeff. *Miracles and Manifestations of the Holy Spirit in The History of the Church*. Seffner, Florida: Walking Barefoot Ministries, 2008. Doles provides an excellent overview of healing and the gifts of the Spirit throughout Church history.

Dvorak, Becky. *Dare to Believe: The True Power of Faith to Walk in Divine Healings and Miracles*. Shippensburg, Pennsylvania: Destiny Image, 2012. This book is a practical work on the ministry of healing from a Charismatic missionary living in Guatemala.

Dye, Colin. *Healing Anointing: Hope for a Hurting World.* London: Hodder & Stoughton, 1997. In this work, Dye provides a balanced, biblical approach to controversial questions about miracles, death, and dying.

Dye, Colin. *The Lord Your Healer*, London: Dovewell Publications, 2015. In this practical guide, Dye introduces the healing ministry of Jesus and positions his readers to experience breakthrough.

Dye, Colin. *Revival Phenomena.* United Kingdom: Sovereign World International Book, 1996. This book examines the controversial subject of bodily affects in revival meetings.

Evans, Rick, and Tom Wadsworth. *Willing: Are You Willing to Pray for the Sick? God is Willing to Heal!* Cleveland, Ohio: Embrace God Ministries, 2009. Evans and Wadsworth have produced a useful practical work on the ministry of healing.

Evans, Rick. *Ministry Time: Enjoying God's Presence-Inviting Power.* Cleveland, Ohio: Embrace God Ministries, 2013. Evans, once again, discusses praying for the sick.

Frisbee, Lonnie with Roger Sachs. *Not By Might Nor By Power: The Jesus Revolution.* Santa Maria, California: Freedom Publications, 2016. This is an autobiography of Lonnie Frisbee. It discusses the early years of the Jesus People Movement.

Frisbee, Lonnie with Roger Sachs. *Not By Might Nor By Power,* book two. Santa Maria, California: Freedom Publications, 2016. In this second volume, Lonnie discusses later developments in the Jesus People Movement as well as the 1980 Mother's Day Outpouring at John Wimber's church in Yorba Linda, California.

Gore, Chris and Chuck Parry. *Bethel Ministry Team Training Manual.* Redding, California: Bethel Healing Rooms, 2014. This is a practical training manual used by ministry teams in the healing rooms at

Bethel Church. It explains the values and practical strategies for ministry.

Gore, Chris. *A Practical Guide to Walking in Supernatural Healing Power.* Shippensburg, Pennsylvania: Destiny Image, 2014. This is a practical manual that was designed to be used in cooperation with Gore's *Walking in Supernatural Healing Power.* Gore has many insights that he has garnished from working in the Bethel healing rooms in Redding, California.

Gore, Chris. *Walking in Supernatural Healing Power.* Shippensburg, Pennsylvania: Destiny Image, 2013. This is a practical healing guide from the director of healing rooms at Bethel Church in Redding California.

Gray, Steve. *Hope Heals: The Beginning of a Dream.* Kansas City, Missouri: World Revival Press, 2003. This is a practical reflection on the ministry of healing from Gray, the pastor of World Revival Church in Kansas City, Missouri.

Gray, Steve. *Training for Prayer Ministers and Helpers in the House of Hope and Healing.* Kansas City, Missouri: World Revival Church, 2003. This is a practical manual that Gray developed to equip workers in the House of Hope and Healing in Kansas City, Missouri.

Greeson, Joshua. *God's Will is Always Healing: Crushing Theological Barriers to Healing.* CreateSpace Independent Publishing Platform, 2003. This is an overview of the theological foundations of healing by a graduate of Bethel School of Supernatural Ministry in Redding, California.

Greig, Gary S. and Kevin N. Springer, ed. *The Kingdom and The Power: Are Healing and Spiritual Gifts Used by Jesus and The Early Church Meant for Today? – A Biblical Look at How to Bring the Gospel to The World with Power.* Ventura, California: Regal Books, 1993. In this book, Evangelical ministry leaders and scholars explore the viability of signs and wonders.

Harms, Lee. *Healing and Deliverance Fundamentals.* Moravian Falls, North Carolina: King of Glory Ministries International, 2014. Harms, a leader in the International Association of Healing Rooms, oversees two healing rooms in the Kansas City area. In this work, he shares some of his practical insights about healing and deliverance.

Hunter, Joan. *Healing Starts Now! Complete Training Manual.* Shippensburg, Pennsylvania: Destiny Image Publishing, 2011. This is a practical guide on the ministry of healing from the daughter of Charles and Francis Hunter.

Hunter, Joan. *Power to Heal: Experiencing The Miraculous.* New Kensington, Pennsylvania: Whitaker House Publishers, 2009. In this practical work, Hunter provides guidance and inspiration about healing

Horrobin, Peter J. *Healing Through Deliverance: The Foundation and Practice of Deliverance Ministry,* revised and expanded. Grand Rapids, Michigan: Chosen Books, 1991, 2003, 2008. This is a comprehensive work on the ministry of deliverance. Horrobin examines what he considers to be a close association between deliverance and healing.

Jackson, Bill. *Quest for the Radical Middle: A History of the Vineyard.* Cape Town, South Africa: Vineyard International Publishing, 1999. This is a historical account of John Wimber and the Vineyard Movement. Among other things, it recounts many of the wonderful healing experiences that were being encountered.

Jensen, Jeff. *The Believer's Guide to Miracles, Healing, Impartation and Activation.* Murfreesboro, Tennessee: Global Fire Publishing, 2013. This is a study guide and workbook designed to teach people how to walk in healing and supernatural expressions.

Johnson, Bill with Jennifer Miskov. *Defining Moments: God-Encounters with Ordinary People Who Changed the World.* New Kensington, Pennsylvania: Whitaker House, 2016. Bill Johnson, with the help of Jennifer Miskov, has compiled biographical sketches of several revivalists and healers. The book draws fascinating observations about their lives.

Johnson, Bill and Randy Clark. *Healing Unplugged: Conversations and Insights from Two Veteran Healing Leaders.* Bloomington, Minnesota: Chosen Books, 2012. Bill Johnson and Randy Clark, two prominent healing ministers, share some practical strategies for ministering in the realms of healing.

Johnson, Bill and Randy Clark. *The Essential Guide to Healing: Equipping All Christians to Pray for the Sick.* Bloomington, Minnesota: Chosen Books, 2011. Clark and Johnson developed an excellent work that explores aspects of healing's history, theology, and practice.

Jones, Luke T. *Street Healer's Guide,* revised edition. Stratford, Connecticut: Superlife Publications, 2013. This book provides practical power evangelism strategies. Jones wrote this version after attending classes at the Bethel School of Supernatural Ministry in Redding, California.

Kilpatrick, Joel. "Churches Reach Community with Healing Services: Health Care Ministries in Missouri and Michigan Offering Healing Prayer and Medical Care at Unique New Outreach Facilities." *Charisma* (July 2003). Kilpatrick briefly examines some of the ministry expressions of two emerging healing homes.

Kraft, Charles H. ""Christian Animinism' Or God-Given Authority?" In *Spiritual Power and Missions: Raising The Issues,* ed. Edward Romme, 88-136. Pasadena, California: William Carey Library, 1995. In this article, Kraft defends the supernatural approach to evangelism—countering claims that it is little more than animism.

Kraft, Charles H. *Christianity With Power: Your Worldview and Your Experience of the Supernatural.* Ann Arbor, Michigan: Vine Books, 1989. This is an important book that explores how one's worldview shapes their understanding and experience of the supernatural.

Lee, Scott Sang-Hyun. "For Waters Shall Break Forth in the Wilderness: Healing Generation X at the Vineyard Christian Fellowship of Cambridge," in *Religious Healing in Boston: First Findings*, eds. Susan Sered and Linda L. Barnes, 13-15. Cambridge, Massachusetts: Center for the Study of World Religions, 2005. This essay explores some of healing practices being conducted in a Vineyard congregation in England.

Long, Steve. *My Healing Belongs To Me*. Toronto: Catch The Fire Books, 2014. Long, senior pastor of Catch The Fire and one of the major Toronto Blessing leaders, shares some of his observations about the ministry of healing.

Loren, Julia. "California Fire: Heaven has Invaded Earth in Redding, California, Where a Sense of Revival has been Stirring Bethel Assembly for Ten years," *Charisma* (March 2005), 44-47. As Loren explores the story of Bethel Church, she includes a number of healing testimonies.

Loren, Julia, compiler. *Dare to Believe in Your Healing*. New Kensington, Pennsylvania: Whitaker House, 2014. This practical compilation includes insights on healing the writings of Bill Johnson, F. F. Bosworth, Maria Woodworth-Etter, Randy Clark, Andrew Murray, Marilyn Hickey, Jerame Nelson, Smith Wigglesworth, Aimee Semple McPherson, John G. Lake, Kathryn Kuhlman, Guillermo Maldonado, and Cal Pierce.

Loren, Julia, ed. and comp. *Claim Your Healing: How to Access the Faith You Need for Healing*. Camano Island, Washington: Tharseo Publishing, 2013. This book includes a number of different articles from prominent healing ministers including: Bill Johnson, F.F. Bosworth, Randy Clark, Smith Wigglesworth, Maria Woodworth-Etter and others.

Maldonao, Guillermo. *Jesus Heals Your Sickness Today*. Miami, Florida: ERJ Publications, 2009. This book is a practical guide to the ministry of healing from a prominent Latin American leader who resides in the United States.

Maloney, James E. *Theology of Healing and Miracles: A Compilation.* Fort Worth, Texas: Answering The Cry Publications, 2001. Maloney, an itinerate, compiled this work to provide some instruction on the ministry of healing.

Maloney, James E. *The Panoramic Seer: Bringing The Prophetic into The Healing Anointing.* Shippensburg, Pennsylvania: Destiny Image, 2012. This book uniquely connects the ministry of the prophetic with the ministry of healing.

Marais, Cornel, and Simon Wilson. *Administrating The Children's Bread: The Basics of Healing Under the New Covenant.* Charisma Ministries, 2010. This is an overview of healing written by Cornel Marais, a South African author, speaker, teacher, and businessman.

Merrill, Dean. "The Church: Healing's Natural Home?" *Leadership* 6 (Spring 1985): 116-26. This forum on healing ministry in the local church draws upon the insights of John Wimber, John Lavender, Don Williams, and Don Bubna.

Moraine, Jack. *Healing Ministry: A Training Manual for Believers.* Choctaw, Oklahoma: HGM Publishing, 2010. This is a practical ministry guide that provides valuable insights into the ministry of healing.

Nygård, Marian. *I Have a Good Life: The Story of Adrian's Healing.* Pawleys Island, South Carolina: 3DM Publishing, 2016. A mother recounts the story of her seriously ill son's healing. He received his breakthrough at Bethel Church in Redding, California.

O'Neal, Dale. *Transformational Thinking: Healing the Sick.* Vacaville, California: Dale O'Neal, 2015. This is a practical training manual from a prominent leader at the Mission in Vacaville, California. Since O'Neal is in fellowship with Bethel Church in Redding, California, Bill Johnson penned the foreword of this manual.

Oguntola, Sunday, and Ruth Moon. "Antibodies or The Almighty? Ebola Outbreak Highlights African Views About God's Healing Power." *Christianity Today* 58:9 (November 2014): 19. This news article explores the problem of the Ebola virus in Africa and how some of the Pentecostal churches are responding. Candy Brown, a Harvard scholar, is quoted in the article saying, "The striking growth of Christianity in Africa, from 5 to 48 percent, is closely linked to the popular appeal of divine healing."

Otis, Don. "Reopening The Healing Rooms: In the Pacific Northwest a New Ministry Is Reclaiming the Gift of Healing for A New Generation." *Charisma Magazine* (March 2002): 72-76. This is a intriguing article on the healing rooms that were being open in various parts of the United States in the early 2000s.

Paterson, Kevin. *Healings, Miracles, Signs and Wonders Today 101, second printing*. Abbotsford, British Columbia, Canada: Fresh Fire Ministries, 2003. This work is a practical training manual that was used for "healing schools" and other training sessions. It was associated with controversial evangelist Todd Bentley and reflects his understanding of the healing ministry.

Pangilnan, Hiram G. *Healing Is Yours*. Quezon City, Philippines: Revival Publishing, 2011. This book is a vibrant reflection on the ministry of healing from a prominent minister from the Philippines.

Perez, Pablo. *201 Prayers for Healing: Build Your Faith for Healing With 201 Healing Quotes from The Bible*. Elizabeth, New Jersey: Open Heavens Publishing, 2014. This is a practical guide that compiles a number of different prayers for healing.

Pierce, Cal. *Receive Your Healing and Reclaim Your Health: Partnering with the Holy Spirit for Total Transformation of Your Body, Soul, and Spirit*. Lake Mary, Florida: Siloam Publishing, 2012. This book, by the Director of the International Association of Healing Homes in Spokane, Washington, focuses on strategies for establishing a holistic approach to health.

Pierce, Cal. *Healing in the Kingdom: How The Power of God and Your Faith Can Heal the Sick.* Ventura, California: Regal Publishing, 2008. In this work, Pierce focuses on the biblical theology and function of healing.

Pierce, Cal. "A Holy Spirit Healing: How to Partner with The Holy Spirit to Reclaim Your Health." *Charisma* 37: 8 (March 2012): 22. In this essay, Pierce discusses practical ways that healing can be appropriated.

Praying Medic. *Divine Healing Made Simple: Simplifying The Supernatural to Make Healing and Miracles a Part of Your Everyday Life.* Gilbert, Arizona: Inkity Press, 2013. An unnamed Christian paramedic, who goes by "The Praying Medic," wrote this practical guide. Over time, this medical practitioner learned how to effectively minister healing and he wanted to share his insights.

Rocha, Ed. *Supernatural Power: Be Healed, Stay Healed.* Ed Rocha, 2014. Rocca is the primary translator for Randy Clark when he ministers in Brazil. In this work, Rocha shares some of his own insights and experiences of healing.

Ruthven, Jon Mark. "Back to the Future for Pentecostal- Charismatic Evangelicals in North America and World Wide: Radicalizing Evangelical Theology and Practice," in *The Futures of Evangelicalism: Issues and Prospects*, eds. Craig Bartholomew, Robin Parry, and Andrew West, 302-315. Leicester, UK: Intervarsity Press, 2003. This essay provides insights from Ruthven on Spirit-filled theology and practice.

Ruthven, Jon Mark. "On the Cessation of the Charismata: The Protestant Polemic of Benjamin B. Warfield," *Pneuma* 12:1 (Spring, 1990): 14-31. In this well-researched article, Ruthven challenges cessationism and the waning of divine healing

Ruthven, Jon Mark. *On the Cessation of the Charismata: The Protestant Polemic on Post-Biblical Miracles – Revised and Expanded.* Tulsa, Oklahoma:

Word and Spirit Press, 2011. This work thoroughly critiques the belief that healing and the gifts of the Spirit ended with the Apostles.

Ruthven, Jon Mark. *What's Wrong with Protestant Theology? Tradition vs. Biblical Emphasis.* Tulsa, Oklahoma: Word And Spirit Press, 2013. In this ground-breaking book, Ruthven deals with key aspects of Church history and theology. He aptly demonstrates the normative biblical pattern of supernatural activity.

Sapp, Roger. *Beyond A Shadow of Doubt: Faith for Healing by Removing Doubts.* Springtown, Texas: All Nations Publishing, 2001, 2004. Roger Sapp, a Texas evangelist, believes that the most common impediment to healing is doubt. In this book, he exposes this problem and provides solutions.

Sapp, Roger. *Christ Centered Healing Ministry Seminar.* Springtown, Texas: All Nations Publishing, 2006. This is a practical training manual actively positioning individuals to pray for the sick.

Sapp, Roger. *Is There a Conflict Between Healing and Medicine?* Springtown, Texas: All Nations Publishing, 2013. In this practical booklet, Sapp makes the argument that divine healing is not in conflict with medical practices. Jesus and medical doctors are not antithetical.

Sapp, Roger. *Performing Miracles and Healing Performing Miracles and Healing: A Biblical Guide to Developing a Christ-like Supernatural Ministry. A Comprehensive Review and Commentary on the Healing and Miracle Ministries of Jesus Christ and His Disciples.* Springtown, Texas: All Nations Publishing, 2000. This is a practical guide for praying for the sick.

Sapp, Roer. *Release The Supernatural by Meditation On Christ.* Springtown, Texas: All Nations Publishing, 2004, 2011. In this booklet, Sapp explains how heartfelt, scriptural meditation on Jesus opens the door to healing breakthrough.

Sawvelle, Bob. *A Case for Healing Today: Biblical Historical and Theological Perspectives on Christian Healing.* North Charleston, South Carolina: CreateSpace, 2015. This work, from an associate of Randy Clark, argues for the validity of healing from scripture, church history, and contemporary practice.

Sithole, Surprise with David Wimbish. *Voice in The Night: The True Story of a Man and The Miracles That Are Changing America.* Grand Rapids, Michigan: Chosen Books, 2012. This is the autobiography of a prominent minister from Mozambique who has actively worked alongside Heidi Baker. Pastor Surprise shares a number of thrilling stories of healing.

Seng, Jordan. *Miracle Work: A Down-To-Earth Guide to Supernatural Ministries.* Downer's Grove, Illinois: Intervarsity Press, 2012. Seng, in addition to scholarly pursuits, is the pastor of Bluewater Mission in Honolulu, Hawaii. He is widely noted for his insights into healing and prophecy.

Smith, Troy Anthony. *Demonstrate It! Unleashing Healing, Signs , and Wonders.* Los Angeles, California: Dunimis Media, 2011. Smith is an itinerate preacher who has put together a practical guide for ministering healing and operating in the works of the Holy Spirit.

Sparks, Larry. *Breakthrough Healing: 50 Keys to Experiencing God's Supernatural Power in Your Life.* Shippensburg, Pennsylvania: Destiny Image, 2014. This is a practical book that explores key aspects of the healing ministry.

Sparks, Larry, and Troy Anderson, "Randy Clark: The Healing and Miracles Preacher," *Charisma* 40:8 (March 2015): This feature story from Charisma magazine explores the legacy and ministerial impact of Randy Clark.

Springer, Kevin, ed. *Power Encounters: Among Christians in The Western World.* New York: Harper and Row Publishers, 1988. This is a well-edited, collection of testimonies and stories of power encounters from respected Evangelical and Charismatic leaders. This book was written to supplement John Wimber's Power Evangelism.

Springer, Kevin, compiler and ed. *Riding the Third Wave: What Comes After Renewal?* United Kingdom: Marshall Pickering, 1982. This work is an insightful polemic on the Third Wave Movement.

Starr, Susan with Susan Thompson. *Journey to Healing: Living Proof That Miracles Happen Today.* Schaumburg, Illinois: Isaiah 61 Publishing, 2014. This book recounts the healing testimony of Susan Starr.

Strasheim, Connie. *Healing Chronic Illness: By His Spirit, Through His Resources.* South Lake Tahoe, California: BioMed Publishing Group, 2011. This book recounts the story of a woman who was healed from chronic Lyme disease.

Steingard, Jerry with John Arnott. *From Here To The Nations: The Story of the Toronto Blessing.* Toronto: Catch The Fire Books, 2014. This is an insider's account of the Toronto Blessing. It includes several testimonies of healing.

Thomas, Art, James Loruss, and Jonathan Ammon. *40-Day Paid in Full: Healing Ministry Activation Manual.* Michigan: Supernatural Truth Productions, 2014. This work is a practical guide for ministering healing and operating in power evangelism.

Various. *By Their Fruits: The Lasting Impact of Toronto in the United Kingdom.* United Kingdom: Word Publishing, 2001. This is a collection of testimonies from Europeans impacted by the Toronto Blessing. It includes references to healing.

Vegh, Steven G. "Faith Is the Key to Curing Ailments at Healing Room." *Virginian-Pilot*, August 13, 2006. This newspaper article examines the outworking of Charismatic healing room ministries in Virgina.

Venter, Alexander. *Doing Healing: How to Minister God's Kingdom in The Power of the Holy Spirit.* Cape Town, South Africa: Vineyard

International Publishing, 2009. This work is a well-researched overview of healing from a noted Vineyard scholar and practitioner in South Africa.

Wagner, C. Peter. "Healing without Hassle," *Leadership* 6:2 (Spring 1985): 114-15. In this article, a Fuller Theological Seminary professor explains how his conservative Sunday school class practiced healing in a way that minimized conflict in the other parts of the Church.

Wagner, C. Peter. *How to Have a Healing Ministry in Any Church: A Comprehensive Guide.* Ventura, California: Regal Books, 1988. In this work, Wagner provides a practical guide to the ministry of healing for the uninitiated.

Wagner, C. Peter. *Signs and Wonders Today: The Story of Fuller Theological Seminary's Remarkable Course on Spiritual Power.* Altamonte Springs, California: Creation House, 1987. This is an account of John Wimber's influential signs and wonders class at Fuller Theological Seminar in the early 1980s.

Williams, Don. *Signs, Wonders, And The Kingdom of God.* Ann Arbor, Michigan: Servant Publications, 1989. Williams, a theologian in the Vineyard Movement, provides a biblical and practical exploration of signs and wonders.

Wimber, Carol. *John Wimber: The Way It Was.* United Kingdom: Hodder & Stoughton, 1999. John Wimber's beloved wife, Carol, wrote a biographical account of his life and ministry.

Wimber, John. *A Brief Sketch of Signs and Wonders Through the Church Age.* Anaheim, California: Vineyard Ministries International, 1984. This work explores the proliferation of signs and wonders throughout the history of Christianity.

Wimber, John. "Flowing in the Spirit: Risks and Rewards." *Charisma and Christian Life* (September 1990): 78-83. In this article, Wimber discusses some of the ways that people operate in the gifts of the Spirit.

Wimber, John. *Healing: Categories and Operatives*. Anaheim, California: Vineyard Ministries International, 1984. This booklet provides an overview of healing, including sections on causes of disease, inner healing, demonization, resuscitation of the dead and more.

Wimber, John. *Healing Seminar, Volume One*. Placentia, California: Vineyard Ministries International, 1985. In this small work, Wimber provides a useful healing study guide.

Wimber, John. "John Wimber calls it Power Evangelism." *Charisma* (September 1985): 35. This is a feature article on the ministry of John Wimber and the Vineyard. It was published in the leading Pentecostal and Charismatic magazine.

Wimber, John. *Kingdom of Suffering: Facing Difficulty and Trail in the Christian Life*. Ann Arbor, Michigan: Servant, 1988. Why do the righteous suffer and what role does Satan play in illness? John Wimber examines the Scriptures to discover what they have to say about suffering.

Wimber, John. *Power Evangelism*. New York: Harper and Row Publishers, 1986. Wimber's first major work discusses an approach to evangelism that is rooted in displays of supernatural power. At its time of release, this work was extremely influential.

Wimber, John, with Kevin Springer. *Power Healing*. New York: Harper and Row Publishers, 1987. Following up on *Power Evangelism*, his international best-seller, Wimber turns his attention to gifts-based healing.

Wimber, John, and Kevin Springer. *Study Guide to Power Healing*. New York: Harper and Row Publishers, 1987. This study guide was written to assist with the direct application of the precepts introduced in Power Healing. It includes additional bibliographic references, questions, and other practical suggestions.

Wimber, John. "The Church: Healing's Natural Home?" *Leadership* 6:2 (Spring 1985): 116-127. In this work, Wimber argues that the ministry of healing should be most active in the regular practices and worship expressions of local churches.

Wimber, John. "Wimber Breaks Silence to Answer Vineyard Critics." *Christianity Today* 9 (March 1992): 66-68. In this piece, Wimber takes some time to defend his signs and wonders methodology to Evangelical critics.

Wimber, John. "Zip to 3,000 in 5 years." *Christian Life* 44 (October 1982): 19-23. This article tells the story of Wimber's Vineyard Christian Fellowship. He says, "Today we see 50 to 100 people a week healed in our services. Many more are healed as we pray for them in hospitals, on the streets, and in homes. The blind are seeing. The lame are walking. The deaf are hearing. Cancers are disappearing." This is not only a result of Wimber's ministry, but also a result of his people. He says, "Today in our church of over 3,000, I would estimate that as many as 20 percent regularly see someone healed through their prayers."

Yoars, Marcus. "The Radical Revivalists," *Charisma* (June 2011): 42-48. This is a news article from a prominent charismatic magazine that considers the methodology and ministry expressions of Bethel Church in Redding, California.

19. CASE STUDIES

Astin, J. A., Harkness, E. and Ernst, E. "The efficacy of 'Distant Healing': a systematic review of randomized trials." *Annals of Internal Medicine* 132:11 (June 6, 2000): 903-910. This article reviews twenty-three studies of "distant healing." Of these studies, 13 (57%) yielded statistically significant treatment effects, 9 showed no effect over control interventions, and 1 showed a negative effect.

Aviles, Jennifer M., Ellen Whelan, Debra A. Hernke, Brent A. Williams, Kathleen E. Kenny, W. Michael O'Fallon, and Stephen L. Kopecky, "Intercessory prayer and cardiovascular disease progression in a coronary care unit population: A randomized controlled trial," *Mayo Clinic Proceedings* 76 (2001): 1192-1198. This study determined that intercessory prayer had no significant effect on medical outcomes after hospitalization in a coronary care unit.

Badenberg, Robert. *Sickness and Healing: A Case Study on the Dialectic of Culture and Personality.* Nürnberg, Germany: VTR Publications, 2008. This case study of an African individual explores missiological and anthropological questions. This analysis begins with the meaning of embodiment and human sickness. The second part delves into healing, focusing on cultural conceptions. It ends with several missiological deductions.

Benson, Herbert, et al. "Study of the Therapeutic Effects of Intercessory Prayer (STEP) in Cardiac Bypass Patients: A Multicenter Randomized Trial of Uncertainty and Certainty of Receiving Intercessory Prayer." *American Heart Journal* 151:4 (April 2006): 934–942. This study, which elicited distance-based intercessory prayer from St. Paul's Monastery in St. Paul, Minnesota, the Community of Teresian Carmelites in Worcester, Massachusetts, and Silent Unity in Kansas City, suggested that intercessory prayer had no effect on recovery from their surgery. On the negative side, intercessory prayer was associated with a higher incidence of complications. Some of have questioned this study's methodology.

Brown, Candy Gunther, Stephen C. Mory, Rebecca Williams, and Michael J. McClymond. "Study of the Therapeutic Effects of

Proximal Intercessory Prayer (STEPP) on Auditory and Visual Impairments in Rural Mozambique." *Southern Medical Journal* 103:9 (2010): 864-869. This is a fascinating case study, focusing on Heidi Baker's missions base in Mozambique, Africa. The remarkable findings seem to demonstrate healing's efficacy.

Byrd, Randolph C. "Positive Therapeutic Effects of Intercessory Prayer in A Coronary Care Unit Population." *Southern Medical Journal* (July 1988): 826-829. This influential case study validates the effectiveness of healing prayer. Over ten months, 393 patients admitted to a coronary care unit were randomized, after signing informed consent, to an intercessory prayer group (192 patients) or to a control group (201 patients). While hospitalized, the first group received intercessory prayer by participating Christians praying outside the hospital; the control group did not. When they came in, there was no statistical difference between the groups. Afterword, the group who received intercessory prayer received a significantly lower severity score.

Cadge, Wendy, and M. Daglian. "Blessings, strength, and guidance: Prayer frames in a hospital prayer book." *Poetics* 36:5 (2008): 358-373. Analyzing the prayers that patients, visitors, and staff wrote in a prayer book at the Johns Hopkins University Hospital between 1999 and 2005, this paper draws insights from cognitive studies of religion to ask what kinds of requests people make of God in their prayers, how they construct God in their prayers, and what kinds of responses they believe possible from God based on how they frame their prayers.

Cadge, Wendy. "Possibilities and Limits of Medical Science: Debates Over Double-Blind Clinical Trials of Intercessory Prayer." *Zygon* 47.1 (2012): 43-64. In this article, Cadge considers the controversies and debates surrounding the scientific study of prayer.

Cadge, Wendy. "Saying Your Prayers, Constructing Your Religions: Medical Studies of Intercessory Prayer." *The Journal of Religion* 89:3

(July 2009): 299-327. This article considers the findings of several case studies on intercessory prayer.

Collie, P. J. "The Efficacy of Prayer: A Triple Blind Study." *Medical Times* 97 (1969): 201-204. This is a case study on the effects of prayer on leukemia patients. Collie's conclusion was, "The small number of patients in this study precludes definite conclusions about the efficacy of prayer. Our data does support the concept, however, that prayers for the sick are efficacious."

Coruh, Basak. Hana Ayele, Meredith Pugh, and Thomas Mulligan. "Does Religious Activity Improve Health Outcomes? A Critical Review of the Recent Literature." *Explore* 1:3 (May 2005): 186-191. The researchers conducted a comprehensive literature search using MEDLINE to identify studies published in the English language between January 1999 and June 2003 describing the effect of religion on health outcomes. The search strategy used the medical subject headings (MeSH) of religion; religion and medicine; religion or intercessory prayer; prayer; prayer therapy; religious rites; faith; medicine, traditional; religiosity; religion and psychology; and religion and health. The researchers determined that religious intervention (such as intercessory prayer) may improve success rates of in vitro fertilization, decrease length of hospital stay, and duration of fever in septic patients, increase immune function, improve rheumatoid arthritis, and reduce anxiety. Frequent attendance at religious services likely improves health behaviors. Moreover, prayer may decrease adverse outcomes in patients with cardiac disease.

Dusek, Jeffery A., Jane B. Sherwood, R. Friedman, P. Myers, Charles F. Bethea, Sidney Levitsky, Peter C. Hill, Manoj K. Jain, Stephen L. Kopecky, P. S. Mueller, Peter Lam, Herbert Benson, and Patricia L. Hibberd, "Study of the Therapeutic Effects of Intercessory Prayer (STEP): Study design and research methods," *American Heart Journal*, 143:4 (April 2002): 577-584. This study considers some of the methodologies for studying the efficacy of intercessory prayer.

Flamm, Bruce L. "Faith Healing Confronts Modern Medicine." *The Scientific Review of Alternative Medicine* 8:1 (Spring-Summer 2004): 9-14. This article questions the legitimacy of case studies asserting the viability of intercessory prayer.

Fosarelli, Patricia. "Outcomes of Intercessory Prayer for Those Who Are Ill: Scientific and Pastoral Perspectives." *The Linacre Quarterly* 78:2 (2011): 125-137. Scientific literature investigating the efficacy of intercessory prayer is explored in this article. Overall, studies have yielded mixed results and have been criticized (on a scientific basis) as having methodological flaws such as small sample size, varied endpoints, varied definitions of prayer, and varied expertize of "intercessors." Such studies have also been criticized on other fronts. This study seeks to offer statistical conclusions.

Grad, Bernard. "Healing by the Laying on of Hands. Review of Experiments and Implications," *Pastoral Psychology* 21 (Summer 1970): 19-26. This was a case study where researchers examined the efficacy of touch on mice and plants in a controlled scientific environment. Though the findings were inconclusive, some fascinating observations were recorded.

Harkness, Elaine F., Neil C. Abbot, and Edzard Ernst. "A Randomized Trial of Distant Healing for Skin Warts." *American Journal of Medicine* 108 (2000): 448-452. This is a case study on distant, intercessory prayer and its effects on skin warts. The conclusion of this study was that prayer was not effective.

Harris, William S., Gowda, Manohar, Kolb, Jerry W., Strychacz, Christopher P., Vacek, James L., Jones, Philip G. Forker, Alan, O'Keefe, James H., and Ben D. McCallister, "A Randomized, Controlled Trial of the Effects of Remote, Intercessory Prayer on Outcomes in Patients Admitted to the Coronary Care Unit," Archives of Internal Medicine 159 (1999): 2273-2278. Nine hundred ninety patients were randomized to receive remote, intercessory prayer or not. The first names of patients in the prayer group were given to a team of outside intercessors who prayed for them daily for 4 weeks. Patients were unaware that they were being prayed for, and the intercessors did not know and never met the patients. Remote, intercessory prayer was associated with lower coronary care unit course scores. This result suggests that prayer may be an effective adjunct to standard medical care.

Helming, Mary, Blaszko. "Healing through Prayer: A Qualitative Study." *Holistic Nursing Practice* 25:1 (January-February 2011): 33–44. This is a fascinating case study on the clinical practice of healing from a member of the Society for Pentecostal Studies.

Hobbins, Peter Graeme. "Compromised Ethical Principles in Randomized Clinical Trials of Distant, Intercessory Prayer." *Journal of Bioethical inquiry* 2.3 (2005): 142-152. Hobbins asserts that intercessory prayer studies often fall short of the World Medical Association's ethical standards. He alleges that these studies did not provide adequate standards of care, patient confidentiality, and informed consent. He argues that since these studies did not meet basic ethical standards required of clinical trials of biophysical interventions, the application of their results are ethically problematic. Hobbins insists that these shortcomings must be addressed in future studies.

Johnson, Daniel M., J. Sherwood Williams, and David G. Bromley. "Religion, Health, and Healing: Findings from a Southern City." *Sociology of Religion* 47:1 (1986): 66-73. Five hundred and eighty-six adult respondents in the Richmond, Virginia area were asked about their use of prayer in response to physical illness. Fourteen percent of the respondents reported recovery that they attributed to prayer or regarded as a divine healing.

Joyce, C. R., and R. M. C. Welldon. "The Objective Efficacy of Prayer: A Double-Blind Clinical Trial." *Journal of Chronic Diseases* 18:4 (April 1965): 367-377. This is an early case study examining the effectiveness of prayer on diseases. Nineteen pairs of outpatients from two clinics in London, with chronic stationary or progressively deteriorating psychological or rheumatic disease made up control and intervention groups. The intervention group received prayer by silent meditation from Quakers and few other Christians. There was only incidental knowledge about the needs. The intervention was conducted over a period of at least six months, and it was determined that "No advantage to either group was demonstrated."

Leibovici Leonard. "Effects of Remote, Retroactive Intercessory Prayer On Outcomes in Patients with Bloodstream Infection: Randomized Controlled Trial." *British Medical Journal* 323:7327 (2001): 1450–1451. This study found that retroactive intercessory prayer was associated with a shorter stay in the hospital and shorter duration of fever in patients with a bloodstream infection and should be considered for use in clinical practice.

Lentos, J. D. "The Association of Physicians' Religious Characteristics with Their Attitudes and Self-Reported Behaviors Regarding Religion and Spirituality in the Clinical Encounter." *Medical Care* 44 (2006): 446–453. This study examines the relationship between physicians' religious views and their self-reported behaviors during clinical encounters with patients.

Kaufman, Yakir, David Anaki, Malcolm Binns, and Morris Freedman. "Cognitive Decline in Alzheimer's Disease: Impact of Spirituality, Religiosity, and QOL." *Neurology* 68 (2007): 1509–1514. This study determined that higher levels of spirituality and private religious practices are associated with slower progression of Alzheimer's disease.

MacNutt, Francis, Dale A. Matthews, and Sally M. Marlowe. "Effects of Intercessory Prayer on Patients with Rheumatoid Arthritis." *Southern Medical Journal* 93:12 (December 2000): 1177–1186. In this case study, the researchers explored the effects of intercessory prayer on individuals with rheumatoid arthritis. It objectively shows the benefits of healing prayer. Patients receiving in-person intercessory prayer showed significant overall improvement during 1-year follow-up.

O'Laoire, S. "An experimental study of the effects of distant, intercessory prayer on self-esteem, anxiety, and depression." *Alternative Therapies in Health and Medicine* 3:6 (November 1997): 38-53. This is a randomized, controlled, double blind study on the effects of healing prayer. The ill were randomly assigned to a prayer group. Photos and names of subjects were used as a focus. Subjects were randomly assigned to three groups: those prayed for by non-directed agents, a control group, and those prayed for by directed agents. Prayer was offered for 15 minutes daily for 12 weeks. Each of the subjects improved significantly on all 11 measures. Agents improved significantly on 10 measures. A significant positive correlation was found between the amount of prayer the agents did and their scores on the five objective tests. Agents had significantly better scores than did subjects on all objective measures.

Roberts, Leanne, Irshad Ahmed, and Steve Hall. "Intercessory Prayer for the Alleviation of Ill Health." *The Cochrane Database of Systematic Reviews* 2 (April 15, 2009). This review examines ten intercessory prayer case studies. The researchers conclude that intercessory prayer is neither significantly beneficial nor harmful for those who are sick. However, they suggest that further studies which are better designed and reported will be necessary to draw firmer conclusions.

Sicher, Fred, Elisabeth Targ, Dan Moore, and Helene S. Smith, "A Randomized Double-Blind Study Of The Effect Of Distant Healing In A Population With Advanced AIDS. Report Of A Small Scale Study." *The Western Journal of Medicine* 169:6 (December 1998): 356–63. The researchers performed a double-blind, randomized study of 40 patients with advanced AIDS. The patients were randomly assigned to receive distant intercessory healing or none at all. The intercession took place by Christian and non-Christian groups in different parts of the United States who never had any contact with the patients. Both patients and physicians were blind to who received or did not receive intercession. Six months later the prayer group had significantly fewer AIDS illnesses, less frequent doctor visits, and fewer days in the hospital.

Vannemreddy, Prasad, Kris Bryan, and Anil Nanda. *American Journal Hospice and Palliative Care* 26:4 (August-September 2009): 264-269. This study evaluates the effect of prayers on the recovery of the unconscious patients admitted after traumatic brain injury. It was determined that patients with a severe head injury who received prayer recovered more rapidly.

20. PHYSICIANS AND ACADEMICS

Andrews, Courtney Jones. "Health and Salvation: The Social Construction of Illness and Healing in the Charismatic Christian Church," Ph.D., diss., The University of Alabama, Tuscaloosa, 2012. This is an analysis of healing and the deeper works of God within a mid-sized Charismatic congregation in Alabama.

Bararacco, Claire Hoertz. *Prescribing Faith: Medicine, Media, And Religion in American Culture.* Waco, Texas: Baylor University Press, 2007. This is an analysis of religion and health care in American culture. Bararacco traces the convergence of medicine, media, and religion from mid-nineteenth century American culture to the present day.

Barnes, Linda L. and Susan S. Sered, eds. *Religion and Healing in America.* New York: Oxford University Press, 2004. This is a fascinating work examining the relationship between religion and healing within the American experience.

Barnes, Linda L. and Ines M. Talamantez, eds. *Teaching Religion and Healing.* New York: Oxford University Press, 2006. This work examines the study of faith and healing in educational institutions. Most of the articles advocate unorthodox religious perspectives. While there are valuable criticisms of Western biomedicine, as a whole this work leaves much to be desired.

Belcher, John R., and Brent B. Benda. "Issues of Divine Healing in Psychotherapy." *Journal of Religion & Spirituality in Social Work: Social Thought* 24:3 (2005): 21-38. This article peers into the intersection of divine healing and psychotherapy.

Benson, Herbert with Marg Stark. *Timeless Healing: The Power and Biology of Belief.* New York: Scribner, 1996. Benson is an associate professor of medicine at Harvard Medical School and the Deaconess Hospital. While Benson is not a Christian, he has conducted significant research on the power of faith and religious belief.

Bialecki, Jon. *A Diagram for Fire: Miracles and Variation in an American Charismatic Movement.* Oakland: University of California Press, 2017.

This book is a socio-cultural study of the Vineyard, an American Evangelical movement that originated in Southern California.

Blanton, Anderson. *Hittin' The Prayer Bones: Materiality of Spirit in The Pentecostal South*. Chapel Hill, North Carolina: University of North Carolina Press, 2015. In this work, Blanton shows how prayer is intertwined with the technologies of sound reproduction and material culture in the Pentecostal worship of southern Appalachia.

Bonser, Wilfred. *The Medical Background of Anglo-Saxon England*. London: Oxford University Press, 1963. While Bonser's goal in this work was to study the medical history of England, he actively examines how early English monastics prayed for the sick. He references some difficult to find sources.

Bowler, Kate. *Blessed: A History of the American Prosperity Gospel*. New York: Oxford University Press, 2013. This is a well-researched analysis of contemporary Pentecostal-Christianity. It includes an entire chapter on divine healing.

Bramwell, Edwin. "A Physician's Attitude Toward Spiritual Healing." *Edinburgh Medical Journal* (February 1928): 58-67. In this essay, a medical professional examines the viability of spiritual healing.

Burkill, T. A. "Miraculous Healing in The Gospels." *Central African Journal of Medicine* 19 (1973): 99-100. This is a perceptive essay on biblical healing written from an African perspective.

Cary, Benedict. "Long-Awaited Medical Study Questions the Power of Prayer." *New York Times*, March 31, 2006. This article summarizes Herbert Benson's 2006 study on the efficacy of prayer. Benson's findings were mixed. The study included prayers from unorthodox religious groups. That factor needed to be considered.

Chamberlin, Theodore J., and Christopher A. Hall. *Realized Religion: A Bibliographic Essay on the Relationship of Religion and Health*. Radnor, Pennsylvania: Templeton Foundation Press. 2000. This source documents more than 300 studies published by reputable scientific journals on the interrelationship of health and faith.

Chesnut, R. Andrew, *Competitive Spirits: Latin America's New Religious Economy*. New York: Oxford University Press, 2003. Chesnut, a professor of History at the University of Houston, explores Pentecostalism's growth in Latin America. A significant factor contributing to the rapid evangelistic growth is divine healing.

Csordas, Thomas J. "Elements of Charismatic Persuasion and Healing." *Medical Anthropology Quarterly* 2:2 (1988): 121-142. This article considers the implications of Charismatic healing practices. Csordas examines the efficacy of Charismatic healing by interviewing 75 ministers and looking at their curing processes.

Csordas, Thomas J. "Imaginal Performance and Memory in Ritual Healing," in *The Performance of Healing*. Eds. Carol Laderman and Marina Roseman, 91-114. New York: Routledge, 1996. This is a well-researched sociological article on the methodologies and forms of Christian healing.

Csordas, Thomas J. *Language, Charisma, and Creativity: The Ritual Life of a Religious Movement*. Berkley, California: University of California Press, 1994. This is the culmination of Csordas' decades-long sociological analysis of the Catholic Charismatic Renewal.

Csordas, Thomas J. "The Psychotherapy Analogy and Charismatic Healing." *Psychotherapy: Theory, Research, Practice, Training* 27.1 (1990): 79. This article considers analogies between Charismatic healing practices and psychotherapy.

Csordas, Thomas J. *The Sacred Self: A Cultural Phenomenology of Charismatic Healing*. Berkley, California: University of California Press, 1994. Csordas has written a penetrating sociological analysis of Catholic Charismatic healing modalities.

Davis, Frank Stafford. "Charismatic Christian Spiritual Healing in Two Cultural Contexts: Existential-Phenomenological Approach," Ph.D., diss., Duquesne University, 1990. This thesis explores the meaning of spiritual healing, trying to avoid reductionistic analysis that permeates the academic community.

Doniger, Simon, ed. *Healing: Human and Divine*. New York: Association Press, 1957. This book is a collection of articles by doctors, psychologists, psychiatrists and theologians, including such well-known names as Earl Loomis, John A. P. Millet, Carl Rogers, Paul Johnson, George Albert Coe, Paul Tillich, Cyril C. Richardson and Wayne E. Oates. The articles explore the relationship between religion and the mind, as well as the effects of prayer on the body, mind, and spirit. The book examines how science, faith, and prayer work together for healing. This work includes many valuable insights.

Dossey, Larry. *Healing Words: The Power of Prayer and the Practice of Medicine*. San Francisco, California: Harper, 1993. Dossey shares evidence that links prayer, healing, and medicine, showing which methods of prayer show the greatest potential for healing.

Dossey, Larry. *Prayer Is Good Medicine: How to Reap the Healing Benefits of Prayer*. New York: Harper Collins, 1996. Physician, Larry Dossey, offers fascinating insights about the effects of prayer on the health of people.

Droege, Thomas A. *The Faith Factor in Healing*. Philadelphia: Trinity Press International, 1991. Medical research has confirmed that "faith" has a bearing on patient recovery. Droege examines this, arguing that patients should be treated as whole persons, not just bodies.

Droogers, Andre. "Normalization of Religious Experience: Healing, Prophecy, Dreams and Visions," in *Charismatic Christianity as a Global Culture*, ed. Karla Poewe, 33-49. Colombia, South Carolina: University of South Carolina Press, 1994. This essay considers healing and unusual phenomenon in Charismatic Christianity.

Ellens, J. Harold, ed. *Miracles: God, Science, and Psychology in the Paranormal, Volume 1, Religious and Spiritual Events*. Westport Connecticut: Praeger, 2008. This collection of academic diatribes explore the meaning and scope of miracles.

Fiorello, Michael D. *The Physically Disabled in Ancient Israel According to the Old Testament and Ancient Near Eastern Sources*. Milton Keyes, United Kingdom: Authentic Media, 2014. This multifaceted study probes the semantics of the physically disabled in the ancient Near East. Fiorello examines law collections, societal conventions, and religious obligations toward those were physically disabled. Fiorello describes the world a disabled person encountered in the ancient Mediterranean world.

Gardner, Rex. *Healing Miracles: A Doctor Investigates*. London: Darton, Longman and Todd, LTD., 1986. In this book, a Christian physician explores the validity of divine healing. Gardner writes, "The conclusion seems inescapable, in the light of the evidence presented in this work, that we have a living God, intimately interested in our affairs, prepared to intervene in a specific practical way in response to prayer. This being the case it is logical to pray about our health, and that of our patients and friends."

Gell, C. W. M. "A Philosophy of Healing: Miraculous Cures and The Nature of Health." *London Quarterly and Holborn Review* 178 (1953): 215-219. This is a critical academic article that examines the claims of those who practice miraculous healing.

Grad, Bernard. "Healing by the Laying On of Hands: A Review of Experiments," in *Ways of Health: Holistic Approaches to Ancient and Contemporary Medicine*, ed. David S. Sobel, 267-287. New York: Harcourt, Brace, Jovanovich, 1979. This article explores laying on of hands as a healing practice.

Griffith, Ezra E. H. "The Significance of Ritual in a Church-Based Healing Model," *American Journal of Psychiatry* 140:5 (1983): 568-572.

This is an interesting academic article on the psychological implications of healing methodologies.

Griffith, R. Marie. *Born Again Bodies: Flesh and Spirit in American Christianity.* Los Angeles, California: University of California Press Berkeley. 2004. This book explores notions of embodiment in American Evangelical culture, taking focus on the popular fitness and diet culture.

Hahn, Robert A. *Sickness and Healing: An Anthropological Perspective.* New Haven, Connecticut: Yale University Press, 1995. In this scholarly work, Hahn explores the meaning of sickness outside of the industrialized Western ethos. It provides a constructive analysis of the limits of biomedicine.

Haider, S. L. "Divine Healing." *Journal of Royal College of General Practitioners* 36 (1986): 223. A European physician critically examines the claims of divine healing.

Hankoff, L. D. "Religious Healing in First-Century Christianity," *The Journal of Psychohistory* 19:4 (Spring 1992): 387-407. This critical essay examines early Christian healing claims through the lens of social sciences and psychotherapy.

Hieger, Roy R. "Divine Healing: The History of Faith Cures and Their Status Today." *The Journal of the Kansas Medical Society* 58:12 (December 1957): 838-858. This is an article on the history and foundations faith healing practices. Hieger emphasizes the early contributions of Charles F. Parham.

Hines, Taylor Spight. "Of Perfection: Illness, Disability, and Sin in American Religious Healing, from the Civil War to World War I," Ph.D., diss., University of California, Santa Barbara, California, 2013. This dissertation explores the implications of sin, sickness, and healing within the antebellum faith-cure and holiness movements.

Jantos, Marek, and Hosen Kiat. "Prayer as Medicine: How much have we learned?" *Medical Journal of Australia* 186 (2007): S51–S53. This is an introductory article examining the contours and meaning of healing prayer, looking at it from a scientific perspective.

Kinsley, David. *Health, Healing, and Religion: A Cross-Cultural Perspective*. Upper Saddle River, New Jersey: Prentice-Hall, 1996. This scholarly work attempts to explore the challenging intersection of disease, healing, and religion.

Koenig, Harold G. and Harvey Jay Cohen, eds. *Psychoneuroimmunology and the Faith Factor: The Link Between Religion and Health*. New York: Oxford University Press, 2002. This is an insightful work on the expanding scope of psychoneuroimmunology—the study of how emotions and thoughts affect health. Koenig and Cohen are concerned with how religious faith impacts the mind, emotions, and body.

Koenig, Harold G. *The Healing Power OF Faith: Science Explores Medicine's Last Great Frontier*. New York: Simon and Schuster, 1999. Koenig was the director of Duke University's Center for the Study of Religion, Spirituality, and Health. In this work, he presents case studies and findings that demonstrate a positive relationship between health and religious faith.

Koenig, Harold G. *Medicine, Religion, And Health: Where Science and Spirituality Meet*. West Conshohocken, Pennsylvania: Templeton Press, 2008. In this notable work, Koenig provides an overview of the relationship between religion and health, drawing insights from several previous studies.

Koss-Chioino, Joan D., and Philip Hefner, eds. *Spiritual Transformation and Healing: Anthropological, Theological, Neuroscientific, and Clinical Perspectives*. Lanham, Maryland: Alta Mira Press, 2006. This collection of articles explores the anthropological, psychological, medical, theological, and biological realities of healing. The book's findings are mixed and often from non-Christian perspective.

Kub, Joan. "Miracles and Medicine: An Annotated Bibliography." *Southern Medical Journal* 100 (December 12, 2007): 1273–1276. This bibliography for health care providers puts them in touch with tools to better comprehend the meaning of "miracles."

Levin, Jeff. "How Faith Heals: A Theoretical Model." *Explore* 5:2 (2009): 77. This is a sympathetic article on the health benefits of religious faith. Physician, Jeff Levin, explores the compelling evidence of the connection between health and religion. He examines an array of beneficial spiritual practices including prayer and attending religious services.

Levin, Jeff. God, *Faith, and Health: Exploring The Spirituality-Healing Connection*. New York: John Wiley and Sons, 2001. This work, from a well-respected physician, discusses the connections between health and religious faith.

Lewis, Todd Vernon. *Charismatic Communications and Faith Healers: A Critical Study of Rhetorical Behavior*. Louisiana State University A&M, 1980. This concentrated study explores the rhetorical patterns and orality of the healing evangelists.

Lindström, Lars G. *Christian Spiritual Healing: A Psychological Study: Ideology and Experience in the British Healing Movement*. Uppsala: Academiae Ubsaliensis, 1992. This is a penetrating examination of healing practices in Great Britain.

Lindström, Lars G. "Religious Faith Healing and Its Psychological Conditions: A Methodological Study." *Psychological Studies On Religious Man* 7 (1978): 219. This is a sociological study examining healing methodologies among religious practitioners.

Lucas, Ernest, ed. *Christian Healing: What Can We Believe? Doctors and Theologians Reach a Unique Consensus*. United Kingdom: Society For Promoting Christian Knowledge, 1997. This book attempts to bring together physicians and Bible scholars to establish common ground on healing. Those drawn together in this exercise reflected a wide range of positions. Some expected miraculous healing and others were extremely skeptical. A theologian and a medic jointly author each chapter; covering the following topics: How are people healed today? What the significance of Jesus' healing ministry? The relationship between psychiatry, religion, and suffering.

Masters, Kevin S. "Research On the Healing Power of Distant Intercessory Prayer: Disconnect Between Science and Faith." *Journal of Psychology and Theology* 33.4 (2005): 268. In recent years, research about distant intercessory prayer has become widespread. Several double blind, randomized, controlled studies have examined whether a statistically significant effect can be found when prayed for groups are compared with control groups. The central premise of this article is that most of these studies lack any theological or rational theoretical foundation. Consequently, many produce non-interpretable findings.

Matthews, Dale A., with Connie Clark. *The Faith Factor—Proof of The Healing Power of Prayer.* New York: The Penguin Group, 1998. A gifted medical doctor and researcher provide a fascinating look at how an individual's faith affects their healing.

Mattingly, Cheryl, and Linda C. Garro, eds. *Narrative and The Cultural Construction of Illness and Healing.* Berkley, California: University of California Press, 2000. This book is a fascinating collection of academic articles that consider American cultural assumptions about sickness and disease. The authors point out that several issues influence the way people understand illnesses.

Mullin, Robert Bruce. *Miracles and the Modern Religious Examination.* New Haven, Connecticut: Yale University Press, 1996. This is a vital academic work that explores the American understanding of miracles at the turn of the twentieth century. Mullin includes insightful anthropological and sociological observations.

Nolen, William. *Healing: A Doctor in Search of a Miracle.* New York: Random House, 1974. This work recounts Nolen's investigation of the claims of Kathryn Kuhlman and other divine healing practitioners. Nolen claimed to find no evidence of efficacy of faith healing. However, some of Nolen's claims were later contested by Alfred Stelter and other researchers.

Oursler, Will. *The Healing Power of Faith*. New York: Hawthorn Books, 1957. Oursler studied extant records and corresponded with healing proponents as he critically examined the viability of physical deliverance.

Pattison, E.M., Labins, N.A., and Doerr, H.A., "Faith Healing: A Study of Personality and Function." *Journal of Nervous and Mental Disease* 157 (1973): 398. This is a critical article that explores "faith healing" practices from a clinical perspective.

Peters, Shawn Francis. *When Prayer Fails: Faith Healing, Children, and the Law*. New York: Oxford University Press, 2007. Based on a wide array of primary and secondary source materials—among them judicial opinions, trial transcripts, police and medical examiner reports, news accounts, personal interviews, and scholarly studies—this book explores the conflict between divine healing proponents, the medical community, and courts.

Pinches, Charles. "Miracles: A Christian Theological Overview." *Southern Medical Journal* 100:12 (2007): 1236–1242. This is a journal article exploring the contours of the Christian understanding of miracles. It was written for doctors and other members of the biomedical community.

Pullum, Stephen J. *Faith Healers and The Bible: What Scripture Actually Says*. Santa Barbara, California: Praeger, 2015. This work is a renunciation of healing evangelists and their practices. A college professor from North Carolina penned it.

Pullum, Stephen J. *Foul Demons, Come Out: The Rhetoric of Twentieth Century American Faith Healing*. Westport Connecticut: Praeger, 1999. This is a sociological assessment of several twentieth century healing evangelists. The book explores the rhetoric of the evangelists and the participants in their meetings.

Reinders, R. C. "Training for a Prophet: The West Coast Missions of John Alexander Dowie, 1888-1890." *Pacific History* 30:1 (1986): 2-14. In this well-researched article, the initial American outreach efforts of John Alexander Dowie are examined.

Roebling, Karl. *Is There Healing Power? One Man's Look at America's Faith Healers.* New Canaan, Connecticut: Keats Publishing Company, 1972. In this biting critique, Roebling examines the ministries of Kathryn Kuhlman, Oral Roberts, Don Stewart, Kenneth Hagin, and others.

Sax, William, Johannes Quack, and Jan Weinhold, eds. *The Problem of Ritual Efficacy.* New York: Oxford University Press, 2010. Nine scholars, from the fields of history, anthropology, medicine, and biblical studies, try to answer the question, "How do rituals work in the lives of the participants?"

Schuman, Joel James and Keith G. Meador. *Heal Thyself: Spirituality, Medicine, And The Distortion of Christianity.* New York: Oxford University Press, 2003. Joel James Shuman is Assistant Professor of Theology at King's College in Wilkes-Barre, Pennsylvania. Keith G. Meador is Clinical Professor of Psychiatry and Behavioral Science at the School of Medicine, and Professor of the Practice of Pastoral Theology and Medicine and Director of the Theology and Medicine Program at The Divinity School at Duke University. They argue that popular culture's fascination with the health benefits of religion reflects not the renaissance of religious tradition but the combination of consumer capitalism and self-interested individualism. They suggest that a faith-for-health exchange misrepresents and devalues the true meaning of faith.

Sims, Andrew, C.P. "Demon Possession: Medical Perspective in a Western Culture," *in Medicine and The Bible*, ed. Bernard Palmer, 165-189. Exeter, United Kingdom: Paternoster, 1986. This article attempts to provide a Western medical analysis of the meaning and effects of "demon possession."

Sloan, R. P., E. Bagiella, and T. Powell. "Religion, Spirituality, and Medicine." *Lancet* 353 (1999): 664-667. This brief article provides analysis on the role of faith within the realm of medicine and disease.

Stolz, Jörg. "All Things Are Possible: Towards a Sociological Explanation of Pentecostal Miracles and Healings." *Sociology of Religion* 72:4 (2011): 456-482. Stolz argues that healings are seemingly produced in Pentecostal-Charismatic services: paralytics arise from wheelchairs, cancerous ulcers disappear, legs grow, cavities are mysteriously filled, and the deaf suddenly hear. Yet, they are not what they appear. Drawing on case studies and qualitative interviews, Stolz believes "social techniques," context factors, and causal mechanisms are what produce so-called, "miracles" and "healings."

Studer, James N. "Toward a Theology of Healing." *Journal of Religion and Health* 21 (Winter 1982): 280-289. Struder, a member of Saint John's Abbey in Collegeville, Minnesota and a chaplain at Saint Mary's Hospital in Minneapolis, reflects on the biblical foundations of healing.

Sulmasy, Daniel P. "Exousia: Healing with Authority in the Christian Tradition," in *Theology and Medicine: Theological Analyses of the Clinical Encounter*, ed. Gerald P. McKenny, and Jonathan R. Sande, 85-107. The Netherlands: Kluwer Academic Publishers, 1994. This is an academic exploration of healing, considering how it is understood within the current medical environments.

Taurnier, Paul. *A Doctors Casebook*, ed. by Edwin Hudson. New York: Harper and Row, 1960. This down-to-earth book, written through the lens of a Christian physician, explores the meaning of biblical healing.

Tolson, Chester L. and Harold G. Koenig. *The Healing Power of Prayer: The Surprising Connection Between Prayer and Your Health.* Grand Rapids, Michigan: Baker Publishing Group, 2003. This work, by two medical professionals, is an exploration on how prayer can affect one's health.

Van Buskirk, James Dale. *Religion, Healing, and Health.* New York: Macmillan, 1952. In this work, a Christian medical doctor explores the relationship between faith, medicine, and health. He writes, "My medical studies and practice, and my religious experience, both confirm me in this conviction of the importance of religion for healthy living for the cure of the sick, and for the prevention of much suffering."

Waddle, Charles W. "Miracles of Healing." *The American Journal of Psychology* 20:2 (1909): 219-268. This early twentieth century essay was published in a professional psychology journal. It takes a very critical look at healing and miracles.

Wallis, Claudia. "Faith and Healing: Can Prayer, Faith and Spirituality Really Improve Your Physical Health? A Growing and Surprising Body of Scientific Evidence Says They Can." *Time Magazine* 157:26 (June 24, 1996): 58-68. This Time magazine article explores how faith and religion can shape the outcomes of one's health.

Walsh, Arlene Sanchez. "Salvación, Sanidad, Liberación: The Word of Faith Movement among Twenty-First-Century Latina/o Pentecostals," in *Global Pentecostal and Charismatic Healing*, ed. Candy Gunther Brown. New York: Oxford University Press, 2014. Walsh produces an insightful case study about Latino Word of Faith adherents.

Watts, Fraser, ed. *Spiritual Healing: Scientific and Religious Perspectives.* New York: Cambridge University Press, 2011. This is an anthology of articles examining the relationship between science and religion. The authors suggest that religious and scientific perspectives answer different questions about healing, and conflict does not necessarily reside between the varying perspectives.

Weatherhead, Leslie. *Psychology, Religion, and Healing: A Critical Study of All Non-Physical Methods of healing, with an Examination of the Principles Underlying Them and The Techniques Employed to Express Them, Together with Some Conclusions Regarding Further Investigation and Action in This Field.* London: Hodder & Stoughton, 1951. This book provides analysis of healing modalities that differ from standard biomedical approaches of the West.

Village, Andrew. "Dimensions of Belief About Miraculous Healing." *Mental Health, Religion and Culture* 8:2 (2005): 97-107. This is an analytical article examining varying perspectives on divine healing.

Wire, Antoinette Clark. "Ancient Miracle Stories and Women's Social World." *Forum: A Journal of the Foundations and Facets of Western Culture* 2:4 (1986): 77-84. Wire provides a serious examination of miracle stories and their implications for social and gender identities.

Wire, Antoinette Clark. "The Structure of the Gospel Miracles Stories and Their Tellers," *Semeia* 11 (1978): 83-113. Wire, with a thorough eye, analyzes the trajectory and structure of the various miracle stories in the gospels.

Wirth, D.P. "The Significance of Belief and Expectancy Within the Spiritual Healing Encounter," *Social Science and Medicine* 41 (1995): 249-260. This is a critique examining the sociological and anthropological contours of healing prayer.